The Rise of the People's Bank of China

THE RISE OF THE PEOPLE'S BANK OF CHINA

The Politics of Institutional Change

Stephen Bell

Hui Feng

HARVARD UNIVERSITY PRESS

Cambridge, Massachusetts

London, England

2013

To Jo, Hillary, Qian, and Ellie

Library of Congress Cataloging-in-Publication Data
Bell, Stephen, 1954–
The rise of the People's Bank of China : the politics of institutional change /
Stephen Bell and Hui Feng.
pages cm
Includes bibliographical references and index.
ISBN 978-0-674-07249-7 (alk. paper)
1. Banks and banking—China. 2. Monetary policy—China. 3. China—Politics and
government—1976–2002. 4. China—Politics and government—2002–
I. Feng, Hui. II. Title.
HG3336.B45 2013
332.1'10951—dc23   2012041751

Contents

PART THREE

The PBC and the Politics of Money
and Financial Development in China

Abbreviations Used in Text

ABC	Agricultural Bank of China
AFC	Asian financial crisis
AMC	asset management company
BA	bureaucratic authoritarianism
BCB	Brazilian Central Bank
BIS	Bank for International Settlements
BOC	Bank of China
BOCOM	Bank of Communications
BSA	bilateral swap agreement
CBA	central bank authority
CBI	central bank independence
CBRC	China Banking Regulatory Commission
CCB	China Construction Bank
CCP	Chinese Communist Party
CFWC	Central Financial Work Commission
CIC	China Investment Corporation
CIRC	China Insurance Regulatory Commission
CLG	central leading group
CLGFEA	Central Leading Group on Financial and Economic Affairs
CPI	consumer price index
CSRC	China Securities Regulatory Commission

EIS	Electronic Interbank System
FA	fragmented authoritarianism
FDI	foreign direct investment
FSB	Financial Stability Bureau
FSI	foreign strategic investor
FTC	foreign trade company
GDP	gross domestic product
GFC	global financial crisis
HI	historical institutionalism
ICBC	Industrial and Commercial Bank of China
IMF	International Monetary Fund
IPO	initial public offering
ISR	Internal Settlement Rate
KNB	Khazanah Nasional Berhad
MOF	Ministry of Finance
MOFCOM	Ministry of Commerce
MOFERT	Ministry of Foreign Economic Relations and Trade
MOFT	Ministry of Foreign Trade
MOFTEC	Ministry of Foreign Trade and Economic Cooperation
MPC	Monetary Policy Committee
MPD	Monetary Policy Department
NBFI	nonbank financial institution
NDRC	National Development and Reform Commission
NPL	nonperforming loan
OMO	open market operation
PBC	People's Bank of China
PRC	People's Republic of China
PSC	Politburo Standing Committee
RBA	Reserve Bank of Australia
RBI	Reserve Bank of India
RMB	renminbi
RRR	required reserve ratio
SAFE	State Administration of Foreign Exchange
SDPC	State Development Planning Commission
SOE	state-owned enterprise
SPC	State Planning Commission
SWF	society-wide financing
WTO	World Trade Organization

PART ONE

Aims and Theoretical Context

I

Introduction

In the grueling transition from a centrally planned economy, one of the most daunting challenges confronting the Chinese state in the post-1978 era of market-oriented economic reform has been to transform old institutions and to establish a flotilla of new institutions capable of managing and regulating the emerging market-oriented economy (Yang 2004). A particular challenge has been to try and build a sound market-oriented monetary and financial infrastructure. Monetary and wider macroeconomic stability has been a major challenge for China. Consumer price inflation is among the "primary" problems confronting transition economies (Maxfield 1997, 10). This has been especially so in China, for several reasons: economic transition entails extensive readjustments of the price system, putting upward pressure on consumer prices (Naughton 1991); the Chinese Communist Party's (CCP's) high-growth model aimed at quelling social unrest and high unemployment adds to inflationary pressures (Hu 1999); and China's process of economic and administrative decentralization and the CCP's linkage of cadre promotion to local economic performance has prompted considerable local investment fetishism and economic overheating (Huang 1996, 2002). Housing reforms and rising household and business debt are also transforming China into a more inflation-prone and inflation-sensitive society. More recently, as-set price inflation in the housing and property sectors has loomed as a major challenge. Hence, excessive inflation on several fronts has posed a major challenge to the party-state's growth strategy and to political stability.

Institutional reforms in the monetary and financial arenas have also been prompted by the incessant challenges of a transitional (and thereby imma-ture) financial system. For example, the state-owned enterprises that used to enjoy literally no-cost policy loans from the big state-controlled banks now have to participate in market exchanges on a more commercial basis, thus exposing more entities to market disorders and financial risks. There have also been wider banking reforms aimed at attempting to transform the major state banks into more market-oriented commercial banks, financial market reforms aimed at establishing stock and bond markets for government and corporate finance, and regulatory reforms aimed at establishing and enforcing modern prudential and securities regulation. The sheer size of China's rapidly growing financial markets, China's ballooning foreign exchange reserves, the problematic and worrisome intermediaries represented by the largely insol-vent state banks (whose bad loans constituted around 40% of the total bank portfolio at the turn of the new century), and the omnipresence of political distortions and economic disruption, as well as increasingly articulated foreign pressures (especially on exchange rate management), have all been packed into the wild ride of China's market transition.

In this book we focus on a key institution that has played an increasingly central role in attempting to manage these challenges, China's central bank—the People's Bank of China (PBC). Studies of central banking in developing countries and postcommunist transition contexts are now central in under-standing the economic growth and governance dynamics of key emerging markets (Johnson 2003; Maxfield 1997). Thus far, the PBC has helped to keep the Chinese economy on the rails and has been important in helping to build a more sophisticated and market-oriented monetary and financial in-frastructure. The PBC has also emerged as an increasingly authoritative insti-tution in the realm of monetary and financial policy. These changes and es-pecially the rising authority of the PBC are the main focus of this book. Yet this poses a puzzle. How are we to explain the Bank's rising authority within the steep hierarchy of the Chinese party-state, where the party elite has tradi-tionally guarded its monetary and financial policy autonomy?

Our answer is that the rise of the PBC has been based on a relationship of growing mutual dependency with the party leadership. This was a contingent, not inevitable, outcome, based primarily upon the increasingly enhanced institutional capacities, expertise, and policy track record of the PBC, especially since the mid-1990s. It was then that the PBC was awarded new legislative foundations defining its role as a central bank charged with fighting inflation. Even more importantly, the PBC has developed specialized resources and capacities—information, monetary expertise, and a range of policy instruments—that have substantially boosted its role as an inflation-fighting central bank. The PBC has also established a reasonably credible policy track record in monetary policy and in dealing with inflation. In the initial era of market reform from the late 1970s to the early 1990s, economic growth averaged 10.1% while inflation averaged 7.7%. In the subsequent era of reform between 1995 and 2011, however, the PBC was more effective in fighting inflation. In that era economic growth averaged 9.9% but CPI inflation fell to an average of only 3.1%. As Figure 1.1 shows, despite various minor cyclical peaks in recent decades, inflation has been effectively managed since the mid-1990s, especially compared with the full-blown inflationary crises of the late 1980s

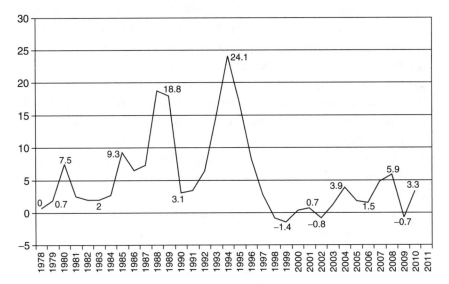

FIGURE 1.1. China's consumer price index, 1978–2011 (%).

Source: National Bureau of Statistics of China, *China Statistical Yearbook,* various years.

and early 1990s. Moreover, as the rest of the world was battered by the global financial meltdown that began in 2007, China's banking and financial sectors have been relatively unscathed. Although huge challenges, from asset price inflation, to banking reform, to managing China's foreign exchange system and the huge pileup of reserves, still remain, the PBC has *thus far* established a credible track record. The PBC has also been active in exchange rate and wider financial reforms to help augment its monetary policy capacities. Although it has experienced setbacks, these resources and capacities far surpass those possessed by the PBC at the beginning of the reform era.

The Rise of Central Banks—and the PBC

Mounting monetary and financial challenges in recent decades have seen central banks rise to unprecedented worldwide prominence (Mahadeva and Sterne 2000; Siklos 2002). There has also been a new wave of central bank formation and modernization in emerging market and transition economies, including China's (Marcussen 2005). The growth in the scale of financial market activity, the increased integration of financial markets, the growth in systemic risks to financial stability, and the quest to control inflation have all ensured the growing prominence of central banks. But another development has also catapulted central banks to prominence. Across an astonishing array of countries, governments have given central banks substantial increases in authority, in many cases granting them formal independence and the right to implement monetary policy. Since the beginning of the 1990s, the number of "independent" central banks, according to changes in statutes, has grown from around 10 to over 100 in number (Marcussen 2005). Given the increasing importance of monetary policy as the key discretionary instrument of macroeconomic management, this is a very substantial gift of authority by governments. It also represents a striking pattern of international policy convergence.

Central banks have thus become a critical institution underpinning monetary policy and financial stability in modern economic systems. As the "bank of issue," they are granted the monopoly of note issue and, as such, they function as "banker to the banks" and also a "lender of last resort," providing guarantees to the domestic and international payments system in a general liquidity crisis. Central banks also act as the "banker to the government," a key agent that provides financial services to the public sector. As a range of national currencies lost the anchor of either gold or the U.S. dollar and became "fiat money," central banks were left to craft monetary policy, which has led to new central bank responsibilities, especially the management of macroeconomic targets, of which price stability has been held as the primary goal by central banks, especially since the 1990s (Bofinger 2001, 234–39). To many, a central bank constitutes a universal symbol of modern nationhood and rational statehood (Jordan and Carlson 2000; Maman and Rosenhek 2007; Maxfield 1997).

Prior to 1978 and the beginning of the market reform era in China, the PBC was a mere subordinate to the Ministry of Finance (MOF) and a cashier of the government under the central planning regime (Guo 2002; Saez 2003). Since then, as we chart and explain, the PBC's rising authority has seen it become the key bureaucratic player in Beijing's policy apparatus dealing with monetary and financial affairs. The rise of the PBC essentially refers to the formal and informal powers of the central bank in the policy arena and in relation to the leadership of the party-state. The central bank's institutional powers include the formal political, economic, and financial relationship between the central bank and the leadership of the party-state (and other bureaucratic institutions in the wider government) and the central bank's statutory discretion in setting certain elements of monetary policy and in overarching financial regulation. The PBC's informal authority is also important and includes the de facto weightings of its policy input in monetary and wider economic policymaking, personal ties and influence between central bankers and top political elites, and horizontal relationships between the central bank and other key bureaucratic institutions in the policy circle.

The highlights of the PBC's rising authority, covered in detail in later chapters, have involved formal changes including new legislative mandates in the 1980s and 1990s that strengthened and clarified the PBC's role as a central bank and as an inflation fighter. Although not mandating formal independence, these reforms nevertheless enhanced the PBC's authority and institutional insulation from rival agencies, such as the MOF, as well as from local governments. The latter was an important step in giving the PBC greater clout in attempting to rein in local growth fevers and credit surges, historically an important inflationary impulse in China. Like many other Chinese bureaucratic institutions nowadays, there is a broad ideational division within the PBC between advocates of more liberal market reform and conservatives who tend to give greater weight to hierarchical and administrative controls.

The former have been ascendant, although the unique combination of administrative controls and the growing use of market-oriented monetary policy measures have meant that the PBC has developed a wide policy toolkit, especially compared to the single instrument of controlling official interest rates found in many other countries.

The intense coverage and scrutiny by the global media and the international market over the Bank's every move can be attributed to the growing weight of the Chinese economy in general, but also to the PBC's rising authority in Beijing's decision-making hierarchy. As China more deeply integrates into the world market, the consequences of its domestic reforms, including its central banking reform, are also spilling over into the wider international community. The PBC oversees the economic performance of the world's third largest trader, it oversees an economy that is a key destination for foreign direct investment (FDI), and it manages the world's largest foreign reserve holdings. The PBC is thus becoming the talk chip of global fund managers, international bankers, and policy elites alike. The impacts of key policy moves by the PBC nowadays tend to ripple out toward stock exchanges in New York, iron ore mines in Australia, car makers in Detroit, oil fields in Russia, and more generally the shopping basket of the rest of the world. Even casual remarks from Chinese central bankers can move the international financial markets. The fact that a brief proposal on alternative international currency arrangements by the PBC's governor, Zhou Xiaochuan, named China's "banking tsar,"[1] stirred up global attention is further evidence of recognition by the international community of the Bank's status in China's internal policy circle.[2]

The PBC's growing policy clout has been evidenced in a series of policy successes. For example, in targeting inflation, the PBC has been influential in opening up discretionary space around China's highly sensitive managed exchange rate system, especially when it argued for a non-devaluation strategy in the wake of the Asian financial crisis. In dampening the inflationary impacts stemming from its exchange rate interventions, the PBC has also used quantitative instruments to help sterilize domestic money holdings and has issued innovative central bank bills designed to soak up liquidity. These endeavors to augment monetary policy were supported when the PBC was successful in mid-2005 in convincing the leadership to shift to a partial liberalization of the exchange rate regime. The PBC has also spearheaded reform of the financial system and ailing state banks, as part of wider efforts to support monetary policy. However, the PBC has probably been most assertive in directly tackling inflation. This was particularly apparent from the mid-1990s when, for the first time, the PBC, under the governorship of Zhu Rongji, managed to contain inflation and help engineer a soft landing in 1996. The PBC also tested the authority of the party leadership in its unilateral action against asset price inflation in early 2003, an unusually bold move for a central bank on this front. The PBC was adamant that there were signs of a systemic shift to inflation and that preemptive action was needed. In this instance, the PBC's measures were rolled out in June 2003 in the form of window guidance; a move designed to "technically" avoid invoking an interest rate hike that would have needed formal approval by a hesitant State Council. Subsequently, the PBC persuaded Premier Wen to raise interest rates in October 2004, the first time in nine years. In commenting on these moves, Ba Shusong, a renowned economist, argues that "the recent several important decisions of the PBC demonstrate . . . evidence of the rise of the operational independence of the PBC" (Du 2003, 7). Key China watcher Barry Naughton (2004a, 3–4) similarly reflected on this episode, arguing that the "PBC is beginning to interact with other economic decision-makers in China in a way not terribly different from the way that Alan Greenspan does in the United States."

We adopt a more cautious view. Although the PBC has clearly displayed rising authority and has thus far established a reasonably credible policy track record, talk of independence goes too far. The fact remains that the PBC formally operates under the leadership of the State Council, China's central cabinet. Hence, the rise of the PBC in the reform era has occurred in the shadow of the CCP that sees delegation of monetary and financial authority as a potential threat to its political power. This is why the PBC has not been granted independence and why major policy moves on interest rates and exchange rate policy have to be approved by the State Council. The party elite sees the financial sector as one of its central concerns in relation to political stability and economic growth and is therefore an extremely sensitive area over which the Party has traditionally been reluctant to relinquish power. Decades of central planning practice have also reinforced the idea that fiscal and monetary policies, to be effective, are inherently inseparable and therefore should be under a single central authority, that is, the leadership of the party-state. Such hierarchical dynamics thus form the basic constraint, rather than support, for the PBC's rising authority.

Nor has the PBC's rise been smooth. It experienced a slow and difficult start in the 1980s, followed by a surge in capacity and influence in the 1990s and early 2000s. It has also experienced setbacks. For example, the PBC lost some momentum on banking reform after 2005 in a turf war with the MOF. Walter and Howie (2011) argue that the change in party leadership in the mid-2000s also impacted the PBC's banking reforms, although it still managed to sustain the reform momentum on a number of fronts, including finalizing the initial public offerings of the major state banks, pushing through reforms in the domestic bond market, and pushing for the resumption of the renminbi's (RMB's) gradual appreciation. The PBC also experienced a temporary setback when the party leadership insisted on a massive stimulatory credit expansion in 2008–9. Moreover, although the PBC is credited with establishing a more sophisticated and market-oriented framework for monetary policy, the rapidly growing informal sector poses challenges to the PBC's policy reach, especially the growing level of local public debt and local government financing platforms (PBC 2011), growing off–balance sheet operations in the banking sector (Fitch Ratings 2011), and an unsustainable level of informal finance in the private sector (Chen and Qiu 2011).

These ongoing challenges remind us that the PBC is deeply enmeshed in intense bureaucratic politics within the Chinese party-state and faces constant battles to enhance its authority and disciplinary capacity in the monetary realm. Clearly, the PBC's rise and reform momentum has experienced ebbs and flows and the Bank faces evolving challenges. Nevertheless, we suggest that the PBC has established itself as a substantial force within Chinese macroeconomic policy. Although the party leadership has final policy authority, the PBC plays a key role in establishing policy options, offering advice, and at times pressuring the leadership. In most instances monetary policy is finalized through negotiation primarily between the Bank and the party leadership, although other players such as the powerful National Development and Reform Commission and the MOF also play a role. Overall then, PBC has managed to build institutional capacities, expertise, and a range of policy instruments in the monetary arena. It has also managed to develop a credible policy track record in dealing with inflation, all of which has helped cement its policy authority, at least thus far.

The apparently competing agendas noted above, of state control versus the delegation of authority to the central bank, have led to polarized assessments of PBC's capacity in the policy realm and its place within the party-state.

Based on the first dynamic, there is a view that in reality the PBC is a puppet agency of the central state and a mere implementation body of monetary policy (Gilley and Murphy 2001). Alternatively, the formal-legal approach, based on a de jure interpretation of central bank laws, emphasizes the PBC's authority, in some studies producing striking results. For example, using one well-known index of central bank independence, Arnone et al. (2009) conclude that by the end of 2003, the central bank in China was politically more independent than that in Australia and on par with those in Canada and the United Kingdom, while by using another well-known measure, the Cukierman index, China achieved an overall central bank independence score higher than that of New Zealand (Arnone et al. 2009, Appendix, Table 10).

We argue that these polarized depictions of the PBC are misleading, reflecting limited efforts to systematically examine the black box of Chinese central banking in relation to how the monetary and financial policy system actually works, how it is evolving, and how inflation control, exchange rate intervention, and banking and financial reform have been tackled within what some observers have called a "bizarre hierarchy" of monetary authority in China (Gilley and Murphy 2001, 49). Of the limited works, Holz's (1992) introduction to China's central banking system focuses on the operational dimensions of the PBC in China's financial system, while Guo (2002) devotes a major part of his analysis of China's central banking to the sequential reforms of the banking system in general. Most of the existing literature on China's central banking and monetary and financial policy is based primarily on examining formal legal-institutional arrangements and economic variables. This means that the historic relationship and policy interaction between the central bank and the CCP leadership has been largely neglected in current research. Yet this is crucial in understanding the politics of monetary and financial policy and the path China has taken in fighting inflation and building a capable central bank and modern financial infrastructure.

We therefore seek to chart and explain the complex and nuanced pattern of institutional change and institutional relations that have underpinned the rising authority of the PBC. The PBC is not a puppet agency, nor is it independent of the central state leadership. By deriving a specific argument on central banking from a highly generalized assessment of the nature of the Chinese political regime, the puppet agency view underestimates the institutional flexibility and authority the Chinese central bank has gained during the reform era and especially since the 1990s. As for the central bank independence view, this again highlights the problems of drawing on an often abstracted body of literature and its proxy measures to arrive at detailed country-specific claims. Instead we show how policymaking in the monetary and financial arena involves, most centrally, an evolving relationship between the Bank and party leadership. We show how the PBC's influence in this relationship has increased substantially over time, underpinned by growing resource exchanges and mutual dependencies.

Explaining the Rise of the PBC—the Central Bank Independence Literature?

There is now a substantial literature that seeks to explain the rising authority of central banks, the main strand of which is the central bank independence (CBI) literature. Despite the fact that the CBI end point has not been substantively reached in China (or in many other developing countries, despite statutory changes), the primary institutional shift—growing institutional authority—is common across many cases, including China. A range of causal drivers are isolated in the CBI literature, some relating to domestic politics (usually in liberal democratic settings) and others relating to international dynamics or the pressures of globalization. The domestic causal factors isolated in this literature focus on the dynamics of government decision making or on factionalized or competitive party dynamics in democratic settings (Banaian et al. 1986; Goodman 1991; Lohmann 1994). Some scholars have focused on coalitional politics, especially the role of the financial sector in pressuring government for policies of low inflation or "sound money" and central bank independence (Bowles and White 1994; Epstein 1992; Posen 1993). There are also arguments that governments grant authority to central banks in order to help shift blame if policy decisions go wrong, thus providing the government with a handy political buffer. The problem with these accounts, however, is that they focus on the dynamics of government decision making or on party dynamics in democratic settings, which simply do not apply to the Chinese case, where the political system remains dominated by one authoritarian party. Are accounts focusing on external or international factors better at explaining the growth of central bank authority in China? Given that the growing authority of central banks has been something of a worldwide shift, and one, according to some analysts, that is indicative of global (neoliberal) policy convergence (Polillo and Guillen 2005), it is not surprising that relevant explanations have increasingly featured accounts based on externally oriented pressures related to institutional isomorphism or the pressures imposed by global financial markets. Bowles and colleagues (2000) make the interesting observation that the widespread shift toward rapidly rising central bank authority occurred not during the height of inflationary challenges experienced in many countries in the 1970s and 1980s but in the relatively lower inflationary context of the 1990s. "This temporal paradox," they argue, "is resolved by viewing CBI not as a response to inflation but to the deregulation and liberalization of financial markets and the corresponding increase in international capital flows" (59).

Within the CBI literature that deals with external pressures on developing countries, the most influential accounts focus on international factors, arguing that greater exposure to international financial markets potentially exposes governments to influential policy demands for low and stable inflation and central bank independence (Maxfield 1997). In relation to the China case, however, such external financial pressures have little explanatory purchase. First, these approaches exaggerate the importance of central bank authority in reassuring investors and signaling policy credibility, especially given the difficulties in actually measuring central bank authority from afar or in interpreting formal indices of CBI (Forder 1998). Investors respond more to the lure of potentially profitable investment opportunities than to the legal status of the central bank. Johnson (2002) argues that many profitable ventures in postcommunist states have attracted capital inflows, regardless of the status of the central bank. This experience is certainly borne out in China, which has very high rates of FDI inflow but has a central bank that is not formally independent. The dynamics surrounding international credit markets and the alleged need to signal creditworthiness in debt or bond markets via an independent central bank are also not particularly applicable to the China case. The Chinese economy has been designed to be relatively insulated from international financial market pressures, rendering arguments about creditworthiness signaling to markets (Maxfield 1997) as not applicable to the China case, largely because China has emerged as one of the world's leading creditors.

True, there are mounting foreign pressures on the value of the yuan and the Chinese exchange rate regime, which has become a key agenda for the international community, especially the United States (IMF 2004). But thus far China still manages its own exchange rate. It is also the case that China's

World Trade Organization (WTO) obligations in the case of its banking reform mean increased foreign presence in domestic banking. Crucially, however, China's regulated pattern of financial opening, its strong role in international credit markets, its high rate of national savings, its success in attracting
FDI, and its success thus far in managing inflation has reduced potential
foreign pressure on domestic monetary arrangements. The Chinese practice of
extreme caution toward financial opening instead suggests that the institutional
capacity of the state is far more resilient than neoliberal talk of a shrinking or
weakening state confronted by globalization.

As we shall see in Chapter 5, the effects of international policy diffusion
and elite networking have influenced China's central banking and monetary
policy, but these influences have not granted authority to the People's Bank.
Our analysis instead points to the importance of *domestic* arrangements. The
main problem with the "outside-in" approaches above is that they ignore the
fact that (domestic) institutions matter in filtering and mediating the pressures of the international system, and in framing domestic preferences and
policy choices (Keohane and Milner 1996; Weiss 2003). A further striking
characteristic of the CBI literature and of the broader policy diffusion literature is that much attention is focused on international pressures and sometimes on the motives of governments, but little attention is given to central
banks themselves. This is especially so in terms of their specific institutional
characteristics and capacities in the monetary and financial arena, and to the
nature of the resource exchanges and mutual dependencies between the central
bank and state leaders. This is a substantial lacuna, and we argue that China's
central banking and the growing authority of the PBC have been shaped more
by domestic institutional change dynamics in a transition context and in the
shadow of the party leadership.

As Tsou (1995, 156) rightfully argued, "Chinese history is so complex that
it provides many hard tests for theories, models and general propositions
based on Western cases. In turn, the Chinese experience might form the basis
for new general propositions enriching the theories and models that have
been built on the Western experience." A review of the extant literature on
the CBI literature suggests that this is also the case for the evolving authority
of the PBC, and that we need a more compelling theoretical framework in
explaining the dynamics behind the process.

Explaining Institutional Change and
the Rise of the PBC

We analyze the rise of the PBC and China's evolving monetary and financial architecture as a process of large-scale institutional change, covering more than three decades since the beginning of the reform era in the late 1970s. Yet if underlying institutional change and capacity building have been central to the PBC's rise, how should we conceptualize and explain this? Johnson (2003, 289) argues that institutional change in postcommunist transitions "remains poorly understood." Certainly, the empirical story of large-scale institutional change that has provided the foundation for the rise of the PBC does not fully accord with institutional accounts of postcommunist transitions that emphasize a pattern of constraining "path dependency" born of the legacies of communist central planning and state hierarchy (Liew 2005, 335). Institutional theory has been a core component of political science in recent decades, but it confronts difficulties in explaining institutional change. It is widely argued in the relevant institutionalist literature that institutions constrain agents and are inertial, rule bound, and resistant to change. Consequently, any minor changes that do occur are seen in terms of constraining, path-dependent processes or, in the case of major change, as the result of extrainstitutional factors, such as "exogenous shocks." Given this "sticky" view of institutions, it is often claimed that institutional theory has tended to be better at explaining institutional stasis and persistence rather than change (Thelen and Steinmo 1992). However, the substantial examples of dynamic institutional change in China in recent decades suggest there may be something wrong with this kind of sticky institutional theory.

A key problem is that all of the main versions of institutional theory, including historical institutionalism (HI), sociological institutionalism, and rational choice approaches, have all emphasized sticky institutional theorizing. In this book, we use HI as our main theoretical approach. However, we critique the sticky version of HI and attempt to move beyond the current bounds of such theory and its highly constrained view of agency and its circumscribed notions of change. Our aim is to develop and use an alternative HI approach to explaining institutional change. We opt instead for a more agent-centered version of HI and argue for a more active notion of agency than that found in sticky versions of HI. This approach recognizes that institutions are mutable and that agents, who are ultimately the drivers of change, have contingent and varying degrees of choice and discretion within institutional settings (Bell 2011). Hence, agents are not passive or locked into institutional formats but can be proactive in shaping institutions. We need to model active agents operating with varying degrees of initiative and discretion, in environments that are not only constraining but also potentially empowering. In contrast to sticky versions of HI that stress the constraining effects of institutions or constrained path-dependent choices, our approach recognizes the impact of institutions but also opens out space for agency. We also see actors as interpretive; they are able to make sense of the world and forge new patterns of change by utilizing ideational resources and discursive practices. Actors are able to exploit institutional resources and wider contexts that enable them to effect change. We also model agents as operating in multiple institutional settings and wider contexts that can evolve and open up new opportunities for agents. Indeed, we argue that the impact of a series of wider contexts helped shape the capacities and empower agents within the PBC.

Thus far the question of context has not been central in institutional theory and considerations of it have been ad hoc, driven by particular and diverse theoretical perspectives. For example, sticky HI theorists rely on crisis contexts to explain change. Other approaches have also separately highlighted the impact of, for example, ideational, policy, and structural contexts. Our aim here is to treat the question of context more systematically and address it through a more unified and coherent theoretical approach. In this book we show how agents within the PBC interacted with key contexts, including economic crises, changing historical contexts, wider constellations of political power (especially within the party leadership), changes in public policy, and changing ideational as well as structural contexts (especially the economic transition), all of which were important in shaping change and institutional development at the PBC.

We show how key agents operated, first within the PBC, a proximate institutional environment, and second, in wider environments. For example, economic crisis contexts in the late 1970s and again in the late 1980s and early 1990s facilitated a change in the distribution of power within the Chinese central state, especially at the elite leadership level. Interactions between the leaders of the party-state and the leaders of the PBC are important in explaining the rise of the latter, but these actors do not operate on a level playing field because the steep hierarchy of the party-state is dominated by the "political elite"; the members of the CCP's Politburo, particularly members of its Standing Committee, the party-state's paramount decision-making group. However, power relations within the party-state have not been static; the changing power context mattered. By the early 1990s, the restructuring of power within the party leadership saw the decline of older conservative elites and the deep factional contests that had in part inhibited the rise of the PBC in the 1980s. The subsequent rise of a new generation of elites pursuing more decisive market-oriented policies and reforms helped cement the rising authority of key institutions, such as the PBC, that could help successfully navigate the economic transition. The ideational context was also important, particularly norms of central bank professionalism and the commitment to fighting inflation that the leaders of the PBC increasingly shared with the wider international community of central bankers.

Crucial also was the changing structural context of the economic transition. Economic reform and the structural transition in China since 1978 can roughly be divided into two periods (Naughton 2008b). In the so-called first era of reform and transition until the early 1990s, reforms gradually saw market elements added to the older planning regime, creating a hybrid "plan-market" system (Liew 2005, 333). As we show in Chapters 3 and 4, this was an era when the legacies and constraints of the previous planning era constrained the development of monetary policy and the role of the PBC. China's authoritarian politics, its transition status, the initial legacy of its plan-oriented economic system, and the political and ideological conflicts surrounding China's economic transition and opening all meant that the transition did not entail a leap of faith into the "free market," as was the case in the "big bang" transition approach adopted in Russia or a number of other eastern European countries. Instead, the process of economic reform was gradual, particularistic, and highly regulated by the state, aimed all along at keeping the process on track and shoring up ongoing political support for the reforms and for the regime (Shirk 1993, 1996). As we argue more fully in later chapters, the dynamics of transition and institutional change have been shaped by tensions between the old and the new, by factional contests within the elite and the bureaucracy, and by the huge technical and institutional complexities of gradually shifting away from central planning toward more market-oriented processes.

During China's second era of reform from the early to mid-1990s, the leadership dynamics of the party-state and the impacts of the economic transition increasingly became more permissive and enabling. Indeed, a major challenge in China's economic transition has increasingly been the need to confront new market pressures, build new instruments of market-oriented economic policy, and create a complex regulatory and institutional infrastructure for a more market-oriented economy, virtually from scratch. The economic transition changed the way the economy was managed, from a mandatory central plan to more flexible adjustments through market-oriented macroeconomic management. The shift in the wider economic system invariably, albeit gradually, led to a shift of authority and power from the old bureaucratic institutions to new more market-oriented institutions, a shift attested to by the gradual wane of the old planning apparatus and the gradual rise of the PBC.

These changing contexts all helped to foster the institutional development of the PBC and to set the stage for the growth of resource exchanges and strong mutual dependencies between the PBC and leadership of the party-state, all of which helped underpin the growing authority of the PBC. Increasingly, the transition context rewarded those technocrats able to develop knowledge, expertise, and policy capacities in monetary and financial affairs and who were able to successfully steer the grueling market transition and its manifold challenges. The developments in the market sector demanded a new type of regulatory institution that the old party-state could not offer, an institution that had the expertise and authority to oversee price and financial stability in a volatile market. The PBC's success was also due to the fact that it was able to develop techniques of institutional change and adaptation that allowed it to *gradually* develop market instruments that proved uniquely suited to Chinese political and institutional requirements for bargained gradualism. These capacities increasingly cemented strong *institutional* dependencies between the PBC and the leadership of the party-state, with the latter depending increasingly on the expertise of the former. In turn, these dependencies deepened into wider forms of *political* dependency between the party elite and the PBC as the latter increasingly became a key player in the internal politics and policy circle within the Chinese state. The PBC was thus able to forge strong mutual dependencies with the party leadership by becoming indispensable to it. Ultimately, the growing authority of the PBC was an artifact of the changing relations between it and the party leadership. We thus see the sources of the Chinese central bank's growing authority as primarily located in the dynamics of the PBC's growing institutional resources and capacity in the transition context and in the evolving nature of the PBC's relations with the party leadership. Hence, an important solution to the puzzle of rising central bank authority in China lies in the structural component of the transition process and the emerging imperatives of the market economy and how this context shaped institutional change and growing mutual institutional and political dependencies between the PBC and the party elite.

Chinese Reforms?

This book also addresses certain deficiencies in extant accounts of China's financial reforms and more generally the assessment of economic reform and state building since 1978. Here, the contradictions associated with China's experience of liberal reforms under political autocracy have largely polarized the literature into camps that are either critical or laudatory. China's contradictions include double-digit economic growth based on an unsustainable development model; internationally renowned achievements in poverty reduction combined with growing income inequality; state-led institutional reforms on a sweeping scale plagued by rampant micro-level corruption; and a dynamic private sector combined with continuous dominance by state enterprises in key sectors.

In recent accounts, the optimists maintain that the so-called Beijing Consensus or the Chinese trajectory of a "state-directed capitalism" serves as a credible alternative to the neoliberal-inspired Washington Consensus (Ramo 2004; Halper 2010). For other sympathetic scholars, the success of a range of state-led reform is acknowledged and is attributed to factors such as regulatory reforms that have rendered the Chinese state more accommodating to and compatible with the emerging market economy (Yang 2004; Naughton 2008a). These arguments are in tune with arguments about the capacity and flexibility of the ruling CCP in adapting to a changing socioeconomic environment (Zheng and Brodsgaard 2006; Shambaugh 2009).

In stark contrast, a group of skeptics question the direction and momentum of the reforms and the capacity of the Chinese state to build effective institutions. For example, Pei (2006) asserts that China's gradualist transition has planted the seeds of crony capitalism and interest group rent seeking, which have increasingly stalled, captured, and trapped the reform process and stymied institutional development. In a similar vein, Y. Huang (2008) sees the reforms as having slipped into a form of "bad capitalism," focused more on urban industrial development and inequality at the expense of the private rural entrepreneurial innovations of the previous decade. Moreover, in the financial realm, Walter and Howie (2011) interpret key reforms from a perspective of crony capitalism and as "business as usual," aimed at luring both domestic and international investors into funding a state-controlled financial system that continues to support indebted state-owned enterprises as well as the party elite's patronage system.

By examining the institutional evolution of the Chinese central bank in the reform era, this book seeks to present a more nuanced assessment within this mostly polarized debate. We argue that an increasingly professionalized and more market-oriented PBC constitutes a form of modern regulatory infrastructure that has been gaining traction at the heart of China's macroeconomic management. In relation to the PBC, this reflects a partial reconfiguration of institutional relationships between the state and the market, between party and government organs, and between the traditional planning and market-oriented elements within the party-state. We also argue that the rise of the PBC points to steps toward a more professionalized "regulatory state" in China, at least in the monetary policy arena. The notion of a regulatory state implies the rise of relatively authoritative, professional institutions charged with the regulation of an increasingly market-oriented economy. In many countries the rise of independent central banks or other forms of independent regulatory agency are good examples of this trend toward greater institutionalization (Moran 2002). However, Pearson (2005) argues that in China the emergence of a regulatory state is being stymied by the centralizing hand of the party-state that refuses to relinquish control to markets or devolve substantial authority to relatively independent regulatory authorities. We partially question this view, at least in relation to the PBC, which has experienced a very substantial increase in institutional capacity and authority.

Nevertheless, a textured account of the PBC's role within the Chinese political hierarchy also suggests a somewhat sober view on the state of the reform process. Despite growing authority, the lack of institutional independence for the central bank suggests a work in progress, even perhaps potential vulnerabilities. Certainly, in the monetary policy arena, reform momentum is subject to more or less persistent political pressures, such as elite and bureaucratic power plays, as well as bargaining between and within central and local governments. In other words, we see positive developments in institution building and change in Beijing's efforts in establishing a modern central banking system and monetary policy framework. But we also argue that there is still a long way to go in terms of the secure institutionalization of these reforms. Moreover, the PBC is always potentially vulnerable to policy miscalculations that could easily damage its reputation and authority.

Our book also seeks to establish a more convincing model in explaining the informal exchanges within the party-state, particularly the behavioral dynamics of key agents, such as party elites and senior bureaucrats. There have been contradictory assumptions and interpretations of the determinants of elite preferences regarding reform policy. For example, Shih (2008) attributes China's macroeconomic cycles and policy deliberations mostly to elite politics and factional struggles, and argues that policies are invariably made on the basis of short-term political calculations, even on the part of those who are commonly seen as reformers, such as Premier Zhu Rongji. On the other hand, despite their critical views on China's financial reforms, Walter and Howie (2011) argue that the reforms under Zhu's premiership were genuine. In this book, we argue that an exclusive focus on elite politics is not adequate because it obscures another key dimension of the drivers of institutional change in reform China, that is, the institutional resources and the informal exchanges between political elites and senior bureaucrats. We treat elite (and bureaucrat) preferences as a complex matrix of both ideational and political factors, and argue that these different combinations formed the backbone of the informal coalitions that then influenced the policymaking and institutional reform process. Moreover, in contrast to factional or purely political accounts, we suggest that the preferences of bureaucratic elites are shaped by the norms and goals of policy and professional competence and performance. This has certainly been true of elites within the PBC.

The Interviews

A key focus of our analysis is the ongoing interplays between political and institutional players that have shaped the path of monetary policy and central banking reform in China. Access to credible sources often makes things difficult for scholars of contemporary Chinese politics. Many accounts have relied on hearsay in overseas media, particularly those based in Hong Kong.[3] The empirical research of this book is based on two main sources, critical engagement with documentary writings and, more importantly, elite interviews in Beijing.

We conducted a series of elite interviews between 2005 and 2011 in Beijing, mostly with current or former central bankers with at least medium-level bureaucratic rank. The material gained was cross-checked with interviews with officials from other related government institutions, such as the National Development and Reform Commission, the MOF, and the China Banking Regulatory Commission. Given the lack of transparency of China's central decision-making regime, this direct access to the "insiders" equips this research with unique, firsthand empirical evidence of what really happens behind closed doors. This gives the study a firm grounding in advancing our understanding on the inner mechanisms of the operation of the Chinese central bank, the informal (but important) hierarchy of Chinese monetary authority, and the elite and bureaucratic politics involved in the monetary and financial policy process.

The Chapters

We divide this book into three parts. Part I includes an introduction to the book and its theoretical framework and analytical method. Part II charts the formal and informal institutional and political dynamics that have formed the basis for the rise of the PBC. These dynamics for the 1980s are discussed in Chapters 3 and 4, and for the so-called second reform era, for period since the early 1990s, in Chapters 5 to 7. Based on the argument in Part II, that the PBC has gained increasing authority, Part III discusses in detail how this enhanced authority and relationship with the party leadership has been reflected in the actual policy processes, including monetary policy, exchange rate policy, and banking reform. Hence, establishing and explaining the institutional and political foundations for the rise of an authoritative central bank and then further illustrating its strengths and setbacks in various key policy arenas define the logic of our exposition.

Following this introductory chapter, Chapter 2 develops the theoretical model of an agent-centered historical institutionalism that will be deployed in our explanation of institutional change and the rising authority of the PBC. The chapter first charts a way beyond one of the major impasses in institutional theory, the tendency to see institutions as sticky, featuring highly constrained patterns of change. The chapter makes the case for a version of historical institutionalism that places active, interpretive agents at the center of analysis but which also traces the mutual shaping of agents, institutions, and wider contexts over time.

In Part II, we trace and explain the gradual rise of the PBC. In Chapters 3 and 4 we deal with the impact of institutional and structural constraints on the PBC and on monetary policy imposed by the initial transition era and by the legacies of central planning in the first reform era in the period between 1978 and 1992. Here we highlight the unique nature of the Chinese transition, the continuing centrality of China's one-party rule, and a strong central state. Chapter 3 first sets the scene by outlining the nature of the Chinese party-state and the wider economic policy and institutional system. The slow and difficult evolution of the PBC in the first reform era under the "shadow of the plan" is then examined. In accord with the so-called legacy school of institutional change in transition settings, we highlight the impact of the old planning regime and factionalized party-state on central bank reform in China and on monetary affairs, especially during the first reform era until the early 1990s. Chapter 4 then deals with the evolution of China's monetary policy during this period. We first briefly review the prereform era and the issue of repressed inflation and this is followed by a detailed discussion of monetary policy in the 1980s. In particular, we discuss the PBC's weak position in the bureaucracy, its initial lack of expertise and knowledge in dealing with the market transition, and the PBC's dilemmas in developing monetary policy instruments under the constraints of the "plan-market" system. We then examine unfolding monetary developments over three inflationary cycles during this period, culminating in the inflationary crises of the late 1980s and early 1990s.

Chapters 5 and 6 chart and explain the rising authority of the PBC during the second reform era from the early to mid-1990s. In Chapter 5, we first trace how the rising authority of the PBC was shaped by the way in which it interacted with a series of wider contexts in which it was embedded, including inflationary crises, changes in the complexion of elite power within the party-state, as well as the wider forces unleashed by the market transition, particularly the imperative of developing market-oriented policies and more effective institutions of economic governance. In Chapter 6 we further explore the wider power context, especially the deepening institutional and political dependencies between the PBC and the leadership of the party state that helped elevate the PBC. In Chapter 7 we examine the follow-up effects of this change, especially the main formal institutional changes to the central bank's role during the second reform era, including the central banking law in 1995 and associated regulatory reforms. We argue that this series of formal institutional changes both reflected and further strengthened the hand of the PBC.

In Part III we show how the PBC's enhanced authority and relationship with the party leadership has been reflected in the actual policy processes, influencing key policy issues in the second reform era. This includes developing a monetary policy framework and fighting against consumer and asset price inflation (Chapters 8 and 9), the PBC's role in exchange rate policy and reserve management (Chapter 10), and in wider financial and banking reforms (Chapter 11). Hence, Part II charts and explains the institutional and political foundations for the rise of a more authoritative central bank and Part III then illustrates the PBC's strengths and setbacks in various key policy arenas.

Chapters 8 and 9 explore the PBC's impact on China's monetary policy in the second era of economic reform since 1992. We argue that as the central bank gradually gained greater institutional authority, the crafting and implementing of monetary policy in the post-1992 era marked a significant departure from the previous period. In Chapter 8, we see the PBC embarking on a quest for a new, more market-oriented monetary policy framework during this period. This included establishing a set of policy objectives and operational targets, as well as crafting a combination of direct and indirect instruments that awarded the Bank a degree of policy discretion. In Chapter 9, we examine the PBC's role in China's monetary policy through the lens of three major economic cycles since the early 1990s. Under Zhu Rongji's governorship in the early 1990s, the PBC managed to reign in inflation for the first time with a soft landing in 1996. In the wake of the Asian financial crisis and domestic deflation during 1998 and 2002, it struck a delicate balance between playing a supportive role to a proactive fiscal policy and refraining from a more expansionary monetary policy. And since 2003, the PBC has become a more assertive central bank in its efforts to manage inflation and tackle new challenges such as asset price inflation amid both internal and external imbalances and crises. We also review the emergency expansion of credit mandated by the party leadership in 2009, which constituted a setback for disciplined monetary policy and for the PBC.

Chapter 10 deals with the PBC's growing role in exchange rate policy. We briefly review China's dual-track foreign exchange regime before 1994, when it was unified into one system that featured a fixed peg to the U.S. dollar. We then examine the PBC's role in Beijing's non-devaluation policy in the aftermath of the Asian financial crisis and argue that the central bank began to be more assertive in the policy process. We then elaborate on the recent global debate on the revaluation of the Chinese currency amid the systemic imbalances between China and the United States and argue that the PBC, under the reformist governorship of Zhou Xiaochuan, has been the major force behind the move to reform the exchange regime in 2005 amid political resistance, in which Beijing replaced the dollar-peg regime with a managed system in which the value of the RMB is determined by a basket of currencies. This effectively led to an appreciation of the RMB and awarded the PBC with more room to maneuver in the realm of monetary policy.

In Chapter 11 we examine the PBC's efforts in leading financial reforms since 2003 in addressing the challenges posed by China's accession to the WTO, in establishing a sound monetary transmission mechanism, and in pursuing macrofinancial stability. We argue that the PBC has been the major force in reforming financial intermediaries in the banking sector and the stock market. The PBC has also injected new ideas and approaches in China's reserve management. The chapter also looks at the PBC's efforts in building a modern payment infrastructure in China.

In Chapter 12, the conclusion, we review our argument and major findings, as well as their theoretical and empirical implications. We also place our findings in a comparative context, comparing experiences from other developing countries, such as India, and other transition economies, such as Russia.

2

Explaining Institutional Change:
An Agents-in-Contexts Approach

The rise of the PBC is a story about institutional change and political relationships. In this book we focus on the leaders of the PBC and how they molded and changed the Bank as an institution and enhanced its capacities. In turn these leaders used their enhanced institutional capacities to forge mutually supportive relationships with the leadership of the party-state, all of which helped elevate the Bank's policy influence and authority. The approach we use in explaining such change foregrounds agency and recognizes that institutional and wider contexts of action are not only constraining but are also potentially *empowering*, offering agents important resources and opportunities. Furthermore, we argue that agents not only operate within specific institutions but also interact with other institutions and wider "meta-institutional" contexts that also help shape behavior and patterns of constraint and opportunity.

Much of established institutional theory is not good at elucidating such dynamics. All versions of such theory—historical, sociological, and rational choice approaches—argue that institutions matter because the rules, norms, and standard operating procedures they embody shape the choices and behavior of agents. Yet these approaches have trouble explaining change because of their highly constraining or "sticky" notions of institutions. A key problem is the assumptions that institutional environments are highly constraining, which leads to a highly restricted account of agency. In this book we give greater scope to agency, accepting that agents and institutions are mutually shaping over time and that agents ultimately propel change.

We also seek to expand the domain of causal influences. We argue that agents interact not only with the proximate institutions in which they are embedded but with wider meta-institutional contexts that also shape behavior and opportunities. Instead of focusing solely on the minutia of institutional rules and norms and their effects on given actors, institutions often look more flexible if we see them as situated within and shaped by wider contexts, for example, wider ideational, power, or economic contexts. Such contexts can help foster change and provide agents with resources and rationales for reform. We thus place agents (albeit institutionally situated agents) at the center of analysis and trace the mutually shaping interactions of agents (especially in the PBC) and their institutional and wider contexts over time.

Thus far the question of wider contexts has not been central in institutional theory, and considerations of it have been ad hoc, driven by particular and diverse theoretical perspectives. For example, sticky historical institutionalism (HI) theory tends to rely on major crises to explain institutional change. Other approaches have separately highlighted the impact of, for example, ideational, policy, or structural contexts. Our aim here is to treat the question of wider contexts more systematically and address it through a more unified theoretical approach. We show how agents within the PBC interacted with key meta-institutional contexts, including crises, wider constellations of political power, changes in public policy, and changing ideational as well as structural contexts (especially the economic transition), all of which were important in shaping change at the PBC. These contextual relationships all helped to foster the institutional development of the PBC. Interactions within the wider political context were particularly important because this arena saw the growth of strong mutual dependencies between the PBC and leadership of the party-state, which helped underpin the growing authority of the PBC. Our agent-centered institutional approach—essentially a variant of HI theory—focuses on how agents operate in relations of constraint and opportunity within institutional and wider meta-institutional contexts; essentially an "agents-in-contexts" approach.

This approach also poses questions about another facet of sticky institutional theory, its emphasis on highly constraining notions of "path-dependent" change. This notion sees institutional change essentially occurring in historical grooves where prior choices or events shape future outcomes. The impacts of sunk costs or institutional legacies are often cited as causal mechanisms in this regard. We accept that such underlying mechanisms can be important, but we question the value of aggregating such effects into a relatively inflexible account of path dependency. Instead we invoke a more agency-centered account that allows us to explain how the path of institutional change followed by the PBC was more dynamic than the relatively constrained notions that path dependency theory implies.

Later chapters explore the empirical dimensions of our account, but in this chapter the key theoretical resources for our approach to institutional analysis are unpacked.

Explaining Institutional Change

Historical institutionalism appears to be bifurcating between, on the one hand, recent constructivist accounts that downplay institutional constraints and overemphasize the role of ideas in shaping institutional life (Blyth 2002; Hay 2007; Schmidt 2008; for a critique, see Bell 2011) and, on the other hand, accounts that present overly sticky depictions of institutional life featuring deeply constrained notions of agency and strong versions of path dependency. In this latter literature, institutions are often depicted as inertial, rule bound, and highly constraining. As Pierson (2000b, 490) puts it, "Institutional arrangements in politics are typically hard to change." Indeed, critics claim that many established versions of "new institutionalism" (rational choice, historical and sociological institutionalism) are unable to effectively explain institutional change because the actors or agents in question are said to be highly constrained by their institutional environments. Hence, Weyland (2008, 281) argues that "institutionalism has emphasised inertia and persistence," offering a "static" view of institutional life. Schmidt (2008, 314) sees the established institutionalisms as "subordinating agency to structure," while Crouch and Keune (2005, 83) argue that "institutional configurations are often presented as a straightjacket from which endogenous actors cannot escape." Such themes have been apparent in HI, with Blyth (1997, 230) arguing that HI sees institutions as "constraining rather than enabling political action."

For their part, rational choice scholars generally see institutional arrangements as "equilibria" from which actors have few incentives to diverge. This approach also uses a priori assumptions about agents' preferences, verging on a "calculating automatons" approach (Hay and Wincott 1998, 952). The norm-bound, "over-socialized" (Wrong 1961) conceptions of agency often found in sociological institutionalism also make explaining change difficult (Koelble 1995, 232). Thus Fligstein (2001, 110) argues, "The critique of both the sociological and rational choice perspectives that I want to make suggests that neither opens up the problem of action and gives real people much leeway in creating their social worlds."

Within HI, these sticky or constraining notions of institutions have led to a focus on noninstitutional factors, such as exogenous shocks or crises, to explain change. Yet critics such as Hay and Wincott (1998, 502) worry that a "latent structuralism" can be discerned in much of HI, while, more recently, Olsen (2009, 3) argues that the approach is "overly structuralist and does not grant purposeful actors a proper role" (see also Peters 2005). These sorts of criticisms are not new and, according to pioneering HI scholars such as Thelen and Steinmo (1992, 16), a "critical inadequacy of institutionalist analysis has been a tendency towards mechanical, static accounts that largely bracket the issue of change and sometimes lapse inadvertently into institutional determinism." The key missing element, of course, is a role for agency and some kind of plausible analysis for the dialectical or mutually shaping interplay between agency and institutional and wider contexts.

To help explain dynamic institutional change, we need to move beyond standard sticky notions of constraint and path dependency, toward what Crouch (2007) calls a "post-determinist" institutional analysis. In particular, the approach used here gives greater scope to agency, accepting that agents and institutions are mutually shaping over time and that agents are the ultimate propellant of change. We argue that agents have a degree of discretion in institutional environments, more than established theory suggests. We also argue that institutional environments are not only constraining but also potentially empowering. The main problem with established institutional theory, such as sticky HI, is that it begins analysis by considering the impact of institutions on agents, largely a top-down, constraining view. Agents are seen as enmeshed and constrained by institutions, leaving consideration of agency almost as a secondary issue. We utilize a somewhat different ontology, which starts with agents and their behavior. Our approach works outward

from agents and examines how they build and shape institutions and negotiate institutional constraints and opportunities. Also, agents not only operate
in institutions but are also influenced by wider contexts, hence our agents-in-
contexts approach.

It is often assumed that HI is a monolithic whole, but this view is incorrect. In fact, HI is best seen as being constituted by two different types of
approach. The first of these, as outlined above, features strong elements of
institutional stickiness and path dependency, with the resultant emphasis on
exogenous shocks to explain change. Arguably, this is an overly determinist
account with a limited view of agency. However, a second strand of HI analysis also provides the basis for a robust account of institutional change and
major shifts in institutional paths. This approach focuses on active agency
operating in relations of constraint and empowerment within institutional
and wider settings. As Thelen and Steinmo (1992, 17) have argued, we need to
unpack the institutional black box and focus on "strategic actors" and how
they are capable of acting on discretionary "openings" (see also Cortell and
Petersen 1999; Campbell 1997, 2002, 2004; Crouch 2005, 2007). As Crouch
(2005, 3) puts it, the challenge "is to devise theories of action that retain all
the insights of neo-institutionalism concerning the constrained nature of human action, while also being able to account for innovation."

Some scholars, like Schneiberg (2007, 50), however, worry about abandon-
ing the "institutional determinism" and the emphasis on the "constraining
power of context" that allegedly gives HI its "analytical edge." He argues,
"Either we preserve institutional insights about path dependence and the
constraining power of context and deny the prospects for fundamental or
qualitative transformation. Or we preserve observations about fundamental
change and new path creation and deny our insights about path dependence
and the explanatory power of the institutional context." By contrast, we argue that such a choice is unnecessary because we reject the notion that institutional determinism within HI provides a useful analytical edge. A more
nuanced approach that moves beyond such deterministic accounts is needed,
one that can model agents operating with variable and contingent degrees of
constraint and empowerment within institutional and wider settings.

Institutions matter because of the ways they reflect, refract, restrain, and
enable human behavior, while, in turn, it is the behavior of agents that repro-
duces or transforms institutions over time (Clark 1998). However, actors are
interpretive, partly constructing the experience of their institutional situa-

tion using cognitive and normative frameworks. This approach recognizes that ideas, language, and discourse provide crucial building blocks for establishing meaning and understanding and thus of purposeful action in politics and institutional life (Hay 2007; Schmidt 2008; Bell 2011). Also, institutions define roles, not final behaviors, and roles always need to be interpreted. As Streeck and Thelen (2005, 14) argue, "applying a general rule to a specific situation is a *creative* act . . . the meaning of a rule is never self-evident and is always subject to and in need of interpretation" (our emphasis). Institutional life then is not about dull conformity or blind compliance; agents are not simply rule bound nor completely locked into the trajectories shaped by path dependency. Rule imprecision and ambiguity during rule enforcement or implementation all open up space for agents (Mahoney and Thelen 2010, 11–13). As is well known, actors can also be very creative in interpreting or bending rules or finding loopholes to suit their agendas. Sometimes whole careers in law or tax accounting can be devoted to such tasks. This underlines the argument made by North (1990) that the *informal* institutional arrangements worked out on the ground by agents are an important component of institutional life. In applying this reasoning to the China case, Tsai (2006, 117) argues that "adaptive informal institutions" or "informal coping strategies" can play an important role in endogenous institutional change: "the etiology of formal institutional change may lie in the informal coping strategies devised by local actors to evade [or modify] the restrictions of formal institutions" (118). As we show in later chapters, the leaders of the PBC were adept at such practices in a range of policy arenas.

Hence, far from being just being constraining, institutional and wider contexts can also be positively empowering and can offer agents important resources and opportunities (Cortell and Peterson 1999). Harty (2005) thus argues for a "resource-based" approach that investigates how agents might use rules, institutional sources of authority, expertise, or other institutional resources to help effect change. In later chapters we show how the leaders of the PBC were able on a number of occasions to deploy such institutional resources and capabilities, especially by developing expertise in arcane monetary affairs and in efforts to develop new policy agendas and complementary institutions in the monetary and financial arenas, all of which helped increase the authority of the PBC.

The Importance of Wider Meta-institutional Contexts

Besides operating in given institutions, agents also operate in multiple institutional settings, with multifarious or even competing rules and agendas or "friction among multiple political orders" (Lieberman 2002, 703), all of which potentially opens up at least some space for discretionary behavior within institutional settings (see also Beckert 1999, 780; Schneiberg 2007). Beyond specific institutional environments, the constraint and empowerment possibilities offered by wider contexts can also be important. As Thelen (1999, 384) argues, "institutional arrangements cannot be understood in isolation from the political and social setting in which they are embedded." Established theory has tended to focus on intermediate institutional dynamics, and, to the extent that wider contexts impinge, they have often been modeled as exogenous crises that propel change (Krasner 1984), as external political factors that reinforce path dependency (Pierson 2000a, 2000b), as changing "environmental conditions" that alter institutional power distributions (Mahoney and Thelen, 2010), as ideational contexts that shape actor preferences (Hay 2006; Blyth 2002; Schmidt 2008), and as policy contexts (Taylor 2009) or as external structural environments that shape institutional change (Pontussen 1995). Institutional theory, however, has treated wider contexts in an ad hoc way. Some studies consider the impacts of wider context; others do not. Moreover, the theoretical assumptions underpinning studies that do consider wider contexts have varied widely. For example, crisis and path dependency approaches are often associated with sticky HI theory while theories that emphasize the ideational context tend to be critical of sticky HI theory.

The approach here is to treat the impact of wider meta-institutional contexts more systematically and to do so through a more unified theoretical approach that posits an active role for "situated agents" within institutional and wider settings who respond to the constraints and opportunities presented to them. The account being developed here thus analyzes agents who are dialectically engaged in shaping and being shaped by their relevant institutions and wider contexts over time. Such environments can shape the behavior of agents by imposing costs or benefits on agents, by shaping actor interpretations and preferences, by the scope of agents' discretion, and by the resources and opportunities that are available to actors. Such effects, however, are always "agency actualized" because as Archer (2000, 465) puts it, "structures [and wider contexts] only exert an effect when mediated through the activities of people."

In Chapter 5 we show how agents within the PBC interacted with key contexts, including exogenous crises, changes in public policy, and changing ideational as well as structural contexts, all of which were important in shaping change at the PBC. We argue that these contextual relationships all helped to foster the institutional development of the PBC. They also set the stage for an even more significant contextual relationship in the political environment, namely the growth of strong mutual dependencies between the PBC and leadership of the party-state. Key party leaders and the PBC were also able to forge relationships of mutual dependency, both institutionally and politically, that over time became mutually empowering. The institutional dependencies reflected the PBC's growing specialized expertise and its increasingly indispensible role in managing and developing new monetary policy instruments, while the political dependencies reflected a reciprocal alliance relationship between party elites and the PBC. The relationship between the political leadership and key bureaucratic institutions such as the PBC is that of command as well as cooperation, in which the elites of the party-state control the strategic direction but at the same time delegate parcels of authority and policymaking to the central bank.

Path Dependency?

Sticky versions of HI are closely linked to theories of path-dependent change, based on common assumptions about the highly constraining nature of institutions. As noted above, however, such an account does not allow us to fully explain the relatively dynamic pattern of change associated with the rise of the PBC.

According to Kay (2005, 553), "a process is path dependent if initial moves in one direction ellicit further moves in that direction." The concept of path dependency was derived originally from studies in economic history, especially arguments about technology development, which showed how decision points such as the adoption of the QWERTY keyboard amounted to a form of technological "lock-in" that could constrain the scope of future choices (Arthur 1989; David 1985). A key insight when applied to institutional settings is that initial or unfolding institutional choices may have strong ongoing conditioning effects on agents. Path dependency theorists variously point to the impact of sunk costs or institutional legacies, with Pierson (2000b, 493) arguing, "Social adaptation to institutions drastically increases the cost of exit from existing arrangements." Another prominent and related mechanism is "reactive sequences," which Mahoney (2000 507, 509) argues have "deterministic properties," and which he defines as a "causal chain in which each step is a reaction to antecedent events." This essentially backward-looking perspective has been labeled by Raadshelders (1998) as "causality in retrospect" (see also Peters et al. 2005). On the other hand, the "pull of the future" is emphasized in so-called increasing returns or positive feedback mechanisms involving, for example, learning effects, coordination effects, adaptive expectations, or the development of complementary institutions (North 1990, 95; Pierson 2000a).

Overall, the view emanating from such theory emphasizes institutional *constraint* or highly circumscribed notions of institutional change. Agents are tightly bound; change does not occur easily and when it does, it occurs along slowly changing path-dependent lines or, more precipitously, as the result of noninstitutional factors, such as exogenous shocks or "critical junctures," which break or explode the normal bonds of institutional constraint. As Krasner (1984, 234) has argued, "Change is difficult. . . . Institutional change is episodic and dramatic rather than continuous and incremental. Crises are of central importance" (see also Ikenberry 1988, 223–24). In this view, change is seen as an abrupt episode of "punctuated equilibrium," typically followed by a period of stasis or slow-moving path-dependent change. Katznelson (2003, 283) sees periods of crisis as those periods when "constraints on agency are broken," thus opening up new opportunities. In this view, crises allow for agency; "normal" institutional life does not, or at least radically limits it. Such theorizing sets up what Krasner (1984, 240) calls a "basic analytical distinction" between "periods of institutional creation and periods of institutional stasis." The former is essentially driven by an exogenous force, the later by endogenous or institutionally embedded processes that allow little scope for agency.

This type of account provides a number of useful insights into the pattern of institutional change at the PBC during the reform era. Hence, the economic and political crises of the late 1970s called into question the efficacy of central planning and helped spur the market reform and economic opening agenda from 1979. This is a classic crisis-induced pattern of institutional change, as explained by the theory above. In the first era of reform in the 1980s, market elements were gradually added to the central planning system. One of the mechanisms invoked by path dependency approaches—the impact of institutional legacies—was important during this period. Party elites took a cautious approach to "growing out of the plan," implementing a hybrid "plan-market" system (Liew 2005, 333). This saw earlier institutional and political legacies from the era of central planning substantially constrain the development of monetary policy and the role of the PBC, as we show in Chapters 3 and 4. Monetary policy innovation and the development of the PBC were constrained by the policy legacies of the past such as centralized credit controls, by the gradualist dynamics of the transition economy, by China's immature financial markets and its managed exchange rate system, and by its hierarchical political and administrative order. Constraints were also imposed by the sheer technical and institutional complexities involved in slowly reducing reliance on the central planning system and slowly boosting the role of market mechanisms and new instruments of monetary policy. Such institutional legacies only slowly yielded to change. This pattern of constraint is broadly consistent with a path dependency account because the constraints imposed by institutional legacies were substantial. As Pierson (2000b, 493) argues, "the dead weight of previous institutional choices seriously limits room for maneuver." This was apparent in relation to the PBC in the 1980s as it struggled under the shadow cast by the planning regime amid the emerging plan-market system.

A subsequent economic and social crisis of the late 1980s and early 1990s involving high inflation and social unrest helped foster regime change in the party leadership and usher in a second, more assertive era of economic reform that accelerated the process of market reform and China's economic transition. Gradually, the market path strengthened while the central planning system weakened. This marked a turning point. From the mid-1990s, institutional change at the PBC was shaped by the impact of increasing institutional returns as the deepening impacts of market forces and associated or complementary institutional change increasingly gained momentum and depth. As we argue in Chapter 5, the market transition provided agents within the PBC with important new opportunities to garner authority, based especially on their rising capacities and expertise and in helping the party leadership develop market mechanisms, stabilize inflation, and negotiate the transition.

In the patterns of change outlined above, we have two periods of crisis-induced path-shifting institutional change. According to path dependency accounts, such bursts of change should subsequently settle into periods of relative stasis, as the constraints associated with "normal institutional life" reassert themselves and limit change or at least drive it along predetermined grooves.

The problem, however, is that this type of path dependency approach and the sticky HI on which it is based does not provide a fully rounded account of what actually happened in this case. Our first criticism is that the above approach is too sticky. It gives insufficient scope to agency within institutional life and assumes that crises are the only or at least the main source of substantial change. We thus question the "basic analytical distinction" between change and stasis found in sticky path dependency theory. Our agency-centered approach, by contrast, blurs the distinctions between exogenous shock processes of change and more endogenous, agency-driven, incremental patterns of change. Indeed, these two patterns of change can be "inextricably intertwined" (Thelen 2004, 31). In this view, change is a function of actor discretion in changing and contingent environments. As we show in this study, patterns of change were wrought by active agents throughout the period under study, in both crisis conditions and during more incremental periods of change. It is this focus on active agents and their capacities to exercise a degree of discretion within institutional settings that underpins recent theories of *endogenous* institutional change (Streeck and Thelen 2005; Thelen 2003, 2004). Moreover, even a supposedly exogenous account of change—such as the impact of a crisis—cannot in any reasonable sense be thought of as just that. Only agents operating within institutions can ultimately produce change; hence it is hard to see how exogenous and endogenous change dynamics can be separated. As Blyth (2002) explains, "Theoretically, no exogenous factor can in and of itself explain the specific forms that institutional change takes." Only agents can do this, and there is no reason to segregate evolutionary from more crisis-driven patterns.

As we show in later chapters, key leaders in the party-state and in the PBC were relentless in their efforts to pursue institutional change, both under crisis conditions (as in the late 1970s and again in the late 1980s and early 1990s) but also in evolutionary modes as well throughout the period under study. It is true that the constraints on change imposed by institutional legacies were pronounced during the 1980s. However, even here agents were able to effect endogenous change. During the second reform era the scope for agential discretion and change widened further. Not only was the PBC able to build institutional resources, but the increasing returns of the market transition began to accumulate, rewarding institutions that were able to help steer the transition. The nature and degree of institutional constraints thus changed systematically over time, from relatively constraining to more accommodating or even empowering. Hence, to fully explain the dynamics of change it is useful to move beyond sticky versions of path dependency. We need to model agents as both partially constrained by past institutional patterns and as also operating simultaneously in wider contexts that constantly evolve and potentially open up new opportunities for agents.

This leads to a second critique. Path dependency approaches are too static, notwithstanding their emphasis on the temporal dimensions of change. As just noted, such approaches pay too little attention to how the nature and extent of institutional constraint (or empowerment) can change over time. We need a more *dynamic* approach. In the case at hand, the impact of earlier institutional legacies waned and change began to accelerate, particularly from the mid-1990s. Instead of being primarily about institutional constraint or change along predetermined paths, the rise of the PBC is better reflected in an account that emphasizes the impact of agency and, particularly as events unfolded, widening opportunities for change. More broadly, the sheer scale and dynamism of the changes in question sit oddly with the highly constrained notions of change implied by concepts such as path dependency; an approach that Crouch (2005, 23) labels the "most heavily deterministic set of arguments in neo-institutionalism." The Chinese story is more complex and dynamic than this. Change accelerated and became a cumulative process, driven increasingly by highly resourceful agents in more empowering contexts.

While the impact of mechanisms such as institutional legacies or increasing returns was influential, we question the value of aggregating such mechanisms into a full-blown account of path dependency and the high levels of determinacy and stickiness thus implied. Moreover, to the extent that underlying path dependency mechanisms are invoked, we see these not as tight constraints but as *contingencies* that agents negotiate. As Johnson (2003) argues, "path contingency" rather than the more determinist path dependency may be a better way of framing the issues at stake. As Peters et al. (2005) suggest, the path dependency approach may well "accord history a more logical trajectory . . . than actually may be the case." We thus see mechanisms such as institutional legacies or increasing returns as both potentially constraining and empowering. We trace agents within the PBC moving along a path of institutional change covering over thirty years. Crucially, the patterns of constraint and empowerment changed over time, generally in the direction of greater empowerment. Hence, the shaping role of the institutional context changed in nature. This was a function of changing institutions and how this process was shaped by agents pursuing change.

Conclusion

This chapter has charted a way beyond one of the major impasses in institutional theory, the tendency to see institutions as sticky, featuring highly constraining, path-dependent patterns of change. The more dynamic nature of institutional change explored in this study suggests there is something wrong with such theory. Instead, the argument was made for a more flexible version of historical institutionalism that places active, interpretive agents at the center of analysis and which subsequently traces the mutual shaping of agents and their institutional and wider contexts over time, which we refer to as an agents-in-contexts approach. This chapter has outlined the nature and capacities of relevant agents in such a theoretical account and how the agents in question interact with their environments. We have also suggested the need to focus on a wide range of potential causal factors in explaining institutional change. In particular, we need to model active agents operating in environments that are both constraining and also potentially empowering. We also need to model agents as both partially constrained by the past and as operating in current environments that constantly evolve and potentially open up new opportunities for change. We have also emphasized the need to embed intermediate institutions within wider contextual terrains, for these have been important facilitators of change in this case, as we show in Chapter 5. In subsequent chapters we add the key empirical dimensions to our account of institutional change in China.

PART TWO

The Institutional Rise of the PBC

3

The People's Bank in the Shadow
of the Plan, 1978–92

This chapter and Chapter 4 deal with the impact of the institutional and structural constraints imposed by the party-state and the legacies of the central planning era on the rise of the PBC and on the dynamics of monetary policy during the first era of economic reform from the late 1970s to the early 1990s.

As the PBC governor Zhou Xiaochuan (2006, 8) suggests, "the traditional planned economy leaves a mark in people's mentality." In the first part of this chapter we examine the key structural dynamics of the transition and the impact of the Leninist legacy on the PBC. This is followed by a section that unpacks the formal structures of the party-state. We then examine the PBC's limited role in the prereform era prior to 1978, followed by an examination of the PBC's slowly evolving status during the initial reform years from 1978 to 1992 as the central bank was increasingly tasked with managing the dual-track, plan-market economy.

We then show how the PBC's role was also shaped by earlier institutional legacies. Under the command economy in the prereform era, the People's Bank played a peripheral and limited role due to the systemic subordination of finance to state plans. The PBC was a mere agent for the central planning apparatus and the Ministry of Finance (MOF) in maintaining financial flows for material balance. In the initial transition period the PBC thus remained a relatively weak and junior organization, with little expertise in modern central banking. The persistence of the planning system under the plan-market arrangements also limited the PBC's options and constrained its role. Nor did the PBC have ready-made instruments and a modern financial infrastructure for conducting monetary policy in the slowly emerging market environment; these had to be developed over time. In some ways, however, the slow-moving nature of the transition was a good thing, providing time for the Bank to learn and adjust to an evolving environment. Here the PBC slowly gained status through its institutional independence from the MOF, improvements in its legislative mandate, and a broadening of its role in macroeconomic governance.

Transition Dynamics and the Leninist Legacy

In contrast to "big bang" market transitions in other transition economies, notably Russia's, the initial reform era in China and the PBC's transition toward greater authority were marked by *gradualism*. Under the plan-market system, this meant that new, market-oriented institutions were built atop, not in place of, the old state institutions. The lengthy coexistence of the institutions associated with the old and the new and the slow embedding of a market-oriented economy in a residual Leninist system formed the wider structural context in which the two evolved. Moreover, the fact that the Communist Party stayed in power rather than competing for office as in other transition economies, combined with the relatively conservative and divided power structure within the leadership of the party-state, produced an even more prolonged transition and more substantial adjustments between central state and market-oriented institutions. The juxtaposition between the old Leninist state on the one hand and emerging market and regulatory imperatives on the other hand thus formed, especially in the first reform era, a key institutional context for the development of the PBC.

There are two competing approaches to transition issues. The legacy school sees the dynamics of transition as a function of the institutions and structures established under Leninist regimes (Breslin 2003; Jowitt 1992), while the school of market imperatives attributes regime change to the power of the emerging market, to the requirements for market-oriented institutional reform, as well as pressures from international markets and institutions for liberalization and market-oriented reform (Aslund 1994; Brada 1993). The first approach emphasizes the way in which Leninist legacies and the accretion of established vested interests constrain future options and limit reform (Crawford and Lijphart 1997; Jowitt 1992). From an institutional change perspective, this accords with the inertial and/or path-dependent view of institutional change. Reflecting the criticisms of institutional theory developed in Chapter 2, Beyer and Wielgohs (2001, 360) correctly argue that this type of transition perspective "lacks the room for systematic explanations of institutional innovation." The market imperatives approach, on the other hand, places greater emphasis on agency and on the role of key political elites in seizing opportunities to force through change in an evolving market context.

It is important, however, to avoid seeing these positions in either/or terms. First, as argued in Chapter 2, sophisticated historical institutionalist research sees the interaction between structure and agency as a dialectical process in which agency and structures shape each other over time. This temporal dimension is also important in the China case for a second reason, mainly because the inertial and constraining impact of institutional and structural legacies was most apparent during the initial period of reform in China until the early 1990s, a period when conservative elites and the imprint of the old planning regime exerted considerable influence. However, as we argue in Chapters 5 and 6, this was followed by a subsequent elite-driven period of structural reform, which essentially broke the shackles of the old planning regime. The transition context was thus a dynamic environment; its basic institutions and structures changed over time and helped empower agents.

We therefore argue that the distinction between the legacy and the market schools is not as polarized as their supporters often assume and that neither of them can explain China's unique set of historical or more contemporary institutional dynamics by itself. In fact, a more convincing explanatory model should incorporate both legacy and market variables, though, as we argue, these need to be combined in a temporal, indeed "transitional," manner in which the initial rigidities gradually give way to more market-oriented and empowering contexts. In this chapter, however, and in Chapter 4, in accord with the legacy school and the inertial view of institutional change, we highlight the impact of the old planning regime on monetary affairs and central bank reform in China. We also highlight the unique nature of the Chinese transition, especially the continuing survival and centrality of China's one-party rule and its statist hierarchy. These core elements of the party-state remained in place despite growing tensions with emerging market imperatives. Nevertheless, the legacies of the planning regime continued to exert a powerful influence over politics, policymaking, and institutional development during the initial period of the Chinese reforms.

Such gradualism was partly rooted in the nature of the power structure of the Chinese state. In the first reform era the elite power structure was fragmented. Although the ultimate leader in the post-Mao era was Deng Xiaoping, power at the top was dispersed across an array of contending revolutionary elders within the party-state. This pattern essentially established competing coalitions and a number of important veto points regarding policy initiatives. As is well understood in policy analysis, the proliferation of veto players tends to produce a relatively gridlocked policy regime marked by gradualism, remorseless bargaining, and compromise between contending interests (Tsebelis 2002). The prevalence of deal making was amplified by the multifarious channels of informal power and influence that exist in Chinese politics (Dittmer 1995; Fewsmith 1996; Tsou 1995). These dynamics saw elites engaged in efforts to forge as wide a reform coalition as possible within and beyond the state in order to further their agendas, in helping to lubricate the politics of reform, and in helping to overcome some of the inefficiencies of the command system. The latter, in particular, entailed an emphasis on attracting skilled bureaucrats, professionals, managers, and risk-taking entrepreneurs. As Shirk (1993, 62) comments, "In the 1980s Deng Xiaoping and his allies decided that, although they wanted to retain essential elements of the existing system, they had to modify the party-government relationship if they were serious about improving economic performance. . . . The party had to trade off a degree of control to gain greater economic efficiency." Hence the Communist Party elites parceled out patronage and resources in order to shore up a reform coalition. A key aspect of this pattern of coalition building and bargaining that was designed to help circumvent conservatives within the party leadership in the Politburo involved devolving greater authority to the bureaucracy and to local governments during this era, a shift that would help generate considerable inflationary pressures by the late 1980s.[1] As Shirk (1993, 1996) argues, these elements were a crucial part of a centrally orchestrated "political logic" that was central to the first decade of economic reform in China.

The transition context was thus an arena of fierce ideological debate and political struggle between liberal reformers and ultra-left conservatives, and an internal rift within the reformist camp between moderates led by Chen

Yun and more radical reformers led by Deng.[2] These inner-party dynamics led to ever-changing official lines that were frustratingly ambiguous and riddled with political compromises that shaped reform in the 1980s.[3] This gradual reformist approach was less threatening to a wide range of vested interests in transition China, yet it also provided room for experimentation and correction if needed. Compared to Russia's big bang, the Chinese approach to market reform proved more politically sustainable and economically viable.

These contextual dynamics reflected the established political congealment of the Leninist regime, but the dependencies of the past were also reflected in the sheer institutional difficulties in developing market mechanisms and running them in a dual-track mode with the established planning regime. This is best demonstrated by the sequencing and achievement of the reforms during the first reform era. The market-oriented rural reforms in the early 1980s that heralded Beijing's economic restructuring were an instant and huge success, with a surge of rural output and household income, largely due to the fact that rural areas were traditionally under weak control of the planned economy (Oi 1999). Meanwhile, the subsequent reforms of urban enterprises, the central focus of the planning regime and the major constituency of the Communist Party, yielded limited achievement in the face of fierce ideological debate and resistance (Huang 2008). This was also the case for the finance sector. As we argue more fully in Chapter 4 where we deal with monetary policy during the first reform era, the problems of monetary management in a system still operating in the shadow of the plan were manifest. Although the PBC became organizationally independent from the MOF and an exclusive central bank during this period, China's monetary policy largely continued to be subject to the parameters of the production and credit plans supervised by the still-powerful planning apparatus. Therefore the central bank had to rely on centralized financial planning to help steer the emerging market. This process of institutional change thus impeded both the development of a market-oriented monetary policy and the rise of the PBC during the first reform era.

Nevertheless, the PBC's capacity to develop and follow through with appropriate and gradualist change mechanisms was a source of empowerment. The mechanics of the change process had to be designed and worked through in a way that was compatible with prevailing institutional and political imperatives, and in a way that could solve huge policy and institutional design challenges. The PBC was able to develop techniques of institutional change and adaptation that allowed it to gradually develop a combination of market as well as administrative instruments that proved uniquely suited to Chinese political and institutional requirements for bargained gradualism. Over the years, the PBC's bargaining power vis-à-vis the party-state has continued to strengthen while marketization gives the monetary technocrats the leverage and space to pursue their institutional interests within a political marketplace.

The Party-State and the General Power Structure

A study of the growing authority of a central bank under one-party rule in China essentially begs the question of how to conceptualize the "party-state," a concept that has prevailed in comparative studies of former communist countries, including China. The party-state conception has been heavily influenced by the model of totalitarianism, which stresses the central role of the Communist Party within communist countries (Brzezinski 1960; Friedrich and Brzezinski 1956; Schapiro 1972). The post-1949 Chinese state followed the institutional signature of Leninist state building, which saw state institutions deeply penetrated and profoundly controlled by a strong revolutionary party. This was achieved through institutional embedding and blending the party apparatus into the leadership of the state and wider institutional system. This was further fortified by a *nomenklatura* system that ensures the Party's leadership over the state and social apparatus as well as a hierarchical power structure within the Party (Hamrin 1992; Lieberthal and Oksenberg 1988).

The end of the Cultural Revolution and subsequent economic liberalization since 1978 saw the party-state evolve from a totalitarian to an authoritarian regime as the Party's grip on the ideological and institutional systems was partly relaxed (Barnathan 1994; Burns 1999; Hannan 1998). Nevertheless, the party leadership's control of state institutions remained in place, with party members occupying most of the key positions in state institutions. In S. Zheng's (1997, 13) words, "The Party is in the state institutions, but it is also above and around the state institutions. In this sense, the Party is not another bureaucracy of the state. It is not even another key institution of the state." The party-state concept is thus useful in stressing the Party as the power center of the Chinese state. Therefore, we generally adopt the party-state concept in this study with reference to the political control by the party leadership of the state.

Before moving to conceptually and empirically examine the PBC's slowly rising authority in the first reform era, we need to map the institutional structure of the party-state, which often appears to the external world as a gigantic labyrinth enclosed in a black box. We will also discuss in this section the major government or bureaucratic agencies that jockey for authority in China's monetary and financial policymaking, as depicted in Figure 3.1.

As the nature of party-state governance was gradually transformed from totalitarianism to authoritarianism, the state's all-intrusive power has been somewhat relaxed through greater decentralization of authority and resources (Barnett 1986; Harding 1986; Yan 1995).[4] Despite this development, societal representation and participation in public management and policymaking has remained systematically constrained by the continuity of one-party rule (Hu 2000; Saich 2000; White et al. 1996), with public opinion playing an increasingly vocal but still limited role, often manipulated by the state (Gries 2001; Rosen and Fewsmith 2001).[5] Given a largely disenfranchised society, reform in China has so far remained dominated by a "statist" state, with the top elite and government bureaucrats dominating the policy process. As Naughton (2008b, 93) puts it, "In such a system, change comes primarily from within the system and primarily from the top leaders."

Within the party-state apparatus, however, scholarly inquiries diverge on the center of gravity of authority and decision making. Given the authoritarian nature of the Chinese regime, elite studies, which thrived in the 1960s and

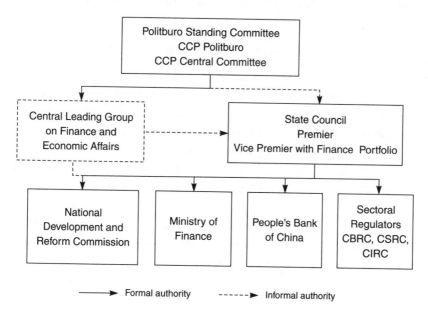

FIGURE 3.1. The power structure of China's financial policymaking.

1970s (see, for example, MacFarquhar 1981; Nathan 1973; Pye 1968; Teiwes 1979; Tsou 1986), continued to be a major approach in explaining Chinese politics and policymaking in the post-Mao era (for a collection of authoritative accounts, see Unger 2002). The term "elite" is often used vaguely in political science. In the Chinese context, elites broadly include party leaders or politicians and top bureaucrats in the government. However, in this book, "elite" refers exclusively to the Communist Party leaders, as it is useful to differentiate politicians and bureaucrats in this study.

The elite-centered approach emphasizes the commanding capacity of senior party leaders over their subordinates and therefore looks at the formal and informal dimensions of elite politics, embodied in intraelite ideological contention and policy disputes (Fewsmith 1994), factional struggles (Dittmer and Wu 1995), or a combination of "informal politics, formal structure and political issues" (Fewsmith 1996, 2001).[6] To these analysts, the steep power hierarchy of the authoritarian regime means that party elites retain ultimate power over the complex system of official patronage, including the distribution of physical rewards, and the *nomenklatura* system, which entails distributing managerial jobs and promotions to the favored (Burns 1993). Through these mechanisms of shoring up patronage and support, the party elite largely dominates decision making and shapes the path of economic reform.

The Politburo and Its Standing Committee

The power configuration in an authoritarian regime, such as China's, is thus highly centralized and hierarchical. The top political leadership of the party-state is embodied in the Chinese Communist Party's (CCP's) Political Bureau (Politburo), consisting of twenty to thirty members, who determine general programs and major policies, and select top personnel for the party, government, and military apparatus. The Politburo also serves as a reservoir and training ground for future leaders of the party. Ultimate decision-making power rests with the Politburo's Standing Committee (PSC), a smaller group of less than ten key (often in odd numbers) leaders headed by the party's secretary-general, which presides over the day-to-day operations of the Politburo (Lieberthal and Oksenberg 1988).[7]

The running of the political system is divided into six major functional sectors (*xitong* or *kou*), each supervised by a member of the PSC, who is also held accountable to PSC peers and to the paramount leader for the performance of the sector. These sectors include military affairs, political and legal affairs, economic and other administrative affairs, publicity and education, and the party's external relationships, as well as mass organization affairs (Ning 2001, 39–40). In particular, the PSC member who also serves as the premier in the State Council (the central cabinet, see below) is in charge of the economic and financial sector. The PSC usually meets once a week and major decisions are based on consensus. The secretary-general has the agenda-setting power of the meeting, but consensus is required on important issues, though on occasions of major dispute, decisions are made by internal voting. Because of area specialization and information advantages, particular PSC members usually have considerable influence in the PSC's decisions in their policy arena unless the policy proposal seriously violates the core interests of other PSC members.

The Central Leading Group on Finance and Economic Affairs

The PSC's decisions are heavily influenced by information and recommendations provided by a number of research and advisory bodies called central leading groups (CLGs, *zhongyang lingdao xiaozu*). The CLGs are the key institutions that bridge political elites to the country's vast bureaucratic network, acting as a forum for the political leadership to meet face-to-face with top bureaucrats. The CLG system divides most of the major bureaucracies into broad functional clusters, each led by one or two PSC members in charge of the area and composed of leading members of the ministerial-ranking government, party, and military agencies. When necessary, department-level *(si)* officials from relevant bureaucracies and academic specialists are also invited to sit in some of the CLG meetings.[8] The CLGs may have different roles in their respective areas, but they all serve very important functions in the policy process. They discuss and exchange ideas and put forward proposals as policy alternatives to be considered by the Politburo or the PSC, initiate and supervise policy research, resolve issues that cannot be handled at a lower level, and coordinate activities among the various bureaucracies in each functional cluster (Liew 2004). Although some of the CLGs are not decision-making bodies, the nature and high-profile composition of the CLGs means that their recommendations are often rubber stamped by the PSC or approved with minor modifications.

The corresponding group for the economic area is the Central Leading Group on Finance and Economic Affairs (CLGFEA), which is typically headed by the premier and his deputy (both of them are usually PSC members). Its membership typically includes vice premiers in the SC with agriculture, industrial, and finance portfolios, as well as heads of the ministries with "comprehensive duties," particularly the National Development and Reform Commission (NDRC), the MOF, and the PBC.[9] The centrality of economic development in the post-Mao era has seen the CLGFEA become one of the most powerful institutions in Beijing. One indication is that, while CLGs are generally not decision-making bodies, the CLGFEA describes itself as "the advisory and coordinating agency for the CCP's Politburo in managing economic affairs, and a core leading and decision-making body for the Chinese economy."[10]

In particular, the CLGFEA can "unilaterally make decisions on important issues that do not pertain to the entire economy. For example, the CLGFEA routinely allocates fiscal and financial subsidies to various sectors and localities by issuing orders to the ministries" (Shih 2005, 8). The Group does not have permanent staff, except an administrative office attached to the NDRC and a cluster of subgroups or bureaus in charge of research and secretarial support.[11] Interviews suggest that the director of the administrative office has considerable "technical flexibility" and discretion in determining which issues to bring before the Politburo for decision and which to refer to the secretariat of the party's Central Committee or State Council for implementation; which issues should be brought to full plenary sessions or just to the executive standing committees; and which issues need full discussion or merely informal approval.[12] Given the CLGFEA's de facto authority in the policy process and the ministerial occupancy of its key posts, it is an important forum for the institutions to exert their influence. Indeed, as we show in Chapter 8, the directorship of the CLGFEA's research office by a PBC official played an important role in the PBC's victory in maintaining a nondepreciation policy in the aftermath of the Asian financial crisis.

The State Council

The State Council is the central cabinet of the party-state, with a ranking similar to the CLGs in the power hierarchy (the head of the State Council, the premier, also heads one or more of the CLGs, such as the CLGFEA). In terms of policymaking, both the premier and the deputy vice premier have been PSC members since the Thirteenth Party Congress in 1987. With such a high level of representation within the Politburo and the CLGs, the State Council is generally preoccupied with day-to-day administrative operations and the substantiation and implementation of strategies, policies, and programs forged by the Politburo or the CLGs. Major issues and issues with cross-ministerial implications, such as monetary policy, are discussed in the executive meetings, comprised of the premier, vice premiers, state councilors, and the secretary-general of the State Council (Oksenberg 1982, 23–24). There are also leading groups within the State Council, most of which are temporary and focused on a particular issue or problem. Leadership in such groups also reflects the institutional authority of the agency in that area. For example, the daily operation of the State Council's leading group on state bank reforms since 2003 was directed by the PBC governor instead of the head of the China Banking Regulatory Commission (CBRC), an indication of the former's superior status.

The National Development and Reform Commission

The NDRC has been a major power contender against the PBC in the finance sector in the reform era. A successor to the once-mighty State Planning Commission (SPC), the dominant economic apparatus in the planned economy, the NDRC still remains the most prominent agency in the State Council, overseeing a comprehensive economic portfolio. Although state plans of a command nature have been shrinking during the reform era, the NDRC continues to formulate five-year and ten-year guidance plans, to regulate prices in strategic sectors, and to draft and oversee national industrial policies, thus playing a significant role in national economic policies.

Despite its retreating influence in recent years, the NDRC has fought hard to maintain its formidable but narrow power in the financial sector.[13] The NDRC has direct authority in distributing fiscal and credit resources. It controls approval power for large-scale fixed-asset investment projects as well as major public works projects requiring state funding, which is financed by bond issuance or the state banking system (Shih 2005). More relatedly, the NDRC sets price controls in a number of economic sectors, including the financial sector (Naughton 2008a). In terms of price stability, the NDRC cares more about growth than inflation, and tends to advocate administrative approaches in the monetary arena, especially temporary price controls, as opposed to the market-based approach favored by the PBC. Since the NDRC provides administrative support to the CLGFEA, it understandably has important influence over the leading group. In sum, despite its diminished influence, the NDRC's traditional claims to economic management and its connections with former NDRC cadres who are now high-ranking party members have given the agency a strong foundation on which to maintain a substantial foothold in overall economic and financial policymaking.

The Ministry of Finance

Another serious contender for authority in relation to the PBC is the MOF. As the Chinese economy has been increasingly marketized and monetarized and the national budget has faced increasing constraints, the MOF's role in national economic management has inevitably clashed with the rise of the central bank. As we argue in Chapter 11, the turf war between two institutions in the financial sector since 2003 has partially shaped the dynamics of financial reforms, particularly banking restructuring and foreign exchange reserve management.

To date the MOF has had considerable presence in the financial sector. It managed to retain its control of the Big Four state banks through a de facto control of Central Huijin, the Big Four's dominant shareholder.[14] The MOF also retains an enormous influence over the stock market through the National Social Security Fund, which can invest one-third or half of its funds in the stock market. The MOF also has a strong presence in the Board of China's sovereign wealth fund, the China Investment Corporation. In addition, the MOF determines all accounting rules and taxation policies, both of which have great influence on the profitability of financial institutions.

In summary, financial and monetary policymaking in China is embedded in the political hierarchy of the party-state. While major issues have to go through the Politburo and its standing committee, the CLGFEA is the major arena of policy deliberation, which further boils down to the premier, vice premiers, and the contending institutions, which, in the case of central banking and monetary policy, included the PBC, and more or less the NDRC and the MOF.

The Sectoral Regulators

The PBC retained its institutional monopoly as the sole financial supervisor in the 1980s and early 1990s. However, the emergence and rapid diversification and development of financial markets called for more targeted and sophisticated regulation. Thus, the PBC's monopoly in this arena was gradually broken up into a regime of sectoral regulation. This saw the establishment of the China Securities Regulatory Commission (CSRC) in 1992, the China Insurance Regulatory Commission (CIRC) in 1998, and the CBRC in 2003, in charge of the equity, insurance, and banking sectors respectively. In particular, the CSRC and the CIRC were split from the relevant departments of the PBC, while the CBRC was formed on the backbone of the party institution, the Central Financial Work Committee.

The PBC was initially reluctant to relinquish regulatory authority (see, for example, Green 2004), but largely managed to regain its leading position as a metaregulator in the finance arena. With a mandate for overall financial stability, the Bank presides over an interministerial meeting, coordinating policy deliberations and implementation with the sectorial regulators (see Chapter 7).

The Process of Monetary Policymaking in China

Monetary policy remains more or less an exclusive turf of the PBC, especially given its institutional mandate, professional dedication, and institutional capacity in information gathering and research. To be sure, decisions on major policy issues, such as interest rates and exchange rates, are formally in the hands of the State Council, but increasingly the PBC has had a major influence over the policy process.

Our account here of the process of monetary policymaking is based upon and has been cross-checked through a number of interviews with PBC and other government officials, as well as impressions gained from various open publications. First, the PBC has full authority over issues that fall under its discretion. The Monetary Policy Committee (MPC) of the PBC is under the leadership of the PBC governor, and is mostly a forum for consultation rather than a decision-making body. Consisting of representatives of other major bureaucratic players in the financial arena, the MPC serves as a forum for these institutions in registering their interests, concerns, and suggestions for monetary policy. The thrust of discussions within the MPC are communicated to the State Council but have no binding impact on the PBC. On other issues of monetary policy, the PBC will typically initiate policy proposals, which are sent to the State Council and circulated among relevant bureaucratic peers. This is then followed by an internal process of consensus building among the institutions within the State Council *(hui qian)*, often under the supervision of the vice premier with the finance portfolio, or overseen by the premier directly. Issues with profound implications may involve deliberation and co-ordination under the CLGFEA on the basis of the PBC's policy draft. Decisions on routine issues and policies are formally approved in the executive meeting of the State Council, and announced and implemented by the PBC, the timing of which is often at the Bank's discretion.

Issues of critical and systemic impact on the economy, such as a reform of China's exchange rate regime, are subject to decisions by the PSC based on recommendations from the CLGFEA headed by the premier. As discussed earlier, given the highly specialized nature of monetary policy, and the support of the premier and bureaucratic consensus represented by the CLGFEA, such recommendations are often likely to be approved by the PSC unless, in rare cases, they seriously violate the interests of the other members of the PSC. In the latter scenario, the proposal is either killed permanently or bounced back to the CLGFEA and the relevant ministries for further deliberation.

This set of transactions and power flows in Beijing's monetary policy process has two major implications. First, the PBC has the initiative in setting the policy agenda by proposing policy adjustments, backed by its institutional specialization and expertise in the financial arena. Such agenda-setting power is important. Policy recommendations and research by the PBC are highly influential within the State Council and the CLGFEA, albeit in a competition with policy inputs from other institutional players. Second, gaining support from the vice premier in charge of finance, and more importantly from the premier, is instrumental in gaining a green light from the CLGFEA and ultimately the PSC. Therefore, the political and working relationship between the PBC (and its governor) and the premier is an important variable in defining the informal authority of the PBC in China's monetary policymaking.

Central Banking under Central Planning

The PBC's evolving authority in the early years of the reform era was deeply rooted in the institutional structure and policy practices of the prereform era. After the CCP seized power from the Nationalists in 1949, it basically copied the Soviet model of political and economic governance, the latter being a central planning or command system (Riskin 1991; Ward 1980).[15] To understand China's central bank and monetary policy in the prereform era, one has to understand the nature and operation of this planning system, with its own inherent logic shaping financial practices in a direct and profound way. Under this system, virtually all means of production were owned by the state and, to a lesser extent, collective ownership, all of which guaranteed the state's control over resources and compliance with the planning authority. The allocation of resources was subject to state plans through administrative commands that were drafted, implemented, monitored, and enforced by a vast and complex bureaucratic structure (Donnithorne 1967). Bureaucratic promotion and career development of government officials and enterprise managers were in large part centered on the business of fulfilling the plan, not necessarily on achieving economic success (Lee 1991).

A common feature of the socialist financial system was the exclusive concentration of credits in the state banking system (He 1998). As Lenin ([1918] 1964, 106) had proclaimed, "A single state bank, the biggest of the big, with branches in every rural district, in every factory, will constitute as much as nine-tenths of the socialist apparatus. This will be country-wide book-keeping, country-wide accounting of the production and distribution of goods, this will be, so to speak, something in the nature of the skeleton of socialist society."

Following this Leninist doctrine, China's banking system in the command economy was essentially a monobank regime with the PBC acting as "a single state bank." The PBC was established on December 1, 1948, by the consolidation of the banks in the then communist-controlled areas, the Huabei Bank, the Beihai Bank, and the North-western Peasant Bank. After the communist regime, the People's Republic of China, was founded in 1949, thus becoming the center of the state banking system.

From the outset, the PBC performed a number of central banking and commercial banking functions. It had a monopoly on the issuance of the national currency (renminbi), management of government accounts, transaction settlement, deposit collection, short-term corporate lending, and foreign exchange management. In 1950, it was authorized as the "center of cash, clearing and credit" to "support the proportionate development of the national economy and to serve socialist construction" (Yang 1984, 425). After a series of consolidations in the 1950s, the PBC finally became "the biggest of the big" in China's banking system (see Figure 3.2 for an illustration of the financial system). Like the party's political penetration into society, the Bank's vast network of branches extended from regional centers to remote localities, from urban to rural areas, and from savings outlets to post offices and cooperatives. In 1957, which marked the final year of the First Five-Year Plan, the People's Bank had

20,000 branches and subbranches, and managed 100,000 rural credit cooperatives. As a result, the Bank became the nerve center of the financial system. By 1952, 90% of the total financial transactions and 92.8% of total savings and deposits were handled by the PBC (Miyashita 1966, 117).

A Big but Marginalized PBC

The financial system of the classic soviet economies, such as China's, was an extreme case of financial repression (McKinnon 1993; Shaw 1973). This was reflected in the passiveness of finance and its subordination to the planning process. Thus, despite its institutional monopoly in the financial system, the PBC's role in Beijing's macroeconomic management was nevertheless limited and marginal.

In systemic terms, the command economy is "an interlocking whole," as Naughton (1995, 27) puts it (see also Ericson 1991, 11), running with its consistent logic, strategy, and institutional structure. A defining characteristic of a planned economy was its central focus on *material* balance, a quantitative equilibrium between supply and resource allocation. Under this system,

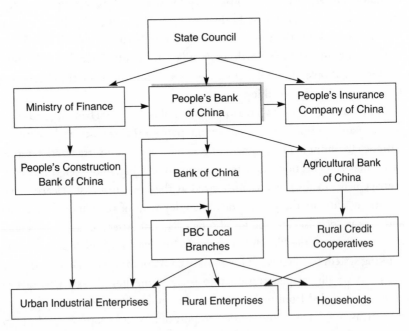

FIGURE 3.2. China's financial system, 1952–79.

incremental output targets on top of previous achievements would first be set out in an output plan. Taking into account material usage coefficients, the planners were then able to work out a schedule of inputs for all producers in a supply plan (Naughton 1995, 29). Here, what counted to the planners was the *physical,* quantitative balance between input and output in order to achieve an expected growth rate. Prices were largely irrelevant since they were bureaucratically set according to the material balance and the desired usage of specific resources, not by the scarcity of commodities. As a result, this severed the relationship between finance and the economy. Production and distribution were subject to the physical plan, whereas the financial plan was a mere reflection of the physical plan with financial flows reflecting officially set prices. The major role of money and finance, therefore, was to supplement and facilitate the planning process.

The centrality of economic planning was represented by the supremacy of the planning apparatus, especially the SPC, within the government (see Figure 3.3). The SPC emerged as the largest, most powerful, and most comprehensive institution, similar to its counterpart in the former Soviet Union, the Gosplan. At the bureaucratic core of the planned economy, it was in charge of the entire planning process, enjoying almost limitless authority in the economic sphere and often referred to as the "little State Council." The SPC not only controlled the planning commissions at all subordinate levels but also oversaw the work of

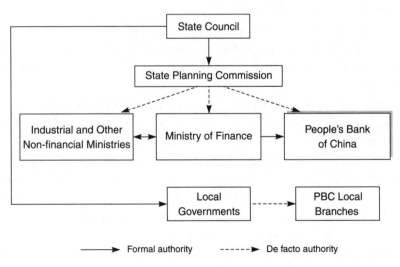

FIGURE 3.3. Power hierarchy in the planning regime.

the various economic and industrial ministries. Each specialized section in the SPC directly interacted with a counterpart specialized ministry or subordinate bureau of the State Council, a relationship referred to as "functional leadership" *(yewu lingdao)*. For the finance sector, both the MOF and the PBC were assigned to the Financial Section of the Financial and Monetary Division of the SPC (Wang and Fewsmith 1995, 52–54).[16]

Within the financial sector, the banking system was subordinated to the MOF that controlled most of the state revenues and extended most of the funds. The banking system could neither increase its funds on its own nor decide the scale and direction of its credits, except for the extrabudget working capital for enterprises, which in any case was an insignificant part of the total portfolio (He 1998, 26). In addition, as an agent of the MOF, the financial position of the PBC had been an implicit part of the state budget. For example, in 1962, 20% of the working capital quota (under the plan) provided by the Bank was transferred into the accounts of enterprises with no compensation to the Bank. Of the 19.9 billion yuan in unpaid agricultural credits extended by the Bank and rural cooperatives in 1978, 5.2 billion yuan was exempted by 1981 and about 70% of the outstanding debt was overdue (Jin 1994, 141).

Due to the passiveness of the banking system in the financial arena, the institutional position of the PBC was quite weak under the planning system. Unlike Gosbank, which had ministerial ranking under the Council of Ministers in Soviet Russia,[17] the People's Bank was an administrative body directly subordinate to the State Council; quite different from the ministries and commissions that were the "component elements" *(zucheng bumen)* of the central government (Miyashita 1966, 112). Under Chinese bureaucratic rules, this meant that the Bank was of a lower status compared to the ministries, particularly the MOF.

This bank-government relationship was copied at local levels, in which local bank branches, including those of the PBC, were aligned with and controlled by local party elites and governments. Before reform, local party committees had nomenklatura power over bank personnel in areas under their jurisdiction. Therefore the Bank and its branches lost substantial organizational independence. Indeed, during the period 1958–62, all local bank branches were merged with the local treasuries; during the period 1968–77, the whole banking sector became part of the treasuries at various levels, with the PBC's head office becoming a department under the MOF with only eighty staff (Jin 1994, 142–43; Walter and Howie 2011).

In short, although it had a vast network of branches, the People's Bank was institutionally marginalized by the financial repression and bureaucratic hierarchies of the command economy. Despite rare cases of active participation in economic adjustment in times of disorder, the general role of the Bank, in P. Yang's (1984, 414) words, was "nothing but a bookkeeper, cashier and mint-master."

Gradual Change: The PBC in the Initial Reform Era

If the PBC had been a mere intermediary in maintaining financial flows for material balance under the central planning system, the economic reforms initiated in the late 1970s marked at least the beginning of a turning point in the Bank's fortunes. Given the increasingly parlous state of the economy and what Naughton (2008b, 94) describes as the "near collapse of state capacity after ten years of the Cultural Revolution," economic reform was a new departure for China and a clear admission that central planning had failed. Indeed, by the late 1970s, the Communist Party found its revolutionary legitimacy in tatters. The relics of the "continuous revolution," the Cultural Revolution, were the last straw that broke the camel's back in the wake of Mao's absolutist rule since 1949. After Mao's death in 1976, the only way out for the party leadership was to shift course, from Mao's mass ideological campaigns against the "comeback of the bourgeoisies" to Deng Xiaoping's practical concerns for bread and butter. The bankrupting of Mao's political capital meant the survival of the regime was clearly perceived to hinge on the re-creation and expansion of its social capital, and the sustained generation of economic growth and social wealth. Given the fact that more than two decades of planning-centered state socialism had brought the national economy to the brink of collapse, the reformist leadership was desperate to change track. A key choice in this context was to open up and slowly liberalize the economy, thus heralding China's transition to a more market-oriented economy.

The transition that subsequently unfolded not only slowly transformed the economic system but also the institutional mechanisms of economic governance, which ultimately affected the party-state itself. Like most major institutional transformations, it altered the balance of power and authority in the institutional and political firmament. In particular, it began to gradually tip the power balance in favor of the regulatory institutions for the emerging market, particularly the central bank. In subsequent years the effect of this institutional dynamic would increase and the PBC would eventually become the pivotal body in the financial system and one of the most authoritative forces in Beijing's economic apparatus. However, the most significant shifts in this direction occurred in the second era of market transition, after 1992. In this section we focus on the initial reform era when the central bank's road to prominence experienced a bumpy start.

To understand the slow ascendancy during this era we need to examine the gradual but steady progress in legislation and the PBC's status. Given the sheer weight of past institutional legacies in the initial years of the reform era, together with the torturous political bargaining and adjustment that characterized Chinese economic reform during this period, institutional change above all was an *incremental* process. Indeed, the first era of reform from 1978 to 1992, as Naughton (2008b, 104) argues, saw "Chinese policy makers unable to adopt a reform policy that dramatically broke with the planned economy past. . . . In transition policy there were remarkably few milestone events or turning points."

One reason for this was that Chinese reformers had few lessons they could draw on for their departure from a planned economy, except for limited examples in Yugoslavia after 1948 (Gomulka et al. 1989). At the same time reformist elites were also constrained by their limited knowledge of the modern market economy, the imperative to maintain political and social stability, and constant scrutiny and pressure from the wary Maoist conservative ideologues within and beyond the state (Bucknall 1989). The results were twofold. First, a radical structural therapy to the old system was ruled out. The whole idea of reform was handled cautiously on a consensus basis. Second, the lack of transition precedents, particularly gradualist transitions, meant the reforms were of an experimental, trial-and-error style, best captured in Chen Yun's and subsequently Deng's slogan of "grappling for stones while crossing the river." The potential to reverse course if needed with particular policy experiments was also considered important. Unlike some of the more zealous neoliberal reforms in the West under governments like Thatcher's in the UK, or reforms inspired by crash-through neoliberal experiments in the former Soviet Union, the reforms in China were not guided by a conscious *ex ante* design but were shaped by responses to spontaneous bottom-up innovations, entrepreneurship, demands of the emerging market, and demands for social stability, as well as crises associated with domestic and international incidents.

As we have argued, the reform process also involved elite accommodation, wider coalition building, and greater devolution of authority to regions and administrative agencies. The economic transition has thus seen the gradual transformation of state governance in China, thus far a relatively successful process of self-reinvention of the Party and the party-state in terms of the relationship between it and the wider institutions of government (Liew 2005; Shambaugh 2008; Zheng and Brodsgaard 2006). But there were also more technical rationales for delegation. In the arena of economic management, the Party used to be the locus of policymaking via its institutional "police patrol" of the government bureaucracy, a system of "parallel rule" in which the hierarchy of government agencies was overshadowed by a parallel hierarchy of Party committees or leading groups to ensure the implementation of the Party's line, a critical imperative of a Leninist planned economy (McCubbins and Schwartz 1984; Shirk 1992, 63). However, the enormous information and efficiency costs inherent in this dual administrative leadership were unsustainable in the wake of the market sea change, which gradually demanded a transformation and modernization of state governance. As then-Premier Zhao Ziyang (1987, 16) envisaged, "leaders must . . . avoid getting entangled in a pile of routine affairs. They cannot truly play a leading role if they are entangled in trivia all day long." As a result, the Party initiated the process of separating the Party and government *(dang zheng fenkai)* in the mid-1980s, with the former delegating routine authority to the latter, thus shifting the locus of routine economic decision making to the government bureaucracy (Shirk 1992).

Yet the whole process was also strongly mediated by institutional factors, especially the long shadow cast by the previous planning regime. It was an era in which many of the older political and institutional entrenchments of central planning were maintained, with market dynamics only slowly being added to the mix. Over time the reforms amounted to a process of slowly "growing out of the plan," a dual-track approach that sought to foster the development of a new market sector as an outgrowth of the planning regime (Naughton 1995). Any major "outgrowths," however, were slow in coming. During the period between 1978 and 1992, some basic issues of the transition had been tackled, such as rural reform in the early 1980s, together with subsequent urban enterprise reform and price reform, albeit with limited achievement. This was mainly a function of contending elites blocking reform measures that were likely to impose substantial costs on their supporters or coalitions; a process sometimes referred to as "reform without losers" (Roland 2002). For example, despite putative market opening, the number of workers in the privileged sectors under central planning, such as the highly inefficient state-owned enterprises, actually grew during this period.

These unique characteristics also shaped the reform parameters for the central banking, monetary, and financial systems. It is true that a soviet-style bureaucratic leviathan had already been up and running in the planning era, but the various agencies (such as the People's Bank) were deliberately dwarfed against the planning apparatus (the SPC), with the Bank's organizational interests invariably aligned with and submissive to the fulfillment of the planned targets as well as Party imperatives. Moreover, although a key component for the success of the transition, financial reforms were not taken all that seriously compared with state-owned enterprise reforms during this period and were only understood in the very narrow sense of banking reform (Saich 2001, 264).

Nevertheless, it is notable that the monobank system was dismantled during the first half of the 1980s. This was heralded by the reestablishment of a cluster of state banks that were institutionally independent from the PBC. As the economic reform was launched first in the rural sector, the Agricultural Bank of China was among the first to be split off from the PBC on March 13, 1979, to facilitate rural reform and provide financial support for the fast-growing agricultural and rural industries. On the same day, the State Council approved the PBC's proposal to separate the Bank of China from the PBC to exclusively deal with foreign exchange-related finance, investment, and clearance. The People's Construction Bank of China (renamed China Construction Bank in 1986), formerly acted as an agent for the MOF in extending the state's budgetary grants for fixed capital investment, and was officially integrated into the banking system in January 1983.

As the financial system was diversified away from the PBC's monopoly, the reform of the PBC was also on the agenda. The PBC's institutional status had reached an earlier nadir when it was relegated and absorbed into the MOF in July 1969. Nearly ten years later, the State Council approved the PBC's independence from the MOF, granting it ministerial ranking in March 1978 (Tam 1986, 430).[18] As noted above, the old financial order under the planning regime had been centered on the PBC acting as a monobank performing both central and commercial banking functions to ensure proper financial flows for physical production. Given the resurrection of a series of state banks that engaged in commercial businesses from 1979, the question of how to position the PBC in the new system became an inevitable and hotly debated issue for the central authorities.

Three options were tabled for consideration.[19] The first plan was to rewind the financial reforms and restore the old order of the PBC monopoly in the face of fears of a possible "loss of control" of the financial system. This conservative plan was easily discredited by reformers. According to the latter, the administrative and fiscal decentralization process put pressure on the old, centralized financial system (Guo 2002, 16–17). The emphasis on local development therefore required financial services that were more flexible and targeted than the rigid control of the monobank. More importantly, the emerging market, in particular the increasingly intensive and extensive market transactions and China's rapid expansion of international economic exchange, demanded professional and sophisticated financial intermediation to finance production, investment, and consumption, which the PBC's universal system was unable to provide.

However, the reformers did not arrive at a consensus on the business of the PBC. Some argued that the existing state banks should be retained and that the PBC should act as both a central bank and a commercial lender, while others insisted that the PBC should be made an exclusive central bank and its existing commercial businesses split off. As a PBC veteran recalls, "as early as 1981, the then vice premier Yao Yilin set the tone for the reform in a PBC national branch executive meeting, arguing that the PBC should be turned into a real central bank for our country. However, we found from our survey that those 'real' central banks in the Western economies do not perform any commercial functions as we do."[20] This look to the West was more likely to have prompted Beijing to dismantle the monobank system.

After lengthy discussions and internal debates, the central government officially confirmed the status of the PBC as China's central bank in the *Decision of the State Council Concerning the People's Bank of China Exclusively Performing Central Bank Functions*, released on September 17, 1983 (hereafter called the 1983 Decree).[21] The aim of the institutional restructuring that subsequently took place was to functionally and institutionally separate the monobank system into a modern two-tiered banking system, in which the PBC was made to be an exclusive central bank, while its commercial functions were taken over by four state banks. Apart from the Agricultural Bank of China, Bank of China, and China Construction Bank, the major chunk of the PBC's commercial operations in the urban and industrial sectors went to the Industrial and Commercial Bank of China, which was created in January 1984. The two-tiered regime, with the PBC as the central bank together with the Big Four, would become the skeleton of China's financial system.

The 1983 Decree marks the beginning of a new era for China's central banking modernization, which centers on a reconfiguration of the authority and function of the Bank in relation to the government, market, and policy. The decree also, for the first time, clarified the nature, status, and institutional mandate for the central bank. According to the historic document, the PBC was defined as "a government agency in charge of national financial affairs under the leadership of the State Council." In particular, it was empowered "to conceive and forge macroeconomic policies in the national financial sector, to strengthen the management of credit funds, and to maintain currency stability." Its major duties included crafting principles, policies, ordinances, and basic institutions of financial works, control of the money supply, regulating interest rates and exchange rates, control of credit funds through Credit Plans, regulating financial institutions and markets, managing the nation's foreign reserves, and representing the government in international monetary engagements (Article I).

The 1983 Decree also granted a degree of authority to the central bank governor over monetary policymaking. Under the stipulated version of the Bank's institutional structure, the decision-making body of the PBC is an "authoritative" council (the forerunner to the current Monetary Policy Committee in the PBC) that includes the governor and vice governors of the PBC, and vice ministers from the MOF, the SPC, and the State Economic Commission, as well as officials from key state financial companies. The council is chaired by the PBC governor, and in cases where no consensus can be reached by the council, the chairman has the power of arbitration (Article II).

The authority of the central bank in this round of reform was, however, limited, even in terms of statutory development. The PBC had to institutionally report to the central government. Its governor was in charge of the decision-making council, but significant decisions on monetary policy again had to be approved by the State Council. Apart from the legal constraints, the Bank during this period was also politically and institutionally weak. Most notably, the authority of the PBC had been considerably constrained by governments at central and local levels. The institutional "leadership" of the State Council over the PBC meant that the latter's monetary policy was in effect dictated by the political agenda of the central government. Although the notion of currency stability appeared in the 1983 Decree as one of the central bank's policy goals, the Bank had little power in resisting pressures of the government that had been eager to pump the economy at the expense of price stability. An indication of the PBC's supplementary status was that the central bank continuously financed the central government budget deficits in the form of overdraft before the passage of the PBC Law in 1995 (Pei 1998, 328).

Within the central government, the actual authority of the central bank was not commensurate with that of the SPC and the MOF, both being able to constrain the PBC's sphere of authority and actions. Moreover, the PBC and monetary policy were still dominated by the routines of central planning. The Cash Plan and Credit Plan managed by the PBC that had prevailed in the prereform era were integrated into the Comprehensive Credit Plan in the early 1980s, which sought to control money supply so as to indirectly affect aggregate demand. According to Bank insiders, key parameters of the plan were determined by several macroeconomic variables,[22] most of which were set not by the PBC but by the SPC's annual plans and the MOF's fiscal plan.[23]

In addition, local branches of the PBC were heavily influenced by local governments. Although the government stated in 1983 that "in principle, the branching of the PBC should be based on economic (not administrative) regions" (Article II), the actual setting still applied the traditional principle of "one level of local government, one level of bank branch" (Jin 1994, 149). As such, the local PBC branches were under dual control of both the head office (central government) and local government, a typical feature of the Chinese bureaucratic system to balance functional and territorial interests (Halpern 1992; Naughton 1992). Under this arrangement, local governments were in charge of the local bank branch's personnel management and social welfare, which presented local leadership an effective leverage to condition, bend, and exploit the central bank's policy agenda in favor of local preferences. Local governments could also subvert PBC directives. In 1985, for example, the PBC phased out a system of certificates that were issued to foreigners when they converted foreign exchange. However, the government of Guangdong province, which had established a lucrative trade in such certificates, objected to the policy, and it was subsequently abandoned, with the certificates finally being phased out ten years later in 1995 (Naughton 2008b, 105).

The PBC's institutional capacity during this period was also constrained by a lack of expertise in guiding the development of a transitional financial system. The PBC thus fell short of becoming a reliable, trustworthy, and authoritative agency the leadership could rely on in the policy process. The education, experience, and careers of the PBC's staff were invariably aligned to a regime of economic planning, rather than financial regulation and indirect monetary policy. Universities resumed recruiting students in 1977, but for a considerable period of time the teaching of economics was still dominated by doctrinal Marxist political economy as Western economics were only slowly introduced. The PBC leadership was well aware of the critical importance of the quality of its staff, and pushed to have established a graduate school directly attached to the Bank as early as 1981, with first recruitment beginning in 1982. Aimed at producing higher-level financial personnel that were equipped with modern knowledge, the school later turned out to be a success for the Bank. However, it played a limited role in lifting the overall staff quality in the first decade after the reform because of the school's small scale at that stage and the slow process of injecting young blood into the Bank.

At the same time, the Bank also faced technical barriers in the regulation of the market, particularly an outdated financial infrastructure. During most of the 1980s, the central bank largely inherited a manual-based clearing system from the old planning era, which made cross-region, interbank settlements complicated and time consuming (Feng 2006a). On the one hand, it retarded the improvement of the Bank's capacity in managing capital and liquidity. On the other hand, the infrastructural inefficiency constrained the central bank's capability in monitoring banking performance and regulating bank practices.

The lack of a radical overhaul of the old system led Peebles (1991, 9) to conclude, "obviously, economic reform in the 1980s had not changed the basic nature of the money supply process, and planners' attitudes and the same institutional assumptions are valid for the entire period." Given such systemic constraints, it was not a surprise to see that the central bank's monetary policy, mostly embodied in the Credit Plan, failed to achieve its targets as monetary expansion exceeded economic growth in eight out of ten years between 1983 (when the PBC was designated as the central bank) and 1992. The lack of policy capacity also saw a series of inflationary cycles, which are discussed more fully in Chapter 4.

Conclusion

In summary, the rise of the central bank to a more prominent place in the Chinese polity had a slow and bumpy start. The most notable development during this period was the transformation of the monobank into a two-tiered system with the PBC authorized as the central bank, functionally and institutionally aligning the bank to manage monetary policy and financial supervision. As it turned out, however, the Bank's authority was limited by the continuance of planning instruments, by a lack of political clout in the party-state's power echelons in both the center and local regions, and by an initial lack of expertise and experience in regulating the emerging market.

Therefore, although the market opening and reform process began in 1978 as a bold and desperate measure to try and restart the economy and shore up the legitimacy of the communist regime, we have seen in this chapter how conservative and incremental the reform process actually was until the early 1990s. The regime's power structure and the politics of contending veto powers, as well as the huge shadow cast by the legacies of the central planning system, both conspired to limit the pace and scale of reforms. This pattern was also evident in the limited gains made by the PBC. However—and this is crucial—the shadow of the past and the trajectory of the reform process were being negotiated and channeled into what was initially a slow but still remorseless process of institutional change. It was the elites in the party-state and the PBC, as we argue in Chapters 5 and 6, that increasingly began to decisively drive more rapid and substantive change in the second reform era.

4

Monetary Policy in the Shadow of the Plan, 1978–92

Under the central planning regime between 1978 and 1992, monetary policy took the form of rigid financial planning in conformance to the physical plan. However, the rigid control of cash and credit did not eliminate inflation, but disguised it under pervasive shortage and repressed consumption (Kornai 1980). As production factors were gradually liberalized and market forces increased in salience, inflation became more prominent. Despite the initiation of market reforms from 1978, we see a substantial continuity of financial planning in the 1978–92 period in that the Credit Plan remained and played a major role in the PBC's efforts to control money and credit. At the same time, the emergence of a growing market sector and a new type of financial system increasingly restrained the application of planning instruments. This formed the basic tension in the plan-market system.

The genie of inflation has been deeply embedded in China's economic transition and its evolving institutional structure. Not only is macroeconomic stability vital for the course of transition, but inflation is among the "primary" problems confronting transitional economies (Maxfield 1997). Institutionally, the PBC's weak position in the government and bureaucracy during this period confronted it with competing central political agendas and a constant game between the center and the localities over financing and investment. The consistency of monetary policy was also marred by the PBC's lack of knowledge and experience in establishing a sound operating framework for monetary policy in a transition context marked by increasingly severe tensions between the constraints of the plan and the pressures of an emerging market system. The ultimate register of such contradictions was a series of inflationary outbreaks that threatened China's macroeconomy in the 1980s.

Here we first review major explanations of macroeconomic volatilities and inflation during the first era of reform and explore the challenges confronting China's emerging central bank. We then discuss the PBC's dilemmas in developing monetary policy instruments under the constraints of the plan-market system and how this unfolded in monetary developments in the three inflationary cycles during this period.

Monetary Policy and Inflation in the Prereform Era

Given the priority of physical balance over price equilibrium, the quantity of money under a central planning regime is automatically adjusted to planned physical flows at given planned prices. One could argue in such a system that there is no scope for monetary policy in its modern guise, with the lack of true money under administrative planning (Lavlan 1973; Portes 1981). As one senior official recalls, "Before our country's reform and opening up . . . monetary policy had not been considered a serious issue in macroeconomic adjustment. Except that monetary measures were taken in the wake of national economic imbalances, [the government] had not frequently and actively used it to adjust the economy. Therefore there had been no such concept as monetary policy."[1]

Without competitive markets and profit-maximizing private enterprises, the balance between material and financial flows was up to the planning bureaucrats instead of market transactions. Under such a system the planners resorted to drafting, implementing, and enforcing a series of physical and financial plans for various components of the economic system. The financial plans consisted of Cash Plans, Credit Plans, and Fiscal Plans, which aimed at ensuring that no planned action was disrupted by lack of funds and no unauthorized, unplanned action was made possible by the availability of funds (Garvy 1977). Although the three plans in the financial sector were relatively independent until their integration into the Comprehensive Fiscal Credit Plan in 1984, Cash and Credit Plans were mostly subordinated to the plan since it collected and distributed the majority of the national income. China's prereform monetary policy, or at least monetary control measures, thus largely dwelled on these planning tools in the financial sector.

Compared with modern practices in market economies, the old planning regime was very different and in many ways flawed. In the current era, monetary policy authority in most countries has been commonly designated to central banks with more or less independence. By contrast, as we saw in Chapter 3, the role of the PBC in this regard was extremely weak under the planning regime. Given the passiveness of finance to material balance, the basic tone of monetary management was set in physical plans configured by the planning apparatus. This meant that monetary authority was in the hands of the State Planning Commission (SPC), not the PBC, as the SPC had been effectively in control of the key variables of the PBC's financial plans. As part of the administrative system, the Bank was also under firm control from both central and local governments. Furthermore, the superior status of the treasury over the central bank constrained the latter's capacity in financial and economic management, and forced the central bank to subsidize fiscal deficits, thus jeopardizing price stability.

Moreover, governmental officials had little knowledge of finance. More importantly, financial markets were virtually nonexistent. Enterprises, treasury, and the banking system had not developed a set of sterilization mechanisms against the soft budget constraint and the strong investment incentives of the government (Kornai 1980, 1986). As a result, the state could not implement monetary policy via indirect adjustment but had to resort to monetary control through central planning. In addition, there were the endogenous problems of financial or monetary planning. The financial planning parameters were mostly set by the physical plans, which were inaccurate at best due to inevitable problems of imperfect information and decision-making and implementation problems (Ericson 1991).

Thus, on the policy front there had been little expertise or practice in developing and utilizing modern monetary policy instruments, including interest rate instruments (Bowles and White 1993). Decision making also often suffered from distorted goals. Although money supply was used as an interim policy goal, aggregate supply was subject to physical plans rather than changes in base money. The ultimate goal of traditional monetary policy was to promote economic growth as well as price stability, but in reality, since money was subordinated to an expansionary production agenda, the physical plans were often exceeded. As a result, the financial plans had to be adjusted accordingly to accommodate the demand for growth, so that the dual goal eventually evolved into a single goal of growth promotion or, to put more accurately, the high-speed growth of the industrial sector, especially heavy industries.

In evaluating macroeconomic performance, Bowles and White (1993, 65) find it "surprising" that "at the macro-level, inflation was kept under control in the pre-reform era . . . a major achievement [given that] high rates of growth and investment were accompanied by low rates of inflation." Indeed, apart from periods such as the post–civil war transition in the early 1950s and the great famine in the early 1960s, official figures show a relatively stable and low price trend before 1978, whereas at the same time the share of investment in GDP rose from 23% in 1957 to 31% in 1979.

On the other hand, this performance is less surprising if the real nature of macroeconomic management is taken into account. Under the traditional socialist regime, prices were administratively set by the planning agencies (Ericson 1991, 17). As such, prices provided irrelevant or incorrect information about scarcities or relative values and instead primarily reflected planners' priorities and objectives. The fact that official price indexes suggest that price levels largely remain fixed and were kept low in part reflected the technical parameters of price control in such a system. Hence, without a relatively fixed price level, the manual setting of prices for tens of millions of goods and services according to their true and constantly changing economic values would have been an overwhelming if not impossible task for the central planners.

It was also politically important for the socialist state to keep prices at a low level. Many consider the hyperinflation during the last years of the old Nationalist regime as one of the major reasons for its demise. The Communist Party was eager to demonstrate "the superiority of the socialist system" and, given a powerful planning apparatus, price control was thus attainable. Wages were also kept low, partly to accelerate capital accumulation, and partly because welfare services, such as housing and public health, were provided mostly free to workers in state enterprises. Furthermore, the egalitarian wage structure was also set to ensure a socially acceptable gap between urban and rural areas in a political regime that claimed to be "a coalition of proletariat and farmers."

Nevertheless, the inflexibility of planning, the information mismatches between relative scarcities and administered prices, and the soft budget constraints in the production and finance systems led to systemic inefficiency and waste. Moreover, the net effect of such price and wage "suppression" led to a chronic "shortage economy" (Kornai 1980), which one economist has characterized as including "long searches; queues and waiting lists (including sometimes queues to join waiting lists and waiting lists to join queues); transactions at prices higher than official norms even in state shops (sometime disguised by nominal changes in product or labels) but more often in alternative black, grey and multi-colored markets" (Nuti 1986, 38).

The economic phenomenon of shortage was reflected in the government's reliance on a rationing system that was "so Byzantine in its complexity that many Chinese themselves [were] at a loss to understand it." In Kornai's (1980, 1982) words, this was typically "hidden" or "repressed" inflation. The former was reflected in "higher price indices than officially recorded" and the latter in "excess demand at official prices" (Nuti 1986, 38). Estimates indicate the substantial nature of these forms of hidden or repressed inflation under the Chinese system of central planning (Song 2004). Measuring inflationary pressure by the aggregate retail values per yuan in circulation, Song's (2004) study of the repressed inflation rate in the prereform era reveals the substantial differences between official and real inflation under the Chinese system of central planning.

Despite a relatively flat curve for money supply, Figure 4.1 suggests that the intensity of the repressed inflation peaked during the second Five-Year Plan

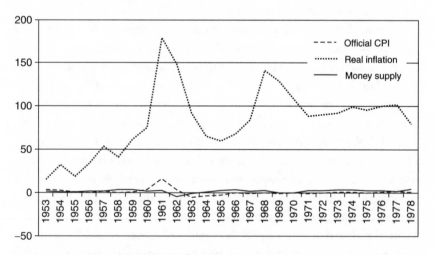

FIGURE 4.1. Money supply and inflation, 1953–78 (%).

Note: Broad money (M2), a major indicator of money supply, was not recorded in China until 1990. Here, money supply is calculated by its definition, including money (currency in circulation) and quasi-money (term deposits held by residents, enterprises, organizations, army units, etc.). Official inflation is measured by "general retail price index" *(quan shehui lingshou wujia zong zhishu),* which is a weighted average of list prices, negotiated prices, and market prices.

Source: National Bureau of Statistics of China, *China Statistical Yearbook*; real inflation figures calculated from Song (2004).

period (1958–62), followed by another peak in the late 1960s. The first peak occurred at a time when central planning was the most rigidly implemented in the prereform era (Naughton 1987), indicating monetary imbalances driven by the systemic problems of the socialist economy. In the years 1962–65, 1969–71, and 1977–78, inflation rates were relatively ameliorated due to economic adjustments, while the rate plateaued during the latter half of the Cultural Revolution (1971–76), resulting from the rampant inefficiency driven by a lack of effective discipline of key industries.

The Missing Link

While the Chinese economy was plagued by a planning-induced stagflation in the prereform years, the first era of reform was marked by mounting inflationary pressures and macroeconomic volatility. Annual inflation started at just 0.7% in 1978, but then peaked at 7.5, 9.3, and 18.8% in 1980, 1985, and 1988 respectively (see Figure 4.2). According to Laurenceson and Rodgers (2010), prior to the mid-1990s, output gaps fluctuated in a band equal to around 5% of GDP, compared with 2% of GDP since then.

The existing literature provides several hypotheses on the causes of the volatilities and inflation. For Chai (1997), this has been mainly rooted in the nature of the evolving central-local relationship in the reform era. To shore up support

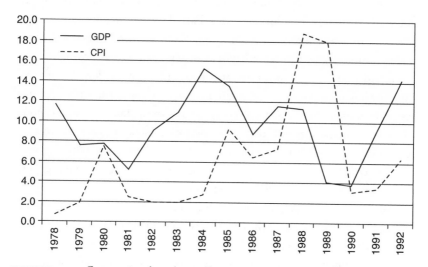

FIGURE 4.2. Gross national product and consumer price index, 1978–92.

Source: National Bureau of Statistics of China, *China Statistical Yearbook*; PBC Research Bureau, *Almanac of China's Finance and Banking,* both in various years.

for reform, the party leadership carried out a bandwagon strategy of coalition building, particularly involving local governments and officials (Shirk 1992, 1993, 1996). The resulting institutional arrangements granted considerable administrative and fiscal authority to local (especially provincial) governments, a process generally labeled as decentralization (Montinola et al. 1996). At the same time, the Communist Party's linkage of cadre promotion to local economic performance prompted considerable local investment fetishism and economic overheating (Huang 1996, 2002). These changes predictably saw funds being channeled away from funding investment in basic industries, which then became bottlenecks to output growth. The central government was thus forced to invest in these sectors directly. However, as funds had been diverted to projects favored by local government officials through their control of local branches of the state banks, the central government had to rely on money creation to finance these investments. This situation was made worse by the fact that central government tax revenue as a percentage of GDP had deteriorated markedly as the traditional tax base, the retained profits of state-owned enterprises (SOEs), had dwindled due to partial price liberalization as well as from competition with the emerging nonstate sector. The combination of fixed asset investment in both price-liberalized and nonliberalized sectors, and the money creation that made this possible, resulted in spikes in both output growth and inflation (Chai 1997; Zhang 1999).

Brandt and Zhu (2000) offer a related but distinct hypothesis for the pronounced economic cycles during the first half of the reform period. They argue that the fundamental cause was not so much the decentralization of decision-making authority as the central government's commitment to maintaining employment in the state sector. Because the state sector was less efficient than the emerging nonstate sector, maintaining employment in the former required resource transfers in the form of cheap credits from state banks and money creation. When the Credit Plan became indicative, banks began diverting more funds to the more efficient nonstate sector. While this increased output growth, it also forced the government to rely more heavily on money creation to finance transfers to the state sector, thus fueling inflation.

The two perspectives above are not mutually exclusive, as the decentralization-induced local expansion and the central government's concern over SOEs both contributed to the output volatilities and high inflationary pressures. Apart from their influence over the banks, local governments also developed other financial levers, such as bond issues, extrabudgetary revenues, and nonbank financial institutions (Tang 2000). These pressures led to uncontrolled credit expansion and growth in the money supply and ultimately inflation. In fact, locally driven economic overheating has been behind the major episodes of inflation in China over the past three decades. At the same time, the Communist Party's high-growth model, aimed at quelling social unrest and high unemployment, particularly in the state sector, the party's key constituency, also added to inflationary pressures (Naughton 1991; Hu 1999). However, what is understated in the extant literature is the fact that the government's role in money creation has largely been taken as given, and that the government had full discretion in relation to the scale of monetary expansion. After all, Beijing had established a central bank back in the early 1980s, which in modern terms would have served as a more conservative gatekeeper for expansionary impulses of the government. In other words, this is the missing link in the extant literature between analyses of money demand and supply, that is, the dynamics of money creation, particularly in relation to the newly erected People's Bank. We explore the PBC's role in monetary policy and macroeconomic management during this period in the following sections.

Monetary Policy, 1978–92

As discussed in Chapter 3, monetary management had played a secondary role to the material plans and fiscal balances under the central planning regime. But as the economy was gradually liberalized and increasingly monetized, monetary policy, particularly the need to tame inflation, became a pronounced imperative of the party leadership. First of all, excessive inflation could easily derail the party-state's all important growth strategy and lead to political instability. For an authoritarian regime that rules by coercive power, inflation serves as an open demonstration of the opposite, weakness of the party-state and its lack of control and governing capacity. In China, inflation is widely seen as leading to chaos *(luan)* and therefore a direct threat to stability and ultimately to regime survival. Time and again this has proven to be the case in China (Tsou 1995).

The series of economic reforms launched in late 1978 initiated a gradual transition not only in the way resources were allocated but also in the way the economy was managed by the state, particularly its monetary policy. This meant that monetary policy was gaining weight at the expense of fiscal policy in economic management. In addition, an increasingly monetized economy ushered in a gradual process of financial deepening, thus giving monetary policy a more central role in macroeconomic management.

Despite this general trend of growing significance in a new environment, the operational framework of monetary policy in the 1980s bore the major hallmarks of the economic transition from planning to greater market orientation. First, an institutionally weak central bank became the monetary authority for the emerging market but found its clout, knowledge, and experience wanting in fulfilling key tasks in a highly politicized context. Second, the dual-track plan-market regime dictated that financial planning continued to be a major means of monetary control. But this was increasingly compromised by decentralized decision making, burgeoning nonbank financial institutions (NBFIs), and the financing of the fast-growing nonstate sector that ran largely out of the Credit Plan, thus limiting the effectiveness and efficiency of the PBC's policy efforts. More importantly, the implementation of the Credit Plan became an impossible task for the PBC. Figure 4.2 clearly indicates the cyclical as well as volatile pattern of output and inflation between 1978 and 1992, which is in line with the characteristic cycles through which the Chinese economy was moving in this period (Khor 1991).

Instruments of Monetary Policy

The existence of a dual-track system during this period, in which the sectors regulated by state plans ran parallel to those operated under market mechanisms, found the PBC in a rather awkward position with two conflicting objectives for its monetary policy. On one hand, the Credit Plan, with its inherent expansionary and inflationary bias, remained the primary objective of the government's policy, but at the same time the PBC was endeavoring to use monetary policy settings to control inflation.

Accordingly, the operating procedures for monetary policy were forced to evolve into a dual-control system as indirect control methods gradually supplemented direct controls. Economic planning, physical and financial, still played a major role during this early stage of transition. The central bank was expected to use indirect, "economic" measures in regulating financial institutions and money supply in the 1983 Decree (Article III), and the PBC made some efforts to experiment with a number of indirect policy tools, such as reserve ratios, rediscount policy, and interest rate structures (Jin 1994, Chapter 6; Zhou 1993, 109–22). However, the scope, scale, and effectiveness of these practices were limited at best due to distorted transmission channels and rudimentary markets. Furthermore, the political imperatives, legacies, and institutional inertia from decades of central planning forced the central bank to resort more to direct, administrative measures, that is, financial planning.

The Credit Plan

As discussed above under central planning, the Credit Plan (and to a minor extent the Cash Plan) was the financial counterpart of the physical plan, specifying the amount of credit needed by (state) enterprises to meet their targeted output. The relaxation of the planned economy, with a gradual phase-out of centralized physical planning, cut both the number and proportion of goods under central government control.[2] Nevertheless, although some of the measures and principles were modified, the Credit Plan remained a major instrument of the central bank. Institutionally, the Credit Plan was developed annually by three agencies, the SPC, the Ministry of Finance (MOF), and the PBC, and was subject to approval by the State Council. Thus, at the macroeconomic level, the need for credit was determined by the State Council's broad targets for output growth, investment, and inflation, ultimately reflecting the Party elite's political agenda. Monetary policy during this period was thus deeply enmeshed in elite factional struggles along competing ideological and political lines.

After the purge of Mao's radical associates, the Gang of Four, and the sidelining of Hua, Mao's chosen successor, Deng and other pro-reform party veterans, such as Chen Yun, seized power and leadership within the Party. Although Deng and Chen were closely allied at the beginning of the reform period, the differences of the two lines began to emerge in the early 1980s when Deng rejected Chen's approach to urban reform. As far as economic policy was concerned, Deng's line was to emphasize a higher rate of growth, bolder experimentation, and allowing nonsocialist economic forms to grow, as well as extensive marketization of the economy. In contrast, Chen's more conservative policy orientation was to work within the basic framework of the planned economy and to maintain the leading position of the SOEs. The conflict between the two groups shaped the dynamics of reform in the 1980s, with a cyclical pattern of periods of high growth sanctioned by Deng followed by retrenchment and austerity programs orchestrated by Chen (Dittmer 1992; Teiwes 1995). As a result, monetary policy also recorded volatile swings between rapid credit expansion and sudden contraction, all the result of elite oscillations.

Institutional legacies were also important. With less authority than the traditional heavyweights in macroeconomic management, the SPC and the MOF, the PBC's drafting and implementation of the Credit Plan was inevitably an institutional compromise over conflicting preferences. The SPC's interests lay in ensuring that the Credit Plan provided sufficient funds for fulfilling the annual and Five-Year Plans. The MOF, on the other hand, tried to minimize the budgetary costs of financing the loss-making SOEs and, therefore, was inclined to include as much of this funding as possible in the Credit Plan, leaving the financial burden to the banking system (Mehran 1996, 41). Both these demands were inherently expansionary. In addition, although the PBC was charged to "maintain currency stability" in the 1983 Decree, it was the National Price Bureau that had formal responsibility for stabilizing price levels (Liew 2004, 39).[3] Therefore, the PBC was not compelled to make the plan prudential. According to a PBC veteran, "Institutions do only what they are slated to do. . . . We did not have to agitate the SPC. We did not have to be a troublemaker."[4]

The institutional decentralization process also contributed to the inflationary bias of the Credit Plan by altering the relationship between the PBC's branches and headquarters, on the one hand, and the local governments, specialized banks, and SOEs on the other. Local branches of the PBC used to follow strict rules and guidelines in implementing the Credit Plan before the reforms (Huang 1994). After the reform, the PBC delegated certain authorities to its local branches in approving credit quotas within the plan. However, as discussed in Chapter 3, local authorities had substantial influence over PBC branches so that the latter were increasingly considered departments of local governments. Hence, these branches were pulled away from the supervision and influence of the PBC headquarters and were instead used as instruments in the promotion of local economic growth.

Moreover, the branch structure of the state banks was the same as that of the central bank and, as such, the local bank branches were subject to the dictation of the local governments. The banks themselves were SOEs and thus shared the same problem of soft budgets. In this case, all the profits of the banks went to the central budget and losses were ultimately subsidized by the central budget, a source of moral hazard that led to reckless lending. More importantly, this asymmetrical cost-benefit structure encouraged local leaders to pressure the banks to provide loans to finance nonstate small and medium-scale enterprises in order to accelerate local economic growth, a prevailing phenomenon of "investment hunger" stimulated by the decentralization strategy (Huang 1996). In practice, local governments could either obtain extra-plan credit created by the bank branches due to loopholes in the overall credit control system, or could ask the banks to divert designated funds (quota) of the plan to local borrowers, where the banks would then force the central bank to finance priority projects, which the latter often found hard to refuse. As a result, local interference in bank decisions led to large credit expansions during 1984–86 and 1988–89, a major cause of inflationary pressures (Figure 4.3).

Meanwhile, the PBC had made some gains in relaxing and restructuring the Credit Plan during this period. For example, in the late 1980s, the specialized banks were given more discretion to lend working capital, thereby allowing for some departure from the credit quotas and adding certain flexibility to the Credit Plan. In line with the diversification of the financial system, the scope of the Credit Plan was broadened in 1988 to include credit to NBFIs and direct financing of enterprises, in addition to credit to specialized and universal banks (Tseng et al. 1994). More importantly, in the latter half of the 1980s,

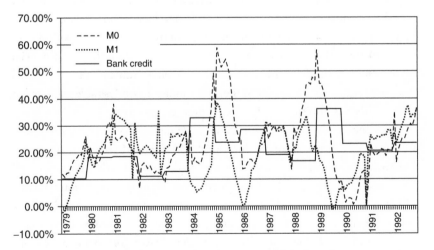

FIGURE 4.3. Money supply and bank credit, 1979–92 (annual percentage increase).

Note: Bank credit figures are based on the annual increase of outstanding loans issued by financial institutions at the end of each year.

Source: PBC Research Bureau, *Almanac of China's Finance and Banking,* various years.

the PBC began to evaluate the consistency of the Credit Plan with the broader macroeconomic objectives of price stability, the balance of payments, and economic growth. The target for aggregate domestic credit was formulated in line with money supply targets and no longer as a purely demand-driven, bottom-up process. Thus, it signaled the authorities' recognition of the increasing role of market mechanisms in a dual-track system (Mehran 1996).

At the same time, the PBC found itself with a lack of effective alternative policy tools, such as indirect instruments, reserve requirements, lending facilities, and flexible interest rates. Again, these developments reflected the PBC's weak position in monetary control and, as argued below, the rudimentary nature of financial markets. The Bank tried to downplay the role of the Credit Plan in the wake of a rapidly growing market sector, but the political authorities were reluctant to give up the plan.

Indirect Instruments

In a slowly marketizing economy, the effectiveness of indirect instruments largely relies on a series of transmission mechanisms that convey policy signals to market entities.[5] In a transition economy, however, the distortions resulting from a dual-track pricing system and institutional inertia mean that sound transmission mechanisms were underdeveloped. In studying inflation reductions in former Soviet countries in Eastern Europe, Brada and Kutan (2002, 8) argue that "monetary policy as yet rests on relatively weak financial markets and institutions, and it operates in an environment where the agents it seeks to influence may react to monetary policy in undesirable ways or not at all." This was also the case for the Chinese central bank.

The central role of the Credit Plan on the macro level and the prevailing institutional distortions in the industrial and financial sector on the micro level meant that indirect instruments of credit control either were not well developed or malfunctioned. These instruments, mainly reserve requirements, PBC lending facilities, and interest rates, were meant to supplement the credit quotas to enable the PBC to respond more flexibly to changing economic conditions. However, instead of being a lender of last resort in a market economy, the PBC largely remained "a lender of *first* resort" during this period, in that it played more of a direct, hands-on administrative role in controlling bank credit, and was the first resort in taking full liability for the losses appearing in the bank's books. Thus, the lack of a fundamental change in the role of the PBC from a lender of first resort to a lender of last resort constrained the flexibility and effectiveness of these alternative control methods throughout most of this period.

Reserve Requirements

Reserve requirements were introduced in 1984 to influence liquidity and liquidity management in the financial system (for adjustments during this period, see Table 4.1). To meet the requirements, banks were required to keep reserve accounts at the PBC. Required and excess reserves were remunerated at the same interest rate. Compliance was based on outstanding deposits at the end of each month. Shortfalls in the required reserves were subject to a penalty interest rate of four basis points of the shortage per day. The excess reserve requirement can be seen as a second tier of reserves that has to be held on an average basis, as banks could use these reserves for settlements of payments, interbank lending, or cash withdrawals. Therefore, technically speaking, the two-tier reserve requirement system amounts to a de facto single requirement.

A distinctive feature of this reserve regime is the high level of excess reserves, which at times were greater than required reserves (see Figure 4.4). This can be traced to the fragmentation and inefficiency of the interbank market, structural problems in the payments and settlement systems, and high remuneration at the same interest rate as required reserves (Girardin 1997, 59). The consequences of these large holdings of excess reserves made the reserve requirements of little use. Reducing PBC lending to banks or increasing the required reserve ratio in no way deflated these extra reserves, since the state banks that borrow from the PBC did not hold extra reserves, while the ones

Table 4.1.   Adjustments of bank reserve requirements, 1979–92

	Before adjustment	After adjustment
1984	Set according to deposit categories: Urban deposit: 40% Rural deposit: 25% Enterprise deposit: 20%	
1985	Various rates unified by the PBC at 10%	
1987	10%	12%
September 1, 1988	12%	13%

Source: PBC Web site, http://www.pbc.gov.cn/publish/zhengcehuobisi/608/index.html.

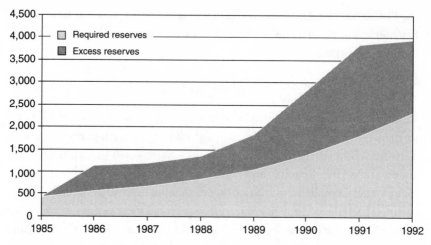

FIGURE 4.4. Required and excess reserves, 1985–92 (100 million yuan).
Source: PBC Research Bureau, *Almanac of China's Finance and Banking,* various years.

that did hold them did not require loans from the central bank. The result was to inflate both the asset and liability sides of the PBC's balance sheet. Moreover, while it is not easy for a restrictive credit policy to be effective, any relaxation in this control led to very rapid expansion of credit because of the extra reserves held by state banks.

PBC Lending Facilities

The PBC's lending facilities to specialized banks were introduced in 1984 to manage overall bank liquidity and to enable banks to meet their Credit Plan targets by filling the gap between bank deposits and lending (Girardin 1997). In addressing the liquidity issue, PBC lending comprises four different types of lending: annual, seasonal, daily, and a rediscount facility that is mainly for commercial paper with six-month maturity. These loans were meant to be "temporary," but at the end of the 1980s, an average of 60% of total PBC lending to specialized banks was annual lending, with seasonal and daily lending only accounting for 35% and 5% respectively. With annual lending as the dominant component, the PBC lending facility was thus closely linked to the Credit Plan.

Access to PBC lending was extended from the specialized banks to a number of NBFIs approved by the PBC. In the first years of the PBC lending facilities, PBC branches had significant autonomy in providing credit to financial institutions in their jurisdiction. In the wake of mounting pressures from local governments, however, the PBC headquarters centralized this authority during the 1989 austerity program from all of its branches, except those in Shanghai and Shenzhen.

Interest Rates

Because the financial system was exploited by various levels of government as a discretionary tool, China's interest rate structure has always been very complex, with more than fifty rates administered by the PBC (Dai 1998, 112). On the lending side, besides the basic distinction between working capital loans with different maturities and fixed-asset loans, industrial and commercial loans, agricultural loans, and household loans were all treated differently. On the deposit side, a distinction was made between individual and institutional depositors (Girardin 1997, 41).

Starting in 1985, and particularly since 1988, interest rates have been adjusted more frequently, primarily in response to inflationary pressures but also because of the profitability considerations of SOEs and specialized banks (see Figure 4.5). Banks were also allowed to adjust loan rates within a 10%

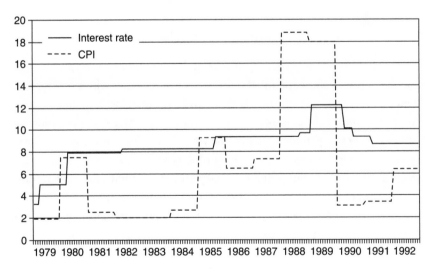

FIGURE 4.5. PBC's interest rates and CPI, 1979–92 (%).

Note: Interest rate figures are based on the PBC's one-year benchmark lending rates.
Source: PBC Research Bureau, *Almanac of China's Finance and Banking,* various years.

margin above the administered rate (Dai 1998, 112–14). This partial liberalization of the interest rate regime was reversed in the economic retrenchment in
1989 (see below).

The introduction of more flexibility in interest rates seems to have been constrained by at least three factors. First, in a clear illustration of the centralized
constraints facing PBC officials, interest rates administered by the PBC require
prior approval for adjustment from the State Council, thus making each rate
change a cumbersome and lengthy process. Second, the complex structure of
interest rates, as a form of financial repression, was aimed at providing subsidies, in the form of easy and low-cost credits, to the SOEs and to certain pro-
ductive activities and investments. Third, the heavy reliance by the state banks
on borrowing from the PBC (up to one-third of their resources) proved to be
another constraining factor, as changes in the PBC's lending rates affected the
average cost of the banks' resources directly and dramatically.

Although used increasingly to control monetary aggregates, the effectiveness of interest rates, as a key monetary policy instrument, remained limited
under the shadow of the plan. This is partly because the soft budget constraint of the SOEs makes them insensitive to the costs of borrowing. In fact,
the impact of interest rate changes was felt much more on household savings
and nonstate-sector financing than on SOE lending.

Inflationary Cycles

As outlined above, the monetary and financial system in reform China in the
1980s was pro-cyclical and inflation prone, a result of the awkward combination of the lineages of central planning and the emerging pressures of marketization and the high-growth strategy. There were three major inflationary
cycles during this period, largely in line with the cyclical pattern of economic
growth (see Figure 4.2). Having laid out the rationale and limits of the monetary authorities in controlling monetary and credit aggregates, this section
concentrates on the monetary aspects of those cycles, analyzing the relationship and interactions between the instrument framework and monetary developments during these cycles.

The First Cycle (1978–82)

The main engine of economic growth during the first cycle was agricultural
reform. Mao's commune system was dismantled and replaced by a family-

based contract system, restoring material incentives to farmers. This led to a significant increase in rural output as well as incomes. There was also a nationwide investment boom as the top reformers were eager to establish their policy credentials after the defeat of the Mao's loyalists. As a result, broad money (M2)[6] grew by nearly 25% in the latter part of 1979 and during most of 1980, and the annual inflation rate reached 7.5% during this period. This generated serious concerns about economic overheating so that in 1981, price controls, direct credit controls, and trade policies were tightened in an effort to restore orderly conditions.

The Second Cycle (1984–Early 1986)

The second cycle was initiated with the introduction of the dual-track pricing system, the granting of greater autonomy to enterprises in setting wages, the initial liberalization of foreign trade, and the establishment of a two-tier banking system. However, increased investment spending and the large wage increases granted by many enterprises were not confronted with hard budget constraints, which led to the overheating of the economy. Credit expanded from a 9% annualized growth rate at the beginning of 1984 to 76% in the fourth quarter of that year. Inflation rose to 17% in early 1985.

It was also the first cycle in which the PBC was formally recognized as a central bank in the newly established dual-track or two-tier financial system. The problems encountered in controlling monetary developments can to a large extent be attributed to the central bank's (and more generally the central authorities') unfamiliarity with using monetary policy instruments other than credit quotas in an increasingly decentralized financial system. In other words, the new monetary terrain was difficult to interpret, and new ideas and procedures for how to navigate it were urgently needed. For the reasons discussed above, even though reserve requirements had been introduced and the PBC was in a position to regulate its credit to the banking system, it had to rely on strict administrative enforcement of credit quotas to contain the overheating in 1985. Additional measures consisted of raising interest rates and devaluing the renminbi.

The Third Cycle (Mid-1986–Late 1989)

The third inflationary cycle originated in concerns over the slowdown in economic growth that resulted from the tightening of policies in 1985. Subsequently, credit policy was eased in 1986, and the banks had more freedom in setting their interest rates. In addition, regional interbank markets emerged. However, the combination of these measures and innovations fueled broad money and domestic credit growth to annual rates of nearly 30%, as shown in Table 4.2.

The growth in these aggregates was largely brought about by a significant reduction of the bank's reserves. At the end of 1985, total reserves were at 27% of bank deposits, compared with the required levels of 10%. The establishment of interbank markets encouraged banks to sidestep the credit quota and to use the reserves for additional lending. By the second quarter of 1988, total reserves had shrunk to 17% of total deposits. This revealed the inconsistency of the PBC's approach in credit control—the relaxation of the credit quota system could not be offset by an effective tightening via raising reserve requirements. There was thus a mismatch between the old planning system and the new market instruments. In fact, the PBC increased the reserve ratios twice (see Table 4.1), but further increases were hitting banks that were suffering from liquidity shortages as liquidity was spread unevenly across the country. The political authorities also resisted further increases, which would have prevented the banks from fulfilling the Credit Plan targets. Thus, even though the PBC drastically reduced its loans to the banks, it did not have enough freedom to use this instrument and effectively absorb the banks' excess reserves.

To make things worse, the political leadership, particularly Deng, pushed for radical price reform at the wrong time. Despite reluctant acquiescence of the then party secretary-general Zhao Ziyang, Deng was determined to take a great leap forward in unifying the dual-track price system into a single regime based on market demand and supply, which led to enormous upward pressure on price levels. However, without complementary wage reforms, this

Table 4.2. Monetary and macroeconomic indicators, 1987–92 (%)

	1987	1988	1989	1990	1991	1992
M2	22.4	21.2	17.5	27.4	26.2	31.0
Official price inflation	7.3	18.8	18.0	3.1	3.4	6.4
Market price inflation	16.3	30.3	10.8	−5.7	−0.9	2.5
Real GDP growth	11.1	11.3	4.3	3.9	8.0	13.6

Source: Official price inflation from *China Statistical Yearbook,* various years; the rest adapted from Girardin (1997, Table 2.3).

move generated nationwide panic in early 1988. Households and consumers reacted with large-scale bank runs and hedged against expected inflation by stocking up on consumer goods, which pushed inflation even higher.

The PBC successfully eased inflationary expectations by the fourth quarter of 1988, and promptly stopped the bank run by introducing an indexing scheme that linked the return on bank deposits to the inflation rate. As a result, by the end of 1989, total deposits reached 514.69 billion yuan, which was 134.54 billion yuan higher than the year before. At the same time, the PBC's experimentation with the partial relaxation of the Credit Plan was reversed, and credit quotas became mandatory again; interest rate liberalization measures were reversed; and interbank activities were controlled more tightly (Zhang 1999). But to deal with exceptionally high investment growth, the PBC and the central government had to use restrictive administrative measures. Investment quotas were established for each province, and the provincial leaders were made personally responsible for their enforcement (Naughton 1995). All investment projects were also required to be approved at either the provincial or the national level (Huang 1996).

The restrictive monetary policy implemented in 1988–89 was successful to the extent that it brought down the official inflation rate to 3.1% in 1990 (see Table 4.1), but it had serious costs. Politically, Zhao, instead of Deng, was made the scapegoat for the ill-fated price reform and economic overheating, which damaged his political credentials and led to his open confrontation with Deng in the Tiananmen Incident in 1989. There was also an economic hard landing. The fall in growth was much sharper than the authorities had wished. The growth rate of industrial output declined drastically to 6% in 1990, the slowest one-year growth since 1979, while GDP growth dropped by two-thirds. Total retail sales decreased by 2.4% in 1990. As a result, thousands of township and village enterprises went bankrupt and numerous rural workers employed in urban areas lost their jobs. Clearly, there was a need for substantial improvements in the monetary system, which would require further moves beyond the rigidities of the old planning system.

Conclusion

The early history of China's transition to a market economy did not present a clear break from the earlier institutional regime of planning and central command. The PBC had formally become a central bank but was constrained and largely sidelined by established political hierarchies and struggles as well as the legacies of the planning apparatus. Given this situation, the PBC's leaders faced considerable constraint on their room to innovate or maneuver. Despite a number of formal institutional changes that helped sharpen the role of the PBC, this era was not particularly empowering for the central bank. The main challenge faced throughout this period and that confronted the leaders of the PBC was how to navigate the transition and slowly build market-oriented instruments that could slowly supersede the planning apparatus.

This proved a difficult challenge during this period, and the macroeconomic volatility and the limited ability to control inflation in an orderly manner are testimony to this. In terms of monetary policy, the fundamental reasons behind the inflationary monetary expansions were distortions in the financial system and the inability of the central bank to resist pressures of local governments for economic growth. Indirect instruments were applied on an experimental basis and with limited scope, mainly to complement the Credit Plan. The central bank also found it hard to establish its credibility in the financial system, particularly in the 1985–86 and 1987–88 inflationary episodes, in which contractionary policies were very soon abandoned, making it difficult to establish long-term credibility and thus further impairing the short-term effectiveness of monetary policy. All in all, the PBC had great difficulty in "growing out of the plan" in the shadow cast by earlier institutional and political legacies.

5

The Second Reform Era:
A New Context for the PBC

We have seen how China's gradualist transition, the persistent legacies of the planning regime, and the centralized Leninist state all posed stark problems for the institutional rise of the PBC during the first reform era. Yet if this era was marked by institutional legacies and the long shadow cast by the central planning system, the second reform era from the mid-1990s slowly saw these effects wane as the process of "growing out of the plan" gathered pace (Naughton 1995). Indeed, a series of interlinked and increasingly important wider contexts helped shape the institutional rise of the PBC. The impact of these contexts was cumulative. The crisis context of the late 1980s and early 1990s helped alter the complexion of power within the party elite and saw the rise of more liberal-oriented reformers who introduced policies that accelerated the market transition. In turn, the transition produced a series of new challenges from inflationary pressures in an increasingly price-based market system, to the challenges of designing a more market-oriented monetary policy framework. These challenges helped empower those that could deal with them, especially within the PBC. Indeed, China's second reform era was one in which the PBC rose to a central place in Beijing's economic hierarchy.

According to Johnson (1997, 26), "We need to be thinking about how institutions created to serve the needs of a command economy can develop the desire and ability to operate according to market principles in a changing, politicized environment." In this chapter we show how the leaders of the PBC operated within and were shaped by the institutional context of the PBC itself. We also show how the PBC operated within a wider array of important institutional, political, and economic contexts that shaped institutional change and development at the PBC, which in turn helped elevate the authority of the Bank in its relations with the party leadership. In this chapter we focus on how wider contexts helped shape institutional development at the PBC.

The PBC as a Proximate Institutional Context

Institutional theory suggests that the rules, norms, and operating procedures of given institutions will shape the behavior of agents within them, which is certainly true for central banks. Around the world these institutions are increasingly animated by a broadly common set of goals, norms, and expectations about how central bankers should behave and operate. These typically feature a commitment to central bank professionalism and expertise as well as a commitment to fighting inflation. Central bank independence (CBI) and the authority and policy discretion it affords are also valued by central bankers. These institutional agendas have been broadly reflected in a new wave of central bank formation and modernization in emerging market and transition economies (Marcussen 2005). The PBC's leaders have generally been oriented toward liberal reforms and have been committed to central bank modernization, a greater role for market-oriented policy instruments, and developing greater expertise, professionalism, and policy influence (Dai 1998). In part, these commitments have reflected processes of international policy diffusion and the impact of an international epistemic community of central bankers, as we explain below. However, the institutional development of the PBC has also reflected institutional and political factors with a distinctly Chinese character.

For example, unlike many other central banks the PBC is not independent. As discussed in Chapter 3, key monetary policy decisions, such as moves on interest rate and exchange rate policies, are in the hands of the State Council and, ultimately, the party leadership, although the PBC plays a key advisory role. The PBC also has to compete with other institutions and think tanks in the policy sphere. Indeed, monetary policymaking is deeply enmeshed in intense bureaucratic politics within the Chinese party-state. This entails bureaucratic struggles and turf battles between the PBC and other key bureaucracies, such as the Ministry of Finance and National Development and Reform Commission, as we detail in later chapters. This fragmented and contested institutional context also compels the Bank and its leadership to enhance their own institutional capacity in a bid to gain traction and authority in the policy process. The PBC's capacities to build expertise, develop bureaucratic prowess, exploit a range of policy instruments, and enlarge discretionary opportunities within its institutional mandate have all been the core institutional foundation for its rise. Beyond this, the rise of the PBC has entailed increasing relations of mutual dependency and reciprocity, both institutionally and politically, with the party leadership, which we explore in detail in Chapter 6.

It is true that many parts of the Chinese state are raven by self-serving activities and corruption (Lü 2000; Pei 2006; Wedeman 2012). On the other hand, the profile and widely understood performance criteria of modern central banks, the concentration and professionalism of senior staff with Western educational backgrounds at the PBC, and ideational influences and engagement with international epistemic communities (see below) all suggest that the institutional interests of the PBC broadly align with the institutional development of the PBC. On the whole, therefore, the PBC has attempted to promote broader collective agendas, such as inflation control, financial restructuring, and macroeconomic stability. As we show in later chapters, the PBC has championed a range of reforms, from building and enhancing its own institutional capacities, to promoting a greater role for market-oriented monetary policy and enhancing its policy tool kit, to the pursuit of wider complementary policies such as partial exchange rate liberalization and financial and banking reform.

Wider Contexts and the Rise of the PBC

It is important to also locate the PBC within wider institutional, political, and economic contexts and to trace out their impact on institutional change and development at the PBC. As Thelen (1999, 384) argues, "institutional arrangements cannot be understood in isolation from the political and social setting in which they are embedded." We argued in Chapter 2 that the inter-actions between institutions and wider contexts can play an important role in shaping institutional change. In the case of the PBC, as we show below, these contexts included economic crises, wider changing constellations of political power (especially within the party leadership), changes in public policy, and changing ideational contexts including policy diffusion from overseas that fostered policy learning. Changing structural contexts, especially the economic transition, were also important. The PBC's interaction with these contexts shaped institutional development, which in turn helped elevate its role and authority. In Chapter 6 and subsequent chapters we show how the PBC's rising institutional capacities, expertise, and policy track record placed it in a posi-tion where strong *institutional* dependencies between it and the party elite increasingly developed. Such dependencies also formed the basis for growing *political* dependencies between the PBC and the party leadership, all of which helped further empower the central bank.

The Impact of Crises

As we argued in Chapter 2, sticky historical institutionalist theorizing tends to see institutional change as a crisis-induced episode of "punctuated equilib-rium," typically followed by a period of stasis or slow-moving path-dependent change. Katznelson (2003, 283), for example, sees periods of crisis as those when the normal "constraints on agency are broken," opening up new opportunities. In contrast, other institutional accounts posit more agency-driven patterns of incremental or evolutionary change (Streeck and Thelen 2005; Mahoney and Thelen 2010). The historical institutionalism (HI) literature tends to divide along such lines, with Taylor (2009, 488) commenting that "theories of institu-tional change can be loosely categorised according to whether they describe causation by exogenous or endogenous forces and whether change occurs un-der exceptional or ordinary circumstances."

Such either/or conceptions are problematic, and a more flexible, agency-centered approach can help overcome such dualisms. There is no reason why exogenous or critical juncture dynamics and endogenous, more incremental change dynamics cannot be handled by such an approach. In this view, the level of actor discretion may increase under crisis conditions when existing ar-rangements might be seriously called into question, but even in more "normal" periods, agency-based processes typically underpin evolutionary or incremental patterns of change through ongoing actor engagement with institutional environments and wider contexts. As argued in Chapter 2, it is possible to combine these approaches by emphasizing how active agents are able to pursue incremental patterns of change as well as change facilitated by crises or critical junctures.

In the case at hand, institutional change at the PBC was spurred by two critical junctures as well as by more continuous patterns of incremental change. The two crisis periods, in the late 1970s and again in the late 1980s and early 1990s, heightened questions about existing arrangements and were important in helping reformers push new agendas. In the late 1970s, the party leadership began to experiment with economic liberalization and external opening in the wake of the obvious and growing limitations of central planning and the near economic collapse following the Cultural Revolution. A second critical juncture occurred in the late 1980s and early 1990s with outbreaks of high inflation and threats to the regime's legitimacy and rule. The late 1980s were particularly important. By then a number of major difficulties with the first era of economic reform were coming to a head. As we have seen, progress with market reforms had been gradual and incremental. The legacies of central planning cast a long shadow over the embryonic market reforms, and by late in the decade conservative forces within the leadership of the party-state were resisting further reforms. There were also significant economic shocks. In particular, major outbreaks of inflation were an indicator of deeper problems. As we saw in Chapter 4, in 1985 inflation rose to 9.3% and then in 1987–88 inflation surged to almost 19%. Inflation had become a new and salient issue confronting the Party leadership. Along with concerns about corruption, the breakout of inflation in the late 1980s contributed to the student demonstrations in 1989 that resulted in the bloodshed and crackdown at the Tiananmen Square. As we have seen, inflation surged again in 1993–94, again driven by local investment overheating. The impact of these economic (inflationary) and political crises helped spur changes in the complexion of power within the party elite, and these junctures helped drive subsequent reform surges.

It is also the case that crises or critical junctures are not just exogenously imposed but can also be generated by endogenous, institutionally embedded processes. In the current case, the inflationary crises of the late 1980s and early 1990s were not simply exogenous shocks from the macroeconomy. They are perhaps best seen as a product of endogenous institutional relations, stemming especially from limited discipline imposed by an institutionally weak PBC, especially in the 1980s, over the banks and local governments. Therefore, exogenous crisis-induced and more endogenous incremental patterns of change were all linked. The pattern of change was propelled not only by critical junctures but also by institutionally embedded patterns of informal, incremental change. This series of crises may have helped further propel market reforms that helped strengthen the PBC, but wider patterns of incremental change within the PBC itself were also working in the same direction. For example, the PBC's growing monetary expertise, its development of a growing range of policy instruments, and its control over burgeoning foreign exchange reserves were all ongoing institutional changes that were important in shaping the PBC's institutional capacities and rising authority. Hence, there is no need to analytically distinguish between exogenous or endogenous forces or between changes under exceptional or more ordinary circumstances. Crises should simply be seen as yet another context with which agents interact within given institutions.

Wider Dynamics of Political Power

Wider contexts of political power shape institutional life. In recent years, agency-oriented approaches within HI have given greater attention to power struggles as actors exploit their institutional positions and deploy resources to win battles and reshape institutions. Mahoney and Thelen (2010, 14) argue that this is "what *animates* change." These scholars argue that institutions can be seen as "distributional instruments laden with power implications" that are "fraught with tensions," creating "winners and losers" amid power and resource struggles. Weyland (2008, 282) similarly argues that institutions can shape change by "empowering the beneficiaries of existing arrangements."

A number of studies have focused on internal institutional power dynamics, yet wider power dynamics can also constrain or enable institutionally situated actors. Powerful agents who are *external* to given institutional environments can play an important role in institutional change. In this case, party elites, as powerful external agents, were important drivers of reform and institutional change, seeing their legitimacy increasingly resting on economic performance and associated institutional reforms. Importantly, the crisis of the late 1980s and early 1990s saw major changes in power alignments within the party elite and associated changes in policy agendas. During the 1980s, progress with market reforms had been gradual, reflecting the compromises and the search for consensus between contending elites, which Shirk (1993) sees as underpinning China's "political logic of economic reform." Reforms gradually saw market elements added to the older planning regime in a system Liew (2005, 333) labels the "plan-market" system. As we have seen, it was an era in which many of the older political and institutional entrenchments of central planning were maintained, with market dynamics only slowly being added to the mix, a process aimed at gradualism and "reform without losers" (Lau et al. 2000. Indeed, by late in the decade conservative forces within the party-state were resisting further reforms.

However, mounting social unrest and significant economic shocks, especially major outbreaks of inflation from the late 1980s, helped spur new reforms. The crackdown at Tiananmen Square and soaring inflation led to a three-year economic retrenchment by party conservatives between 1989 and 1991, in which some of the previous reform policies were "rectified" if not unraveled. There was also the steep decline in the state's fiscal revenues, as well as declines in the profits of the state-owned enterprises (SOEs). As Naughton (2008b, 114) puts it, "through the early 1990s, the Chinese government seemed to be facing a gathering crisis of effectiveness." These challenges as well as generational change in the party elite and the "sudden collapse of 'elder power' in 1992" (Naughton 2008b, 114) helped restructure power and overturn the earlier patterns of veto power within the leadership that had been instrumental in the purge of the then party secretary-general Zhao Ziyang and his close associates (Manion 1993). These changes helped usher in a new era of reform driven by a more cohesive and reform-minded elite led by Jiang Zemin (secretary-general of the party, 1989–2002) and strongly supported by key reformers such as Zhu Rongji (vice premier 1991–98; premier 1998–2003).

The reform process in China has thus been composed of two distinct eras, shaped in important ways by the changing structure of power within the leadership of the party-state. In the first reform era the dynamics of change reflected a fragmented elite, with power at the top dispersed across an array of contending revolutionary elders within the party-state. By contrast, in the second reform era, under the leadership of Jiang, elite power became more consolidated and assertive. This move helped alter the ideological debates that had shaped the reform process in the 1980s and for the first time presented an articulated goal for the reforms, that is, to establish a "socialist market economy with Chinese characteristics."

It had taken three years for the political climate in Beijing to change in favor of the reformers by 1992. As in the late 1970s, a mood of crisis prepared the ground for more radical change, exemplified when the aging Deng Xiaoping made his tour of southern China in 1992. Deng rallied local support for more radical reforms and called for an ideational shift aimed at rethinking the nature of socialism and the market economy (Fewsmith 2001). Deng's ideological breakthrough against the conservatives in the early 1990s thus further accelerated the pace and scale of economic reform, producing a more decisive reform momentum. Deng's proposition for a "socialist market economy" was endorsed as the ultimate goal of China's reform path in the Fourteenth Party Congress in September 1992. A year later the party resolution was substantiated into a number of broad principles for the systemic transition to a market economy in the "Decisions on Issues Concerning the Establishment of a Socialist Market Economic Structure," adopted by the Third Plenum of the Fourteenth Party Congress in November 1993.

Importantly, if devolution during the first reform era had seen a fragmented elite seeking to win the support of the localities, the new, more cohesive elite in the second reform era pursued a policy emphasizing the recentralization of authority, especially in relation to local governments. Substantial fiscal, monetary, and administrative authority had been delegated from the center to local (provincial) governments in the 1980s, but this trend was largely reversed in the latter half of the 1990s when the center found it lacked the capacity to implement national priorities (Yang 2004). As Naughton (2008b, 114) argues, "China did move away from the policies of decentralization of power and devolution of resources that characterized the first fifteen years of reform. As in the late 1970s, the gathering crisis propelled drastic action, but the different structure of political power in the 1990s resulted in a qualitatively different response."

The new reform agenda was further spurred by a second inflationary outbreak in the early 1990s. From 1992 inflation surged again in China, reaching an annual rate of 24% by 1995. Again, a key driver was the local investment hunger that had been revived after Deng's southern tour (Huang 1996). The inflation surge can also be attributed to the leadership's attempt to replace the dual-track pricing system prevailing in the 1980s to one that was largely market driven and which led to a convergence of the planned price with the (higher) market price. Spurred by such crises and by shifts in the power structure within the party leadership, the reform of the central banking system and the wider financial sector entered into a new and vital stage during this period as economic reform in general accelerated and the country was inundated with the challenges of internal imbalances and external integration.

The Policy Context

Many institutional studies tend to equate, indeed conflate, public policies with rules and hence with institutions. However, Taylor (2009) distinguishes between policies and institutions, arguing that exogenous policy changes can be an important source of institutional change. As he suggests, "while institutions have a demonstrable effect on policy choices, the opposite path is also highly significant. . . . Policy change occurs relatively frequently and, like water flowing daily through a riverbed, can gradually mold institutions to its flow" (487, 491). For example, in the case of the Brazilian Central Bank (BCB), Taylor (2009) shows how policy shifts, such as the Brady Plan for sovereign debt repayment, moved foreign debt management from the BCB to the Treasury and allowed the Bank to hone its focus on monetary policy, a shift that helped accelerate a raft of slipstream institutional changes which helped build the capacity and authority of the Bank. Similarly, Bell (2004) shows how the Australian federal government's policy decision to liberalize the exchange rate system in 1983 promoted the institutional status of the Reserve Bank of Australia (RBA) by focusing monetary policy on managing official interest rates, the key remaining monetary instrument that remained in the postderegulation context, and one controlled by the RBA.

In contrast to many other transition cases, the Chinese central state has remained relatively intact and authoritative throughout the reform process (Breslin 1996; Huang 2008; Hu 2000; Liew 1995; Shambaugh 2008). This particular Chinese characteristic has proved crucial, for it has meant that there has existed a powerful source of policy authority able to push through change or clear logjams in particular settings as needed. One aspect of this was a major reorientation of economic strategy during the second reform era. Instead of a focus on local, township, and village enterprises in the vast rural regions that had dominated the development agenda of the 1980s, the reform focus shifted to larger-scale industrial development in the coastal provinces featuring state-led investment drives fueled by foreign direct investment funneled into the Special Economic Zones (Huang 1996). The reform process thus entered a new phase, in which China's economic transition widened, deepened, and accelerated. Since the early 1990s, many of the planning elements have been gradually phased out in economic management and slowly replaced by a more market-oriented albeit state-orchestrated system. Over time the dual-track pricing mechanism was largely unified into a more market-determined price system. Critical reforms involving greater market discipline of the SOEs were also pushed through, albeit with painful costs in terms of massive urban unemployment, shedding over 40 million workers between 1995 and 2005 (Johnston and Li 2002). Unlike the first era of reform in the 1980s, the reform process in the second era was less concerned with balancing interests or compensating losers. The reform front was also widened to include fiscal policy and foreign trade. In terms of the latter, the Chinese economy was increasingly integrated with the world market, culminating in China's accession to the World Trade Organization (WTO) at the turn of the century. There was also an acceleration of market-oriented reforms of the central bank, financial intermediaries, and financial markets.[1]

In relation to the PBC, local administrations had exerted heavy influence on its monetary policy up until the late 1990s, but this situation was arrested through organizational and administrative changes that strengthened the PBC, as we detail in Chapter 7. From early 1993 the party-state also beefed up the system of patronage politics that also helped recentralize authority. Also, although the bandwagon strategy and decentralization of the first reform era had seen greater authority devolved to the bureaucracy in the 1980s, rapid developments in the emerging market in turn demanded a more responsive, efficient, and sophisticated mode of governance, which the older fragmented bureaucracy could not offer. A second wave of administrative reforms was thus rolled out, aiming at transforming state governance from an older pattern of administrative supervision to a more modern form of market regulation (Yang 2004). From the late 1990s Zhu Rongji pursued a comprehensive program of bureaucratic restructuring, a program of reform that abolished most of the economic bureaucracies and reduced the size and consolidated the administration of key planning agencies (Chan and Drewry 2001). Even more significantly, the central state raised the rank of a number of regulatory agencies and created a number of new ones (Bach et al. 2006; Feng 2006c, Chapter 5). Further evidence of the clout of the party-state was the party's creation of the Communist Party Central Financial Work Commission that operated during the late 1990s and early 2000s to further centralize oversight and authority over the banking, securities, and insurance sectors (Heilmann

2005): in Premier Zhu Rongji's efforts to aggressively restructure the bureaucracy in a bid to speed up internal consensus building for the external talks on the WTO accession (Feng 2006c, 91–135; Fewsmith 1999), in Beijing's attempts to pursue a mercantilist standards-setting practice in the wireless technology sector (Bell and Feng 2007), and, more recently, in Premier Wen Jiabao's role in pushing through structural reforms in the stock market (Bell and Feng 2009).

Overall, the Chinese state has been gradually transformed from the central planning state, in which the state apparatus used to control the national economy through a centralized administrative system, toward an emerging market-oriented "regulatory state" (Levi-Faur 2005; Pearson 2005; Yang 2004). Although the central role of the state persists, there has been a shift toward a somewhat greater reliance on legally mandated and professionalized regulatory institutions to oversee more market-oriented activities. It is this shift in the mode of governance and policy on the part of the state, from arbitrary planning to more modern forms of market regulation, that has set the stage for the rise of a new generation of market-related state agencies, including the central bank, at the expense of the old planning apparatus.

If the policy approach of gradual market reforms and the adoption of the "plan-market" system had initially constrained the role and authority of the PBC, the growing shift toward more market-oriented policy changes of the 1990s helped alter this situation. The reshaping of power within the party elite saw a more determined market reform agenda unfold. As we outline in Chapter 7, this was associated with the promulgation of a formal central bank law in 1995 and other institutional reforms of the PBC that helped insulate it from local interests in a regional restructuring in 1998. Similar to the above-noted cases with the BCB and RBA, the separation of banking regulation from the PBC to a designated banking regulator in 2002 also helped the Bank focus its business and resources on monetary policy deliberations. Furthermore, although market processes in China remain heavily administered in many cases, the market push did see significant initiatives. For example, a major step in the 1990s was the phasing out of financial planning. As a PBC official commented, "in strict terms, China's genuine monetary policymaking actually started from 1998 when we abandoned the credit plan."[2] Yet the PBC continued to maintain a range of direct administrative controls in the monetary arena, reflecting the impact of traditions of hierarchical authority. The PBC also needed to factor in the party-state's economic agenda of forced-draft economic growth and the constraints imposed on monetary policy by the party-state's external balance agenda and managed currency regime. All of these policy factors forced the Bank to operate with an intermediate control system involving direct administrative controls combined with efforts to develop more market-oriented indirect instruments such as open market operations and interest rate setting. The increasing range of instruments at the disposal of the PBC, however, has meant that it has been able to open up space for initiative and a degree of discretion in shaping monetary policy, as we show in later chapters.

The Ideational Context

In recent years one response to sticky HI theory has been to establish a new "constructivist" or "discursive" version of institutionalism that elevates the role of agency and especially the ideational and discursive practices that agents use in interpreting and defining their realities (Blyth 2002; Hay 2006; Schmidt 2006). This approach "puts agency back into institutional change," according to Schmidt (2008, 316). For Hay (2006, 63), this means a focus on "strategic actors . . . who must rely upon *perceptions*" of their environment and whose "desires, preferences and motivations" are "irredeemably ideational" (our emphasis). However, this approach has been criticized by Bell (2011). When Hay and Rosamond (2002, 147), for example, argue that what matters is the "ideas that actors hold about the context in which they find themselves *rather than* the context itself" (our emphasis), they overemphasize the role of ideas and underemphasize or neglect the role of institutional and wider contexts in shaping behavior. Agents cannot simply make up their realities in ways that are disconnected from the institutions and contexts they inhabit at any given point in time.

Despite these problems in extant work, constructivist perspectives are nevertheless correct in pointing to the importance of subjective and intersubjective ideas and wider discourses in shaping institutional life. In this context scholars have highlighted the impact of policy networks and international epistemic communities and ideational diffusion as factors shaping the transfer and uptake of policies across the world (Dobbin and Garrett 2007; Levi-Faur 2005; Sharman 2008; Weyland 2005). Internationally, central bankers have been increasingly animated by a broadly common set of norms and policies about how they should operate. Here, the leadership of the PBC has been increasingly animated by ideas such as fighting inflation and developing market-based monetary instruments. For example, former governor Dai Xianglong (1998, 12) has argued, "The practical experiences of the past fifty years attest that, resolutely fighting against inflation and stabilizing currency value and finance should always be the primary function and historical responsibility of the central bank." Cross-border policy diffusion has also emphasized agendas such as financial liberalization, inflation-targeting regimes, and CBI (Johnson 2003). While we have argued that external market pressures have not been particularly significant in shaping China's approach to central banking, other external influences such as policy diffusion, policy learning, and the effects of international elite networking have been important. These factors can be linked to studies that emphasize ideational factors and transnational epistemic communities of policy experts (such as central bankers) in shaping worldviews; the policy choices of actors; and policy learning, emulation, and diffusion across borders (Campbell 2004; Drezner 2001; Sharman 2008).

For example, McNamara (2002, 48) has argued along such lines, suggesting that processes of transnational institutional diffusion have shaped central banking in Western Europe. In a similar vein, Polillo and Guillen (2005) argue that the diffusion of CBI across borders reflects the impact of transnational networks, such as the international central banking community (often self-described as the "official community"), which generates "group identity," a shared view of reality, and in uncertain environments generates incentives to "resort to imitating other organizations that they perceive as successful competitors" (1778). This is essentially a sociological institutional approach that focuses on how decision makers may seek legitimacy or emulate the perceived success of other systems in the context of "organizational mimicry and global norms of neoliberal governance" (Polillo and Guillen 2005, 1778). Attention to the international central banking community points to the role of groups of technocrats who share beliefs or a policy vision and who unite to influence practice through persuasion, activism, or standard setting, and whose authority is based primarily on expertise and institutional capacity (Haas 1992; Adler 1992). It seems apparent that central bankers who communicate with each other and meet regularly in international meetings—for example, at G20 meetings and at the Bank for International Settlements (BIS)—have forged such an international epistemic community. Marcussen (2005, 918), for example, emphasizes the role of Western central banks and bodies like the

International Monetary Fund (IMF) and the BIS in "fertilizing the ground for a genuine transnational central bank culture."

Perhaps the most succinct account of such an approach has been applied to central banking in postcommunist transition states in Eastern Europe (Johnson 2002, 2003, 2006b). United by similar institutional experiences, expertise, and a common ideology, Johnson argues that the international club of central bankers has the resources and institutional wherewithal to pursue central banking institutional convergence on an international scale. In explaining the ubiquitous pattern of policy convergence toward CBI in Eastern Europe in the 1990s, Johnson (2002, 1) argues, "A transnational epistemic community of central bankers, possessing a shared neoliberal ideology and significant material resources, actively guided the institutional transformation of post-communist central banks. . . . Established central bankers integrated the post-communist central bankers into their community, changed their ideas about the proper roles of a central bank, and led hands-on efforts within the post-communist central banks to develop modern tools of central banking."

Postcommunist central bankers have been receptive to ideas and assistance packages that promised an already-worked-out institutional agenda and set of policy principles and procedures. They delivered not only a blueprint for institutional construction but also offered central bankers a newfound status, legitimacy, and membership in a powerful international community of central bankers, as well entrée into major international institutions such as the IMF and the central bankers' bank, the BIS.

Such accounts throw useful light on the China case. Certainly the tasks of greenfield institution building in China in relation to central banking and financial sector reform have been daunting, and Chinese officials have been keen to explore Western practices and become a member of the international central banking community. As one PBC official commented, "I feel that central banks are like a club. As a Chinese central bank, we want to be a member of it."[3] Moreover, the international central banking community has been influential, as a former PBC official explains:

> For example, take the Financial Stability Department [within the PBC]. We didn't think of having such an institution within the central bank, but the Bank of England and the central banks in some Scandinavian countries have been conducting this [the duty of ensuring financial stability], and the IMF and World Bank have also initiated the Financial Stability

Assistant Program, and many countries have participated. We feel that we should also establish something like that, and that we should add such a duty to the PBC. So the external influence has been direct.[4]

PBC officials have also had to develop their monetary policy approach virtually from scratch. The same official recalls, "We initially had no expertise in modern monetary economics. Governor Dai Xianglong even handed out a copy of Mishkin's book [*The Economics of Money, Banking, and Financial Markets*] to each and every director of the PBC departments in the mid-1990s and asked them to read it. We would call our monetary policy framework at that time 'the Mishkin Framework.'"[5]

The PBC's exchange with international institutions, particularly the IMF, has also been an important channel for external influence. It has been institutionalized by the IMF's technical assistant programs, personnel training (at the purpose-built IMF Institute in Dalian), and the IMF's annual Article IV consultations with China. For example, as a PBC official suggests, the Article IV consultation,

> has been important in pushing [changes in China]. The final reports feed back to the leadership. If they [the IMF] feel that we haven't done well enough on certain areas, for example, lack of transparency, or if the PBC wanted to say something but would not be in a position to say so, for example, to enhance the independence of the central bank, then these will be reflected in the report. . . . We [the PBC] sometimes cannot say these because [if we do] others would say that we would be biased and not objective, for the sake of our own interests; while if these issues are raised by an independent third party, the result would be different. On the other hand, it is not that we ask them to raise a certain issue. We feed them the facts and if they see it as an issue, they will then raise it.[6]

Although these external dynamics have played a role in domestic changes, a decidedly one-way, outside-in approach tends to obscure the key domestic factors that have also elicited and propelled change. On the one hand, China's transition economy has been a green-field site for market-oriented policy innovation, ripe for the diffusion of foreign policy ideas and models. On the other hand, what is missing in this view, and to an extent in the wider policy diffusion literature, is a focus on the role of mediating domestic dynamics and on the agents that are ultimately responsible for policy choices. Such dynamics—especially relating to China's transition economy and its

hierarchical party-state—have constrained and greatly complicated policy
diffusion and convergence. Hence, while Chinese central bankers have had
close associations with their foreign counterparts and have been receptive to
ideas and approaches that potentially promised already-worked-out policies
and institutional templates, the diffusion and translation process has been
highly selective and nuanced. Many overseas policies and institutional de-
signs could not easily be aligned with the legacies of the past, the gradualist
dynamics of the transition economy, China's immature markets, its managed
exchange-rate system, and its hierarchical order. The unique characteristics of
China's domestic institutions and politics have thus heavily mediated the diffusion process (Bell and Feng 2010).

Hence, China has rejected CBI and has been cautious about market reforms, with much local adaptation. Nor has China followed widespread overseas practices and adopted an inflation-targeting regime or fully embraced
open market operations in its monetary policy, as we show in later chapters.
China's somewhat iconoclastic approach thus points to a "selective state," one
that has embraced only some overseas elements and which has substantially
charted its own course. The approach has also been shaped by the PBC's pragmatic approach to institutional and policy development, especially its unusual
combination of administrative and market-based policy instruments and its
pattern of influence within rather than independence from the leadership of
the party-state. This is not to say that external influences have not been important. Instead they have been selectively adopted and heavily mediated by *domestic* choices and institutions.

In this context the PBC has emerged as a key champion of imported
market-oriented policy ideas in the monetary arena, which has been important in helping to spur policy diffusion. In an early but still useful HI account
of the capacity of agents to use imported economic policy ideas, Hall (1989)
argued that such ideas must have a sufficient degree of "political viability,"
broadly according with the preferences and agendas of the dominant political
elite or coalition. As Hall explained, new ideas "do not acquire political force
independently of the constellation of institutions and interests already present
in a given context" (390). Hall also argued that new imported policy ideas must
be "administratively viable," able to "fit long-standing administrative biases
and the existing capacities of the state" (371).

In the present case, the PBC has worked to enhance the "political viability"
of imported policy ideas by convincing the party leadership that an expanded

array of policy instruments and ideas (including market-based instruments) is vital in fighting inflation. The PBC has also been innovative in melding imported policy ideas with local institutions and policies in a way that has broadly proved to be "administratively viable." In championing diffusion, the PBC has thus worked to overcome Hall's "fitness" tests. Yet in some ways conceptions of such tests are too static, largely because the PBC has done more than simply try to ensure fitness with local conditions. In particular, the PBC has adopted imported ideas and policy models in innovative ways that have helped to empower it, furthering its capacity to act as a champion of policy diffusion in subsequent rounds of such activity. The PBC is thus playing the long game, and in many ways the diffusion process has featured positive feedbacks. Importantly, the PBC has also worked to *change* local institutional conditions in order to better facilitate ongoing diffusion. A measure of success here has helped to empower the PBC and its ability to champion further diffusion.

Policy diffusion has been empowering because the PBC has been innovative in blending and melding imported policy ideas with local policy traditions. In contrast to the predominant use of market-based monetary policy instruments used internationally, the PBC's policy toolbox has featured a mixed bag, meshing imported market-based policy ideas with existing direct administrative instruments, as we detail in later chapters. None of this has been easy. In particular, the challenges raised by China's political hierarchy and transition economy have been well recognized by policymakers. According to a PBC official,

> There have been basically two camps within the central bank. One is the market faction, or camp, consisting of people with experiences of studying abroad or with a background in modern finance and economics. The other camp consists of people that believe in the effectiveness of state administration. Over the years, however, even the major figures from the market camp began to have second thoughts in the applicability of Western ideas in China.[7]

The key issue here has been the recognition that imported policy ideas could not simply be taken off the shelf but would instead need to be carefully tailored and adapted to suit local conditions. As a PBC official commented, "We have to do our own homework. As the reform deepened we came to realize that the economic transition in our country is so unique that few of the Western theories could give us sound explanation and guidance. Also, we operate in a

different political system."[8] This view is echoed by another senior PBC official: "We didn't have a real central banking before [the reform], and we are
genuine students of Western lectures and doctrines. Over the years, some
worked but many didn't. We came to realize that not all Western doctrines
could explain issues in China because of the special and unique situation
here—I mean the transition. We simply don't have the sort of fully fledged
institutions of the advanced economies."[9]

Such challenges have meant that the importation and domestic application of market-oriented monetary policy in China has had to proceed on a
trial-and-error basis, searching for effective hybrid forms of markets and hierarchy within the Chinese setting. The PBC has also been active in pursuing
wider institutional reforms in areas such as banking and exchange rate reform, all aimed at improving the institutional context for the operation of
monetary policy. The ongoing tensions and policy dilemmas of China's economic transition set amid its hierarchical administrative order in relation to
policy diffusion were also underlined by another PBC official in an interview.
Here, hierarchical traditions of administered pricing are a key issue:

> In China, prices are still more or less controlled by the government. The
> National Development and Reform Commission (NDRC) has a Price De-
> partment that sets and coordinates price policies for a number of strategic
> sectors such as energy and major commodities. Obviously, in a state-
> controlled context, price-centered monetary instruments, or qualitative in-
> struments, would have less impact than state administration. One day we
> achieved a low inflation; the next day the NDRC would like to raise the
> price of petrol; then we [the central bank] would go back to the drawing
> board again [to work on containing the potential inflationary impact]. In
> another example, the large SOEs are actually less sensitive to interest rate
> adjustments because they always get easy credit from the state banks. So in
> terms of monetary tightening, an administrative order on bank credit quo-
> tas is always more effective than an interest rate hike. So, it's not that we
> question the validity of the Western monetary doctrines. It is that they
> simply don't work in our scenario. We have to navigate the system and take
> advantage of it.[10]

Hence, the development of market instruments—such as open market operations and interest rate setting—has been applied on an experimental, incremental, and adaptive basis. This means that China's "mixed"-system direct
administrative controls combined with more market-oriented policy instru-

ments has defined the opportunities for policy diffusion, necessitating unique forms of policy adaption and institutional reform within China's unique setting. In this context, the PBC has been adept at combining hierarchical and administrative controls with market-based instruments in novel ways, giving the PBC a wide range of instruments and options with which to conduct monetary policy, of a kind typically not found in more market-oriented, "single-instrument" policy systems found overseas.

The Structural Context of the Economic Transition

Some time ago, Pontussen (1995) rightly criticized HI for focusing too narrowly on "intermediate level institutions" and ignoring wider structural environments. Structures are often materially defined, for example, a demographic structure or the structure of an economy. Broader social phenomena might also be seen in structural terms. For example, Pontussen (1995, 126) argues that "the centralization of state power might be considered a structural feature that underlies various political institutions." More abstractly, structures can be defined as "strategically selective" terrains, establishing incentives or disincentives or other rationales that may lead agents to favor certain developments or choices over others (Jessop 1996). Because structural factors are typically the result of embedded historical processes, they arguably form a broader background context in which specific institutions operate and change. Historical institutionalists often conflate institutions and structures or use the terms interchangeably (for example, Cortell and Petersen 1999). This conceptual muddling is not helpful because it prevents us from examining how agents within institutions dialectically interact with wider structures (Archer 2003). Although "structuralist" accounts in political analysis are often handled in a way that implies deterministic patterns of constraint, in reality, structures can help both constrain and empower agents. Structures thus have institution-like effects in that they shape the options and strategies available to agents. Structural environments can exert potential, though always agency-actualized, effects (Archer 2003) by imposing costs or benefits on agents and by shaping actor interpretations and preferences, the scope of actor discretion, and the resources and opportunities that are available to actors. Structural effects will also typically be mediated by institutions. Hence, from the perspective of given agents, the impact and indeed the meaning of structural forces will be shaped by the institution in which they are located. Structural changes such as tightening labor markets leading to strong inflationary impulses in an economy, for example, could mean very different things to inflation-fighting central bankers, compared to, say, a government carrying a heavy debt burden and potentially interested in monetizing such debt.

The pattern of constraint or enablement embedded in such relationships can also change systematically over time. In the case at hand, an important structural feature that shaped the rise of the PBC has been the market transition. The transition initially constrained the PBC, partly due to immature markets, but over time it became a context that helped empower the PBC, as we show below. The transition itself was thus a dynamic process; its basic structural impacts changed over time and gradually helped empower key agents.

The transition, as a structural element shaping the PBC, reflected forces generated by the transition and broader changes in the sectoral composition of the economy. For example, the transition unleashed new inflationary forces stemming from sectoral economic changes and by new mechanisms of market pricing. As production factors were gradually liberalized, the basic pricing mechanisms (once managed under plan-centered preferential policies and subsidies) needed systemic realignment to reflect supply and demand forces. Coupled with the increasing monetization of the economy, radical price reforms of major commodities tended to lead to open inflation, as did the forces generated by the evolving central-local relationship, which prompted considerable local investment fetishism and economic overheating (Naughton 1991; Huang 1996, 2002). The net effect was to place greater emphasis on the need for a competent monetary authority, namely the PBC.

For the party-state, its responses to challenges in the monetary and financial realm have been for the most part a result of the evolving compromise between the old Leninist state-planning system that refuses to abandon its authority in the financial sector and politicizes monetary policy, and the new market institutions, represented most prominently by the central bank, that have increasingly tended in policy terms to be advocates of price signals, market rules, and transparency, while institutionally valuing notions of authority based on expertise and links to an international central bank epistemic community. On the one hand, the party would retain as much control of the financial sphere as it deemed vital for the ultimate goal of sustaining the regime and its authoritarian rule. On the other hand, the party has increasingly banked its legitimacy on economic development and welfare enhancement in a more market-oriented environment. This momentum has also partly been a function of the ongoing economic success of the market transformation itself. Yet the tensions between the old and the new were a source of institutional change, though largely in the direction of giving greater scope to markets. The impact of inflationary crises in the late 1980s and early 1990s may have helped restructure power within the party-state, as we have seen, but the persistent momentum for further reform unleashed by the market drive also underpinned institutional change as the market reforms slowly displaced elements of the previous planning regime and emphasized the need for new market-oriented institutional and regulatory capacities. As Heilmann (2005) argues, although the leadership for a time resorted to a form of centralized personnel control over the financial sector in a typical knee-jerk response to the external Asian financial crisis in 1998, the demise of this approach in 2002 and its replacement by a more market-oriented regulatory approach represents a triumph of the emerging market over the old Leninist approach. The structural impact of these imperatives and the wider forces of the economic transition, and their associated institutional correlates, have thus slowly helped restructure authority dynamics within the Chinese state. As Naughton (2008, 91) argues, "the political hierarchy itself has been reshaped in response to the forces unleashed by economic transition." And as Liew (2005, 333) observes, "It is the contradictions inherent in a plan-market system and the momentum of pent-up liberal forces unleashed by reform that gradually forces the CCP's leaders to shift China's economy away from the plan towards a market economy."

In such a context, key agents in the PBC were able to develop new capacities, expertise, authority, and supportive complementary institutions as the market transition progressed. The shift toward the new market path increasingly developed a dynamic of increasing returns and self-reinforcing sequences as the new regime was further embedded. These were derived from gains produced by the economic success of the market regime itself, by learning effects as agents developed and mastered new policy and administrative systems, and by the impact of wider complementary institutional reforms that helped further embed the market reforms. The PBC in particular worked to expand the scope of its market-oriented policy capacities by developing wider complementary reforms and new institutions to better embed and support the market transition. As Amable (2000) points out, increasing the levels of complementarity between institutions in a given system can help increase the returns to institutions in such settings. In this regard, the PBC has taken a leading role in pushing wider financial reforms that have been aimed at establishing a sound transmission mechanism for monetary policy, including initial efforts in the liberalization of interest rates and exchange rates, and in the reform of the banking sector. This suggests that systems of institutional change and capacity building can unwind earlier path dependencies and over time produce new patterns of institutional accretions and increasing returns. As Elster et al. (1998, 296) argue, new institutional arrangements can "alter or nullify the determining force of structural legacies or replace them with newly created legacies."

For the PBC, the key challenge posed by the transition has been the need to confront new market pressures, build new instruments of market-oriented economic policy, and create a complex regulatory and institutional infrastructure for an increasingly market-oriented economy. A reasonable measure of progress with such tasks has helped empower key agents, especially within the PBC, by rewarding those with technical expertise and the capacity to steer the course of the transition and to develop techniques of change that fitted with the wider political need for gradual adaptation.

Hence both the transition and the technical capacities to cope with it and indeed prosper from it have thus far at least served as resources for the PBC. The initial, constraining pattern of the transition in the 1980s marked by strong institutional legacies and the shadow of the former planning system gradually gave way to a situation where the transition itself increasingly helped support key agents. In such a context the PBC's leaders were able to garner authority by building their own institutional capacities and supportive relations with the party leaders. As we show in Chapter 6, the evolving pattern of mutual dependency between the party-state and the PBC, both institutionally and politically, has been important in the rising authority of the PBC. The institutional dependencies reflected the PBC's growing specialized expertise and its increasingly indispensable role in managing the economy, while the political dependencies reflected a reciprocal alliance relationship between party elites and the PBC. Overall, then, the contexts above helped elevate the PBC to a position where it could exploit what might be seen as a "higher" context, that of strengthening mutuality between the party elite and the central bank.

Conclusion

This chapter has highlighted the importance of considering how agents operate within proximate institutions and also within wider contexts when explaining institutional change. In this case the rise of the PBC was aided by changing contexts, involving crises, power dynamics, and wider policy, ideational, and structural contexts, all of which increasingly placed a premium on the expertise and resources the PBC was able to develop in meeting key challenges, especially in battling inflation. These contextual relationships all helped to foster the institutional development of the PBC and set the stage for an even more significant relationship, namely, the growth of strong mutual dependencies between the PBC and leadership of the party-state.

6

The Growth of Mutual Dependency between the PBC and the Party Leadership

An important dynamic of Chinese politics stems from the interplay between the party elite and key elements of the Chinese bureaucracy. In this chapter we explore the relationship between the PBC and the leadership of the party-state, a relationship that has been critical to the rise of the PBC. We begin by reviewing elite-bureaucratic relations. While highlighting the importance of institutional dynamics in China's politics and governance, the literature tends to either under- or overemphasize the importance of the party leadership. In this chapter we present a more nuanced account by showing how the rise of the PBC's authority stemmed from increasingly important relations of *mutual* dependency between it and the party elite, both in the Jiang-Zhu era and in the more recent Hu-Wen era.

The Party-State and the Bureaucracy

The pattern of changing relationships between the Chinese government bureaucracy and the Chinese Communist Party (CCP), especially the party leadership, has been extensively explored in the classic literature dealing with the models of fragmented and bureaucratic authoritarianism in the Chinese setting. Below we argue that the model of fragmented authoritarianism (FA) that captured key developments in the 1980s tended to underplay the role of the party leadership. The subsequent revisionist model of bureaucratic authoritarianism (BA) tended to overplay the significance of the party leadership, while saying too little about the capacity of key agencies (such as the PBC) to gain authority through developing mutual dependencies with the party leadership, as we show later in this chapter.

Fragmented Authoritarianism

The FA model emerged in the late 1980s and early 1990s and provided an account of the growing weakness of the central party-state amid processes of decentralization and fragmentation that had been a hallmark of the first reform era in the 1980s. An important step forward in the study of Chinese politics came with the work of Lampton (1987a, 1987b), Lieberthal and Oksenberg (1988), and Lampton and Lieberthal (1992), who pushed beyond the traditional focus on elite power to highlight the importance of the institutional structure of the Chinese state in shaping political dynamics and policy outcomes. The institutional approach embodied in the FA model suggests that "while power at the apex inheres in individuals, formal decisions are made in and implemented through the established bureaucratic institutions" (Zhao 1995, 233). Hence the FA model implied a shift from central control and from Mao's extreme politics of individual dictatorship and ruthless purge to a somewhat more horizontal form of interorganizational bargaining amid a compartmentalized institutional structure. As Lampton and Lieberthal (1992, 36) argue, "in the first decade of reform in the post-Mao era we see that there was a relative *decline* in the use of hierarchical command . . . and a delegation of authority downward."

The FA model argued that authority below the apex of the Chinese political system was fragmented and disjointed, a pattern that grew increasingly pronounced under the reforms of the 1980s. According to this model, China's bureaucratic ranking system, combined with the functional division of authority among various bureaucracies, produced a situation in which it was often necessary to achieve consensus among an array of bodies, where no single body had authority over the others. Therefore intensive and extensive *horizontal* bargaining often took place among these bodies with de facto veto power in the policy process. In reality, according to the FA theorists, the Party principal was often entangled by the bureaucratic subordinates who exploited the scattered power structure and the associated consensus-seeking procedure, as well as the increasing technicality involved in policymaking. Moreover, elite policy agendas, according to this model, could also be distorted, bent, or even sometimes captured by the bureaucracy during the course of implementation, a process that Lampton (1987b) calls the "implementation bias." The effect of such a policy process was that it produced a policy system that relied heavily on bargaining and which, as a consequence, was rather disjointed, protracted, and incremental in nature. Lampton and Lieberthal (1992, 37) explain the increase in such bargaining as a result of an "agenda dominated by complex economic and technical issues, with multiple trade-offs, in a context of collective leadership and bureaucracies of growing size and complexity."

The FA model was useful in highlighting the increasingly important role of the bureaucracy in the 1980s, the growing importance of technical expertise and bargaining in the policy process, and the bargaining and incremental nature of policymaking. However, the approach was deficient because it tended to erroneously downplay the continued importance of the center and of hierarchy within the Chinese state. This tendency reflected not only the policy and administrative decentralization of the 1980s but also a declining interest in the status of political parties in the political science literature during this period, as well as the emphasis given to policy bureaucracies and wider questions of state capacity in models of East Asian developmental states. Another lacuna in the FA approach was that it ignored the reality that the increased role of the bureaucracy was part of a leadership political strategy designed to improve regime legitimacy and strengthen the central state. As Hamrin and Zhao (1995, xxvii) argue, the FA model "implies an uncontrolled process whereby autonomy is being seized by subunit actors against the will of the state." The problem, however, is that this account does "not evoke the state's complicity in its own devolution and overstates the weakness of the center." The FA model is also somewhat dated because it does not account for the considerable recentralization of authority that occurred during the second reform era from the early 1990s. As we saw in Chapter 5, this reflected a change in the party elite from the early 1990s, as well as a deliberate agenda to further strengthen the party after the political turmoil and threat to the party in the late 1980s. The literature on Chinese politics has subsequently given much greater attention to the central party-state, especially in works such as Brods-

gaard and Zheng's (2006) *The Chinese Communist Party in Reform* and Shambaugh's (2009) *China's Communist Party: Atrophy and Adaptation.*

Bureaucratic Authoritarianism and the Importance of the Party-State

In their response to the FA model, Hamrin and Zhao (1995) instead proposed
a more top-down bureaucratic account—BA. The advantage of the BA model
is that it emphasizes the rise of bargaining within a *hierarchical* state system.
Under this model, "bureaucratic" refers to the increasing institutionalization
of interest articulation and policy formulation through bureaucratic entities,
as opposed to the centrality of unfettered discretionary power vested in revolutionary party leaders in Mao's era, while "authoritarianism," on the other
hand, pinpoints the monistic leadership of the Party in the overall political
system. The Party commands, controls, and integrates all other political organizations and institutions in China. According to the BA model, "high poli-
tik" issues that have national ideological, political, and strategic significance
remain largely the exclusive territory of the top leadership. The leadership
also retains the ultimate authority and leverage in arbitrating bureaucratic
disputes and, on certain critical issues or in crisis conditions, can resort to
personal involvement and dictation, a mechanism that Shirk (1992, 76; 1994)
calls "management by exception." This enables the political elite, vis-à-vis the
thick bureaucratic institutions, to retain the authority of taking significant
policy initiatives and direct intervention on its key concerns, and have the
final say in balancing conflicting interests, ironing out strong disagreements in
the bureaucracy, and pushing through bold programs on tough issues or issues with "overwhelming urgency" (Shirk 1992, 76). This is evident in action
taken by the central party-state in several rounds of ruthless restructuring of
the bureaucracy and recentralizing authority. Crucially, however, in the context of the move toward the recentralization of authority during the second
reform era, agencies such as the PBC were nevertheless given *more* authority
and their bureaucratic rank was raised.

Overall, the FA-inspired research agenda focused largely on horizontal
bargaining and authority dynamics within the bureaucracy between "parties
of equal bureaucratic rank" (Lampton and Lieberthal 1992, 35), giving less than
sufficient attention to elite-bureaucracy interaction. And when vertical relationships were considered, the main focus was on the changing relationship

between central and local governments, with insufficient attention to power and authority dynamics between the elite political leaders and bureaucratic office holders in the center, a central dimension of the relationship examined in this study. The BA model, by contrast, helps correct such deficiencies by refocusing attention on the power of the center and on how the center has developed strategic relational agendas with lower-level units in the bureaucracy. However, in practice, the BA model largely failed to expand and substantiate its original theoretical and methodological thrust into a conscious and concrete research agenda out of Hamrin and Zhao's (1995) book, which introduced the model in studies of Chinese politics. In addition, scholars that sought to rebalance the FA model's preoccupation with horizontal bureaucratic relations and bargaining more or less shifted back to an elitist or top-down approach, such as the various aforementioned accounts of "management by exception" or, more recently, in accounts such as Pearson's (2005) that suggests that centralized, top-down authority is stymieing the development of a market-oriented "regulatory state" in China. The BA literature also lacks an updated and sophisticated account of the *evolving* dynamics of the relationship between the elite and the bureaucracy in the course of China's economic transition, particularly the way in which the demands and increasing returns of the transition have helped empower key bureaucracies such as the PBC.

Evolving Dynamics of Mutual Dependency between the PBC and the Party Leadership

Institutional Dependencies

A notable institutional feature of modern bureaucracy is its functional specialization. As Max Weber recognized long ago, expertise and knowledge growing out of functional specialization are important sources of bureaucratic authority: "[Even] the absolute monarch is powerless opposite the superior knowledge of the bureaucratic expert" (Weber 1976, 62). This view about the authority of bureaucratic experts has also been prominent in the literature on the "administrative state" (Huber and Shipan 2002). In the case at hand, the enormous complexity and arcane knowledge and expertise associated with monetary and financial management in an emerging market economy has helped underpin the rising influence and authority of the PBC.

Traditionally, top party cadres were not well equipped with essential expertise, especially in complex economic arenas such as monetary and financial affairs. Given their typical skill sets and the requirement to cover a wide range of issues, government leaders do not usually have the time or expertise to deal effectively with monetary policy or the intricacies of the financial system. To be sure, there has been generational evolution of the party leadership from charismatic revolutionary leaders to a more practical technocracy in the post-Mao era, particularly the so-called third-generation party leadership under Jiang Zemin and the current fourth generation under Hu Jintao (Li 2001). But even in the recent party leadership, most of the elites received a poor education in their formative years in a soviet system and were profoundly affected by the political turmoil of the Cultural Revolution.[1] Compared with government recruitment that has increasingly emphasized meritocracy, the party has always been slower to refresh key leaders with higher educational backgrounds, especially in the area of economic management, which is still dominated by political considerations. Although most of the new generation of party elites have been engineers-turned-politicians, they lack essential knowledge in modern economics and finance. For example, the key figures in the third generation (Jiang Zemin, Li Peng, and Zhu Rongji) and the fourth generation (Hu Jintao and Wen Jiabao) are all trained engineers (Li 2001, 27). Such qualifications, as well as the daily pressures of running a complex state system, leave little room for considered or knowledgeable judgments about complex and technical issues to do with monetary or financial policy.

Another problem associated with a collective leadership regime is the relative fluidity of the members of the leading nuclear circle, which cannot provide a stable stock of expertise and experience in the Party's key decision-making bodies. For instance, in explaining the dynamics of the rising authority of China's foreign policy apparatus, Ning (2001, 58–59) observes, "Turnover at this level [top leadership] has been fairly frequent compared with the past. As a consequence of its relative inexperience, the political leadership has had to rely more heavily on professional bureaucrats to reach foreign policy decisions. The bureaucratic institutions, meanwhile, have become more assertive and have occasionally even resisted ill-conceived policy initiatives of members of the leading nuclear circle."

Hence, the imperatives of a transitional economy, the growing penalty of monetary mismanagement in the emerging market, and a relative lack of experience on the part of the political leadership all highlight the need for professionalized institutions, including the PBC, to be in the management circle. However, this is necessary but not sufficient conditions for the rise of the PBC, which also rests on the institutional capacity of the central bank itself, particularly in marshaling the necessary expertise, experience, and institutional and policy capacity to conduct an effective monetary and financial policy.

As the FA and BA models suggest, the fragmented structure of the Chinese bureaucracy lends itself well to the development of specialized expertise. This has several implications. First of all, because information is such a valuable resource, each agency has an incentive to attempt to monopolize the information necessary for an understanding of its particular policy sphere. Agencies also tend to enlarge their own sources of information and expertise. More importantly, lacking the information and expertise necessary to fully evaluate the recommendations of lower-level units, political leaders will often permit those units to become increasingly influential in their own policy spheres.

Another important dimension of bureaucratic authority in China is the bureaucracy's crucial involvement in the gestation stage of the policy process, which is relatively understudied compared to extant research focused on subsequent policy processes such as policy formulation, implementation, and review (Liew 2004, 23–24). Policy gestation, as the initial part of policy formulation, includes aspects such as policy inputs, information collection and analysis, and the formulation of alternatives or options for final decisions to be made and executed by those responsible. Apart from the relevant government agencies (and their sponsored think tanks), other possible participants at this stage include think tanks attached directly to the State Council (such as the Development Research Center) and the Party Central Committees (such as the Central Policy Research Office), sponsored by a particular leader (such as the research centers under Zhao Ziyang's wing in the 1980s), or based in universities and the national research apparatus (such as the Chinese Academy of Social Sciences). It could also include the protégés or close friends of a party leader, such as Zhu Rongji's extensive exchange with his personal (informal) advisers. The makeup of the team depends in a large part on the personal style of the party leader in charge of the issue area.

The fact that multiple parties take part in policy input and analysis representing different institutional backgrounds and interests, all vying for attention and influence from the top leadership, leads Halpern (1992) to ascribe a model of "competitive persuasion" to the process. Ideas and the construction of realities are of course central to this process. Nevertheless, the actual influence of different institutions is rather *asymmetrical,* commensurate with the formal authority, informal resources, and institutional capacities of the actors.

Major players in this regard include institutions with comprehensive, cross-sector authority, particularly the National Development and Reform Commission (NDRC, successor to the State Planning Commission), and specialist institutions with a strong tradition of expertise and experience, such as the Ministry of Foreign Affairs and, in this case, the People's Bank. By occupying key posts in the policymaking regime and playing a coordinating role in the policy process, these bureaucratic heavyweights are influential in crafting and filtering information and ideas selectively and thereby shaping elite preferences, options, and agendas.

Here, the institutional fragmentation of the Chinese bureaucracy has major implications for institutional authority and the policy process. On the one hand, the policy process often entails bargaining and consensus seeking among related bureaucratic players. Typically, a policy proposal can be submitted for formal consideration by the upper authorities only after it has been signed off by the chiefs of all the related agencies (hui qian) (Xu 1996). At the same time, the upper authorities in normal circumstances would not make a decision in the face of stark opposition from lower-level agencies. This arrangement thus invites (sometimes lengthy) bureaucratic bargaining and trade-offs that lead to a prolonged policy process, often resulting in delays. For instance, a major disagreement between the PBC and the NDRC on the macroeconomic outlook in 2003 had the effect of postponing a crucial interest rate hike suggested by the PBC well into 2004 (see Chapter 9). On the other hand, because of functional divisions and exclusive expertise, other related agencies would usually respect the special role and hence the informal authority of the agency that puts forward and coordinates a given proposal. In the monetary policy sphere, the PBC has been the proposal originator in most cases and thus has special influence. As one official from the NDRC comments, "unless we have major differences, we wouldn't say too much [on policies proposed by the PBC]. Their business is very hard [for outsiders] to meddle with even if we wanted to. . . . We will [also] consult with them [the PBC] if we are going to have any moves on pricing."[2]

Apart from such horizontal bargaining and coordination, the one-on-one persuasion of the leadership is even more important. Here the "recommending power" of the central bank in China's monetary and financial policy is crucial. In the Chinese policy process the political leadership often makes its choices from a range of analysis and recommendations from government agencies. Here information monopoly and area specialization help confer considerable power on key bureaucratic players. As George Yang aptly asks in relation to foreign affairs, "if the Ministry of Foreign Affairs drafted all Zhao Ziyang's speeches on foreign policy, who was directing whom?" (quoted in Hamrin and Zhao 1995, xxxix). The following quote from a former head of the British Treasury and secretary of the Cabinet illustrates another way in which this almost subliminal pattern of influence can work: "Obviously I had great influence. The biggest and most pervasive influence is in setting the framework within which questions of policy are raised. . . . We set the questions which we asked ministers to decide arising out of that framework and it would have been enormously difficult for any minister to change the framework, so to that extent we had great power" (quoted in Wilenski 1986, 213).

These arguments about knowledge and expertise as an important basis for bureaucratic authority should only be amplified when it comes to central banks. Indeed, Xie Ping, a senior PBC veteran with experience in its research and executive branches, argues that the central bank could gain "technical independence" from the leadership by deliberately limiting policy options, often to just one or two, which has left the party elites often with no alternatives but to adopt those favored by the Bank (Xie 1995). The PBC and indeed successful central banks more generally have built up specific and very substantial expertise in relation to the workings of modern financial markets and the monetary system. This expertise is arcane, conferring special authority on central bank technocrats.

Central bankers are also increasingly able to trade on the rising international status of their organizations, particularly since the 1990s when many governments granted independence to their central banks (Marcussen 2005). True, some central banks, such as the U.S. Federal Reserve, have had their reputations damaged amid the financial crisis that began in 2007, but the Fed has continued to play a central role in monetary and financial policy in the United States (Wessel 2009). Central banks have also established close relationships with the markets and financial intermediaries and are in constant 24/7 touch with market developments, able to react at a moment's notice. Very few other bureaucracies or regulatory agencies face the need to develop such specialized capacities or occupy such a critical, real-time market-state interface. In other words, central banks are now performing crucial functions in complex monetary and financial environments that governments and politicians can no longer adequately deal with. The inevitable division of labor between central banks and governments in such arenas is increasingly conferring a great deal of authority on central banks.

The PBC's expertise is also embodied in the quality of the Bank's personnel. As we saw in Chapter 5, the PBC has faced a major challenge in building up its monetary policy and financial expertise. One aspect of this has been to learn from and adapt overseas policy ideas and templates. But recruiting and training top talent in the labor market and develop its own experts has also been a challenge. As part of this effort, a younger generation of Western-trained Chinese economists and academics has been invited or promoted into the senior management of the PBC, such as PBC Vice Governor Yi Gang. To attract and retain such personnel, the PBC has also undertaken substantial measures to elevate the remuneration and welfare of its staff. In a welfare system that is highly centralized and distributed strictly according to hierarchical and administrative rankings, the PBC leadership had to go the extra mile to improve the welfare of its staff, especially in the early days of the reform era when it had broken free from the control of the Ministry of Finance (MOF). Hence Li Baohua, the first PBC governor during this time, saw improving the accommodation of the staff working in the Bank's headquarters as urgent.[3] Chen Muhua, the PBC's second governor in this period, contributed much to the improvement of the bank's equipment and use of modern technology, especially after the lost decade of the Cultural Revolution. Chen initiated a long and painstaking process of computerization of the PBC and a nationwide payment and settlement network. Li Guixian, Chen's successor, is remembered for granting higher pay in the banking sector, including the central bank. Under Li's governorship, working for the Bank became one of the most sought-after jobs for university graduates, which helped ensure that the PBC could pick the most talented from China's vast human resource pool.

The PBC's Graduate School has also been playing an important role in providing a platform for the Bank's recruitment and ongoing training. Established in the 1980s, the school attracts many of the most talented graduates in China. Over the years, the school has become "a critical intellectual home for China's financial talents, an active participant in China's opening up to the world, and a faithful facilitator of the nation's financial reform." It has an influential alumni network with over 2,000 graduates, many of whom occupy key posts within the PBC and other financial and economic institutions. To further elevate its educational quality, the school was merged with Tsinghua University in March 2012 and renamed PBC School of Finance.[4] Apart from its own graduate school, the PBC has also been recruiting its higher-level personnel from academia, especially those who have Western educational (doctorate) backgrounds. Since the 1990s, and especially under the governorship of Zhou Xiaochuan, a number of prominent economists returning from overseas joined the central bank and have become a key element of the PBC's management team, as Table 6.1 illustrates.

At the same time, the PBC has also been working with foreign institutions such as the International Monetary Fund (IMF) to provide quality training of its staff. Under its scheme of technical assistance, the IMF built a five-story training center in the northeastern city of Dalian to provide exclusive training courses to PBC staff. Training courses are also offered at the IMF Institute in Washington, DC. The Hong Kong Monetary Authority has also delivered training for more than 800 staff of the PBC at its Beijing headquarters (PBC 2007). "It's safe to say that at any given time, there are PBC officials sitting in the classroom somewhere in the world."[5] Frequent exchanges with the central banks of other countries and with the general international

Table 6.1.   PBC's top recruitment with Western training background

Name	Education and career before joining PBC	Year joining PBC	Current post
Yi Gang	PhD, economics (Illinois); taught at Indiana University (with tenure)	1997	Deputy governor of the PBC, chief of the State Administration of Foreign Exchange
Zhang Xin	PhD, finance (Columbia); worked for Merrill Lynch, the IMF, and World Bank	2004	Deputy director of the PBC's Second Head Office in Shanghai
Li Bo	PhD, economics (Stanford); JD (Harvard)	2004	Director of the PBC's Monetary Policy Department II (in charge of exchange rate policy)
Zhang Tao	PhD, international economics (California); worked for the World Bank and Asian Development Bank	2004	Director of the PBC's International Department

Source: Author-collected data.

financial community have also helped improve expertise and professionalism within the Bank. The systematic efforts of cultivating, recruiting, and training its personnel have ensured that the PBC is capable of maintaining and enhancing its expertise, making it an intelligence center and core institution in Beijing's macroeconomic management. An experienced bank analyst speaks highly of the PBC's technocrats in this regard: "Compared with other major central banks, the People's Bank of China is less independent, but its increased professionalism means more of its proposals will be endorsed by the leadership" (Yao 2011).

Other institutional supports to the PBC have included establishing a second head office in the financial heartland of Shanghai in August 2005 (PBC 2005), a move designed to mimic the kind of key role played by the New York branch of the Federal Reserve in the United States. Being a key financial center, Shanghai offers firsthand market information and allows the PBC to better trace on-the-spot market activities. Elevating the status of the PBC's Shanghai branch has been an important strategic move to facilitate the implementation of monetary policy and open market operations for the Bank (PBC 2005).

In line with many other central banks, the PBC has also taken steps to improve the transparency of its policy deliberations and more widely circulating its views. It now routinely publishes monetary and financial statistics as well as reports of its Monetary Policy Committee meetings. It also produces quarterly reports on monetary policy implementation and annual reports on financial stability, domestic financial market developments, and financial services.[6] In terms of financial services, the central bank has built up a nationwide credit information system and a payment and settlement infrastructure that "position[s] China amongst the best of the breeds in the payments system world" (Keppler 2005, 11; see also Feng 2006a). In addition, the PBC sponsors a daily newspaper *(Financial News)* as well as a number of academic and sectoral journals (such as *Financial Research*). These are important platforms for the PBC to express its policies and ideas and to help strengthen public relations and foster financial research. Another important channel is verbal communications from central bank officials, particularly senior officials, in the form of statements and public interviews. As the PBC increasingly became the focus of the domestic and global financial media, its leadership has developed a more sophisticated (Fed-speak) way of communicating with the market. Using daily data between 2006 and 2010, Ji (2011) argues that the

PBC's external communications, both written and verbal, have helped shape the expectations of money and equity markets, and in this sense can be seen as a new policy tool.

On top of its growing expertise, the PBC has been able to exploit its growing institutional capacities and make strategic choices that have helped open up a degree of discretionary space. As we show in later chapters, there have been crucial moments when the PBC's leaders have been able to innovate, bend the rules, or use specialized institutional capacities and resources (such as access to China's huge foreign reserves to recapitalize the banking system) in efforts to pursue key agendas and build the PBC's authority.

The rise of the PBC's institutional capacities can be seen as part of a wider process of building up the institutional capacities of the Chinese state in the reform era. Dali Yang (2004) argues that such "institutionalization" has been an important aspect of the modernization of the Chinese state. As we saw in Chapter 1, however, some have cast doubt on such assessments, arguing that the Chinese state suffers from endemic corruption and other institutional pathologies. For example, Pearson (2005) has argued that the kinds of professional and relatively independent regulatory agencies that are central to the rise of the "regulatory state" in the West are not taking root in China and are instead being stymied by the centralizing hand of the party-state that refuses to fully relinquish control to markets or devolve substantial authority to relatively independent regulatory authorities in a range of sectors, including public infrastructure and the financial sector. Pearson argues that institutionally, state ownership of key firms, and the limited status, ambiguous role, and fragmentation of regulatory remits, as well as continuing oversight by more senior ministries and comprehensive commissions, all limit the authority of the new regulatory institutions. This pattern is further entrenched by the strategic preferences of the top party elite in limiting competition in key sectors and breeding national champions among leading state-owned firms. "Such comprehensive oversight is a legacy of central planning" (Pearson 2005, 304). In fact, regulatory agencies have been set up in most sectors (telecommunications, food and drug, airlines, and finance). Yet these regulatory agencies never really achieved substantial independence from the leadership or from more senior bureaucracies and in many cases ended up being, essentially, reabsorbed into the bureaucratic hierarchy.

Yet the PBC does not fit this pattern of the "subordinated" regulator. Although it has oversight of the three financial regulatory agencies—the

CBRC, CSRC, and CIRC—the PBC is more than a regulator, largely because of its specialized policy capacities and its key role in a critical state-market interface. This specialized policy role is arguably what sets the PBC apart and helps explain its authority. The party leaders have increasingly deferred to the PBC's monetary expertise and authority, especially since the 1990s. In the hierarchical Chinese context, this is a significant outcome. The PBC's growing expertise and institutional capacities are also forming the foundation for increasing political dependencies between it and the political leadership.

Key Political Dependencies between the Party Elite and the PBC

Our approach to this kind of mutual political dependency reflects the fact that bureaucratic authority in China has both formal and informal dimensions. We cover the former in more detail in Chapter 7, but here we focus on the latter, more informal dimensions of authority relations and suggest they have been composed of two factors, the political ranking or clout of the director of a given institution, and director's relationship with the top leaders. More often than not, top bureaucrats in major ministries are concurrently Party members. In the party-state featuring a strict vertical power hierarchy, rankings in the Party echelon of the bureaucratic executives and the authority of their institutions are mutually reflective. The higher the director's political ranking in the Party, the more authoritative and powerful the institution, and vice versa. For instance, the status of the central bank was significantly boosted by the governorship of Zhu Rongji in the mid-1990s. Zhu was vice premier at that time and later became premier and number three in the Party.

In a relationship-based society such as China, personal relationships (guanxi) between party leaders and top bureaucrats form an important facet of informal bureaucratic authority. The nature of such relationships reflects a form of patron-client symbiosis, with "reciprocal accountability" (Shirk 1994, 18–19). Top government officials are accountable to their patrons, the party elites, who appoint and promote them. At the same time, party leaders also rely on the loyalty and support of bureaucratic clients as their power base in political competitions. The older generation of party leaders, such as Mao and Deng, were able to legitimize and sustain their personal authority through past revolutionary legacies, popular charisma, and extensive networks in the Party, government, and military. These assets are now somewhat scarce for their successors, most of whom have only a technocratic background with a much narrower career path. This has made it imperative for the new breed of party leaders to enlarge their power bases by expanding networks of supporters and clients (including those in the bureaucracy) and elevating the formal or informal status of the institutions under their spheres of influence, exchanging institutional authority for political support.

These kinds of patron-client relationships and the fact that top bureaucrats also hold party rank begs a question about the career and policy incentives of senior central bankers, which is important in our discussion of central bank authority in China. In other words, how is political obeisance to the Party weighed in the top bureaucrats' policy choices vis-à-vis their institutional mandate? And to what extent are institutional interests compromised by political directives of the Party, especially when these two are in conflict?

In the many accounts of China's policymaking in the reform era, there has been a general lack of discussion on the motivations of senior bureaucrats in policy processes. In elite-centered studies, these officials are often perceived as trivial compared with the political leaders. And in many institutionalist accounts, the emphasis is usually given to institutional parameters rather than agency. The vagueness in interpreting the incentives and preferences of senior bureaucrats is also due to their dual identities as government officials as well as party cadres. Even the notion of "bureaucrat" is blurred with that of "politician." For example, in Shih's (2004, 2008) framework of China's financial policymaking, Zhu Rongji is categorized as one of the "top bureaucrats" or "central bureaucrats," despite the fact that Zhu was the third most powerful man in the Party at the peak of his career.

The result is a polarization, as bureaucratic executives are implicitly taken as either Weberian bureaucrats or Machiavellian politicians. There are two streams in the former camp. The rationality model believes that policymaking, especially in the economic arena, is usually based on reasoned debates over perceived policy problems (Barnett 1981; Lardy 1992b; Wang 2000). Under this model, government officials are seen as rational technocrats whose policy choices are determined by their personal values, ideas, ideology, and preferences, often squaring with what they perceive as national interests. The institutionalist model, on the other hand, follows the logic of "where you stand depends on where you sit," depicting policy outcomes as the result of bureaucratic competition for budget, power, authority, and prestige in China's fragmented institutional structure (Feng 2006c, Chapter 5; Liew 2003; Shih

2005; Wang 2001). Under this model, bureaucratic executives are seen as natural promoters and utility maximizers of institutional interests. The "politician" camp, however, suggests that senior bureaucrats are clients fighting for their elite patrons in power struggles for political survival. Hence, factional politics is seen as the key to understanding both policy process and outcomes (Shih 2004, 2008).

These narrowly defined assumptions are questionable. The rational-technocrat assumption is simply idealistic, given the imperfect nature of its implicit prerequisites in the real world, such as information availability, clear sets of priorities, sufficient time to evaluate alternative choices, and, most importantly, their absolute insulation from the political arena. In this regard, the institutional and factional models have the merit of bringing (bureaucratic and elite) politics back in, but actors' values and ideas tend to be understated, which invariably influences policy advocacy. For example, Shih (2007) suggests that because "administrative accomplishments are evaluated by short-term results," actors have incentives to ignore longer-term issues and have "strong disincentives to carry out fundamental reforms." It is true that the choices of the key actors such as politicians and bureaucrats are inevitably informed by their political calculations, but longer-term reformist ideas and ideology cannot be excluded from the equation. Decision makers in the party-state constantly face a trade-off between political and ideational or normative preferences, which is contingent upon the nature of the issue area, the strategic importance of the policy, and the specific political environment in which they are embedded. The above argument by Shih is based on a study of Premier Zhu Rongji's financial policies in the late 1990s. Shih argues that in the financial realm, Zhu focused on the short term in that meaningful banking reform was postponed in a bid to support his political career. However, if Zhu's *overall* policy framework during this period is taken into account, it becomes apparent that financial restructuring was not a high priority for him at that time. Despite a number of earlier successes, such as debt restructuring between state-owned enterprises (SOEs) and the economic soft landing in 1996, Zhu's position in the top circle of the party was constantly challenged by opportunistic attacks from Li Peng (number two in the hierarchy) as well as by provincial governors who were discontented with the fiscal recentralization program Zhu had pushed. The then president, Jiang, was broadly in support of Zhu, but Jiang had to play a balancing role between reformers and conservatives, a consummate conciliator staying carefully out of the disputes himself (Fewsmith 1998). Moreover, although banking reform became an urgent issue in the wake of the Asian financial crisis, Jiang and Zhu's priority had been SOE restructuring and the shedding of tens of millions of workers, as well as staging a desperate bid for China's WTO membership amid fierce bureaucratic resistance (Feng 2006c). This put Zhu in a more vulnerable position in domestic politics and his enemies wasted no chance in attacking him and his allies on issues such as the non-devaluation policy amid the Asian financial crisis (see Chapter 8), Zhu's highly anticipated but largely empty-handed visit to the United States during WTO entry negotiations, and the subsequent U.S. bombardment of the Chinese embassy in the former Yugoslavia in May 1999, which almost cost Zhu his premiership (Zweig 2001). The fact that Zhu pushed major reforms with little foreseeable short-term political benefits but huge immediate costs suggests that the reformist vision and ideas of political and bureaucratic elites in reform China do or at least can matter, and have shaped the dynamics of institutional change in China.

In fact, the unique, interlocking structure of the Leninist party-state and the reciprocal relationship between informed elite leaders and their key bureaucratic allies mean that their incentive structure is inevitably a multifaceted matrix of ideational, institutional, and political considerations. Among these factors, we argue that institutional considerations have often been more prevalent than political or factional ones. The reason is straightforward. In China's political system, the head of a line ministry, including the governor of the central bank, may be a political appointment sanctioned by the appointee's elite patron, but future career development is ultimately determined by the performance of the institution he or she is in charge of. After all, the Party needs problem solvers in the administration more than incompetent loyalists. This is especially the case for senior officials of the central bank because of the commanding position of finance in an increasingly marketized economy and the almost universal agreement regarding key performance indicators of a central bank. Factional politics is more likely to play a greater role in determining policy processes and outcomes in other arenas, such as industry policy, where policy frameworks and criteria of performance are more open to contest and debate.[7]

As Shih (2007, 1245) argues, for top technocrats, the best strategy for accumulating political capital and ensuring political survival within the regime is "making oneself the indispensable problem solver. . . . As the post-reform era experience has shown, the perceived ability to solve pressing problems greatly increases the likelihood of promotion and of retaining power." On this issue, a PBC veteran said,

> Western media usually analyze our policy making from the perspective of factions, and I noticed that some domestic media had started mimicking this in our country. To be frank, I don't know how they make up the stories, but I do know that if inflation is out of control, no one can save our Governor Zhou [Xiaochuan], no matter who is his political support *(kaoshan)*. No one can save him [laughs]. He will definitely have a hard time when briefing to Zhongnanhai.[8]

This does not suggest that political factors are irrelevant. In fact, personal relations and coalitional associations between elite leaders and top bureaucrats play an important role in Chinese policymaking. Yet from the perspective of bureaucrats, the factional model tends to exaggerate factional interests over institutional concerns. Moreover many of the so-called factions are actually loose groups, or broadly defined political coalitions, whose membership is based on similar values, ideology, and career experience, not rigid cliques that are well organized, mobilized, disciplined, and require maximum compliance (Dittmer 1995; Shih 2008). Therefore, our working assumption is that top bureaucrats in the functionaries normally stand for their institutions, albeit with certain preferences for advancing their political patrons.

This institutional priority leads to behavioral consequences, which partly explains the use of persuasion and bargaining over open dispute between ministers and top leaders when disagreement among them exists. A paradox of China's political system has been the coexistence of a hierarchical but fragmented institutional structure, and a political culture of unity. This sense of unity is partly rooted in the Confucian philosophy of harmony *(he wei gui)*, and partly due to the political necessity of the Communist Party to build an image of a united and strong party-state as a capable public administrator. This has two implications. On the one hand, inner-elite disputes are rarely made public, unless they serve critical political purposes, such as the open trial of the Gang of Four after the Cultural Revolution. The institutional control of the Party over the administrative agencies also forbids the latter to shift internal disagreement into an open dispute in public. On the other hand, the policy process is normally consensus driven to accommodate and coordinate among various preferences. Given that institutional interests top their concerns, top bureaucrats and their institutions, particularly the powerful ones, could forestall potential conflict with political imperatives and achieve their goal by persuading the leadership in their favor. As argued above, this can be done by utilizing the agency's institutional capacity in the formal process of policy formulation and advice. It can also be done through informal channels based on personal relationships between elite leaders and line ministers.

Political Relations between the PBC and the Party Leadership in the Second Reform Era

The Jiang-Zhu Era

None of the PBC's governors before 1993 was a political heavyweight. This was both a result and an indicator of the central bank's actual status within the party-state. For instance, Li Baohua (1978–82), son of CCP founder Li Dazhao, was a provincial governor and a member of the party's Central Committee before taking up the governorship of the PBC. Lü Peijian (1982–85) was a vice minister of the MOF and also a member of the Central Committee before his term at the PBC. Chen Muhua's (1985–88) status was higher than that of her predecessors, as a vice premier in the State Council. However, being an alternate member of the CCP's Politburo, she was only marginally involved in key decision making regarding party-state affairs. Chen's follower, Li Guixian (1988–93) had a rank similar to that of Li Baohua.

The relatively marginal status of the PBC changed in the 1990s, which reflected the reform push by the new generation of party leaders intent on dealing with economic instability and pushing forward market reforms. In this era, a key indicator of the Bank's rising stocks was the appointment of Zhu Rongji as PBC governor in July 1993. Zhu had long been widely recognized as a reform-minded economic thinker and political leader fashioning a can-do and iron-fisted style, which was rare among party politicians and earned him the title of China's "economic tsar."[9] He was politically resurrected by Deng Xiaoping after the Cultural Revolution, largely for his insight and expertise in economic management, and was further elevated from the mayorship in Shanghai to the central government in Beijing in 1991, part of a clear roadmap to enter the Party's paramount power circle backed by Deng (Gao and He 1993, 86–88). Zhu established his reputation in Beijing by taking the lead in addressing tough issues such as triangular debt among SOEs and other enterprises and national fiscal reform, which greatly strengthened the financial capacity of the center (Shih 2004).

For the Bank, Zhu's political profile was unprecedented. At the time of appointment, Zhu was already a member of the Politburo Standing Committee, deputy director of the Central Leading Group on Financial and Economic Affairs (CLGFEA), and the deputy premier of the State Council. A rising star who later climbed to number three in the Party, Zhu's governorship and long-term legacy greatly boosted the PBC's status within the center. On the one hand, as a relative newcomer in the central government, Zhu needed bureaucratic support from the Bank to tackle some of the serious problems in the economy. Success here was vital for him to establish his reputation. On the other hand, to achieve this, Zhu needed to delegate authority to the Bank and elevate its de facto authority to make it a powerful platform for his ambitious reform agenda. The use of such reciprocity bonding by the party elite is well illustrated in Zhu Rongji's ongoing relationship with the central bank and its successive governors (Zhu's protégés), so that the rising authority of the Bank became an indispensable link in Zhu's ongoing strategy of political success.

Despite Deng's support, Zhu initially lacked a broad network of support in the central government as a new transfer from his provincial post (Zweig 2001). He also lacked political support among provincial governors, who were unhappy with his partial recentralization programs in fiscal and banking reforms. This made him vulnerable to his major rival in the central government, then-Premier Li Peng, who was an adopted son of party veteran Zhou Enlai and had developed his entire career in the central bureaucracy. Zhu had to face subtle political resistance from Li, who felt more or less threatened by Zhu's promotion. The dire political atmosphere in Beijing helped forge mutual reciprocity between Zhu and the central bank. Zhu had to cultivate his own power base within the central bureaucracy, most conveniently the agencies he presided over during the early days of his vice premiership. This was the case for the Production Office of the State Council, which Zhu chaired after he arrived in Beijing, which was promoted from being a trivial body to one of the two most powerful supraministerial agencies (beside the NDRC) in charge of China's economic and trade affairs, the State Economic and Trade Commission (Gao and He 1993; Wang and Fewsmith 1995). This is also the case for the PBC. Treating it as his own backyard, Zhu was willing to grant the central bank more authority in the policy process. For example, as we show more fully in Chapter 7, Zhu initiated a series of institutional reforms of the central bank, particularly its regional structure, to make it more immune to influence from provincial governments.

At the same time, Zhu also promoted a number of like-minded, younger-generation technocrats as leadership reserves for the central bank during his years in Beijing between 1991 and 2003, such as Dai Xianglong (a banking expert handpicked by Zhu to be his successor at the PBC in 1995), Zhou Xiaochuan (a liberal reformer promoted by Zhu from the directorship of a state bank to head the stock market watchdog group in 2000 and governor of the PBC since 2003), and Yi Gang (a U.S.-trained doctorate and vice governor in charge of monetary policy of the PBC since 2007). Moreover, officials from the central bank were given some of the key posts in top decision-making bodies. For example, Dai Genyou, director of the PBC's Monetary Policy Department, was concurrently head of the research office of the CLGFEA, which was a position of high influence in the supreme economic policymaking organ of the party-state (Liew 2004, 28).

The central bank also needed support from Zhu, a political contact for the Bank at the top of the Party, to reinforce its newly gained legislative authority in the 1995 PBC Law (detailed in Chapter 7), as well as to enhance its de facto authority in the top policy circle. As one insider commented, "It was very much like I look after you, and you look after me."[10] In particular, Zhu and Dai had established strong working relations. For instance, during the PBC's regional restructuring, Zhu and Dai worked hand-in-hand to ensure a smooth implementation as the reform reshuffled local, institutional, and personal interests. As premier, Zhu took measures to placate provincial protests, while Dai, as head of the central bank, presided over the bargaining within the PBC.[11]

As we show in Chapter 8, Zhu's tenure at the PBC saw him tackle a runaway economy rapidly heating up after Deng's southern tour in 1992, which was caused by local investment manias and the lack of effective control by the central bank. Through a package of mostly administrative measures, Zhu helped bring the economy to a soft landing in 1995–96. Not only was this experience a great personal victory in Zhu's political career, it was also a huge credit for the central bank in the domestic polity as it managed, for the first time, to rein in inflation. Moreover, Zhu's ruthless campaign against corruption and wrong dealings in the financial sector transformed the PBC from a relatively toothless regulator to one that was "frightening" for many government officials and market practitioners.[12]

As we argue in Chapter 9, as the Asian financial crisis unfolded in 1998, the Bank successfully supported the non-devaluation strategy advocated by Zhu. In the wake of the crisis, Dai also ensured that Zhu's economic rescue package, centered on the stimulation of China's domestic demand, was accompanied by a favorable monetary policy, cutting interest rates six times between 1998 and 2001. Dai was also a key supporter of Zhu's leadership in China's talks to enter the WTO. One of the critical issues of these talks had been the terms of China's financial opening, in which Dai, as the central bank governor, had a vital say in forging the internal consensus. In the final stage of the bilateral talks with the United States, it was Dai who lent his full support to Zhu's concessions in financial market entry in exchange for a speedier accession for Beijing, a difficult trade-off that saw Zhu hesitant for nearly six months.[13]

The central bank's ascendance also benefited from a leadership change, which saw Zhou Xiaochuan taking over the PBC's governorship in December 2002. Zhou was regarded by both domestic and foreign analysts as "the brightest financial star in government" (Murphy 2003, 30). Zhou was an engineer-turned-economist, a staunch promoter of market initiatives, and, in Alan Greenspan's (2007, 298) eyes, a Chinese technocrat with "fluency in English and international finance." He was also an experienced central banker and commercial banker, whose long career at the top of the financial sector included serving as vice governor of the PBC, chief director of the State Administration of Foreign Exchange, governor of the China Construction Bank (one of the Big Four), and the chief regulator of China's securities market, the CSRC.

Most importantly, he was a party heavyweight with close ties with both the outgoing Jiang Zemin–Zhu Rongji administration and the new Hu Jintao–Wen Jiabao regime that was installed just months after Zhou's appointment. Zhou is one of the few high fliers who not only survived the purge of former Premier Zhao after the 1989 turmoil, but who flourished. This is less surprising given his family connections. Zhou's father was a mentor to Jiang and facilitated Jiang's promotion at key moments during his early career (Murphy 2003, 30). Zhou was highly regarded by Zhu Rongji, who took him as his right-hand man and who had a vital say in Zhou's PBC tenure.

The Hu-Wen Era

The leadership transition from Jiang and Zhu to Hu Jintao and Wen Jiabao beginning in late 2002 brought new dynamics to the relationship between the PBC and the party-state. Hu became the secretary-general of the Party in November 2002, but it took until March 2005 for Hu to acquire the de facto top leadership post, chairman of the Military Committee, from his predecessor, Jiang. Compared with Jiang, Hu was rather slow in consolidating his power base in the central apparatus (Miller 2005). Meanwhile, Wen took over the premiership from Zhu in March 2003.

The change of leadership also led to a shift in emphasis between the two administrations. While the former leadership was deeply concerned with chronic problems in the SOE sector and China's external integration into the global economy, especially through steering China's WTO accession in 2001, the latter is more concerned with the externalities of liberal reforms, in particular poverty and income inequality (Liew and Wu 2007; Naughton 2004c). To put this another way, the Jiang-Zhu regime was preoccupied with enlarging the size of the economic pie, while the Hu-Wen regime has sought to achieve a more equitable distribution of the pie. In particular, the new leadership is concerned with domestic imbalances between agriculture and industry, between the coastal and the inland regions, and between the rich and the poor, despite overall rapid economic development in the last three decades. A staple in the Chinese press that has been ascribed to the new leadership transition has been the term "scientific developmentalist viewpoint." It calls for "putting people first" (yiren weiben), implying a broad, human capabilities–based perspective on growth. It also advocates the establishment of a "Harmonious Society," which sees tackling social inequalities and polarization as the foundation for comprehensive, coordinated, and sustainable development (Naughton 2005). While the shift of focus from reform and external integration to domestic inequality does not necessarily represent a U-turn or a rollback of the general direction of the reforms, it led to a more cautious stance toward the liberalist and internationalist theme of the Jiang-Zhu reforms and a partial scaling-down of the previous programs. For example, Jiang and Zhu initiated SOE restructuring in the late 1990s. By shedding the small and medium-sized SOEs and building state champions, the leadership hoped that the capital consolidation would help to turn the SOEs into more market-oriented, profit-generating enterprises. However, under Hu and Wen, these national champions cemented their monopoly in almost all the strategic and most profitable sectors, such as energy and telecommunications, at the expense of a more efficient and dynamic private sector, a phenomenon referred to as *guojin mintui* (the advance of the state sector and the retreat of the private sector). This trend has apparently deepened in the aftermath of the global financial crisis, as the majority funds from Beijing's stimulus package went to the state sector, thus crowding out private investment (Feng 2009).

Similar to previous arrangements, Hu opted out of leadership in economic and financial affairs, leaving Wen as the major decision maker in this area (Liew and Wu 2007). Prior to his premiership, Wen had assisted Zhu in financial affairs as vice premier and head of the Central Financial Work Commission (restructured into the CBRC in 2002). The vice premier with a finance portfolio under Wen's leadership has been Huang Ju, who died of cancer and was replaced by Wang Qishan in 2008. Huang is associated with Jiang's power base in Shanghai, and has been very supportive of Governor Zhou and the PBC in the State Council (Walter and Howie 2011). Wang, once a vice governor of the PBC (1993–94) under the then PBC governor Zhu, is considered as Zhu's protégé and a trusted firefighter used to being assigned to tough jobs, such as mopping up the mess after the collapse of the Guangdong International Trust and Investment Company. According to former U.S. Treasury secretary Henry Paulson (2009), Wang is "the man China's leaders look to for an understanding of the markets and the global economy," who "managed the largest bankruptcy restructuring in China's history in 1998 and thereby prevented a banking crisis that could have crippled the country's growth." More importantly, there was a special relationship between Zhou and Wen, both of whom were longtime followers of the key reformers, such as Zhao Ziyang in the 1980s and Zhu Rongji in the 1990s (Gao and He 1993; Naughton 2002). This relationship flourished under the Wen administration, in which Wen "effectively delegated authority and decisive action to Zhou" (Naughton 2004a, 5).

This lineup of pro-reform leaders at the top of post-Zhu financial decision making ensured that Zhu's legacy has been largely kept intact under the Hu-Wen regime, at least in the finance sector, recognizing the fact that only by reforming the ailing financial sector, particularly the banking system, can Beijing establish a sound foundation for sustainable development and social stability. On the other hand, however, the general work style of the Hu-Wen leadership explicitly emphasizes collective deliberation and decision making

(Miller 2005, 5), and thus a more balanced position in potential bureaucratic frictions. As we elaborate in subsequent chapters, this has been exploited by institutional players, such as the MOF, that had been wary of the PBC's unilateral activism and emerging dominance in some of its traditional jurisdictions. This is especially of banking reform since 2005, when the PBC's policy vehicle, Huijin, was merged into the sovereign wealth fund under the MOF's control.

At the same time, however, the PBC's efforts in building up its institutional expertise and capacity over the years rendered it an indispensable force in Beijing's macroeconomic management. This in turn has boosted its institutional clout, which the leadership partly relies on in keeping the reform momentum moving forward. Indeed, the PBC has continued to play a major role in key policy fronts, including monetary policy and exchange rate policy, as we see in subsequent chapters. On the exchange rate front, the Bank was also instrumental in pushing for a partial liberalization of the renminbi exchange regime in 2005 and again for moving off the dollar peg in 2008. Even in the financial reform arena, where there had been a setback for the PBC with the loss of Huijin, the reform agenda, which is based on the PBC's more market-oriented approach, has been kept alive.

Reportedly, Zhou was to leave the PBC when his five-year term ended in March 2008 ("Zhou Xiaochuan huo jiang" 2007). Yet given his knowledge of monetary issues and success in presiding over the reform of the exchange rate regime in 2005, he was "strongly supported" by the top leadership to continue steering the central bank for a second term. In addition, Beijing also felt compelled to keep Zhou as the PBC governor as the Chinese and global economy entered into an era of greater uncertainty amid WTO-inspired financial opening ("Huigai huo kending Zhou Xiaochuan" 2008). Indeed, this is the other reason why Zhou and the institution he represents prosper: being an indispensible problem solver. Zhou's achievement as PBC governor has also been recognized internationally on a number of occasions over the years, which also increased the PBC's power at the top. For example, he was elected the Best Asian Banker in 2006 by the British magazine *The Banker;* ranked fourth on the Top 100 Global Thinkers list of the *Foreign Policy* magazine in 2010; named Central Banker of the Year by the *Euromoney* magazine in 2011; and was one of only two mainland officials on *Bloomberg Markets'* 50 Most Influential list in 2012 (Ren 2012). His key role in the debate over China's exchange rate regime earned him the title "Mr. RMB." Zhou also found himself in eleventh place on the *Forbes* list of the World's Most Powerful People, with Ben Bernanke being his only international counterpart to make the top ten.

Conclusion

Although various laws have elevated the status of the PBC, perhaps more important are informal exchanges and accommodations in which the party elite has increasingly been influenced by PBC's central bankers. Central banks can *win* authority if they are able to set the agenda and establish a credible policy and administrative track record and adeptly utilize institutional resources and capacities. This has largely been the case with the PBC, at least thus far. The PBC has also been able to exploit gaps in the statutes to assert authority and exercise a degree of discretion, as evidenced, for example, in the Bank's use of administrative controls to fight inflation in 2003. Therefore, the real issue in this case is how policies are formulated in a two-way street of authority flows, a complex interaction between top-down elite power and bottom-up bureaucratic influence. In this view, the relationship between the political leadership and key bureaucratic institutions such as the PBC is that of command as well as cooperation, in which the elites of the party-state control the strategic direction but at the same time delegate a degree of authority and policymaking to the central bank. But beyond this notion of top-down authority delegation, an important bottom-up process is also at work. Here, the PBC has been able to win authority, mainly by becoming indispensable to the party elite and by asserting distinctive agendas, monopolizing specialized expertise, and performing strongly in the policy arena. Trust relationships and wider political dependencies have also been important in this equation.

Back in 1983, a group of young PBC staff informally proposed to make the Bank a Fed-like statutory body answerable only to the national legislature, the National People's Congress. Not surprisingly, this notion was not accepted by the party-state authorities (Zheng 1995, 34). It is most likely that a similar move today would yield the same result, as control of finance is believed to be vital for the party's monopolistic rule. However, compared with the minor role of the Bank in the planning days and even in the 1980s, what did change in recent decades was a steady increase of both formal and informal authority of the central bank within the party-state and the wider government and in the emerging market. Given the development in the Bank's statutory authority, and its informal political and institutional clout, the PBC has evolved from the once-passive role of bookkeeper and cashier to the government to become a true power center in Beijing's macroeconomic management.

Most of the central banks in the former communist camp gained some measure of independence in the 1990s amid economic and political re-orientation under neoliberal doctrines. Their counterpart in China also gained substantial authority, albeit within a rather different context, in which the Communist Party managed to retain its authoritarian rule over a selectively liberalized economy. The growth in central bank authority in China has been achieved despite the persistence of a hierarchical state and rests mainly on key political and institutional needs of the Party amid the process of economic transition.

This chapter has argued that the policy authority of the PBC was greatly strengthened from the 1990s, particularly since the time when Zhu relied on the Bank to enhance his position in the center. With expanding political prow-ess and more experience in the policy sphere, the Bank has built up its capacity, confidence, and credibility. On the one hand, the economic transition created an institutional need for an authoritative central bank to tackle inflation that is inherent in the transition process and the dynamics of China's central-local relationship. At the same time, the Bank has been beefing up its institutional capacity by strengthening and expanding its expertise and knowledge, which makes it indispensable for Beijing to maintain sustainable growth. In addi-tion, the Bank's bargaining power vis-à-vis the party-state has continued to strengthen while marketization gives technocrats the leverage and discretion to pursue their interests within the political marketplace. In this case, the reci-procity between the Bank and the political leaders significantly boosted the former's authority in the policy process.

Despite evidence of widespread international institutional isomorphism regarding central banks and their evolution, we have focused mainly on the domestic political and institutional sources of rising central bank authority as the key to the China case. Although external influences have been appar-ent, these have not been the primary driver of the changes in question. Nor have international financial market pressures driven or even strongly shaped such changes. Despite increased exposure to international financial markets, China has effectively shielded itself from critical sources of such pressure and has used its huge reserves to service and manage debt and currency markets rather than be led by them.

We have also highlighted something of a gap in the literature dealing with rising central bank authority. In particular, as we have seen, the standard central bank independence literature focuses on domestic political machinations, external market pressures, or institutional isomorphism driven by epistemic communities. Yet this literature says little about the institutional characteristics of central banks themselves. A key focus in this respect has been on the ambitious institutional building strategies of the PBC's leaders and on the role of specialized knowledge, expertise, and institutional capacity in garnering institutional and policy authority in an arena in which central banks perhaps play a unique regulatory and management role in the crucial and specialized 24/7 engagement with domestic and international money and financial markets. This specialized institutional capacity deserves wider attention in central bank studies.

7

Formal Institutional Change and the Rise of the PBC in the Second Reform Era, 1992–2011

During China's second reform era beginning in the early 1990s, in the wake of the economic and political turbulence of the late 1980s, the PBC rose to a central place in Beijing's economic hierarchy. In this chapter we outline the main formal institutional changes to the central bank's role during this era. These changes saw a substantial consolidation of the PBC's formal monetary and financial authority, all part of its becoming a more modern central bank overseeing a monetary order featuring a greater role for market-based policy instruments.

The 1995 Central Bank Law

As we saw in Chapters 5 and 6, the increasing informal authority of the PBC, the growing mutual dependencies between the party leadership and the PBC, and the inflationary surges of the mid-to-late 1980s and early 1990s, helped propel a long-overdue move toward formal legislation that both strengthened the central bank and clarified its role. The traumatic experience of high inflation had a great impact on the political leadership. The view emerged that the Party needed a stronger central bank to supervise and regulate monetary affairs and credit issuance in the emerging market. Until then, the central bank had not had a formal, legal underpinning, except for the State Council 1983 Decree (see Chapter 3), which made its position vulnerable in the bureaucratic process (vs. contending ministries, local governments, state banks, and the emerging nonbank financial institutions).

Hence on March 18, 1995, the National People's Congress adopted and promulgated the Law of the People's Republic of China on the People's Bank of China, which marked a milestone in modernizing the Chinese central bank. Building upon the 1983 Decree of the State Council, the 1995 Law finally confirmed the PBC's status as a central bank in national legislation. The PBC was mandated to "formulate and implement" monetary policy and financial supervision (Article 2). With the abolition of one of the vestiges of the planning era, the National Price Bureau, in the early 1990s, the PBC was also now formally responsible for inflation. In stating, "The aim of monetary policies is to maintain the stability of the value of the currency and thereby promote economic growth," the law follows the spirit of the 1983 Decree, which set currency stability as the priority goal of the central bank. Yet the more or less ambiguous wording of the text suggests a degree of confusion, by which one could argue that economic growth was the "ultimate" goal of the Bank (He 1998). In reality, however, both price stability and economic growth are the objectives of the PBC. In all public speeches and writings, PBC governors have argued that the PBC's policy objective is a comprehensive one, aiming to balance inflation, employment, growth, and balance of payments concerns. But in practice, as we argue more fully in Chapter 8, the Bank views reducing inflation as its primary goal. The Bank's leaders argue, as do most other central bankers, that the best way they can promote economic growth in the longer term is by ensuring price stability. However, its leaders acknowledge the difficulties in pursuing multiple goals simultaneously and that compromises are required. Perhaps this is best illustrated in the Bank's accommodative monetary policy in the immediate aftermath of the global financial crisis in 2009, when overall growth and systemic stability were seen by the leadership as being under threat (see Chapter 9).

The law reiterates "the leadership" of the State Council over the central bank (Article 2), and stipulates that the PBC needs to approach the central leadership for approval on "key issues" concerning monetary policy, such as the annual supply of banknotes, interest rates, and exchange rates (Article 5). Nevertheless, the central bank is also granted a degree of autonomy from the central leadership. For example, the governor of the Bank is appointed through a somewhat less centralized process. The governor is nominated by China's premier, but affirmed by the legislature (or its Standing Committee) and appointed or removed by the president (Article 9). The central bank also has full autonomy in deciding matters of monetary policy other than the "key issues" above (Article 5). Moreover, the central bank is made accountable (albeit indirectly) to the national legislature by submitting to the latter an annual report on monetary policies and financial regulation, which could constrain central intervention, at least nominally.

Importantly, the PBC also enjoys substantial autonomy from the rest of the government under the law, with its role described as an independent operation "free from any intervention by local governments or government departments at all levels, public organizations or individuals" (Article 7). In particular, the central bank was granted high insulation from the MOF. Article 28 stipulates clearly that the PBC must not finance budget deficits or "directly subscribe to or act as sole sales agent for State bonds and other government bonds." The PBC was also delegated to manage the State treasury (Article 23), thus excluding the possibility of the Ministry of Finance (MOF) controlling the PBC through treasury management. In addition, the central bank was given financial autonomy to "exercise independent control over its financial budget" (Article 37). The Bank's budget is incorporated into the central budget while its losses are also covered by the state budget. This further reduces any potential intervention from the MOF through manipulating the PBC's budget and expenditure, and helps ensure greater "economic" independence for the PBC.

The Central Bank Law, together with the Commercial Bank Law promulgated at the same time, is historically significant in China's effort to establish a modern financial system amid its economic transition. As far as the central bank is concerned, the law delegated considerable statutory authority to the PBC in terms of enshrining central bank status, functions, and structure, as well as its role in monetary policymaking and market supervision (Qian 1996). Although it leaves scope for improvement in terms of insulating the Bank from the political leadership, the Bank did gain a measure much operational and financial autonomy, not only from the leadership but from the wider government. And although some of the stipulations of the law remain nominal in the Chinese reality, it nevertheless provides an essential foundation and stepping stone for future reforms. Indeed, many interviewees within the PBC and in other agencies refer back to this period as the beginning of an era in which the central bank became a force to be reckoned with by other powerful players in the government and market, and that by the latter half of the 1990s, the central bank became "the most influential ministry in economic affairs" (Liew 2004, 50).

Beyond these legislative changes, another key dimension of the PBC's rising authority and capacity lies in ongoing reforms to its institutional structure, aimed at building a modern central bank, insulating it from local governments, and enhancing its monetary policy capacity.

Reforming the PBC's Regional Structure

The institutionally induced bottom-up dynamics of inflation in China have also been dealt with institutionally by the center, and one of the key measures has been to delegate greater authority to the central bank to rein in local growth fevers. As we have seen, a key constraint for the central bank's capacity had been its regional structure. Under the old system this structure meant that local branches of the PBC were heavily influenced by local governments. Although the government stated in 1983, "In principle, the branching of PBC should be based on economic (not administrative) regions" (Article II, 1983 Decree), the actual setting still applied the traditional principle of "one level of local government, one level of bank branch." As such, the local PBC branches were under the dual control of both the head office (central government) and local government, a typical feature of the Chinese bureaucratic system aimed at balancing functional and territorial interests (Halpern 1992; Naughton 1992). Under this arrangement, local governments were in charge of the local bank branch's personnel management and social welfare, which presented local leadership with an effective means to condition, bend, and exploit the central bank's policy agenda in favor of local preferences.

In terms of the trade-off between inflation and unemployment, the policy preferences of central bureaucrats also stood in stark contrast to those of local officials.

National policy makers are more concerned with high rates of inflation and thus less concerned about high levels of unemployment; local officials have the opposite preferences. . . . A principal factor is that central leaders absorb a disproportionate share of costs of inflation, whereas to the local governments inflation control is a public good in that the benefits of its provision are small as compared with the costs. For that reason, the central policy makers are "balancers of the last resort," if they do not balance the macroeconomic situation, no one else in the system will. They cannot simply "pass the buck," so to speak. (Huang 1996, 17)

These different incentive structures lead Shih (2008) to categorize two broadly defined factions in China's macroeconomic management, the "generalist" faction, whose members, such as local officials, have comprehensive responsibilities; and the "central" faction. Shih argues that the conflicts between these two groups formed the dynamics of business and inflation cycles in reform China. Since central bureaucrats, including central bankers, are more intrinsically concerned about inflation, they are more trusted by the Party leadership in inflation control. Moreover, given the intimate and particularistic ties

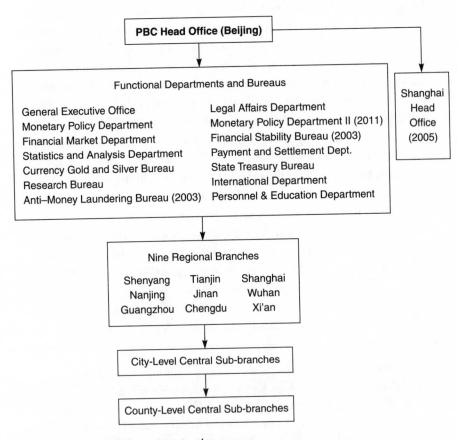

FIGURE 7.1. PBC's organizational structure.

Note: Dates in parentheses indicate the year the institution was established.

between local officials and their patrons in the center, it became more necessary for the party leaders to install a strong, authoritative, and insulated central bank to resist political pressures for monetary expansion that could derail stability and growth.

For these reasons a further key institutional reform has been pursued. While it was undisputed that local interference over bank decisions severely weakened the central bank's authority and capacity in credit control and bank regulation, this was not put on the reform agenda until Zhu Rongji took over the key economic portfolio. Accordingly, the center undertook institutional reforms of the Bank's regional structure in the late 1990s to insulate the Bank from local influences. The final program was a Chinese version of the Fed structure, in which the former thirty-one provincial branches were consolidated into nine cross-provincial (regional) ones, reporting only to the head office in Beijing (Figure 7.1).[1] The zoning of regional branches was based on the principle of proximity of economic development instead of territorial administration, with one branch typically overseeing several provincial areas. The governors of these branches were also subject to interregional transfers, thus severing their traditional links to a particular provincial leadership.[2] Although this organizational arrangement is not sufficient to fully eradicate local influence on bank decisions, it helps diffuse local pressures in large degree and helps promote a greater measure of regional stability (Tao 2003). By reducing local interference, the moves have also centralized the power of the central bank and greatly enhanced its autonomy from local interference.

Establishing the PBC's Second Head Office in Shanghai

Apart from helping to insulate the PBC from local interference, another important step in boosting the PBC's institutional capacity has been the establishment of its second head office in Shanghai in 2005 (see Figure 7.1). According to Governor Zhou, "the outdated organizational structure of the People's Bank of China no longer fits in with its mandate to improve market operation and financial services"; therefore "the setup of PBC Shanghai Head Office is of historical significance."[3] A clear attempt to copy the institutional pattern of the Federal Reserve Bank in New York, the strategic move establishes an operational platform of the PBC's monetary policy in Shanghai, which hosts China's major financial markets, such as the foreign exchange market, gold market, securities market, futures market, and the interbank bond market. Being "on-site" in China's financial capital, this new platform is instrumental in facilitating the acquisition of real-time, firsthand information on the financial markets to feed back to the Bank's monetary decision making in turn. It is also tasked with facilitating the PBC's open-market operations. By doing so, it has strengthened the PBC's capacity for information gathering and analysis as well as policy assessment, which has further enhanced its authority in the market as well as in Beijing's macroeconomic policy apparatus.

The Central Financial Work Commission

In the wake of various financial scandals as well as the Asian financial crisis in 1997, Zhu Rongji urged the Party to establish the Central Financial Work Commission (CFWC).[4] This was a mechanism designed to exert greater central authority over and to attack special insider dealing in China's banking, securities, and insurance sectors. The main focus was on the PBC, state regulatory bodies, and twenty-seven key financial firms. The CFWC operated between 1997 and 2003 and primarily used the Party's control over the *nomenklatura* process to institute a system of recruitment, dismissal, and surveillance of executive personnel. The commission thus implemented a one-off purge of certain key officials in order to stem insider dealing and collusion and also to reduce the influence of local governments on the branches of national financial institutions.

Heilmann (2005) argues the CFWC was not designed to usurp the regulatory functions of the agencies under its surveillance, "The CFWC did not enjoy formal decision making authority with regard to the contents of financial regulation that was supposed to be formulated by government bodies such as the Central Bank or the Securities Regulatory Commission." The cooperation of the PBC and other key regulatory agencies was both important and forthcoming in helping the CFWC with its agenda, and the links between the CFWC and the PBC were close. For example, from 2001 the PBC governor, Dai Xianglong, served as the deputy secretary of the CFWC, while the executive deputy secretary of the CFWC, Yan Haiwang, concurrently served as the vice governor of the PBC.

Contrary to the argument advanced by Gilley and Murphy (2001), who claim that the CFWC undermined the PBC, our study, as well as Heilmann's conclusions, support the view that the CFWC process ultimately helped build a stronger central bank. First, the CFWC had authority to discipline irregular practices of finance officials, including those in the central bank. However, it was not mandated to meddle with the substance of the PBC's monetary policy. In addition, the CFWC represented an important step in recentralizing financial authority from the localities to the center, including the central bank. This was achieved by strengthening vertical hierarchies in the financial sector, which had gradually been weakened by local interests in the reform era. This was also the intention of the restructuring of the PBC's regional offices in 1998. The establishment of the CFWC was thus a further movement to strengthen and insulate the PBC from local intervention.

While illustrating the leadership's recourse to top-down methods when needed, the CFWC's brief period of operation also illustrates a second increasingly important issue. It confirms the reality that excessive top-down political control and intervention is out of touch with the increasingly marketized economy and the need for more nuanced forms of state intervention. As one PBC official stated, "The CFWC warrants its own historical status but let's admit that it was an extraordinary arrangement for an extraordinary time in the wake of the crisis. It's more of a knee-jerk reaction in a traditional [Leninist] way. Once the crisis was over, it [the CFWC] was over."[5] The dissolution of the CFWC in 2003 saw most of its functions passed to state regulatory bodies, including the PBC and the China Banking Regulatory Commission (CBRC; see next section). Indeed, the dissolution paved the way for the establishment of a modern prudential regulatory platform in China, led by the central bank. The Party's agenda used central authority to ultimately establish a stronger set of regulatory bodies, thus "laying the foundations for national market regulation" (Heilmann 2005, 5).

Separating Banking Regulation from the PBC

A further key institutional change was prompted by ongoing problems with the banking sector and China's entry into the World Trade Organization in late 2001 with its associated commitments to financial opening. A key event in this respect was a 2003 amendment to the 1995 Law, ratifying an institutional restructuring that hived off the responsibility for banking supervision from the PBC to a newly established agency, the CBRC. This act has been the final part of a wider process of building a two-tier system of financial regulation, with the central bank overseeing national financial stability and three prudential regulators, the China Securities Regulatory Commission (CSRC, established in 1992), the China Insurance Regulatory Commission (CIRC, established in 1998), and the CBRC (established in 2003), in charge of securities, insurance, and banking businesses respectively (Feng 2007a).

This one-plus-three framework, following the classic specialized model,[6] was aimed at catering for the increasing specialization of various branches of the economy, particularly the diversification of financial markets and the associated imperative for rational and professional industrial regulation (Tang 2003). The need for change in the financial sector was first preceded by an ideational shift by key agents. An argument often made in the literature suggests a potential conflict of interest between the implementation of monetary policy and banking supervision; hence the argument that it is desirable to have the latter function designated to a specialized agency, a practice that is also often observed in the large advanced economies (Arnone et al. 2009; Arnone and Gambini 2007; Courtis 2006). According to the reform advocates, a central bank charged with financial regulation could be tempted to compromise monetary policy to mitigate problems in the financial sector if it falls within the Bank's constituency, and thereby jeopardize both policy and the financial industry. Many senior economic officials had thus argued that the PBC could not be "both an athlete [representing the banks] and a referee [as a central bank] in the new game [a market economy]," suggesting that these two streams of function had to be separated.[7]

This is especially the case in a relationship-based society where the PBC and the big state banks had over the years formed a cozy relationship through routine regulatory linkages and frequent personnel transfers, what Pearson calls the "revolving door" (Lee 2002; Pearson 2005; Xia 2003). In this context the move to a new regulatory model reflected an attempt to insulate the PBC from the direct influence of the large state banks. As Heilmann (2005, 15) argues, "That the Central Bank was too closely intertwined with the interests of the big four banks and could not resist their lobbying effort was one of the main reasons given by insiders for why a separate banking regulator had to be established." This spin-off of detailed regulatory functions streamlined the role of the PBC but also boosted its authority in the monetary policymaking arena. Therefore, freeing the PBC from such regulatory duties further strengthened the autonomy and neutrality of the central bank as well as the credibility of monetary policy. Moreover, although the duty of supervision was assigned to the Bank at the beginning of the reform era, the institutional capacity of the

Bank's regulatory arm had been more underdeveloped than that of monetary policy ("Yinjianhui dansheng ji" 2006).[8] The establishment of a designated watchdog will thus help concentrate the resources of the central bank on monetary policy on the one hand and enhance professional practice in financial supervision on the other (Xia 2003).

It is true that the PBC fought hard to defend its monopoly on regulation and was reluctant to lose sectoral regulatory authority to the new bodies, especially in the securities (Green 2004) and banking sectors.[9] Nevertheless, the restructuring has not meant a retreat of the central bank from the regulatory scene. In fact, the PBC, formally and informally, has secured a superior role over the sectorial regulators in the new configuration. In the new one-plus-three framework, the PBC is essentially a metagovernor, mandated to ensure national financial stability by legislation.

On the other hand, the pluralization of regulatory institutions inevitably increased the costs associated with bureaucratic coordination and at times the PBC has been uneasy about relinquishing its regulatory authority to the three "little brothers." A joint meeting system was initiated in 2000 to include key decision makers from the PBC (then in charge of banking regulation), the CSRC, and the CIRC, aimed at enhancing cross-agency information exchange and policy coordination. However, the first such meeting was not held until September 2003 (Feng 2007a). Neither was the joint meeting institutionalized. Although it was supposed to be a quarterly meeting, in the eighteen months between March 2004 and October 2005, the heads of the regulatory agencies did not meet, and a key reason was the nonparticipation of the PBC ("Jinrong jianguan daibian" 2005). In a gesture aimed at displaying its superior status, this nonparticipation effectively paralyzed the mechanism. Instead, the PBC issued more than ten joint policy documents to individual regulators during this period, most of which could have been discussed at meetings.[10] Facing increasing pressures for sound and coordinated financial regulation, the State Council eventually resurrected the joint meeting mechanism in 2008 and formally confirmed the leading role (*qiantou*) of the PBC in presiding over the prudential regulators and coordinating cross-sectoral issues in relation to broader financial regulation (Miao and Li 2008).

In fact, the above measure was part of a move by the State Council to formally recognize the PBC's previous oversight practices, as well as to grant more authority to the PBC in the State Council's internal review of the Bank, which was finalized in August 2008. According to the State Council's *Provision of the PBC's Major Duties, Internal Institutions and Personnel Scale,* the PBC's role as a central bank and a metaregulator was further strengthened on a number of fronts. It is now responsible for planning and drafting overall reform and development strategies for the financial industry, for conducting comprehensive research on and thereby resolving "serious issues" in finance, and ultimately for promoting the healthy development of the financial system. It is also mandated to assess the implications of major financial merger and acquisition activities in relation to national financial security, to produce policy recommendations, and ultimately to promote an orderly opening of the financial sector. In the area of regulation, the PBC is authorized to coordinate among the prudential regulators on drafting standards and rules in regulating financial holding companies and cross-sectoral financial businesses (State Council 2008; Yu and Li 2008).

Apart from the PBC's official authority over the regulators, it could also circumvent them by directly engaging in their sectoral jurisdiction under its discretion. This can be best demonstrated by the financial reforms since 2003, in which the PBC, through the proxy of Huijin, recapitalized major state banks and securities firms using foreign reserves administered by the central bank (discussed in detail in Chapter 11). By doing so, the PBC effectively bypassed the CBRC and the CSRC and directly controlled the banking and securities institutions. This authority was formally cemented in the State Council's 2008 review, which states that the PBC is responsible for "supervising and monitoring the activities of the financial institutions that have received funds from the PBC in defusing financial risks."

Conclusion

As Naughton (2008b) argues and as we have suggested here and in Chapter 6, the dynamism of the second reform era challenges notions of a "trapped" reform process in China (cf. Pei 2006). This is especially so in relation to forging a new system of monetary and financial sector reforms and the strengthening of the PBC. The passing of the historic central banking law in 1995 and associated regulatory reforms that strengthened the hand of the PBC marked the emergence of at least a segment of a "regulatory state" in China and cleared the way for the emergence of the PBC as a modern, market-oriented central bank. The reforms also saw the long shadow of central planning wane as the PBC set about developing new market-oriented instruments of economic control. The formal institutional changes described in this chapter were in fact the formal skeletal elements of a new system of central banking and financial controls established through the agency of key actors in the party-state and the PBC. In other words, interpretive and empowered agents were able to push against the inertia of the legacies of the past and forge new ties and change strategies. In Part III, we show how the PBC proved to be a key agent, building and winning authority and establishing major policy gains in the monetary, exchange rate, and banking reform arenas.

PART THREE

The PBC and the Politics of Money and Financial Development in China

8

In Search of a New Monetary Policy Framework

In previous chapters we have examined the evolution of the formal and informal dimensions of the PBC's growing authority in the second reform era. Here and in Chapter 9 we show how this has helped shape the evolution of China's monetary policy since the early 1990s.

Equipped with its new institutional mandate and in the context of the market reforms of the 1990s, the PBC has embarked on building a more market-oriented monetary policy framework, including the growing use of indirect instruments. While the PBC eventually phased out financial planning, it nevertheless continued to maintain a range of direct administrative controls in the monetary arena, reflecting both the impact of traditions of hierarchical authority and the ongoing impacts of the economic transition. The latter has been especially related to the inadequacy and immaturity of markets and the nature of institutions and regulations in the financial system and the wider economic environment. The PBC has also needed to factor in the party elite's economic agenda of forced-draft economic growth. Constraints are also imposed on monetary policy by the party's external balance agenda and managed currency regime. All of these factors have forced the Bank to operate with an intermediate control system instead of fully embracing open market operations (OMOs).

This chapter discusses the PBC's quest for a new monetary policy framework that has been taking shape since the mid-1990s, including a discussion of the primary monetary objectives, targets, and direct and indirect policy instruments in the Bank's growing toolbox. As we show in Chapter 9, the PBC's evolving policy system has thus far managed to keep the economy largely on the rails during three major bouts of instability.

Monetary Reform in the Fast Lane

As central banking and monetary policy, in its modern guise, were largely absent in China during the planning and early transition era, it was therefore essential for the authorities to establish an appropriate framework for modern forms of monetary policy, which have become increasingly central in Beijing's macroeconomic management. As discussed in Chapter 7, the new reform push in the 1990s saw the promulgation of a formal central bank law in 1995, a series of institutional reforms of the PBC to help insulate it from local interests in a regional restructure in 1998, and a strengthening of its own policy capacity by handing certain responsibilities to other regulatory agencies (especially the CSRC since 1998 and the CBRC since 2002). All this was done in parallel with more informal processes under successive PBC governorships in building up the Bank's expertise in monetary policy deliberations and expanding its knowledge base in modern macroeconomic management, especially including the slow development of a more market-oriented monetary policy. In addition, the Bank's unique position as Premier Zhu Rongji's key power base greatly boosted its authority in Beijing's decision-making circle.

Reforms in the wider financial system, as well as Beijing's responses in the aftermath of the Asian financial crisis, also provided an empowering environment for establishing a more responsive transmission mechanism for monetary policy. In the banking sector, as we argue more fully in Chapter 11, three policy lending banks were established in 1994, taking over the function of providing policy loans from the state-owned specialized banks.[1] Together with the promulgation of the Commercial Bank Law in 1995, this paved the way for the specialized banks to become more focused on commercial banking, operating with a greater emphasis on profit incentives and risk management. In addition, the ownership of financial institutions was increasingly diversified, including shareholding enterprises, joint ventures, and an increased presence by foreign institutions. Financial markets experienced rapid development as well, particularly the stock market and the interbank market. As the same time, the PBC made painstaking efforts to establish a national payment and settlement system, which provides the essential infrastructure for financial transactions and liquidity management by banks. All this has facilitated the PBC's efforts to expand the application of market-based, indirect monetary policy instruments. Hence, as China's transition to a market economy deepened and as the PBC's institutional capacity and political authority grew, the Bank's capacity to deliberate and implement monetary policy also increased. The basic elements of the PBC's growing monetary policy framework, including policy objectives, targets, and instruments, are reviewed in the sections below.

Policy Objectives

In institutional terms, a clear definition of the central bank's primary objective is important in helping to establish its authority and market credibility. There has been a long and often intense debate on the policy objectives of the PBC since the beginning of the reform era. During the 1980s, the dominant paradigm was the dual-objective model, with price stability and economic growth both regarded as primary goals of monetary policy. This was made official in a key document of the State Council in 1986: "[In relation to] the Central bank, specialized banks and other financial institutions . . . their business activities should be aimed at developing the economy, stabilizing the currency, and enhancing economic efficiency." In practice, however, economic growth tended to be given priority in monetary policymaking. According to a PBC official, this priority directly affected the central bank's functions: "Different policy goals often generate different business [for the central bank]. Once the Bank is responsible for economic growth, we have to undertake all the related businesses. Other government departments, local governments, and [state] enterprises would then have sufficient reason to ask us for capital and credit quotas, and PBC lending had to perform certain quasi-fiscal functions."[2]

This pressure for a growth-oriented monetary policy was the result of a combination of factors. It was partly due to the legacies of the former planning era and a lack of knowledge on the part of the authorities about how to engage with the emerging market economy. The money creation function of the central bank also created a convenient channel for the government to obtain large sums of "ready-made" capital to meet the surging demand for base currency at the initial stage of the economic monetization. At the same time, the reformist leadership felt pressured to generate rapid growth to maintain the momentum of the reforms against the conservatives and to shore up the regime. Nevertheless, the consequences of such an expansionary monetary policy led to opportunistic policy behavior, short-term price volatilities, damaged policy credibility, and, ultimately, two episodes of vicious inflation in 1987–88 and 1993–95.

The traumatic experience of these episodes resulted in a rethinking of the relationship between stability and growth. In a 1993 Party resolution, an important blueprint that guided a new wave of reforms during the 1990s, it was stated that the primary objective of the PBC was "to stabilize currency value, regulate the aggregate money supply, and maintain balance of international payments," a formulation in which the term "economic growth" was notably omitted (Mehran et al. 1996, 2). Furthermore, the 1995 Central Bank Law marked a keystone for establishing a legal framework for central banking in China. Article 3 of the law clearly stipulates that "the aim of monetary policies is to maintain the stability of the value of currency and thereby promote economic growth," a formulation that makes growth dependent on the prior achievement of monetary stability.

One former PBC official admits that had there not been high inflation around 1993, it would have been "extremely" unlikely that price stability would have become a formal priority of the PBC in the 1995 Law.[3] During the drafting of the law, the PBC seized a window of opportunity posed by a surge in fears about inflation and the resultant switch of elite and public sentiment in cementing its inflation-fighting mandate. The PBC initially had favored a single goal of currency stability, but the wording was changed in the final text to avoid hurdles in the legislative process by which officials from other key government agencies and legislators in the People's Congress could well deem this goal "radical" and "impractical."[4] However, as just noted, the wording of this clause clearly acknowledges the assumption that the best way the Bank can promote economic growth in the longer term is by ensuring price stability, and therefore the *primary* objective of the PBC, according to this logic, is to ensure price stability. This "modern" understanding of monetary policy priorities and trade-offs is now widely held among central bankers worldwide.

The desirability of a price stability objective for the PBC was further advocated in an official book commemorating the fiftieth anniversary of the PBC under the editorship of the then governor, Dai Xianglong (1998). In a clear example of policy and institutional learning, and in summarizing the lessons of the Bank's half-century history, it stated that the economic authorities

> could by no means promote the economy by inducing inflation. . . . Events such as the unrealistic Great Leap Forward in the late 1950s, the catastrophe of the Cultural Revolution from the mid-1960s to the 1970s, the runaway investment and consumption in the mid-1980s, and the economic overheating in the early 1990s, have time and again attested that stability of the currency assures economic development. . . . Financial instability is a major hurdle and a fatal pitfall against a sustainable, rapid and healthy development. The practical experiences of the past 50 years attest that resolutely fighting against inflation and stabilizing currency value and finance should always be the primary function and historical responsibility of the central bank. (Dai 1998, 12)

Based on empirical studies of Chinese monetary policy in the reform era, Xie Ping (2000), a former PBC chief researcher and senior executive, also confirms this new orthodoxy by arguing that central banks should set price stability as a primary goal. At the same time, however, he admits that the PBC was in practice constrained by the broader multigoal agenda of the party-state, including price stability, economic growth, employment, state-owned enterprise (SOE) reform, and foreign exchange management. This was more evident after 1997 when the Chinese economy slipped into deflation, which saw the PBC under growing pressure to play "a more active role" (Xie 2000, 1). It is also true, as we shall discuss later, that the PBC's monetary policy was coordinated closely with a proactive fiscal policy in the postcrisis period. Nevertheless, most of the officials we have interviewed share the view that the centerpiece of the PBC's policy stance during this period was a nondevaluation policy, which was aimed at preventing the return of the inflation the PBC had just managed to help bring down in 1996.

Moreover, as China's market reform deepened, the reality and dynamics of a prolonged transition also began to increasingly impact on issues of monetary policy. Indeed, the conception developed that progress with the transition and the reform of monetary policy were closely interrelated and essentially defined the unique policy path in the Chinese setting. According to a PBC official, "We didn't have real central banking before [the reform], and we are genuine students of Western lectures and doctrines. Over the years, some worked but many didn't. We came to realize that not all Western doctrines could explain issues in China because of the special and unique situation here—I mean the transition. We simply don't have the sort of fully fledged institutions as the advanced economies."[5]

Zhou Xiaochuan (2006), the PBC's governor since 2002, agrees with this. In terms of what the Chinese central bank should strive to achieve in its monetary policy, the staunch liberal reformer has a sober view, taking into account the complex relationship between financial stability, economic transition, and the overall reform program. Zhou argued that,

> China is currently in the process of transition. The prices of some resource commodities, services, and production factors are being further marketized, which is bound to lead to extra influences on the price and quantity of the currency. However, this issue does not exist in mature market economies. If currency value volatility were to happen in China, it would not necessarily be induced by money quantity and price, but mostly likely would be due to the [Chinese] economy's nature of transition.
>
> At the same time, China being a low-income developing country, economic growth and employment is an important policy goal of the state, which the PBC has to deal with carefully. Although the most important function of the central bank is to keep monetary stability and low inflation, we have to adopt a multiobjective policy at this stage, that is, we need to check inflation, but also have to consider issues such as economic growth, external balance of payments, employment, and so on, especially pushing through the reform.
>
> . . .
>
> Monetary stability in China, in other words, to achieve the low-inflation objective, largely depends on the progress of the economic transition and external opening. If the financial institutions are in crisis, the currency value cannot be stable; if there is a lack of a transmission mechanism, then we cannot rely on those theoretically tempting monetary policies. Therefore, we need to promote the reform so that the economy can be in a more stable mode. During the process of reform, inflation statistics, neither core inflation nor headline inflation, would be in a stable mode. However, we cannot keep stability at the expense of the pace of reform, since slowing down reform will have a negative impact on overall economic development as well as the smooth implementation of monetary policy. In the long run, it will be more difficult for us to achieve a desirable institutional environment for monetary policy. Therefore, from the view of the central bank, in

the medium term, propelling the reform and transition process is the foundation for achieving currency stability (low inflation) and to establish an effective economic and financial system. We see reform as a priority in our consideration, and we believe that only by undertaking these reforms can we prevent financial crisis in the future. This is also different from those mature market economies. (Zhou 2006, 13–14)

Thus, according to Zhou, the key to improving the effectiveness of monetary policy in China lies not so much in the realm of monetary policy per se, but in the wider transition and an integrated institutional reform process. On the one hand, price stability is theoretically desirable and has largely and increasingly been the Bank's short-term priority goal. As we demonstrate later in this chapter and in Chapter 9, this is best illustrated by the PBC's hawkish stance and preemptive strikes against inflation since around 2003, and its efforts to liberalize China's exchange rate regime since 2005. At the same time, the effectiveness of monetary policy hinges on the soundness of the entire financial infrastructure, which is deeply embedded in the dynamics of the market transition. Therefore, central banking reform, according to Zhou, has to be dealt with from a wider perspective, promoted or constrained by reforms in other financial and economic arenas. For example, SOE reform, banking reform, and bond market reform need to be in place to enable the PBC's benchmark interest rates to take a central role in financial markets (PBC 2008a). However, the inflation priority of the PBC's monetary policy was bent toward stimulating economic recovery in the immediate fallout of the global financial crisis of 2008. In Chapter 10, we argue that the PBC's gradualist agenda on exchange rate liberalization was a compromise between concerns about growth and unemployment on the one hand and concerns about the problematic domestic banking system on the other. The latter also explains the PBC's major efforts in leading banking reforms in China since 2003 (see Chapter 11).

The PBC's trajectory thus suggests two implications for the diffusion of central banking principles, such as the centrality of inflation busting, in the international realm. On the one hand, there has been an increasing acceptance of these principles as general doctrines among money mandarins worldwide. On the other hand, effective policies have to be more embedded in the particular historical and institutional settings of the polity and economy as we discuss the PBC's choice of its policy targets and instruments below. This is the key to understanding China's path to the modernization of its monetary policy framework, a cautious, flexible, and practical approach that features ongoing experimentation within a mixed field of both established doctrines and new and unique processes of economic transition.

Monetary Policy Targets

The choice of operational targets for most central banks is usually between a quantitative variable, such as the central bank's monetary liabilities (e.g., bank reserves or monetary base) or more market-oriented targets such as controlling credit market conditions, particularly short-term interest rates (Sullivan and Sheffrin 2003).[6] Most advanced economies, which have more developed financial markets, typically rely on influencing market conditions, especially short-term interest rates, as their operational targets. However, contrary to widespread Western practice, the PBC has not focused primarily on using short-term interest rates as its operational strategy. The legacy of financial planning has played a role here. Financial planning under a command economy was based on quantitative controls as the price of money was a rather meaningless indicator. Financial planning mainly took the form of the Credit Plan and a credit quota system for the banks. In a financial system that still has strong administrative traditions and is dominated by a few large banks, the PBC still sees targeting money supply aggregates (see below) as more manageable, responsive, and effective than interest rate targeting (PBC 2001b, 6).

Questions about the selection of intermediate and operational targets have also been a central part of the debate on an appropriate framework for China's monetary policy, especially since the 1990s when the PBC began to expand its application of market-oriented, indirect policy instruments as market reforms deepened. Under the current regime, the PBC's *intermediate* target has been monetary aggregates, particularly broad money, or M2; and its *operational* target has been the PBC's base money, particularly the excess reserves and money market interest rates, with inflation and (sequentially) long-term growth as its *ultimate* targets. The logic is that, by implementing a range of monetary policy instruments, the central bank could adjust its base money. Through the effect of a more or less predictable money multiplier, this is expected to lead to a corresponding adjustment in monetary aggregates and, ultimately, the price level and output (Xie 2000).

For countries that adopt such quantitative targets, this is often justified on the grounds that bringing high inflation under control is the central bank's main objective. In China's case, this can also be attributed to institutional legacies from the earlier planned economy, which was based on strict quantitative controls. Moreover, financial markets have not been sufficiently developed to rely solely on price (interest rate) signals. Also, nominal interest rates are still officially controlled, meaning that the prevailing distorted interest rates are unable to convey accurate information for monetary management (Yu 1997; PBC 2009b, 12–13).

Empirical studies suggest that the demand for the three major aggregates in China—currency (M0), narrow money (M1), and broad money (M2)—underwent structural change in 1988, due to the introduction of a secondary market in government securities and of new financial assets at more market-determined interest rates (Tseng et al. 1994).[7] Because of the relatively stable long-run demand functions for the monetary aggregates in the post-1988 period, these studies also suggest that monetary targeting can be a feasible exercise (Xie and Yu 1999). In particular, demand for M2 has been more stable than that for any other aggregates (Dai 1998, 121).

As the older administrative system of credit quota allocation became increasingly ineffective and began to be phased out in the mid-1990s, the PBC began to prepare for a transition to a regime of monetary aggregate management. A key step was that in 1994, the central bank began to publish statistics of aggregate money supply and each year's targets to be achieved by policy instruments. Institutionally, intermediate and macroeconomic targets for the following year, such as M2 and the consumer price index (CPI), are proposed by the PBC in coordination with the NDRC and announced at the National Economic Work Conference usually held at the end of the year, and formally approved at the National People's Congress the next spring. However, this does not mean that the PBC operates on the basis of inflation targeting. These publicly announced figures are often largely indicative of the general policy benchmarks, to which the Bank is not strictly bound (see, for example, the target and actual figures in Table 9.2).

In 1996, the PBC officially defined its intermediate target as M2 (Xie 2000). The domestic deflation in the aftermath of the Asian financial crisis, however, greatly altered the transmission mechanism in China. This led to questions about whether monetary aggregates were an appropriate intermediate target since the money multiplier was seen as unstable, and therefore money supply was perhaps not controllable by the central bank (Liu and Liu 2002; Xia and Liao 2001). However, Governor Dai Xianglong (2002a) argued that money aggregates were still strongly correlated with price and output, and that the PBC was able to adjust them through interest rates, relending, and OMOs, and therefore that money aggregates should remain the PBC's intermediate target. Wu Xiaoling (2007), former deputy governor of the PBC, also argued that both M1 and M2 had high correlations with the CPI, suggesting their applicability as an intermediate monetary policy target for the PBC.

The PBC's intensive intervention in keeping the undervaluation of the renminbi (RMB) in the 2000s has in turn led to a passive release of base money, structural constraint in controlling M2 (see Chapter 10). The PBC had to rely more on reigning in new bank loans through credit quotas. However, a notable development in recent years has been a considerable decline of the share of new bank loans in total financing due to development in financial diversification, particularly direct finance, other nonbank sources of financing, and off–balance sheet activities that aim to evade credit quota restrictions. For example, according to Sheng Songcheng (2011), director of the PBC's Department of Statistics and Analysis, the share of new bank loans in total financing dropped from almost 96% in 2002 to a mere 59% in 2010. Based on his study of monthly and quarterly data during this period, Sheng concludes that a broader concept of "society-wide financing" (SWF) is a more relevant proxy for monetary policy analysis than new bank loans (with stronger correlations in Table 8.1). The PBC made the first step in April 2011 by formally including the SWF figures in its monetary policy report, announcing this broader gauge of financing as one of the "important" indicators under its watch of the macroeconomy. According to the PBC, the SWF includes Chinese yuan (RMB) loans, foreign currency loans, entrusted loans, trusted loans, banker's acceptance, corporate bonds, nonfinancial institu-

Table 8.1.   Correlations of SWF and new bank loans to various economic indicators

	SWF	New bank loans
GDP	0.85	0.73
Consumption	0.75	0.63
Investment	0.78	0.65
CPI	0.65	0.54

Source: Adapted from Sheng (2011, Table 2).

Note: In this table, the correlation between two variables is measured by the absolute value of their relational coefficient, a figure between 0 and 1. The bigger the value (approaching 1), the higher the correlationality.

tions' equities, insurance payouts, real estate investments by insurance companies, and others (PBC 2011, 5). For the time being, the new measure is still under development, with a number of institutional and technical issues to be sorted out before the SWF becomes the key metric to look at rather than M2 (Alloway 2011). It nevertheless represents the Bank's ongoing efforts to sharpen its policy framework in a highly dynamic environment and thereby increase its policy credibility.

Instruments of Monetary Policy

As the reforms sped up and entered a new phase of systemic transition to a more market-oriented economy in the second reform era, the political and monetary authorities also geared up to transform the mode of conducting monetary policy in the new environment, using not only direct but increasingly indirect monetary management. In terms of policy instruments, the PBC's hands were untied by the phasing out of the Credit Plan and the financing of state budget deficits, a process that began in 1994. The Bank also gained more operational authority and discretion under the Central Bank Law in 1995 and increasingly began experimenting with various indirect policy tools. Although the scope of indirect monetary management is still more or less restrained by the overall development of the financial and economic system, the PBC has made substantial progress and at times has been innovative in addressing the unique challenges posed by the transition process.

Phasing Out the Credit Plan

The key prerequisite for shifting to the greater use of indirect monetary management was the abandonment of the Credit Plan in the PBC's policy framework. The corresponding moves in this direction have been the most important development during this period. Under the old framework, the PBC's policy goal was to enforce the aggregate credit ceiling while using the overall Credit Plan and its lending facilities as the main policy tool. As discussed in Chapter 4, the central bank retained the Credit Plan as its major method to enforce monetary policy during the 1980s. For the government, credit allocation was an easy way to replace budgetary grants with bank loans for financing the SOEs and to manage aggregate demand. However, along with the development of the market system, the effectiveness of financial planning had deteriorated, due to a number of factors.

In structural terms, as the Credit Plan had to accommodate the state's growth targets, monetary policy was invariably proexpansion and procyclical, resulting in major price and economic volatilities. At the same time, the administrative allocation of financial resources through the Credit Plans produced serious inefficiencies and led to a deterioration of bank portfolios. Time and again, the PBC was forced to bail out insolvent banks to avoid financial collapse, which created huge problems of moral hazard.[8] In addition, lacking effective regulatory means and tools, the PBC was unable to enforce credit discipline, and banks could easily circumvent preset quota constraints. Moreover, the banks no longer monopolized the credit supply, since agents could seek funds from a number of newly accessible sources, such as capital markets, domestic informal (underground) channels, and foreign sources (Pei 1998). According to a PBC official, this direct intervention in bank lending has had serious consequences:

> [Milton] Friedman often insists that price volatility is mainly attributed to government's inconsistent antiinflation measures. This is more of the case in China than in the Western world, since our government has greater direct control over the economy. In fact, the government did adopt harsh measures, often in the form of compulsory administrative orders rather than economic leverage to combat inflation, which has disturbed economic growth and distorted resource allocation.[9]

A departure from this direct mode of credit governance was heralded in a landmark Party Decision, adopted by the Third Plenum of the Fourteenth Party Congress in 1993 as the reform program gained renewed momentum after Deng's southern tour. According to this blueprint, the central bank "should control the money supply and stabilize the currency value by changing from relying mainly on the control over the scale of credit to using such means as reserve ratios on deposits, the central bank's lending rates, and open market operations" (Mehran et al. 1996, 2). This was followed by a transition period, in which the PBC began to experiment with a new framework of money aggregate management on the basis of base money control through more market-oriented policy tools. The practice of the Credit Plan was finally officially terminated at the beginning of 1998. As a PBC official commented,

> In strict terms, China's genuine monetary policymaking actually started in 1998 when we abandoned the Credit Plan. Yes, without the plan we are facing a lot more uncertainty, but isn't it true that because of the existence

of the uncertainties associated with a market economy that we need a central bank to keep an eye on price fluctuations? Everyone can make plans but in a market economy, we need proper management and indirect control, not rigid plans.[10]

The case of the Credit Plan again demonstrates the legacy of the past that shadows the postplanning era. Hence in recent years, as part of an increasingly desperate effort to reign in domestic inflationary pressures induced by the PBC's intervention in the RMB's exchange rate, Credit Plans have been more or less reintroduced into the Bank's toolbox since 2007 in the form of credit quotas for commercial banks. As discussed above, the share of bank credit in overall financing has been on a steady decline since 2002; therefore the credit quota system has been increasingly eroded and circumvented by new sources of finance, and the PBC has been working on a new framework, centered on the SWF, for its monetary policy deliberations.

Reserve Requirements

The direct regulation of bank reserves is a powerful instrument for managing bank liquidity and lending. The PBC's capacity to manage banks' reserve requirements was rudimentary in the 1980s. Because of the administrative organization of the PBC and the state banks, required and excess reserves were held by each PBC branch at the same administrative level. This made the PBC's monitoring complicated and time consuming, often with considerable delays. Moreover, given the lack of a sound intrabank communication system, bank branches had to go to the interbank market to adjust their reserve positions with the PBC, which further complicated the PBC's aggregate liquidity control. To address this problem, the PBC decided in 1995 to reduce the autonomy of bank branches and have banks meet their excess reserve requirements on a bankwide basis, a significant step in the centralization of liquidity management (Mehran 1996, 45). On the one hand, this held commercial banks more accountable in internally managing their reserves. On the other hand, this change gave the PBC a better overview of liquidity developments in the system and improved its ability to assess those developments so that the central bank could decide on the amount and timing of its market intervention.

Further reforms were announced on March 21, 1998, to merge the required and excess funds into a single reserve account (Dai 1998). Before that, the two-tiered system amounted de facto to a single requirement of 18–20% of the bank's deposits, which reduced the bank's discretionary funds. At the time of the account unification, the reserve ratio was reduced to 13%, 8% of which was official reserves that were inaccessible by the banks, while the rest was for payments and settlements (Xie 2004). In March 2004, amid early signs of economic overheating, the PBC decided to establish a differential reserve regime, in which the reserve ratio for financial institutions whose capital adequacy ratios were under par was increased by half a percentage point. The new regime restrained lending by the country's smaller and weaker banks, which analysts lauded as demonstrating that the central bank had developed the sophistication to target the weaker banks without penalizing the whole financial system.

Reserve requirements are rarely revoked by central banks in advanced economies because of the harsh and immediate impact on banks' liquidity and lending, particularly those with lower excess reserves. However, this approach plays a more active role in China and became an important instrument of the PBC in the cause of inflation fighting. Especially since 2003, it has been much more frequently used than before. In fact, between 2004 and December 2011, the reserve ratio was altered thirty-four times, compared with only six times between 1984 and 2003 (see Figure 8.1). This was due to several

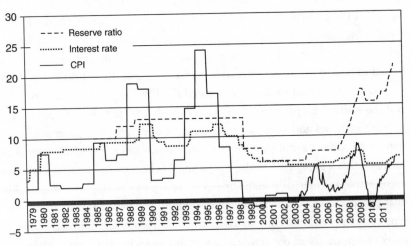

FIGURE 8.1. Interest rates, required reserve ratios, and CPI, 1979–2011 (%).

Note: Interest rate is based on the PBC's one-year benchmark lending rate; required reserve ratio (RRR) regime was established in 1984; the initial differential rates were unified in 1985 at 10%. RRR figures after September 2008 are those applied to large financial institutions. Interest rates and RRRs are based on monthly data. CPI data before 2003 are annual, and after 2003 are monthly.

Source: PBC Research Bureau, *Almanac of China's Finance and Banking,* various years.

reasons. First, as in other developing countries, the banking sector played a predominant role in China's financial system, so much so that "monetary policy in China is actually the monetary policy for the Big Four [banks]."[11] Therefore, changing the banks' reserve requirements had a direct, targeted, and effective impact on money supply and hence on inflation in China. Empirical studies also suggest that changing reserve ratios has a high coefficient relationship with a corresponding change in the amount of M1 and M2 (L. Zhang 2009). Second, an increasingly modernized payment and settlement system in recent years means commercial banks could keep a low profile of excess reserves with the central bank (around 4–5% for major state banks), making a change in official reserve requirements a more effective method in the PBC's monetary management. In addition, the PBC's control over interest rates was mostly tied to the growing interest rate differentials with those in the United States, fearing that any upward change of the rates would further fuel the inflow of international hot money betting on RMB appreciation (see Chapters 9 and 10). Hence the Bank had to resort to raising reserve ratios as part of its sterilization program to reduce domestic liquidity and bring down inflation. For this purpose, the PBC raised the reserve requirements ten times in 2007 alone.

Window Guidance

The PBC started to adopt the policy of "window guidance," also known as "moral suasion" or "jawboning," in 1998. The usual form of window guidance is for the PBC to convene monthly or unscheduled meetings (in special or urgent circumstances) with representatives of selected financial institutions (mainly banks). Sometimes the head of the PBC branches are also present in these meetings.[12] Central banks put administrative pressure on financial players to make them operate consistently with national needs (Geiger 2008). This policy uses benevolent compulsion to persuade banks and other financial institutions to stick to official guidelines. Despite the phrase "guidance" and its implied voluntarism, in the China setting the PBC has a major influence on lending decisions, especially over the four state-owned commercial banks (Ikeya 2002). The PBC regards window guidance as "an important monetary policy instrument [that] can be combined with other instruments to guide market expectations." Through "making the market anticipate its monetary policy," the PBC (2006, 16) claims to achieve a more effective overall monetary policy. This style of institutional coercion reflects China's hierarchical order. The reason that window guidance is relatively successful in China relates to the fact that the governor of the PBC is a higher-ranking official than the leaders of the commercial banks. Thus, the commercial bank leaders have to adhere to orders made within the policy of window guidance. The PBC undertook window guidance in its efforts to prevent economic overheating in 2003, which we discuss later. In commenting on the effectiveness of this traditional administrative lever, a PBC official gave us a good example: "If the PBC had not held exclusive meetings with the Big Four, the increase of credit in 2003 would have skyrocketed to 3.6 trillion yuan. What does this mean? It means this could lead to 500–1,000 million nonperforming loans within the next five years."[13]

Open Market Operations

As the PBC began to search for an expanded policy framework using more indirect policy tools, it also contemplated the introduction of open market–type operations in the form of issuing central bank bills in 1993 and offering banks special deposits at attractive interest rates in 1994 and 1995. It also started some genuine OMOs in the newly established national foreign exchange market in 1994 (Liu and Chen 2008, 32). Given the PBC's limited experience and knowledge, it was considered that OMOs could be used to pursue purely quantitative adjustments in banks' reserves, rather than the more common combination of price and quantity adjustments used in more liberalized environments. The Bank soon realized, however, that changing the volumes of reserves of the banking system without affecting the interest rates could in fact induce additional instability in the system. Subsequently, the PBC suspended its plan to rely on OMOs as its main instrument of monetary policy in the mid-1990s and started to work to establish an integrated interbank market and interest rate liberalization that had hindered the effectiveness of OMOs. Again, detailed institutional reforms were required to pave the way for the wider use of market instruments.

The interbank bond market was initiated in June 1997 and developed rapidly in terms of the number of market participants and the scale of market transactions and liquidity. On May 26, 1998, the authorities officially reintroduced OMOs. Under new circumstances with a better institutional foundation, the operations were an immediate success. Ever since, OMOs have represented an increasingly important instrument for the conduct of monetary policy by the PBC. The OMOs have been conducted mainly in the foreign exchange and treasury bond markets. In addition to its trading in the foreign exchange rate market in Shanghai, the PBC also traded treasury bonds with banks in the bond market in Beijing to align credit market conditions (Xie and Yu 1999). Before February 27, 2003, OMOs were generally carried out once a week—on Tuesdays. Since May 11, 2004, OMOs (central bank bills and repurchases) have been increased to two days per week—Tuesdays and Thursdays ("Yanghang meizhou zengjia" 2004).

A major problem that has hampered the PBC's OMOs, however, has been the limited scale (and therefore the PBC's holding) of government treasury bonds. For example, by the end of 2006, the PBC's holdings amounted to 285.6 billion yuan in its balance sheet, a mere 2.2% of the central bank's total assets, while the same figure in the United States, Japan, and Canada was 88%, 60%, and 85% respectively (Liu 2007; Xie 2004).

The limited scale of the government bond market nevertheless created room for innovations on the part of the PBC. As we will discuss more in detail in Chapter 10, To end a flood of liquidity in the market due to a dramatic expansion of the monetary base as a result of a surge of foreign reserves under its managed exchange rate regime, in September 2002 the PBC began to issue its own bonds, or PBC Bills, as a part of its sterilization program, which increasingly became a major instrument in the Bank's OMOs. By the second quarter of 2008, the total issuance reached 14.8 trillion yuan, more than forty times that of 2003 (PBC 2008b; L. Yu 2008). Nevertheless, there are huge opportunity costs for the issuance of PBC Bills and a possible crowding-out effect for treasury bonds (Goldstein 2004b). Given future expansion in short-term treasury bond issuance, OMOs will become a major instrument for the PBC's routine adjustment of monetary aggregates.

Interest Rate Setting

Because of transition dynamics, the use of price-centered policy instruments, most importantly short-term interest rates, was not on the authority's agenda in the early days of reform. As Zhou Xiaochuan commented in a conference, "The traditional planned economy leaves a mark in people's mentality, which believes in quantitative adjustment, not price adjustment. In the financial sector, this is reflected in the fact that the authority intends to tighten quantitative tools such as liquidity while price tools are secondary options after quantitative tools" (J. Wang 2004). Despite some limited efforts in the 1980s, major steps have been taken since then to further liberalize interest rates. Again, this was heralded by the 1993 Party Decision: "In light of the changes in the monetary supply and demand, the central bank should make timely readjustments of the benchmark interest rate and allow the deposit and loan interest rates of commercial banks to float freely within a specified range" (Mehran et al. 1996, 2).

One of the major problems that had hindered interest rate reforms, reflecting earlier legacies and the hierarchical regime, has been the insensitivities among SOEs and state-owned banks to interest rate adjustments due to a lack of hard budget constraints and the SOEs' preferential access to bank lending under a regime of directed capital (Girardin 1997). Meanwhile, as the transition progressed, the establishment and rapid development of financial markets have facilitated interest rate liberalization. The dual-track pricing of foreign exchange was unified in the 1994 reform, which set the foundation for a national interbank foreign exchange market (Liew and Wu 2007). In the same year a nationwide interbank lending market was established, and a national interbank interest rate (CHIBOR) was taking shape (Dai 2002b).[14] At the same time, the discount and rediscount market based on commercial paper was also experiencing rapid development, becoming a major channel of corporate finance and settlement (Sun 2008). Since June 1997, repurchase rates have been market determined, and the seven-day repurchase is widely accepted as a benchmark rate for interbank transactions along with the PBC's deposit and lending rates (PBC 2009b, 12). The emergence and gradual maturity of a national money market increasingly provides the central bank with the essential external environment in making interest rates more market oriented. According to Xie Ping,

> the basic rule of the [interest rate] reform is to deal correctly with the relationship among market-based interest rate reforms, the stability of financial markets and the healthy development of financial institutions to properly coordinate domestic and foreign interest rate policy, and to gradually reduce the fiscal role of interest rate policy. The steps of the market-based interest rate reform are, first foreign currency, then domestic currency; first lending, then deposit; first long-term, large-deposit, then short term, small-deposit. (Rolnick 2003)

Under this principle the Bank initiated a series of reforms aimed at interest rate marketization after the soft landing in 1996. It improved the rate structure by reducing the number of categories, enlarged the floating band of the lending rates, and abolished most of the preferential lending rates. It also liberalized the interbank rate, and the discount and rediscount rate; policy-oriented financial debts and government bonds were also issued by auction (PBC 2009b; Pei 1998, 342; Sun 2008). As a result, interest rates in the money and bond markets have been gradually liberalized, with the Shanghai Interbank Offer Rate increasingly becoming the pricing benchmark for the money market, commercial paper market, bond market, and derivatives market (PBC 2008d).

The central bank also used its benchmark interest rates to achieve macroeconomic targets. Between 1993 and 1996, the PBC raised interest rates three times in efforts to deal with inflation while economic growth was maintained at a relatively high rate of 8.8%. After that it lowered interest rates eight times between 1996 and 2002 to help deal with deflation (PBC 2003a). In the subsequent fight against inflation, the PBC jacked up its benchmark deposit rates eight times and lending rates nine times in the 2003–7 period. The subsequent global financial crisis has seen the rates path being slashed by the PBC four times before being jacked up again five times as inflation loomed (see Figure 8.1).

Despite the solid improvements in the interest rate regime, there has not been any major breakthrough in liberalization since 2000, for several reasons. First, the PBC has been structurally constrained regarding the flexibility of interest rate setting under the pegged currency regime. Given an undervalued RMB, the Bank could not resort to an interest rate hike to offset the expansionary pressures generated by the dollar peg. At the same time, the PBC was concerned about the viability of domestic banks in the face of further liberalization, which was believed to exacerbate the banks' balance sheets at a time when they were haunted by the return of rising levels of nonperforming loans despite the government's recapitalization in 1998. Hence, despite some progress in the liberalization of the interest rate regime, the PBC has been deliberately retaining the upper ceiling of deposit rates and lower ceiling of lending rates, thus guaranteeing a comfortable margin for the banks. Again, this reminds us that in a transition context, key elements of monetary policy, such as the setting of interest rates, are often constrained by (under)developments in other sectors (in this case, the largely failed banking reform in the late 1990s). Given these constraints, Zhou Xiaochuan, a longtime advocate of rate liberalization, has called for patience based on his philosophy of "systemic reform" and a recognition that market-oriented monetary policy can only proceed on the back of wider market reforms and progress with the transition. As he argues, "The progress of interest rate liberalization is determined by that of the complementary reforms at this stage. We cannot march forward without the proceeding of these reforms. From the perspective of the entire reform, the pace of interest rate liberalization has been very fast indeed" (Ye 2008, 73).

The Monetary Architecture

The discussion above has highlighted the way in which China's monetary policy system has evolved since the 1990s. There has been the substantial use of top-down, direct monetary policy instruments such as quantitative controls and window guidance. On the other hand, there has been the gradual development of more market-oriented policy instruments, such as OMOs and the setting of short-term interest rates, both of which are aimed not only at the quantity of money in the system but at its price. These changes reflect a commitment to the transition process itself and the quest to build a more robust national market architecture, with progress in the development of more indirect market-oriented instruments. In a review of contemporary central banking and monetary policy, Davies and Green (2010, 24) write, "As a general rule, the central bank can only target the price of money . . . or its quantity, but not both, except when markets are not free and either prices or quantities are fixed through administered interest rate ceilings or quantitative lending limits." Yet China is running such a "mixed" system, featuring the continued use of direct, quantitative controls as well as developing more indirect, market-oriented policy mechanisms. The former reflects the traditions of the Chinese hierarchical state as well as the constraints imposed by the economic transition and the immaturity of financial markets and policy transmission mechanisms.

China's distinctive approach to monetary policy has also seen it unreceptive to widespread Western central banking practices, such as the use of an inflation targeting regime. One major consequence of the transition has been the prolonged monetization process. Macroeconomic management, including monetary policy, has had to accommodate price reforms that often have inflationary impacts on the economy. For example, energy prices had been kept low under the planned economy as a subsidy to the SOEs. During the reform era, these prices were made more market oriented. This has raised them with inflationary effects. In order to pursue such reforms, the PBC sometimes has needed to accommodate a higher CPI in the short term. These maneuverings would have been more difficult under an inflation-targeting regime. Moreover, although the PBC now sees price stability as its key goal, there is also the need to balance the demand for growth in a developing country such as China. At times, this has confronted the Bank with the difficult task of striking a fine balance between low inflation and growth. An inflation-targeting regime would make such fine balancing more difficult. In this context, the vice governor of the PBC (2008–11), Ma Delun, accepted the desirability of inflation targeting, but was conscious of the huge challenges it could entail in the transition from aggregates management. "For example, how do we guide and manage public expectations? How do we increase the transparency of monetary policy? How do we establish better transmission mechanisms? These are the new tasks for us" (Zhao 2010).

China's monetary authorities also face a structural constraint in terms of internal and external stability, namely, the "impossible trinity" or "policy trilemma"—a key paradigm of open economy macroeconomics—which posits that the authorities can only achieve two, instead of all three, of the following macroeconomic goals: free capital flows, a fixed exchange rate, and domestic interest rate autonomy (Dai 2006). Given a partially liberalized capital account, Beijing is left with a dilemma between external stability (a pegged currency) and internal stability (low inflation). This has been reflected by growing difficulty in China's macroeconomic management since 1994 when the RMB began to be formally pegged to the U.S. dollar, which has been illustrated by tensions between monetary policy and exchange rate policy (Xie and Zhang 2002). More recently, this is illustrated by increasing domestic inflationary pressure as a result of base money expansion induced by the PBC's intervention in setting exchange rates (see Chapter 10).

Given these constraints, conventional wisdom would argue that managed currency regimes would seriously constrain the capacity of authorities in terms of domestic monetary policy. For example, Davies and Green (2010, 24) write that "with only one main instrument, the short-term interest rate, a central bank can focus primarily on either domestic stability or external stability but not both simultaneously." To be sure, the fixed-rate regime does constrain and complicate domestic monetary policy. Yet as just noted, China's authorities are not running "with only one main instrument." Instead, the inclusion of a range of both direct and indirect instruments in the PBC's toolbox provides a degree of scope for policy discretion and experimentation, allowing the Bank to act more selectively and strategically in the policy arena. In particular, the Chinese central bank can invoke a range of direct instruments to achieve its domestic policy goals, utilizing administrative hierarchy, institutional clout, historical linkages, and personal relationships. This innovative use of institutional resources opens up space for a degree of discretion on the part of Chinese central bankers and has often proved to be more effective than market-oriented means in China's unique setting.

For instance, the PBC adopted strict administrative measures in the enforcement of capital controls to partially alleviate pressures given the difficult choice between interest and exchange rate stability in the latter half of the 1990s. The State Administration of Foreign Exchange, which is institutionally controlled by the PBC, significantly intensified enforcement measures on approval, registration, and authenticity verification for capital account transactions. At the same time, the PBC exerted strong and frequent intervention in the domestic foreign exchange market, in which foreign currencies were traded according to a differential trading band (Xie and Zhang 2002). Another example is the PBC's crunch on inflation in the mid-1990s. The PBC, under the leadership of Zhu, issued administrative orders to the banks to recall their refinancing loans immediately, and reduced a surge of bank credits due to China's mounting foreign reserves. Equipped with the authority to administratively set interest rates, the PBC also conducted frequent adjustments on the interest rate of domestic foreign exchange deposits in financial institutions in achieving an appropriate rate margin and preventing serious capital flight (Xie and Zhang 2002).

Chapters 9, 10, and 11 provide more evidence of the PBC's capacities for discretion in its policymaking in recent years. Despite the constraints imposed by the currency regime, the PBC resorted to a combination of administrative (window guidance) and quantitative approaches (selective bank reserves) to achieve its target goals for inflation during the 2003–4 period. Moreover, since 2003, the PBC has utilized a range of quantitative measures, such as bank reserves and innovative central bank bills, in its painstaking campaign to sterilize the expansion of base money amid the growth of a massive trade surplus and foreign reserve accumulation. It is true that the use of direct, administrative controls (particularly the reinstallment of credit quotas) does not align with the marketization of the Chinese economy, and entails certain financial and institutional costs. Nevertheless, the nature of economic transition under an authoritarian regime means that common practices in the West are often not easily applied to the situation in China. In this way, Zhou Xiaochuan was likened to "a Beijing traffic policeman at a clogged intersection. His white gloves are immaculate and his gestures imperious, but all around him chaos reigns" (Associated Press 2004). On the other hand, the discretion afforded by invoking both direct and indirect tools has in fact awarded the Chinese central bank an advantage in helping to contain the negative impact of structural dilemmas and difficult policy choices.

Conclusion

The PBC's rising authority has been inextricably linked to the process of China's economic reform and transition. This has increasingly been the case as the reform entered a new phase of structural adjustments in the post-1992 period. The transition to a more market-based economy calls for a corresponding shift in the conduct of monetary policy from administrative controls to a wider variety of direct and indirect management. This has prompted the political and monetary authorities to embark on a search for a more flexible monetary policy framework for the emerging market. This has entailed a search for a set of technical and operational targets and instruments. We have also argued that China's "mixed bag" of direct and indirect policy instruments has afforded the PBC greater discretion and clout in relation to monetary policy.

But perhaps more importantly, the new dynamics of monetary policy have entailed a political, institutional, and legal realignment of the relationship between the party leadership and the monetary authority, and the confirming and reaffirming of the central task of monetary stability. The transition itself has also posed a basic dilemma for the PBC, that is, to use market-oriented measures to cure nonmarket institutional problems. This has set the parameters of the options available and the choices made by China's central bankers. It has also helped shape the effectiveness of monetary policy.

9

Monetary Policy in the Second
Reform Era, 1992–2011

We saw in Chapters 3 and 4 how during the first reform era in the 1980s, the dynamics of the economy, the institutional legacy of central planning, a marginalized PBC, an ineffective monetary policy, and the political machinations within the leadership of the party-state helped produce major price and economic fluctuations. Monetary policy throughout this era was broadly expansionary and ultimately helped ignite major outbreaks of consumer price inflation in the late 1980s and early 1990s. By contrast, since the mid-1990s, monetary policy has been more disciplined and inflation better controlled than in the first reform era. Given a similar average rate of economic growth between the two periods of 1978–94 and 1995–2011 (10.1% and 9.9% respectively), the average inflation rate was reduced from 7.7% to 3.1%. Given China's high-growth economy this has been a considerable achievement, at least thus far.

The general shift to a more stable macroeconomic performance, especially the lower level of inflation, can be attributed to a number of factors, such as a consistently high savings ratio, repressed domestic consumption, highly constrained wage growth (at least until recently), a massive restructuring of the loss-making SOE sector that has considerably reduced government bailouts (involving money creation), as well as the deflationary impact of external shocks, such as the Asian financial crisis and the recent global financial crisis (GFC). We argue in this chapter that, apart from these variables, an increasingly authoritative central bank has also played an important role in taming consumer price inflation.

Chapter 8 suggested that, while the economic transition and the hierarchical nature of the Chinese state have continued to shape monetary policy, the PBC has endeavored to pursue a more market-oriented monetary policy framework, including the growing use of indirect instruments. In this chapter we examine the performance of China's monetary policy in the second reform era. During this period, the PBC's major preoccupation turned to inflation fighting. This was particularly apparent from the mid-1990s, when, for the first time, the PBC, under the governorship of Zhu Rongji, managed to contain inflation and help engineer a soft landing in 1996. In the wake of the Asian financial crisis and domestic deflation between 1998 and 2002, the PBC struck a delicate balance by playing a supportive role to a proactive fiscal policy while refraining from a more expansionary monetary policy. It also insisted on the nondevaluation of the renminbi (RMB) to check the potential resurgence of inflation. Since 2003 the PBC has also become assertive in its efforts to tackle asset price bubbles as well as in containing inflation through a massive sterilization program (see Chapter 10). It has also sought to facilitate economic recovery while maintaining price stability in the wake of the GFC. In this chapter we review the empirical developments and key events of monetary policymaking and implementation during this period through four general monetary cycles, containing inflation, 1993–97; dealing with deflation, 1998–2002; dealing with asset price inflation and sterilization issues, 2003–8; and dealing with the fallout from the GFC, 2009–11.

Soft Landing, 1993–97

The austerity program associated with the economic retrenchment after the Tiananmen crackdown and the fight against double-digit inflation in the 1987–88 period resulted in three years of low inflation from 1990 to 1992. However, the economy started to heat up again as the Party leadership reaffirmed Deng's line of market reform and rapid development. 1993 is often called a year of financial chaos. With high inflationary pressure, the year was dominated by several major developments. First, there was acceleration in the growth of money supply, particularly M0 and M1. In fact, the increase of cash in circulation (M0) between 1992 and 1993 had been more than 1.87 times the total cash issuance in the previous forty-two years since 1949 (Dai 1998, 76). Second, semilegal or informal capital-raising activities, beginning in 1992, reached a peak in early 1993, causing a large drop in savings deposits. At the same time, a huge amount of funds were invested in the real estate market in coastal areas. Banks, financial institutions, and local governments had circumvented the central bank's rules and regulations on raising funds and financing their projects. The PBC found that more and more institutions escaped the control of its Cash and Credit Plans. Large amounts of unauthorized loans were used to finance fixed-asset investment with high rates of return, with a significant exposure to real estate, stocks, and local capital investment projects (Girardin 1997). A good example was the overheating in the real estate sector. The main reasons for this extremely large credit expansion had been a renewed nationwide investment campaign sanctioned by local governments, evidenced by a high level of fixed-asset investment in 1993 (Figure 9.1). It was also due to the PBC's inability to discipline the banks and to control the activities of nonbank financial institutions that fell outside of the PBC's Credit Plans. Moreover, there was a lack of limits on the expansion of policy loans, extended to subsidize the state sector, which is equivalent to an injection of high-powered money into the economy.

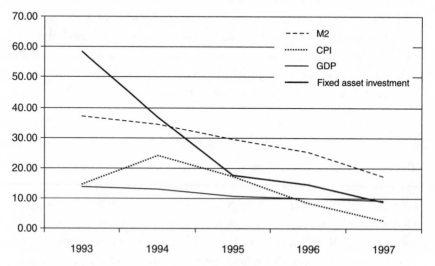

FIGURE 9.1. Money supply, inflation, and selected indicators of macroeconomy, 1993–97 (nominal rate of growth year by year, same period).

Source: National Bureau of Statistics of China, *China Statistical Yearbook*; PBC Research Bureau, *Almanac of China's Finance and Banking*, both in various years.

The result was financial chaos, inflation (peaking at 24.1% in 1994), with resultant negative real interest rates, runs on banks, and rampant disorder in the interbank market (see Figure 9.1). It also caused a real estate bubble in coastal areas, particularly Hainan. The number of real estate developers in China increased from about 3,000 at the beginning of 1992 to more than 12,000 in just a year. Investments in real estate jumped 117% in 1992 compared to the previous year, and housing starts increased by 40.4% in 1992. By mid-1993, the number of real estate developers had reached 20,000 (Zarathustra 2011).

Amid the chaos and overheating, with the temporary retreat of the conservative then premier, Li Peng, Vice Premier Zhu Rongji took over the economic portfolio. Under the auspices of Party Secretary-General Jiang Zemin, Zhu terminated the long hesitation and debate on whether to sustain the growth momentum or to push the brakes. Realizing the weakness of the central bank in resisting local pressures and in regulating the financial system, Zhu took over the PBC governorship himself in July 1993, and designed and implemented a well-crafted austerity program in the summer. The package was adopted in July and consisted of both administrative and market-based measures, but the basic theme was to resort to administrative command (see Figure 9.2). The aim of the package was to remedy the financial chaos by strengthening the capability of the PBC as a central bank in restoring financial

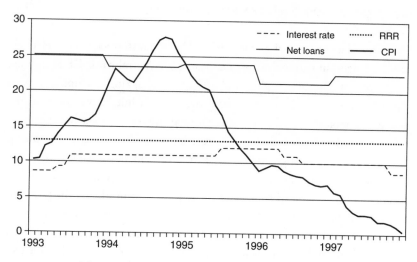

FIGURE 9.2. Monetary instruments and CPI, 1993–97.

Note: Interest rates are based on the PBC's one-year benchmark lending rates. Figures for net loans are nominal rate of growth year by year, same period.

Source: PBC Research Bureau, *Almanac of China's Finance and Banking,* various years.

discipline. The PBC set about separating the state-owned banks from their affiliated trust and investment companies, required all specialized banks to call back all loans made outside the Credit Plan, restricted interregional lending, and sent out working groups to the provinces to check the implementation of these measures. The four main series of policy measures consisted of clearing up and withdrawing loans granted without authorization, raising interest rates on deposits and loans, restraining irregular capital-raising activities, and restoring order among investments in the real estate and development arenas (Gao and He 1993).

These austerity measures were managed more skillfully than in previous attempted stabilization episodes and were almost immediately effective. The real estate bubble was the first to burst as developers went bankrupt due to their difficulties in financing, leaving a huge number of projects unfinished and buildings undelivered and deserted in the following years, as well as a pileup of bad loans in the banks. In a broader scope, the growth of money supply was slowed, savings deposits resumed their rising trend, and efforts to clean up financial activities had some effect. Inflation reached its peak in 1994, but this was mainly because of factors including the reform measures for the tax system, foreign trade, and currency devaluation, as well as an insufficient supply of farm products (Girardin 1997). By 1997, the austerity policy had succeeded in lowering inflation to 2.8% while GDP growth was brought down to a more sustainable level of 8.8%, as shown in Figure 9.1. The economy had made a soft landing.

Under Zhu's governorship, the PBC had been transformed from a relatively toothless tiger into an increasingly authoritative central bank. Zhu's iron fist in enforcing financial discipline and his campaign against corruption earned him the name "Boss Zhu" in the banking sector, while he was awarded the title of "economic tsar" by the international media for his achievement in helping to bring high inflation to a soft landing. Zhu's brief governorship between 1993 and 1995 greatly elevated the PBC's institutional status within the central government and the party-state. It also established the Bank's authority in the financial sector and the market by centralizing the power of monetary policy in the Bank's head office, establishing a modern monetary policy framework, and strengthening the Bank's authority in currency issuance, monetary base control, aggregate credit control, and interest rate adjustments.

Battling against Deflation, 1998–2002

The major event that affected China's monetary policy during this period was the Asian financial crisis. China's exports, a major pillar of its economic growth, slowed down significantly due to the recession in Asian economies and the overall slowdown of world economic growth, as well as the devaluation of other Asian currencies. At the same time, international capital inflows also slowed significantly. The resultant devaluation expectations for RMB discouraged capital inflows and encouraged capital outflows. In 1998, despite China's tight capital controls, official foreign exchange reserves increased by only US$6 billion compared with the current account surplus of about US$30 billion (Yu 2000). Overinvestment in the past inflationary cycle had created an economy of excess supply, which could not be digested by corresponding export growth. Given sluggish domestic demand, the macroeconomic result was deflation (Figure 9.3).

Importantly, the PBC resisted calls from "some voices" in the party leadership to adopt a more expansionary monetary policy aimed at creating 2–3% inflation and to allow a negative real interest rate, all aimed at stimulating growth at the expense of medium-term inflation.[1] Instead, the PBC executed

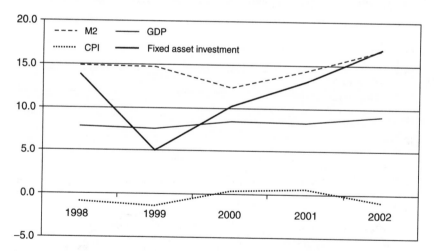

FIGURE 9.3. Money supply, inflation, and selected indictors of macroeconomy, 1998–2002 (nominal rate of growth year by year, same period).

Source: GDP and fixed asset investment figures are from National Bureau of Statistics of China, *China Statistical Yearbook*, various years; M2 and CPI figures are from PBC Research Bureau, *Almanac of China's Finance and Banking*, various years.

a more prudent "moderately loose" monetary policy in coordination with the leadership's proactive fiscal policy (PBC 2001a). As noted, the conduct of the Credit Plan officially ended at the beginning of 1998, which eliminated administrative controls over bank credit, granting commercial banks greater discretion over their lending. The bank's reserve accounts at the PBC were also unified and the reserve ratios reduced. Deposit and lending rates were also reduced five times during this period, thus stimulating investment expectations but maintaining a positive real interest rate (see Figure 9.4). Discount and rediscount rates were also cut to ease corporate financing (Dai 1998, 78).

These measures helped somewhat in cushioning the deflationary pressures in the economy, but failed to achieve their intended targets. As Table 9.1 shows, M1 and M2 deviated from their targets and the economy became trapped in a prolonged deflation.

There are several reasons for these mixed results. First, fighting deflation has been a difficult problem for central bankers around the world. Empirical studies by Cover (1992) and Karras (1996) on the United States and Europe suggest that the effects of monetary policy are asymmetrical, with monetary expansion having little effect on output, compared to the effects of negative shocks or monetary contraction. In China's case, the PBC had only just switched to money aggregates targeting and therefore it still lacked experience in such

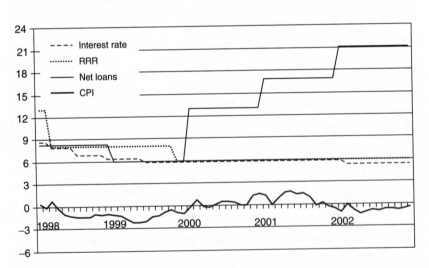

FIGURE 9.4. Monetary instruments and CPI, 1998–2002.

Note: Interest rates are based on the PBC's one-year benchmark lending rates. Figures for net loans are nominal rate of growth year by year, same period.

Source: PBC Research Bureau, *Almanac of China's Finance and Banking,* various years.

Table 9.1. Monetary policy targets and actual growth rate (in %)

Year	M1 Target	M1 Actual	M2 Target	M2 Actual	CPI Target	CPI Actual
1998	17	11.9	16–18	14.8	5	–2.6
1999	14	17.7	14–15	14.7	2	–1.4
2000	15–17	16.0	14–15	12.3	1	0.4
2001	13–14	12.7	15–16	14.4	1–2	0.7
2002	13	16.8	13	16.8	1–2	–0.8

Source: PBC, *China Monetary Policy Reports,* various issues.

aggregates management. Moreover, the deflation was not only a matter of macroeconomic fluctuation, but also an inevitable result of the tardy reforms of the SOEs. With huge amounts of nonperforming loans piling up in the banks, the PBC's policy signals were inevitably distorted in the transmission process. Consequently, the credit crunch worsened and so did deflation.

In terms of the exchange rate, the central bank gained authority to determine both the reference exchange rates and the band within which market rates were allowed to deviate from the reference rates (State Council 1996, Article 36). As the RMB has been made convertible in the current account since 1998, the Bank started to examine its ramifications and the linkage between interest rates and exchange rates. As we discuss in detail in Chapter 10, the Bank argued strongly, as the Asian crisis unfolded in 1998, to maintain China's exchange rate since it was primarily concerned with the potential expansionary effects of an RMB devaluation in the domestic economy, which had just locked the tiger of inflation in the cage.[2] Yet there was mounting popular pressure for devaluation. On the other hand, with the political support of Zhu, the Bank managed to weather the debate and swing elite opinion against devaluation through hard persuasion by its top officials, including then PBC governor Dai Xianglong, the director of PBC's Department of Monetary Policy, Dai Genyou, and, to a lesser extent, Zhou Xiaochuan, then director of the State Foreign Exchange Administration under the PBC (Chapter 6).[3]

A Touchstone: Tackling Asset Inflation during 2003–4

The political transition around 2003 from the Jiang-Zhu administration to one led by Hu Jintao (as the secretary-general of the party) and Wen Jiabao (as the premier) saw the general continuation of a broadly reformist line at the top of the Party, albeit with the priority more or less shifting to address social inequality issues. The central bank also saw a change of its governorship from Dai Xianglong to Zhou Xiaochuan at the end of 2002, the latter bringing a blend of academic expertise, industry experience, and political clout to the PBC's leadership. Combined with the authority the Bank had already gained under Zhu's guidance in the 1990s, the PBC increasingly played a critical role in Beijing's macroeconomic management.

At the same time, the PBC also faced unprecedented policy challenges in a new and changing environment. On one hand, China's accession to the WTO in December 2001 marked a milestone for China's deeper integration into the world market, which generated renewed momentum for China's economic growth in the first decade of the new century. On the other hand, the export-oriented development model, the hallmark of China's reform and integration, contributed to a series of internal and increasingly external imbalances. This development model has led to the economy's overreliance on export and state-led investment rather than indigenous consumption and private entrepreneurship. Externally, an undervalued currency regime pegged to the U.S. dollar has been a catalyst for the export-growth model, but it has also resulted in a massive buildup of foreign reserves since 2002. These have tended to fan inflation as well as to prompt foreign pressures for currency revaluation. The PBC's intervention in the foreign exchange market has also distorted the structure of money supply and the imperative of the currency peg has dominated and constrained monetary policy options.

For the central bank, this highly complicated and contentious macroeconomic environment has called forth both innovative and fine-grained policy responses. The PBC has had to fight against consumer price inflation associated with China's high-growth model, deal with the effects of systemic currency intervention, and increasingly deal with asset price inflation. More recently, it has had to help spur an economic recovery in the face of a major global financial crisis. Indeed, the PBC has faced an increasing trilemma: how to pursue an independent domestic monetary policy and limit exchange rate flexibility, while at the same time facing large and growing international capital flows.

Under Zhou, the PBC has helped guide a high-growth economy in a relatively stable manner, at least thus far, despite a recent slump in external demand, while inflation has so far been largely under control. Under Zhou's governorship, the Bank has modernized China's domestic bond and money markets, and introduced a flurry of short-term instruments to help it control money supply and guide market expectations. In terms of monetary policy, the PBC enhanced its *ex ante* adjustment and engaged in fine tuning with market-based tools. The major events involving the PBC during this period were its preemptive strike against asset price inflation in 2003–4 and its battle against consumer price inflation since then; its push for the liberalization of the exchange rate regime in 2005 (see Chapter 10); and the PBC-led banking reforms (explored in Chapter 11). In this section we examine the battle against asset price inflation.

After building its policy capacities through the 1990s, a critical case in which the PBC tested the authority of the party elites in the monetary arena was its move against asset price inflation driven by the property market in early 2003, a bold move even within international central banking circles (Borio 2006). After five years of deflation following the Asian financial crisis, the central bank was aware of emerging signs of overheating, especially in the real estate sector. By the first quarter of 2003, M2 increased by 18.5%, well above the PBC's target of 16% (see Figure 9.5) (PBC 2003c). High levels of bank lending saw investments in property development increase by 34.9% in 2003, compared with 21.9% in 2002 (PBC 2003a; Du 2003). As a result, despite a general deflation in the CPI, prices of homes rose 9% nationally year-by-year,

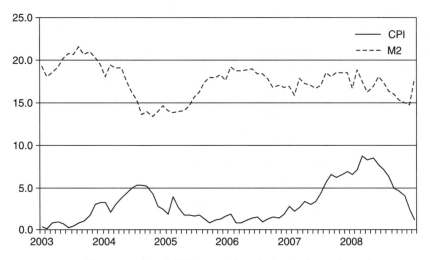

FIGURE 9.5. Money supply and CPI, 2003–8 (nominal rate of growth year by year, same period).

Source: Quarterly data from PBC Research Bureau, *Almanac of China's Finance and Banking,* various years.

while the price of newly built properties increased at a heady 19% at the end of 2002 (Economist Intelligence Unit 2003) (see Figure 9.6).

Another perhaps more direct worry for the PBC was the relationship between the banking industry and the real estate sector. The banking sector was highly exposed to the property boom. Financing real estate was an increasing part of the core business of the commercial banks. By April 2003, total outstanding loans to real estate developers stood at 1,836 billion yuan (US$222 billion), representing 17.6% of the bank's total lending. Mortgages added a further 8.9 to this figure, bringing the bank's overall exposure to the real estate market to over 25% of their total lending (Economist Intelligence Unit 2003). There had thus been an overreliance on bank loans for real estate development. According to the PBC's (2003b) statistics, total outstanding loans for real estate development in 2003 were 2.2 times that in 1998, while outstanding mortgages in 2003 skyrocketed to be almost twenty-seven times the level in 1998, or 75% of total consumer credit. A survey of 3,328 real estate developers by the National Statistics Bureau in 2003 suggests that 28.9% of total funds for the real estate sector came from bank loans. However, if other related items are calculated, including the working capital loans for the

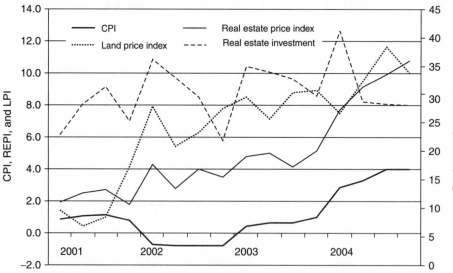

FIGURE 9.6. Early signs of asset price inflation, 2001–4 (nominal rate of growth year by year, same period).

Source: Quarterly data from PBC Research Bureau, *Almanac of China's Finance and Banking,* various years.

developers, loans for advance procurement by builders, and the mortgages used for advance payment, bank loans made up 60% of real estate investment.[4] Thus, the deeply intertwined relationship between the banking and property development sectors saw many analysts raise the prospect of a repeat of the 1993 property market collapse that had saddled China's banks with massive amounts of unrecoverable loans.

There had been a nationwide debate on whether these signs were signals of a systemic shift to inflation and financial instability. The PBC was adamant from the beginning that this was the case and that preemptive actions were needed. As early as July 2002, Zhou Xiaochuan gave the first warnings about the situation in a speech:

> The expansion of credit lending in our country is now too quick and needs appropriate regulation and guidance. Past experiences suggest that there had been a time lag of at least a half year between overexpansion of money supply and the emergence of inflation; this time the lag was even longer and resulted in more damage through the transfer of the inflationary pressures to assets, such as real estate, equities, and other investment prices, which formed bubbles. Therefore, the central bank should greatly enhance the vision and rationality of monetary policy and financial regulation. (Wu 2004)

In contrast to the widespread timidity in directly confronting asset price inflation in the West, and the more favored approach of the postcrisis mopping-up strategy famously advocated by former Federal Reserve chairman Alan Greenspan, Zhou insisted on more direct and proactive measures. As he put it, "we must make correct assessment in advance of potential inflation rather than taking measures after it becomes apparent" (Wu 2004).

A PBC investigation into property market lending in late 2002 reported that the central bank's audit of commercial banks showed percentages of loans involved that violated lending rules, accounting for 24.9% of the total bank loans (PBC 2003b). The PBC's audit result, recalling the property bubble of 1993, finally convinced the government to take action, but differences existed between Zhou and Wen regarding the severity of the action.

Given sluggish growth between 1998 and 2002, the leadership was eager to pump up the economy, but the central bank desired to "order the punch bowl removed just when the party was really warming up" (Greenspan 2007, 111). Initially the PBC was unsuccessful in persuading the top leadership to consider either RMB appreciation in order to reduce aggregate demand or to raise interest rates to dampen the rapid growth of credit (Lardy 2005). In the end, Governor Zhou decided to take the lead, unilaterally, and curb excessive lending for property development. Without consulting the powerful National Development and Reform Commission (NDRC), as was traditionally the case, the PBC's measures were rolled out in June 2003, embodied in a policy statement titled "The PBC Circular on Further Strengthening the Management of Real Estate Credit," commonly referred to as Circular No. 121.[5] The circular took the form of window guidance, addressed directly to the institutions under the Bank's administration and regulation, including the PBC's branches, state banks, and shareholding banks. The circular and the PBC's reliance on window guidance thus cleverly exploited the central bank's place in the administrative hierarchy, especially in relation to the commercial banks. The PBC required the banks to limit lending to real estate developers, to beef up credit management, and to increase down payments from buyers of second or luxury homes. The policy also encouraged the banks to provide loans for low and midpriced housing development (PBC 2003d).

Although Wen may have been notified about this beforehand, the combination of tools was within the Bank's administrative discretion without resorting to an interest rate hike, enabling it to avoid the formal approval of the State Council through a technicality.[6] This is a classic example of the PBC carving out discretionary space and exploiting its institutional position. Following the issuance of the policy, the PBC called for window guidance meetings three times in the second half of 2003. In those meetings on July 18, August 11, and September 12, the PBC invited representatives from all Chinese financial institutions and repeatedly instructed them to pay attention to the proper capital adequacy ratio and to prevent credit and liquidity risks (Geiger 2008). "The most worrying aspect for the People's Bank of China is the safety of the loans of the commercial banks. And the main goal of the circular is to avoid risks in the future," said Zhang Rongfang, spokesman of the PBC's Shanghai branch (Zeng 2003). For the PBC, this was a necessary action. According to a senior PBC official,

> Of course, these policies should have been self-decisions of the commercial banks based on their individual situations, but the lack of effective self-restriction and incentives of the banks means the transmission of monetary policy cannot solely rely on market mechanisms. Therefore, it is still necessary for the central bank to undertake window guidance and regula-

tion; during the implementation [of monetary policy], apart from the aggregate targets, the central bank should also pay attention to credit structures. In addition, this policy also has certain flexibility. For example, the commercial banks have certain discretion over the specific lending criterion on second properties.[7]

The credit crunch encountered fierce resistance from the NDRC, and particularly from the Ministry of Construction and local governments with their direct stake in promoting property development. As an NDRC official recalls,

> The point is, this [the circular] was a unilateral policy document [by the PBC], which excluded us from the consultation. Because if you want to put brakes on real estate lending, this would have a general impact on the overall economy. They should have consulted with us and the Ministry of Construction beforehand. Without the consultation, the release of the policy left us in a rather awkward position.[8]

The new policy also got some real estate developers fired up because it broke their financial links with the banks and increased their costs. Under these pressures, the party leadership caved in and partly rolled back the PBC's initiative.[9]

However, the PBC turned out to be the ultimate winner. As the Chinese economy started to jitter with apparent bubbles forming in property prices, the NDRC's austerity program largely failed to cool it down (Naughton 2006a, 5). The PBC had also started to use further indirect instruments, withdrawing liquidity from the banks. For example, on August 23, the PBC raised reserve ratios by one percentage point. At the end of 2003, the PBC slashed the interest rate for excess reserves. The PBC still thought that the package was insufficient to head off the risk of a credit bubble. Then on April 13, 2004, the PBC raised the reserve ratio for all banks by another half percentage point. Two weeks later, it established a differential reserve regime for commercial banks, restraining the lending by smaller and weaker banks (PBC 2004). As a senior PBC official recalls, "We withdrew the dishes they were enjoying, but to keep a stable currency value, we couldn't care less about the infamy."[10]

As NDRC lost ground at the top and the PBC gained the upper hand, Wen weighed in publicly in favor of slowing down credit growth in February 2004. The central bank managed to persuade Wen to finally raise interest rates in autumn 2004, the first time in nine years. "What can he [Wen] do? He should thank us [the PBC] for taking some preemptive strikes in the early stage. Now he believes Governor Zhou. This time Zhou has completely discredited the fellows at the NDRC."[11] Another NDRC official familiar with the issue recalls,

> Policies are policies, but we did admit later on that we were wrong in the overall assessment of the situation at that time. We used a variety of administrative tools but didn't get desirable effects. The central bank had also been working on their part, including raising reserve ratios, but the overall effect was not too good, so that the central bank got their wish from the top to raise interest rate in October 2004.[12]

As a result of this contest, forward-looking monetary policy and the central bank's unilateral activism against asset price inflation earned it much credit in the top decision-making circle as well as in the market and the media. Wen apparently has learned much from this episode, and the NDRC has had to concede policy authority and at least partially accept the PBC's leading role in macroeconomic policy. In commenting on these events, Ba Shusong, a renowned economist with a major think tank of the State Council, argued, "the recent several important decisions of the PBC demonstrate that the independence of monetary policy and the independence of the PBC's assessment of the macroeconomy have been on the rise. Circular No. 121 is especially evidence of the rise of the operational independence of the PBC" (Du 2003). Even more significantly, Wei Jianing, deputy director of the Development Research Center, a powerful and authoritative think tank attached to the State Council in direct competition with the PBC regarding policy proposals, made a rare acknowledgment: "we have to admit that this time it is the central bank and a few ex-PBC officials who were the first to be alerted by the overheating and took measures against it. . . . The PBC has been playing a critical role" (Wu 2004, 1).

Fighting against CPI Inflation, the PBC, and Monetary Policy since 2003

Except for a brief and abrupt period of deflation in the immediate aftermath of the GFC, the CPI data in Figure 9.7 demonstrate several upward trends in consumer prices since 2003, with the CPI peaking at 8.7% in February 2008 and again at 6.5% in July 2011. There have been diverse interpretations of the sources of such inflation, broadly categorized into two models, "pork" and "money" (Pattis 2008). The pork model claims that inflation in China is a food problem caused by a short-term supply constraint, particularly by temporary and cyclical shortages of pork. Although the National Bureau of Statistics does not release data on the weightings of the CPI, it is estimated that the share of food is about 30%. According to an analysis by an official think tank, the Chinese Academy of Social Sciences, pork makes up a third of the food part of the CPI basket, or 10% of the CPI as a whole, making it the largest single component (Orlik 2011). For some observers, pork prices have such a decisive impact on the CPI that they are referred to as the "China Pig Indicator." Empirical data seem to support this argument. For example, pork prices were 74% higher than the previous year's peak in March 2008, while the CPI had peaked a month earlier in February. And when pork prices returned to a high of 62% above the previous year's peak in mid-June 2011, the CPI peaked a month later in July. Therefore, on this evidence it seems prima facie that inflation in China is primarily, if not exclusively, a food price problem, caused by food supply constraints that are temporary in nature.

On the other hand, as money model exponents have pointed out, these rounds of inflation have been driven more by monetary expansion as a result of Beijing's intervention in its foreign exchange rate, as well as its anti-GFC stimulus program that has seen a flood of bank credits, both of which led to a surge of liquidity in the market. In Rogoff's (2008) words, "Those who believe that the cause of China's inflation is too little pork, rather than too

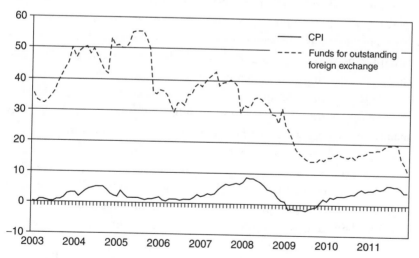

FIGURE 9.7. Correlation between CPI and funds outstanding for foreign exchange, 2003–11 (nominal rate of growth year by year, same period).

Source: PBC Research Bureau, Almanac of China's Finance and Banking, various years.

much money, are seriously mistaken." Indeed, food and pork prices are seen as a mere proxy of an underlying monetary phenomenon, that the surge in China's money supply since 2003 means there is more money chasing less food and pork, thus pushing up inflation.

A major driver behind the surge of money supply has been Beijing's attempt to stabilize the RMB's value in the context of large net foreign currency inflows from both the current and capital accounts, particularly after China's WTO accession in late 2001. To keep the value of the currency within its desired level, the PBC has been compelled to purchase foreign currencies with RMB, which has added to China's foreign reserves, but has also created local currency (indicated by "Funds for outstanding foreign exchange" in Figure 9.7), which is then channeled through both the formal and informal financial sectors into alarmingly high levels of domestic investment. Thus, the PBC has been faced with a policy dilemma, in which monetary policy has largely been constrained by the priority of exchange rate stability.

Given the dominance of exchange rate concerns in Beijing's macroeconomic framework, monetary policy between 2003 and 2008 (before the GFC) was largely distorted in a bid to secure the dollar peg regime. Most importantly, the PBC could have resorted to interest rate hikes to contain inflation during this period, but given increasingly limited capital controls, the growing spread between rates in China and the United States, and persistent market expectations over RMB appreciation, any increase in interest rates was believed to be more likely to spur an influx of speculative hot money. Therefore, for the PBC, rate adjustment was a reluctant last resort. There was nevertheless a cycle of rate hikes between October 2004 and October 2008 before the GFC. Six consecutive rate hikes were announced in 2007 alone, but the Bank struggled to keep real interest rates positive during this period. To withdraw the massive liquidity in the market and offset its inflationary pressures, the PBC has mainly relied on issuing central bank liabilities, accompanied by raising banks' required reserve ratios. In particular, between July 2006 and September 2008, reserve ratios were cranked up from 7.5% to 17.5% in nineteen installments. A more profound move, however, was the PBC-led push for more flexibility in China's foreign exchange regime, culminating in de-pegging the RMB to the U.S. dollar in July 2005. The dynamics of these developments are elaborated in the discussion of China's exchange rate policy in Chapter 11, as the latter dominated the agenda of China's monetary authority during this period.

Asset Price Inflation: More Recent Developments

On another front, however, the PBC was preoccupied with renewed rounds of potential bubbles in property prices. The PBC had been concerned by the correlations between asset prices and domestic inflation since the beginning of the new century and, as discussed above, had resorted to harsh measures against irregular property lending back in mid-2003–4. To the Bank's dismay, however, the bout of overheating in the property sector during 2003–4 was not an isolated episode, but was in effect the start of a long cycle of asset price increases. Figure 9.8 suggests major price surges in the property sector during 2004–5, 2007, and 2009–10, while equity prices experienced a major boom in 2007–8.

The asset price booms during this period can be attributed to surges of liquidity in the market due to the money creation mechanism resulting from the PBC's intervention in the exchange rate system. In the post-GFC era, the property sector was further buoyed by the lending boom that featured in Beijing's stimulus program, part of which found its way into the real estate sector. For housing prices, in particular, other factors have also made their contribution. First, rising inflation, low interest rates, and a lack of alternative

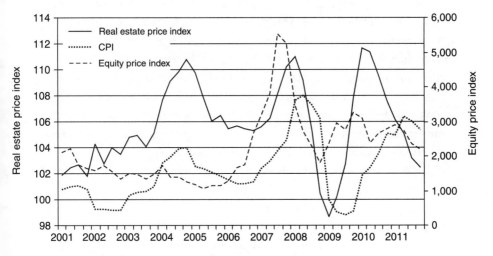

FIGURE 9.8. Consumer prices and asset prices, 2001–11.

Note: The base year for the real estate price index and CPI is the previous year. Equity price index is based on end-of-quarter figures of the Shanghai Stock Exchange Composite Index.
Source: PBC Research Bureau, *Almanac of China's Finance and Banking,* various years.

investment channels (particularly foreign investments) due to financial repression and capital controls increased the appeal of domestic investments, such as property and, to a lesser extent, equity. Second, the real estate sector had been given favorable policies from the government as property development gained the status of a national pillar industry. According to the National Bureau of Statistics, real estate investment accounted for 13% of China's GDP in 2011, making it a leading growth driver for the economy.[13] Given the sector's extensive links to upstream and downstream industries and its significant share in the overall economy, the associated financing arrangements for construction, development, and mortgages have also been enjoying cheap credits and increased bank lending. More importantly, local governments, desperate to expand their revenue base, have relied on land sales for income (accounting for up to 50% of revenue) and have used land for financing collateral (F. Wu 2006). Therefore, the local governments have high stakes and incentives for propping up local land development and housing markets.

Given these drivers, residential housing investment as a share of China's GDP tripled from 2% in 2000 to 6% in 2011 while average housing prices in the country tripled from 2005 to 2009 (Chovanec 2009). As a result, housing prices are now increasingly far beyond affordability for most people, evidenced by exceptionally high price-to-income ratios for real estate in recent years, which is one of the key housing indicators approved by the United Nations Commission on Human Settlements (Malpezzi and Mayo 1997). According to World Bank standards, an affordable housing price in market economies should be no more than three to six times a family's annual income (Lau and Li 2004). In other words, the ratio should be no more than 3:1 to 6:1. As Figure 9.9 suggests, this ratio has been hovering above 6:1 since 2001 with spikes in 2005, 2007, and 2009. The figure is even higher for tier one cities in China, reaching 27:1 in August 2009 (Xu 2009). That means a double-income household would need twenty-seven years of wages to buy a house or apartment.

Ballooning property prices have spurred nationwide social grievances and protests that have started to threaten political stability. Apart from excessive liquidity, and actions by local governments, more fundamental drivers of property price increases have included the tax redistribution regime that favored the central government,[14] and an official promotion system that supports short-term opportunism among local officials. In this context, the leadership has increasingly come to realize that, given the hierarchical nature of China's political and bureaucratic system, the PBC's monetary policy per se could not solely fulfill the task of stemming asset price inflation in the property sector. It also needs a strong top-down policy package that tackles the fiscal, monetary, and administrative aspects of the problem. Recognizing this, the State Council took over the leadership and political responsibility for this issue from March 2005.

Before the GFC, the State Council initiated three major policy campaigns in March 2005, May 2006, and August 2007, with limited success. The policies included the abolition of discount mortgage rates, restrictions on the size of apartments, levying transaction taxes on secondary properties, and the introduction of affordable housing projects. Subsequently, the prospect of a recession in the immediate aftermath of the GFC prompted a policy shift at the top from containing asset inflation to a market rescue. After all, given the entire real estate sector's share of GDP (10–13%), the leadership could not afford a slump on this front. According to Chovanec's (2012) estimate, if property investment plateaus (growth falls to zero), it could shave as much as 2.6 percentage points off of real GDP growth. If it fell 10% in real terms, it could bring GDP growth down to 5.3%, almost a national recession in China's terms. Given

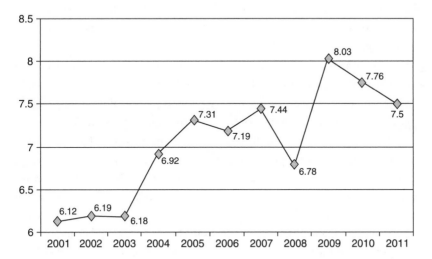

FIGURE 9.9. Cost-to-income ratio for national residential real estate, 2001–11.

Note: Income is based on disposable income per capita. Residential real estate refers to newly built residential properties and does not include the secondary market.

Source: Calculated from National Bureau of Statistics of China, *China Statistical Yearbook,* various years.

the flood of liquidity following the government's GFC-inspired lending spree, property prices jumped again in 2009. Zhang Xin, CEO of Beijing's largest commercial developer, made a candid calculation during an interview:

> I don't know [when the bubble will burst]. We don't really have a view on when it will end; [but] we do have a view that this is a bubble. Real estate is very much driven by government policy. This year we have RMB 4 trillion through the stimulus package, another RMB 6 trillion from municipality bonds, another RMB 10 trillion from bank loans. We have RMB 20 trillion in the system and it all finds its way to real estate. (Roche 2010)

As real estate prices spiraled, again threatening political stability, Beijing's approach shifted back to tightening in early 2010. Harsh policy packages were rolled out in April and September 2010, and January 2011, using a combination of administrative and financial measures that aimed at a retrenchment. The packages, targeting both demand and supply, and both transaction and ownership dimensions, included more government supervision; administrative limits on purchases and land transactions; raising down payments, mortgage rates, and transaction taxes and fees; reducing finance to developers; introducing property taxes; and, more profoundly, increasing the supply of low-cost public housing in the longer term (Lan 2010). By the end of 2011, there were early signs of corrections in the national real estate market. The cost-to-income ratio dropped from the peak of 8.03 in 2009, to 7.76 in 2010, and to 7.5 in 2011 (see Figure 9.9). Such corrections are more apparent in tier one cities as well as tier two cities in the eastern part of the country (Yang et al. 2012). For example, residential property prices dropped 9.5, 5.4, and 11.5% in Beijing, Shanghai, and Hangzhou respectively. Despite only lukewarm support from the local governments that stood to lose from the campaign, Beijing appears to have decided to further reign in property prices. In a press conference at the National People's Congress in March 2012, Premier Wen Jiabao declared, "Now, I can clearly tell everyone, home prices are still far from returning to reasonable levels, and as such, regulation cannot be relaxed. If they are relaxed, our achievements will have come to naught. [It] will cause chaos in the real estate market and will not be conducive to the long-term health and stability of the housing market."[15]

There has been an ongoing debate on whether there is a housing or property bubble in China. Many assert that a property crash is imminent, pointing to alarming signs such as high price-to-income ratios for real estate (Xie 2010), the relatively higher share of real estate investment in total investment in China (Krugman 2011), and the increasing difficulty of financing on the part of developers due to a tightening of policy settings by the party leadership and the regulators that could ultimately lead to fire sales (Chovanec 2009, 2012). While we agree that these factors could lead to price corrections in the short term, we, among others such as the World Bank (2009), the IMF (2011), the Economist Intelligence Unit (2011), and Laurenceson (2012), do not think there is a major real estate bubble in China, for a number of reasons. First, in terms of high price-to-income ratios, Chinese household income has been underestimated. As the World Bank (2009) makes clear, Chinese home prices have not outpaced increases in incomes on a nationwide level. According to a projection by the Economist Intelligence Unit (2011), between 2011 and 2020, Chinese urban per capita disposable incomes are likely to increase by 2.6-fold to RMB51,310 (about US$7,500 at 2011 exchange rates). In addition, a significant amount of hidden or "gray" income is not included in the total disposable income figures. According to Wang Xiaolu (2010), such income reached an estimated RMB5.4 trillion in 2008, compared with RMB17.9 trillion of income that is included in the personal income tax levy.[16] Second, in the long term China should reduce its overall share of investment in the economy and increase domestic consumption. Nevertheless, real estate investment is less likely to lose steam because the demand for housing remains strong due to the ongoing urbanization process in China. Between 2011 and 2020, China's urban population is forecast to increase by 26.1%, or over 160 million people (Economist Intelligence Unit 2011). The urbanization process has been "a fundamental driver of China's economic growth" and is seen by Joseph Stiglitz, along with technology developments in the United States, as the two most important issues that will shape the world's development during the twenty-first century.[17] The massive scale of urbanization will thus help sustain a strong underlying demand for housing during the next decade. In addition, there is a strong cultural propensity toward home ownership in China. A national census in 2005 suggests that 88% of Chinese households lived in homes they owned or were purchasing, one of the highest rates in the world. Moreover, given few alternative investment channels and the fact that there has been relatively light taxation of housing, real estate remains one of the major investment vehicles for Chinese households with a high savings ratio and much less leveraged than those in the West. China's banking sector is also relatively better equipped to fend off a potential drop in real estate prices than its Western counterparts. Indeed, an internal survey by the China

Banking Regulatory Commission found that the national average rate of down payment was about 40% in early 2012.[18] Hence, despite a period of strong increases in property prices, underlying income and property demand dynamics suggest China is probably not sitting on a major property bubble.

For its part, the PBC during this period was more preoccupied with the exchange rate and CPI inflation. As we discuss in Chapter 10, the PBC has been struggling to mop up liquidity in the market. Despite its adept sterilization operations and consecutive increases of bank reserve ratios that aimed to offset the expansionary effect of a de facto exchange rate targeting regime, headline inflation had been on a gradual rise, and hit an eleven-year high at 8.7% in February 2008. In the aftermath of the GFC, the PBC's hands were again tied by its concerns about economic recovery, which compelled the Bank to tread a fine line between checking asset prices and not choking the overall economy.

Nevertheless, the PBC has paid close attention to the relationship between asset prices and domestic inflation, attention sometimes not apparent in overseas inflation-targeting regimes.[19] In a quarterly policy report in 2007, the PBC presented a special discussion on asset prices and monetary policy. In contrast to somewhat more hesitant views among many central banks, the PBC appears to be moving toward its view that asset price inflation should be squarely factored into the monetary policy framework (PBC 2007, 30–31). More recently, Zhang Xiaohui (2009), director of the PBC's Monetary Policy Department, published an article on the relationship between asset prices and monetary policy in the prestigious domestic magazine *Caijing*. Zhang argues that globalization has led to changing inflation dynamics. On the one hand, globalization dampens upward pressure on the prices of ordinary commodities through expanded production and supply networks. On the other hand, the economic expansion has spurred the demand for primary commodities and financial assets. Under the auspices of international speculation, this tends to push up their prices more strongly than before. The net result, according to Zhang, has been a global "structural" inflation, especially featuring higher asset price inflation. Accordingly, Zhang calls for central bankers to rethink how they deal with asset prices and monetary policy. He argues that since asset prices are more sensitive to economic performance and public expectations, their persistent increase can be "early and visual warnings of excess liquidity in the market." Therefore it is necessary for central banks to "pay more attention to price stability in broader terms" and to further explore the methods and approaches in assessing overall price levels. In particular,

Zhang suggests that real estate prices could be among the first to be included in a new overall price index. Zhang's views have since found official reference in the PBC's policy report published in November 2009, in which the Bank argues that it will "pay attention to price stability in longer and broader terms" (PBC 2009a, 32). Given the gravity of rising asset price pressures in China, this policy space will be well worth watching.

Monetary Policy during the GFC and Beyond

Although concerned with potential inflationary impacts from the government's GFC-inspired stimulus programs, the task of fostering economic recovery has become an important focus for the PBC in recent years. Accordingly, the PBC's approach to monetary policy had been accommodative in the immediate aftermath of the crisis. Nevertheless, as the economy stabilized and inflation picked up pace, monetary policy was first neutralized and then tightened in 2011.

Officials in Beijing were shocked when what they believed to be a local infection in the U.S. financial system quickly spiraled into a global pandemic. World trade collapsed, dropping 10.7% in 2009, the sharpest annual contraction since the 1930s. Since September 2008, the external crisis has translated into a dire situation for the Chinese economy. China's exports, a major force that has underpinned China's phenomenal growth and employment in the last two decades, plunged from an annual growth of 26% in July 2008 to a 27% contraction by February 2009 (see Figure 9.10). GDP growth dropped to under 8% in the first half of 2009, a worrying decline by Chinese standards. According to the statistics of the Ministry of Human Resources and Social Security, 20 million migrant workers lost their jobs due to the financial crisis. For policymakers, "China was in the throes of the functional equivalent of a full-blown recession" (Roach 2011).

In this context, Chinese monetary officials have had a roller coaster ride before and after the crisis. One day they were in firefighter mode to check inflation that peaked at 8.7% in February 2008, but two quarters later they were inundated by a credible threat of deflation as external demand fell drastically. In fact, the PBC's governor, Zhou Xiaochuan, was quoted as late as August 2008 in the Chinese media saying that inflation remains a risk, implying that monetary tightening could remain on course. However, the Bank was alarmed by the early signs of a slowdown in external demand as the U.S. subprime crisis quickly spilled over into the GFC. More or less reassured by

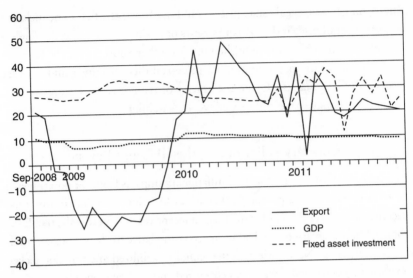

FIGURE 9.10. Selected macroeconomic indicators, September 2008–11 (percentage rate of growth year by year, same period).

Source: Figures for exports are from General Administration of Customs of China; figures for GDP and fixed asset investment are from National Bureau of Statistics of China.

an August CPI of 4.9% (although the producer price index stood at an uncomfortable 10.1%), the PBC cut the one-year benchmark lending rate by 27 basis points on September 16, signaling the beginning of the end of a long monetary tightening cycle in China (see Figure 9.11). This suggested a shift of policy priority from containing inflation to maintaining economic growth.

In retrospect, some question the efficiency of the PBC's policy response in 2008, arguing that the Bank had inadequate knowledge of the impact of the brewing subprime crisis in the United States and did not react quickly enough, pointing to the fact that the PBC had raised bank reserve ratios five times in the first half of 2008, but subsequently dropped interest rates twice and slashed the reserve ratio by half a percentage point between September and December (Tang 2008). In response to such criticisms, a PBC official insisted that one needed to comprehend the context to have "a fair understanding":

> In fact, most of the same people [making the criticisms] had praised us for the monetary tightening, up until the crisis. No one could have foreseen the sudden change of situation in the external environment, and how severe its impact would be to the domestic economy at that time. Even the

European Central Bank raised interest rates as late as May that year. What do you make of that? On the other hand, it was the consecutive [tightening] measures in early 2008 that brought CPI down from 8.7% in February to 4.9% in August. This gave us much greater room in allowing a relaxation of policy in order to stimulate the economy without runaway inflation. . . . Without seeing the big picture, you won't have a fair understanding of our situation and decision at that particular moment.[20]

To the Bank's credit, the response here was indeed vigorous. The central authorities, including the PBC, mobilized political, economic, and social resources in a bid to steer the nation through the storm. A fiscal stimulus package with a face value of 4 trillion RMB (almost 600 billion U.S. dollars) was announced on November 5, an amount equal to 12.5% of China's GDP in 2008 (Feng 2009).[21] There has been criticism that the package was more of a short-term rescue plan than a long-term solution for badly needed economic restructuring that would enable the Chinese economy to transition toward a more balanced path in which domestic and private consumption plays a larger role. To placate the criticisms, the government adjusted the composition of the stimulus plan in March 2009 after discussion in the National People's Congress. Stripping out earthquake reconstruction spending, the revised plan

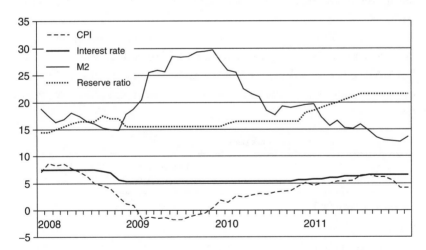

FIGURE 9.11. Inflation (CPI), Money supply (M2), and monetary instruments, 2008–11.

Note: M2 figures are year-by-year percentage rate of growth. Interest rate refers to the PBC's benchmark one-year deposit rate. Reserve ratio figures are those applied to large financial institutions.
Source: National Bureau of Statistics of China; PBC.

reduced government investment in infrastructure and the environment by 10%, but increased spending in technological innovation, public housing, and health care and education (see Table 9.2).

According to a *Wall Street Journal* article, the PBC had held concerns about the inflationary impact of the stimulus program, but its views were "brushed aside" (Davis 2011a). In fact, insiders from the PBC suggested that the Bank was rather more worried about deflation in the short term since employment was believed to be well under the equilibrium level given the massive layoffs in the wake of the crisis. In addition, there had been ample signs of excess capacity in the economy. When asked which industrial sector had the potential for excess capacity, Fan Gang, member of the PBC's Monetary Policy Committee, reportedly answered "each and every" (Feng 2009). Similar to some other central banks, the PBC and monetary policy played a relatively ancillary role compared to the fiscal authorities and fiscal policy in a textbook Keynesian initiative. The PBC saw a relaxation of monetary policy as an imperative. Governor Zhou said at a press briefing held during the National People's Congress in March 2009, "If we act slowly and less decisively, we are likely to see what happened in other countries, a slide in confidence. . . . We would rather be faster and heavy-handed if it can prevent confidence slumping during the financial crisis, and spur fast recovery of the economy amid the crisis" (R. Zhang 2009).

Indeed, the PBC was fast and heavy-handed in implementing an "appropriately loose" money policy. In the remainder of 2008, after September 16, the PBC slashed benchmark interest rates by 2.16 percentage points, and reduced the reserve ratio of financial institutions by 1.5 percentage points (see Figure

Table 9.2.　Composition of China's stimulus package (%)

	Initial plan (Oct. 2008)	Revised plan (March 2009)
Transport and power infrastructure	60	50
Rural infrastructure	12	12
Environmental investment	12	7
Affordable housing	9	13
Technological innovation	5	12
Health and education	1	5

Source: Adapted from Naughton (2009).

9.11). In addition, the Bank released 275.5 billion yuan through the open market during the first half of 2009 (Feng 2009). This dramatic policy relaxation led to a soaring money supply. In August 2009, the nation's money supply (M2) grew 28.53% year-by-year to its highest level since the central bank started disclosing M2 data in 1997 (see Figure 9.11). It also far exceeded the PBC's annual target of 17% for 2009, and was over four times the increase of GDP in the first half of the year (7.1%) (Si 2009).

As the stimulus plan was highly politicized, state banks felt compelled to issue credits for projects listed in the investment plan with an implicit assurance that they would not be held accountable for the potential bad debts resulting from the massive credit expansion. As a result, bank lending has grown at an explosive pace since the announcement of the stimulus efforts, particularly since the beginning of 2009. There was a record 7.37 trillion yuan in loans for the first half of 2009, 2.3 times the amount loaned during the same period in the previous year. To put the figure in perspective, the 8.18 trillion yuan of new loans pumped out between January and August 2009, at 31% of GDP, is more than was seen in Japan in the late 1980s, or in the United States during Greenspan's housing bubble.

However, the PBC began feeling uncomfortable as the lending extravaganza continued into the latter half of 2009 as asset prices skyrocketed. The depth of the credit pool in 2009 had surprised many, even the central bank. Governor Zhou admitted back in January 2009 that the increase in new loans was "out of our expectation" (Huo et al. 2009). In fact, the PBC's expansionary annual target of new credit for 2009 was set at 8 trillion yuan, but the actual figure reached 9.59 trillion, almost doubling from the previous year (PBC 2010). The trend largely continued in 2010 with new credit reaching 7.95 trillion yuan, exceeding the annual target of 7.5 trillion. Apart from the massive increase of bank credits in 2009 and 2010, a return to surplus on the part of exports since May 2010 reignited the accumulation of foreign reserves and hence domestic inflationary pressures, as Beijing switched back to the dollar peg in the face of the GFC. After reaching their lowest point at a negative 1.8% in July 2009, CPI figures in November 2009 entered positive territory and rose, standing at 6.4% in June 2011 (see Figure 9.11).

In mid-2010, policymakers in Beijing were still divided between those concerned about the emerging inflation and those concerned about the resilience of China's economic recovery. PBC governor Zhou has been floating an argument that, amid signs of a more sustainable balance of consumption, investment, and net exports, the central bank should neutralize monetary policy before tightening it in order to "gradually reduce inflationary pressure over two years" (Huo and Yu 2010). For those worried about inflation, there was also a debate on potential measures against the inflation—that is, to revalue the RMB or to raise interest rates—but the PBC has been adamant about using both measures at the same time to rein in inflation (B. Chen 2010). As we shall see in Chapter 11, the Bank finally resorted to an exchange rate correction, announcing on June 19, 2010, that it would switch back from the RMB's precrisis crawling peg to a basket of currencies featuring gradual and modest appreciation.[22] This is clearly a political move to defuse the collective pressures from the major economies amid a painful recovery. It also suggests that the Bank was again gaining an upper hand in Beijing's macroeconomic management, particularly against the Ministry of Commerce, which had been adamant on an undervalued RMB and trade promotion. A revaluation of the RMB would also help alleviate the Bank's pressure on inflation.

On the interest rates front, despite popular pressure to keep the rate on hold, the PBC seized on the pending release of what was anticipated to be an alarming CPI figure for September 2010 (which turned out to be 3.6%) to prompt the leadership to give a green light for a rate hike. The rate move was formally announced on October 19, 2010, for the first time in the postcrisis era. This rate hike was also notable for its pace of 25 basis points, instead of the usual 27 basis points adopted since 2002. The old practice was designed for the convenience of the accounting patterns of domestic banks. The new scale suggests that the PBC has opted for international standards and practices. Since October 2010, the PBC has announced five interest rate hikes. Taking into account the rising CPI during this period, real deposit rates have remained in negative territory. Again, this reflects the PBC's concerns about short-term capital inflows, as well as risks for domestic banks and local governments that have been highly leveraged due to the stimulus programs. But the PBC managed to bring lending rates above the CPI in July 2011 and to leave the real interest rates above 2% by the end of 2011.

Apart from rate adjustments, the PBC has been relying more on quantitative instruments such as bank reserve ratios and PBC Bills, as well as restricting bank lending, to dampen the increase in domestic liquidity. In particular, reserve ratios have been increased six times, in each month from January to June of 2011, reaching a historic high of 21.5% in June 2011. Chinese monetary authorities have addressed the inflation challenge through more aggressive open market sterilization operations as well as by employing window guidance measures when concern about overheating was paramount. Overall, the Chinese central bank has fared reasonably well in postcrisis inflation fighting. Given a red-hot average growth of GDP at 9.5% between 2009 and 2011, average headline CPI had been kept at 2.7% during this period, standing comfortably at 1.7% in October 2012. Bank loan growth was reduced from 31.7% in 2009 to 14% in 2011. By the end of 2012, China seemed to be on track for a soft landing.

For Stephen Roach (2012), former chairman of Morgan Stanley Asia, by deploying both monetary and administrative measures, the PBC "was able to orchestrate a 'passive' monetary tightening," which is "classic central banking at its best." Li Daokui (2012), an academic member of the PBC's Monetary Policy Committee in the postcrisis period, assesses the Bank's performance during this period from the perspective of the Bank's capacity to guide the market:

> A central banker must respect investor sentiments, not because they are correct but because they have an overwhelming momentum, like a huge oil tanker. How do you change the direction of such a huge tanker? Steer early and steadily, while staying patient and not expecting instant response. Since the financial crisis, China's central bank has been carefully steering against investor sentiments. Between August 2008 and June 2009, Chinese investors were largely pessimistic. Monetary policies were then aimed at delicately changing investors' minds through cuts in interest rates and deposit reserve ratios. By mid-2010, however, investor sentiments had swung in the other direction—annual output growth was running at 10 per cent. Tighter policies were then pursued, together with stronger banking and property market regulations. By mid-2011 sentiments finally stabilized.

There had been different approaches to anticrisis strategies but similar consequences in China and the West. The Chinese approach was bank-funded public spending under political command, which generated concerns about bad loans in the banking system, unsustainable local government debt (see Chapter 11), asset bubbles, and inflation. In the West, particularly the United States, crisis management was mainly through public debt financed through central bank liquidity injections, which also potentially poses inflation or asset inflation challenges down the track. The sheer scale of the GFC and the potential prospect of postcrisis stagflation involving a lackluster economic recovery and rising price levels have largely thrown central banking into uncharted waters. Given the prolonged uncertainty over the global economy, particularly a weak and fragile U.S. economy and the deteriorating sovereign debt crisis in the euro zone, China is better positioned to foster stability and growth compared with major Western economies in terms of the policy options at its disposal. Following the lead of the Bank of Japan, the U.S. Federal Reserve, the European Central Bank, and the Bank of England have all taken their short-term policy rates down to the zero bound, neutering the scope for monetary stimulation, other than through untested and dubious liquidity injections. In contrast, the PBC has plenty of ammunition in its monetary policy arsenal, including high required reserve ratios and positive real interest rates, as of early 2012.

Conclusion

The evolution of the PBC's authority in Beijing's policy circle has been reflected in the deliberation and conduct of monetary policy in battling against an increasingly complicated set of internal and external imbalances. The PBC only started to switch to aggregates targeting and indirect control on an experimental basis in the 1990s. In the new century, the central bank has been increasingly adept, skillful, and innovative in fine tuning the economy through a combination of instruments, witnessed by the PBC's relative success since 2003 in containing inflation induced by external shocks through a large-scale sterilization program. More tellingly, an institutionally weak PBC had to rely on the political authority of Zhu to rein in inflation in the 1993–95 cycle. Increasingly, however, a more authoritative and assertive central bank has begun to flex its muscles to guard against asset price inflation and economic overheating since 2003. The PBC's range of policy instruments has helped here. Compared to the "one instrument" model based on using short-term interest rates typically found in the West, the use of direct controls, especially over bank reserves and credit, has helped the PBC since 2003 in directly battling asset price inflation. As we have noted, most Western central banks are hesitant on this front. Such instruments have also helped the Bank in its tightening in the postcrisis period. The PBC has also fought to expand its policy discretion in attempts since 2005 to partially liberalize the dollar peg regime, which we discuss in Chapter 10.

10

The PBC and China's Foreign Exchange Rate Policy

This chapter traces the evolution of China's foreign exchange rate policy, reserve management, and the internationalization of the renminbi (RMB), focusing on the PBC's changing and growing role in this arena. This arena is important to the PBC because the managed exchange rate system and the resultant growth in foreign exchange reserves pose major problems for domestic monetary policy. This is why the PBC has an interest in exchange rate liberalization. Corresponding to the rising clout of the PBC in the monetary policy arena, we argue that a somewhat similar story can be told on the exchange rate front and in the increasing internationalization of the RMB.

In the central planning era, the PBC's role was limited to monitoring foreign exchange transactions, with no say in the setting of the RMB's external value. Despite institutional developments in the first era of reform, particularly the establishment of the State Administration of Foreign Exchange (SAFE) under the leadership of the PBC, the Bank largely remained at the periphery of exchange rate policymaking. However, a series of formal and informal developments in the second reform era, including foreign exchange reform in 1994, the passing of the 1995 Central Bank Law, and political patronage by Zhu, all marked the beginning of the rise of the PBC in the exchange rate policy process.

This is demonstrated clearly in Beijing's non-devaluation policy during the Asian financial crisis (AFC), in which the PBC played a key role in influencing the top leadership. Under the governorship of Zhou Xiaochuan since 2002, the PBC has been a major player in China's exchange rate policy deliberations. As we show in this chapter, constrained by a fixed exchange rate regime, the Bank successfully persuaded the leadership to relax the regime, sought to use a combination of instruments to sterilize inflationary pressures in the domestic economy, and endeavored to seek a new approach in managing China's ballooning foreign reserves and the internationalization of the RMB.

Exchange Rate Policy in the Planning Era

A nation's foreign exchange policy is invariably linked to its foreign trade strategy as well as to the nature of its economic system. Given foreign sanctions on goods and investments and an extreme lack of foreign currency, China's prereform trade regime was an extreme example of import substitution, "designed to develop the indigenous capacity to produce domestically the manufactured goods initially acquired through imports" (Lardy 1992b). Under the inward-looking trade regime, production for domestic investment and consumption was favored over production for exports.

In China's central planning economy, the foreign trade and foreign exchange plan were invariably integrated components in the central plan, which needed to be coordinated and reconciled with the domestic production, investment, and consumption subplans. The tradition in central planning is to price foreign exchange, like most commodities, according to the cost-plus principle, the domestic currency cost of exports, or the cost of earning foreign exchange. In a command economy such as that of China prior to 1978, the domestic currency is typically overvalued so the government can subsidize imports by taxing exports, a policy that is in line with the pursuit of an import-substitution strategy. All foreign exchange earnings of foreign trade companies (FTCs) were surrendered to the government, and demand for foreign exchange would be allocated through state planning. If the foreign trade sector suffered a domestic currency loss in its operations, the government would automatically cover the loss through the central budget. For example, according to Lin and Schramm (2003, 251), in 1979, the national average cost of earning one unit of foreign exchange was 2.40 yuan per dollar, whereas the official exchange rate was 1.50 yuan per dollar. As a result, unprofitable exports accounted for 66% of China's total exports in 1978 (Wu and Chen 1989, 47). Because of this automatic tax subsidy mechanism, exchange rates could be fixed at an arbitrary level, irrespective of changes in prices and other economic variables. In other words, the variations of the exchange rate did not reflect changes in demand and supply, but were adjusted to match the available supply of foreign exchange. In fact, after 1953 when the central planning regime was formally established, there were only minor variations in the exchange rate despite structural changes in both the domestic and international economy, which was fixed at 1.60 yuan per dollar up until the eve of the reform in 1978 (Lin and Schramm 2003, 250).

In this regard, the exchange rate served mainly an accounting function to determine local currency profits or subsidies (the latter, in the case of losses). As such, the RMB exchange rate played a minor role in distribution within the national economy, and the setting of its value was not an important policy issue for the economic bureaucracy. Foreign trade and foreign exchange rate policy in the planning years involved a number of bureaucratic players in the production, trade, and finance realms, including the State Planning Commission (SPC), Ministry of Foreign Trade (MOFT), Ministry of Finance (MOF), and the PBC. A central planning regime centered on material balance meant that the financial planning of foreign exchange was tightly centralized by and subordinated to the physical planning of foreign trade and, ultimately, to the central plan. Hence, the central planning apparatus, represented by the SPC, played a dominant role in setting the parameters of China's foreign exchange policy.

The MOFT was responsible for implementing the foreign trade plan drawn up by the SPC, which was done through its administration over the state-owned FTCs under a state monopoly. The losses the FTCs incurred through an overvalued RMB were not a concern to the MOFT because they were always covered by fiscal subsidies from the MOF as well as state banks. More importantly, under the planning framework, foreign trade volumes were independent of a fixed exchange rate, and the performance of the MOFT was assessed against the fulfillment of the foreign trade plan rather than economic or commercial criteria. Therefore, the MOFT had less interest in the setting of the exchange rate. So did the MOF. Although the state budget had to compensate exporters' losses due to the RMB's overvaluation, this was mitigated, if not covered, by the surplus from imports. In fact, the overall budget for the foreign trade sector had remained in surplus for most of the time before the reform in 1978. For example, during the twenty-eight years between 1953 and 1980, the foreign trade sector was in surplus for nineteen years, with only nine deficit years (Lin 1997, 4).

As discussed in Chapter 3, the PBC did not have ministry status and had been subordinated to the MOF from the mid-1960s. Therefore it had limited influence on macroeconomic issues, including exchange rate policy, and had no authority in setting the external value of the RMB. The major function of the PBC in the realm of foreign exchange was to settle, monitor, and supervise foreign trade transactions through the Bank of China (BOC), which was under the PBC's administration before reform, as well as to facilitate foreign trade and exchange earnings within the wider cash and credit plans (Jiang 1999; Mah 1971).

Exchange Rate Policy in the First Reform Era

The overvalued RMB faced structural challenges after the reform. First, taxing exports to subsidize imports has limits. Sooner or later taxing exports will affect the incentive to export, with direct fiscal subsidies required to compensate for the overvalued exchange rate. When foreign trade becomes a significant share of gross domestic product (GDP), the size of fiscal subsidies required will be prohibitive and cannot be sustained in the long run. In the case of China, export losses in the 1960s and 1970s were still manageable because prices of all commodities during that period were tightly controlled and export quotas were largely mandatory. But export losses grew in the late 1970s on the back of agricultural reform and became more serious in the 1980s with industrial reform. Relaxation of central planning and liberalization of the economy made production more sensitive to state procurement prices, dramatically increasing the export costs of FTCs. However, export revenues of the FTCs could not increase as rapidly because the exchange rate was fixed and overvalued. According to Lardy (1992b), in the years just prior to 1980, 70% of China's exports posted losses, which increased demands on the government's budget and exerted devaluation pressure on the RMB. Pressure on China's exchange rate intensified in the mid-1980s when the government introduced industry reform, which, for the first time since the beginning of central planning, substantially raised the prices of key industrial input materials, thus increasing the domestic procurement costs of the FTCs.

Another structural factor that challenged currency overvaluation was the gradual shift of China's trade strategy from import substitution to export orientation during this period. As one of the central features of China's economic reform, an export-oriented, outward-looking strategy enabled China to integrate into the world market by utilizing its comparative advantage in relatively low labor costs, an increasingly liberalized international trade regime, and a substantially improved relationship with the West in the last decade of the Cold War (Feng 2006c; Shirk 1994). Instead of playing a supplemental role of financing imports in the planning era, exports became the pivotal sector in propelling economic growth, whose share in the GDP tripled in the first reform era, from 6% in 1981 to 18.6% in 1992 (Feng 2006c, 48). The change of trade strategy thus called for a corresponding change in the exchange rate regime; a devaluation of the RMB became increasingly essential for the rapidly expanding export sector.

As it turned out, economic reform after 1978 witnessed the liberalization of a range of institutions in relation to foreign trade and foreign exchange. The state monopoly on foreign trade was gradually broken up. Private trading companies and manufacturing enterprises were allowed to compete with the state-owned FTCs in engaging in the foreign trade business. As an incentive, exporters were allowed to retain a certain part of their foreign exchange earnings in the form of quotas, which could be used to purchase back the foreign exchange from the government at the official exchange rate. From 1980, these retention quotas were permitted to be traded in a foreign exchange trading system established by the BOC for authorized enterprises.

In parallel to the foreign trade reform, a dual-track exchange rate system was established to address the problem of the unprofitability of exports due to an overvalued RMB. In August 1979, the State Council introduced the RMB Internal Settlement Rate (ISR) effective from January 1980, fixed at 2.80 yuan per dollar. Under the new system, the official exchange rate was applied to non-trade-related foreign exchange transactions and the more depreciated ISR applied to trade-related transactions (Jing 2001, 307). The introduction of the ISR was the first attempt to adjust the RMB exchange rate according to the structure of domestic prices since 1953 (PBC 2008c). Nevertheless, a fixed ISR in the wake of a steady increase of domestic prices resulted in international pressure, particularly from the United States, regarding allegations of trade subsidies.

The ISR was subsequently abolished in 1985, and the official exchange rate was devalued to the ISR level of 2.80 yuan per U.S. dollar, which was further devalued to 3.71 yuan in July 1986, where it remained for over three years. After 1987, China's foreign exchange rate was classified as a more flexible arrangement ("other managed float") by the International Monetary Fund (IMF) (Lin and Schramm 2003, 254). At the same time, the foreign exchange swap business run by the BOC was terminated and a new foreign exchange swap center was established in the Shenzhen Special Economic Zone, which had a more flexible approach to prices. Later, other Special Economic Zones were allowed to create similar foreign exchange swap centers. The swap price was determined by buyers and sellers through negotiations. With the rapid development of the swap market, a dual exchange rate system of the official exchange rate and the swap market rate (retention market rate) reemerged in China in 1986 and increasingly became an important tool to offset the distortion caused by the overvalued official exchange rate and to facilitate the competitiveness of the export sector. Subsequently, higher retention ratios, the relaxation of price controls, the expanded supply of foreign exchange, and the permission for domestic individuals to participate in trading greatly stimulated the development of the swap market. By the early 1990s, the swap rate had become an important signal of macroeconomic performance. According to Lardy (1992a), the swap market rate had already been applied to 80% of China's total foreign exchange transactions at the end of this period.

Institutional Dynamics of Exchange Rate Policymaking

The economic reforms and institutional changes within the state also altered the institutional dynamics of China's exchange rate policymaking. In the first era of reform, however, the emerging market elements played only a supplemental role to the state plan. Therefore the planning apparatus, as embodied in the SPC, remained the most powerful bureaucratic player in Beijing's macroeconomic management, including exchange rate policy. Generally speaking, the SPC favored gradual, moderate devaluation of the RMB. As the export sector increasingly became the engine of economic growth, devaluation would facilitate the growth target of the state plan through increased trade and foreign direct investment (FDI). On the other hand, the SPC favored a steady pace of devaluation, fearing that any radical moves would disturb the performance of the state-owned enterprises (SOEs) in the form of rising costs for raw materials and production.[1] In particular, the SPC opposed devaluation pressures in the late 1980s when the Chinese economy was embroiled in inflation as the state lost control over money supply. The SPC was concerned that RMB devaluation would increase market prices and further widen the gap between market and plan prices, which in turn would encourage rent-seeking activities that would divert inputs away from the SOEs and put more financial pressure on them (Liew and Wu 2007). Mainly because of the SPC's opposition, the devaluation, argued for strongly by the Ministry of Foreign Economic Relations and Trade (MOFERT, successor of the MOFT in 1982), was not carried out until the end of 1989 when the SPC's concern about the negative economic and social effects of devaluation had subsided as inflation was brought down by an economic austerity program.

As discussed earlier, the MOFT was more or less indifferent to exchange rate setting in the planning era since it was assessed against the achievement of the foreign trade plan while foreign trade volumes were independent of the exchange rate under the central planning regime. However, this changed after the reform as profits of the export sector became an important performance indicator of MOFERT, which saw the ministry turn into a vocal supporter of devaluation. First of all, an overvalued RMB was a major factor that hampered the competitiveness of Chinese exporters in the world market. To make things worse, agricultural reform in the early 1980s and the subsequent industry and price reform had increased the domestic costs of exports. In addition, enterprise reforms saw the losses of the FTCs no longer automatically covered by the state budget. As a result, rising domestic prices and an overvalued RMB made it increasingly unattractive for producers to help MOFERT meet the compulsory export targets in the mandatory export plan. Therefore, because of its institutional interest in stimulating exports, MOFERT and its successors became the bulwark of RMB devaluation.

Until the high inflation of the late 1980s, the MOF favored a lower exchange rate because overvaluation had resulted in FTCs incurring losses that required massive subsidies from the MOF, thus putting pressure on the latter to fulfill the budget plan. According to F. Yang's (1993) study of the gap between the exchange rate and export costs, to earn one U.S. dollar of export sales in 1990, the government had to pay RMB 4.72 based on the prevailing official exchange rate; RMB 0.35 through the central tax rebate; RMB 0.86 as the "quota price" for every retained dollar, which is considered a bonus to exporters; and over RMB 3 through various local government subsidies. In total, an average exporter in 1990 received about RMB 9, of which over 33% were fiscal subsidies.

In the late 1980s, however, the MOF backed the SPC's case against devaluation based on a similar concern over increased costs to the SOEs. While devaluation was favorable for exporters, the majority of the SOEs were in the nontradable sector. In addition, China's imports had low price elasticity and the MOF believed that devaluation would increase the cost of material inputs to producers, particularly the SOEs (Liew and Wu 2007). According to the National Price Bureau, which was in charge of estimating the impact of the cost of key imported materials on domestic prices, 1% devaluation of the RMB would increase domestic inflation by 1.55% (Yang 2000, 14).

We have seen in Chapters 3 and 4 that, during the first reform era, despite concrete steps in the institutional building of the PBC as a newly appointed central bank, the Bank largely remained in the shadow of the planning apparatus. The gradualist reform under a political compromise with the then powerful conservatives led to a dual-track economy, in which the emerging market elements had to develop alongside or within, rather than replacing, the central planning framework. Accordingly, the PBC's impact on macroeconomic management, including exchange rate policy, was indeed limited. In terms of the exchange rate, the PBC's authority was confined to the management of China's foreign exchange, not the setting of the exchange rate, in the *Decision of the State Council Concerning the People's Bank of China Exclusively Performing Central Bank Functions* (State Council 1983). PBC's management of foreign exchange rested on SAFE, which was established in March 1979 under the BOC, which was also supervised by the PBC, but the Bank took over SAFE for direct administration in 1982 on the eve of the BOC's separation from the PBC (see Chapter 3). The inclusion of SAFE in the PBC's institutional framework has been strategically important for the latter, as it provided the Bank with valuable institutional and financial resources for its ambitious programs, such as the PBC-led banking reforms since 2003 (see Chapter 11).

As discussed in Chapter 7, the National Price Bureau was responsible for domestic price levels between 1978 and 1993. Therefore the PBC was not directly responsible for managing inflation, but was preoccupied with a weak banking system. Given a decrease in the scale of the central budget, the banking sector was increasingly required to perform fiscal functions of providing working loans to the SOEs. Therefore, similar to the concerns of the SPC and the MOF, devaluation would devastate the SOEs, which in turn would produce massive bad loans for the banks. Hence, it was in the PBC's interest to oppose devaluations. However, according to Ou (1995, 7), the PBC, instead of expressing its concerns about the healthiness of the banking sector, argued against devaluation on the grounds that such a move would exacerbate the already serious inflationary situation in the latter half of the 1980s. Compared with the SPC, which had been adamant about a more cautious approach to devaluation, the limited authority of the PBC on this issue made it lack confidence in articulating its own institutional preferences, resorting instead to a more populist concern about inflation.

The PBC and Exchange Rate Policy in the Second Reform Era

As China's reform switched to the fast lane in 1992, so too did China's foreign exchange reforms. A major milestone in China's foreign exchange regime and exchange rate policy during this period was the unification of the official and swap market prices in 1994 and the launch of the foreign exchange surrender system. Moreover, as we argue below, the PBC's growing authority in Beijing's policy circle was reflected in its influence on Beijing's non-devaluation policy after the AFC.

The Foreign Exchange Reform in 1994

The pace of foreign exchange reform started gaining momentum in the wake of the Party's new reform blueprint, embodied in *The Decision of the CPC Central Committee on Several Matters Concerning the Establishment of a Socialist Market Economic System* adopted at the Third Plenary Session of the Fourteenth CPC Central Committee in November 1993 (Mehran et al. 1996). According to this strategic document, the aim of foreign exchange reform was to establish "a managed floating exchange rate regime based on market supply and demand and a unified and well-functioning foreign exchange market" (Hu 2010). There were also external concerns as Beijing had to make dramatic measures and commitments in its bid to accede to the General Agreement on Tariffs and Trade before 1995 when it was to be replaced by the World Trade Organization (WTO). After 1991, the Chinese authorities repeatedly announced on different occasions that a major goal of China's financial reform was to make the RMB a convertible currency. In 1993, Beijing made a formal commitment to the international community that it would achieve RMB current account convertibility by 2000 (Lin and Schramm 2003, 256–57).

The fact that the exchange rate in the swap market had been applied to a majority of China's total foreign transactions by the early 1990s (80% after 1991) provided appropriate timing and foundation for a regime change. Effective in January 1994, the RMB official and swap market rates were unified at the swap market rate of 8.7 yuan per U.S. dollar, which had prevailed at the end of 1993. At the same time, a national interbank foreign exchange market (China Foreign Exchange Trading System) was established in April 1994 to replace the old swap market. Another complementary measure was the launch of the foreign exchange surrender system in which enterprises are required to sell their foreign exchange receipts to the banks and buy foreign exchange from the banks when necessary, which ended the practice of foreign exchange retention and submission. Beijing had also achieved solid developments in current account liberalization. On November 27, 1996, PBC Governor Dai Xianglong, announced in a letter to the IMF that China would accept the obligations under Article VIII of the IMF's Articles of Agreement beginning on December 1, 1996, which meant RMB current account convertibility, well ahead of its previous timetable of 2000 (Dai 1998). By then, China had a US$42 billion surplus on the balance of payments and US$100 billion of foreign exchange reserves (Wu et al. 2001, 110).

A unified exchange rate, a national interbank foreign exchange market, and a mandatory surrender system formed the three pillars of a new foreign exchange regime, which would have pivotal and profound implications for China's economy and macroeconomic management in the years to come. The unified exchange rate on the back of an interbank market turned out to be essentially a regime of a rate pegged to the U.S. dollar, which greatly facilitated Chinese exports in terms of price competitiveness due to the devaluation and stable expectations of exchange rate risks. The mandatory surrender system helped the authorities with foreign exchange control, but, more importantly, by turning private holdings of foreign currency into official reserves, it resulted in a gigantic buildup of China's foreign reserves as China began to run large surpluses in both its current and capital accounts in 2001. In fact, this trend was heralded by the same situation immediately after the 1994 reform. By 1996, after two years of intervention in the market by purchasing the excess supply of dollars, the PBC had tripled its reserve holdings to US$77.9 billion (Lin and Schramm 2003, 259). In other words, the 1994 reform planted the seeds for both the subsequent success of export-led economic growth and the growing headache of an unbalanced economy and external pressures for RMB appreciation.

This was also the case for the PBC because the 1994 reform awarded new tools and authority to the Bank as well as new constraints to its monetary policy. After the reform, the PBC stood at the center of China's foreign exchange management. Instead of more scattered, locally based swap centers, the new national interbank system enabled the central bank to maintain its desired exchange rate by buying and selling foreign exchange as the largest, preponderant player in the market. Doing so provided the Bank with a new, market-oriented instrument, open market operations, in its quest for a new monetary policy framework. At the same time, however, the imperative of a fixed exchange rate under the management of the PBC also constrained the Bank's room to maneuver in terms of monetary policy. Henceforth, exchange rate and balance of payments became central variables of monetary policy that the PBC had to deal with seriously, and later, painstakingly. According to Xie Ping, a PBC veteran, "the PBC began to pay close attention to the relationship between exchange rate and monetary policy" (Rolnick 2003).

As we saw in Chapter 7, according to the "policy trilemma," a country may not simultaneously run a system of exchange rate flexibility and independent monetary policy, and allow full capital mobility (Obstfeld et al. 2005). Ample studies suggest the possibility that a pegged exchange rate is "a trap" in the era of greater financial integration (see, e.g., Aizenman and Reuven 2008; Edwards and Yeyati 2005; Eichengreen 1999; Frankel 1999). Indeed, as we argue below, despite the PBC's efforts to utilize a variety of instruments, China's surging trade surplus and massive inflows of FDI, combined with the objective of a fixed exchange rate, have compromised the independence of the PBC's monetary policy, and with it an incentive to liberalize the exchange rate system.

The PBC and the Non-devaluation Policy in 1998

The PBC began to gain substantial authority in the 1990s under the governorship of Zhu Rongji, who later ascended to number three in the Party (see Chapters 6 and 7). In this respect the Bank's growing authority can be best illustrated by its influence over Beijing's decision not to devalue the RMB in the aftermath of the AFC.

The crisis, which broke out in mid-1997, produced a formidable challenge to China's exchange rate policy. An increasing number of China's Asian neighbors had announced currency devaluations, thus putting pressure on Beijing to lower the RMB exchange rate to salvage the export sector. As it turned out, however, Beijing kept its exchange rate intact during and after the crisis. This decision has been interpreted mainly from a strategic and diplomatic perspective. Many believe that, by avoiding a beggar-thy-neighbor-style competitive devaluation, Beijing's non-devaluation policy was a strategic move to gain trust and prestige from Asian countries as "a responsible great power," particularly in contrast to the largely failed IMF finance packages backed by the West (Yu 2000). It was also seen as a diplomatic maneuver for Beijing to gain essential support for its accession to the WTO (Feng 2006c). While these external political considerations were obviously factored into the policy decision, domestic institutional dynamics should be seen as at least equally important. After all, if the non-devaluation policy faced strong opposition from the bureaucracy, it would have been difficult for the party leadership to go ahead without an institutional consensus.

To be sure, an economic policy with wide and critical significance to the economy, such as exchange rate policy, is ultimately subject to the decisions made by the party leaders within the Politburo and particularly its Standing Committee. However, the Politburo normally rubber-stamped the decisions of the Central Leading Group on Finance and Economic Affairs (CLGFEA), a key decision maker linking the party and the government apparatus (see Chapter 3). The CLGFEA can be dated back to 1954 as the highest-level economic policy organ dominated by the SPC at that time. In the late 1980s it was downgraded to an advisory institution before it was resurrected by the then party secretary-general Jiang Zemin in 1993 to be the supreme economic policymaking body of the party-state. Jiang chaired the Group from 1991 until his retirement (Lam 1999), and had two of his protégés, Zeng Peiyan and Hua Jianmin, take up influential positions within the Group as its deputy secretary-general and deputy director of its administrative office (Liew 2004). However, Jiang deliberately distanced himself from the top job and was happy to let first Li Peng and later Zhu Rongji be responsible for the economy. According to Lam (1999, 78), former party leader Zhao Ziyang's disastrous overseeing of the inflationary economy in the late 1980s reminded Jiang that a poorly performing economy could be fatal for the supreme leader of the party. Let someone else, ideally the premier, be the scapegoat.

Thus, although Zhu Rongji had been the deputy chair of the CLGFEA, he was actually China's chief economic manager and "undisputed boss of the CLGFEA" (Liew and Wu 2007, 151). Of the five subgroups within the CLGFEA at that time, Zhu headed the subgroups on monetary and fiscal affairs himself until 1998 when he became premier and Wen Jiabao formally took over the two groups. Nevertheless, until the middle of 1999, Zhu had been in charge of the major issues in all the portfolios except agriculture (Liew 2004). In other words, Zhu had been the key decision maker in China's exchange rate policy during the AFC.

Wen also chaired the Central Financial Work Commission (CFWC), established in June 1998. As we saw in Chapter 7, the CFWC aimed to curtail rampant corruption and strengthen the party's control of the financial apparatus in formulating long-term policies rather than interfering in short-term monetary policy and exchange rate policy. Therefore, despite serving as the leader for monetary affairs, secretary-general of the CLGFEA, and leader of the CFWC, Wen (and the CFWC) did not exert substantial influence in this realm at that time.

Below the CLGFEA, a number of key ministerial institutions were influential in exchange rate policymaking. In March 1998, the SPC was renamed the State Development Planning Commission (SDPC). By the time of the AFC, however, the SDPC had lost its dominant role in short-term macroeconomic management, but it still had institutional concerns in this area, particularly the negative impact of devaluation on the cost of development projects. The SDPC was responsible for drawing up plans for major state development projects, but also had to ensure their successful completion within budget. Since these projects invariably used imports, any devaluation of the RMB would therefore increase the costs of the planned and existing projects (Liew 2004). Moreover, given a steady fall in central budget revenue in the 1990s (from 35% of GDP in 1978 to only 11.6% in 1997), these state projects were no longer guaranteed to get subsidies from the MOF (Hu and Wang 1994).

The Ministry of Foreign Trade and Economic Cooperation (MOFTEC) succeeded MOFERT in 1993. Like its predecessor, MOFTEC had a vested interest in a low exchange rate given its responsibility for the overall foreign trade performance of the economy. However, its influence over exchange rate policy began to wane after 1994 for a number of reasons. First of all, the unification of the official and swap market exchange rates in 1994 eliminated a vital rationale for MOFTEC in pushing for the convergence of the two rates (a de facto devaluation). In addition, tax reform in 1994 introduced tax rebates to compensate exporters for a value-added tax (VAT) of 17%, so that MOFTEC could seek higher tax rebates for exporters as an alternative to lowering the RMB exchange rate (Bowles and Wang 2008). On the other hand, however, the MOF would favor devaluation rather than increased tax rebates, which would put more strain on the state budget under its management.

More importantly, the 1995 Central Bank Law and subsequent regulations had relocated the primary influence over exchange rate policy from MOFTEC to the PBC. As discussed in Chapter 7, in the landmark Central Bank Law in 1995, the exchange rate was formally made an instrument for conducting monetary policy. In particular, the 1995 Law and the subsequent passing of the State Council's 1996 *Regulations on Foreign Exchange Management* converted the RMB's exchange rate from an instrument of trade promotion to an instrument of monetary policy. The regulation stated that the aim of foreign exchange management was to increase foreign exchange earnings and to economize on foreign exchange expenditures, without referring to external trade. The 1996 regulation stipulates that the PBC has the exclusive right to determine both the reference exchange rates and the band within which market exchange rates are allowed to deviate from the reference rates (Long 1997, 84; State Council 1996).

Apart from the significant increase in formal authority the PBC had gained in the exchange rate arena, its interactions with political leaders, particularly Zhu Rongji, made it a key institutional actor in Beijing's non-devaluation policy during the AFC. Of major significance regarding the 1995 Law was the decision to give the mandate to the PBC to fight inflation and to take this role away from the National Price Bureau. Facing the ultimate question of whether "to devalue or not to devalue," the PBC stood firmly on a non-devaluation stance. In 1998, despite facing a deflationary economy, the PBC was concerned with potential inflationary effects of any RMB devaluation because it had only recently been able to bring inflation under control (see Chapter 9).

We have discussed in detail the mutual dependency relationship between the PBC and Zhu Rongji in Chapter 6. Zhu needed bureaucratic support for a wide range of ambitious reform programs in the face of a political rivalry with the then premier Li Peng (then number two in the party), and the Bank needed Zhu's political profile to elevate its status and influence in the policy circle. In this regard, Zhu had a valuable source of influence in exchange rate policymaking through his right-hand man, Dai Xianglong, who succeeded Zhu as governor of the PBC in 1995 after serving as its deputy governor from 1993. While serving as PBC governor, Dai chaired the PBC Monetary Policy

Committee (MPC), which was established in 1997 as an advisory body on monetary policy. The committee consists of the deputies from major economic ministries as well as limited representatives from state banks and academia, acting largely as a forum for various institutions to voice their concerns over monetary policy. Therefore the MPC did not exercise any real power over exchange rate policy, and its views on policy were largely dictated by Dai Xianglong.

As chairman of the CLGFEA, Jiang appointed his protégés to important positions at its administrative office, and Zhu Rongji had the PBC's Monetary Policy Department (MPD) to counterbalance the influence of the office. The MPD has been at the core of the PBC's monetary policy deliberations, including exchange rate formulations. Dai Genyou was the director of the MPD during and for some time after the AFC and reported directly to Zhu. Dai Genyou was also directing the research office of the CLGFEA, an important institution within the Group that funneled and filtered relevant research by various ministries and official think tanks into the Group's leadership. Taking an important position within the CLGFEA thus provided a vital link between the CLGFEA and the PBC. Another figure from the PBC who was influential was Yi Gang, deputy secretary-general of the PBC's MPC in 1997. As a U.S.-trained PhD in economics, Yi was in a position to forcefully put to Zhu the dominant Western economic approach to analyzing the AFC and China's exchange rate during this period. It should also be noted that the person in charge of SAFE under the PBC during the AFC was Zhou Xiaochuan, who took over governorship of the PBC from Dai Xianglong in 2002.

The initial decision not to devalue was made at the end of 1997. On January 16, 1998, PBC Governor Dai Xianglong announced in a press conference in Beijing that the value of the RMB would be maintained. One month later, on February 16, the PBC's deputy governor and chief of SAFE, Zhou Xiaochuan, reiterated this position at a meeting of SAFE regional bureau chiefs in Beijing, reassuring the delegates that China would not suffer the same fate as other Asian countries and the RMB would not be devalued (Y. He 1998, 2096). The formal announcement came from Zhu Rongji in a press conference during the Ninth National People's Congress on March 19, 1998, that the RMB would not be devalued (Liew and Wu 2007).

However, the severity of the AFC became apparent only toward the end of the first quarter of 1998, with exports growing at only 0.6% for the whole year (Lin and Schramm 2003, 261). The falling value of the yen in June put additional pressure on China's already beleaguered foreign trade sector. The PBC maintained that the substantial foreign reserves held at that time (close to US$150 billion), more stringent restrictions on capital outflows, and relatively solid economic fundamentals would ensure that China would live through the storm.[2] There had been mounting popular pressures for devaluation, but as a senior PBC official recalled,

> It was a hard time back then [in the summer of 1998]. . . . Much local opposition [to the non-devaluation policy] was channeled into the Beidaihe Conference in 1998. Some delegates even proposed a change of the PBC governorship. But make no mistake; the PBC was no longer the weak institution of several years ago. We couldn't afford another round of inflation at that time and I think we did the right thing [in arguing for maintaining the value of the yuan]. . . . [There was] no doubt that Premier Zhu was on our side, and Governor Dai also made the political case very compelling for President Jiang [that] a yuan devaluation could lead to a massive devaluation of the Hong Kong dollar, a big loss of face for the government, which had just taken over the administration of Hong Kong from the British. It was a clear victory that no major modification was made in exchange rate policy after the conference.[3]

The fact that the PBC was singled out for attack by the opposition again suggests that the Bank had played a key role in influencing exchange rate policy decisions by Zhu and hence the party leadership during the AFC. Although the non-devaluation policy was maintained, the leadership and the PBC took various measures to promote exports. For example, the government increased export rebate rates three times between August 1998 and July 1999, while the PBC urged commercial banks, through window guidance, to provide discount loans to support domestic exporters (Bowles and Wang 2008).

Dai was also a key supporter of Zhu's involvement in China's negotiations to enter the WTO. One of the critical issues of these talks had been the terms of China's financial opening, for which Dai, as the central bank governor, had a vital role in forging the internal consensus: "Governor Dai was Premier Zhu's top adviser in the negotiations. . . . Both met frequently during the sidelines of other meetings, and only Zhu's personal secretary was present when the two met, which is highly unusual in our government."[4] In the final stage of the bilateral talks with the United States, it was Dai who lent his full support to Zhu's concessions in financial market entry in exchange for a speedier accession for China, a difficult trade-off that Zhu had been hesitant about for nearly six months.[5]

Exchange Rate Policy since 2003

Beijing's decision in 1998 not to devalue the RMB had been rewarded with praise and compliments from a wide range of countries, from Asia Pacific leaders to the then U.S. president Bill Clinton, for having avoided further destabilization of the international economy amid the pandemic crisis. It was not long after this that China's exchange rate policy once again became headline news in the global media and the focus of debate in international conferences. This time, however, Beijing found itself embroiled in a storm of criticism not just from the Western countries led by the United States, but also from some of the emerging and even developing countries ("The Looming Revolution" 2004). As one MOF official said, "on exchange rate issues, we often face the embarrassment of one against nineteen in G20 meetings."[6] This issue was also part of the growing phenomenon of "global imbalances," which was widely seen later as underlying the dynamics of the global financial crisis (GFC).

The International Context

To be sure, there had been little change of China's exchange rate policy per se between 1997 and 2005—the RMB had been fixed at around 8.2 yuan per U.S. dollar. What had changed, however, was China's rapid rise to star status in global trade in the new century, which was further facilitated by its accession to the WTO in December 2001 (see Table 10.1 and Figure 10.1). China's

Table 10.1. China's balance of payments (US$ billion)

Item	Annual average 1998–2000	Annual average 2001–5
Increase of foreign reserve	8.5	139.6
Share in GDP (%)	0.8	8.8
Current account balance	23.7	65.9
Share in GDP (%)	2.3	4.2
Capital account balance	0.3	68.0
Share in GDP (%)	0.0	4.3
Net FDI	38.5	50.8
Share in GDP (%)	3.8	3.2
Non-FDI capital account balance	−53.6	23.0
Share in GDP (%)	−5.3	1.5

Source: Adapted from Liew and Wu (2007, 185).

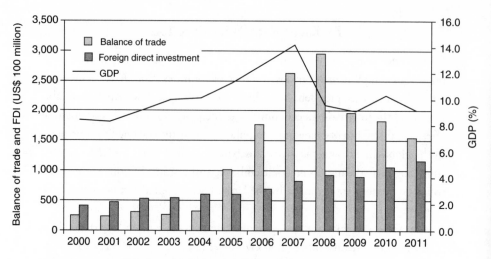

FIGURE 10.1. China's trade surplus and foreign direct investment, 2000–11 (US$100 million).

Source: Trade surplus figures are from the Ministry of Commerce; figures for foreign direct investment are from State Administration of Foreign Exchange.

trade experienced an explosive increase, and its shares of world merchandise imports and exports more than doubled, from 2.7% and 2.8% in 1994 to 5.9% and 6.5% in 2004, respectively. By 2009, China had become the largest exporter and the second largest importer in the world (WTO 2010). At the same time, China has also become a huge magnet for global FDI seeking a slice of the country's export boom. China has been a fixture in the top three FDI recipients in the world and the largest recipient among developing countries since 2000 (UNCTAD 2007). The acceleration in external trade and inflows of FDI in the new century, for an increasingly export-dependent country such as China, played a direct role in boosting its national economy. As a result, China overtook Japan as the second largest economy in the world by the second quarter of 2010, leading many to believe that the days for the United States as the world's number one economy are numbered.

As China grew into an elephant in the world economy, the valuation of its currency, the RMB, and its foreign exchange regime increasingly began to appear on the radar of international scrutiny. For developed economies that run large trade deficits with China, particularly the United States, and some developing countries whose industrial and export sectors are increasingly struggling against the often relentless "China Price," the undervaluation of the RMB under Beijing's sanction has been an important, if not critical, factor in explaining the meteoric strengthening of China's balance of payments accounts in recent years. Before Beijing became complacent about the shift from scarcity to overabundance, its foreign reserve holdings, piling up at record speeds, were a ready and pronounced symbol of an alleged "mercantilist" trade and foreign exchange practice by the Middle Kingdom. Indeed, China has been the largest holder of foreign reserves in the world since February 2006. The accumulation of foreign reserves has greatly accelerated since 2000, leading to a total figure of almost US$3.2 trillion at the end of 2011 (see Figure 10.2). To put the pace of accumulation in perspective, over the two years between 2005 and 2007, China's reserves increased by nearly US$500 million per day, or US$21 million per hour (Feng 2007b).

Consequently, an international debate has raged over whether and to what extent China's exchange rate may have been undervalued. A number of studies have attempted to answer these questions by estimating China's real "equilibrium" exchange rate. Drawing on different models, methodologies, explanatory variables, subjective judgments, and instability in underlying economic relationships, these studies have yielded a wide range of variation in terms of the deviation of RMB's exchange rate to its alleged equilibrium level. For example, while T. Wang (2004) suggests a small overvaluation of the RMB, Goldstein (2004a) sees an undervaluation of 15–30%, Frankel

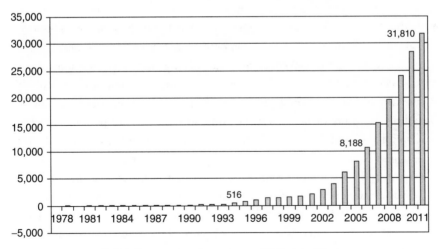

FIGURE 10.2. China's foreign reserves, 1978–2011 (US$100 million).

Source: National Bureau of Statistics of China, *China Statistical Yearbook,* various years.

(2004) of 36%, and Coudert and Couharde (2005) of almost 50% (in terms of purchasing power parity).[7] Despite the variations in the estimates, a general consensus is that the RMB has been undervalued. According to Liew and Wu (2007, 123), China's exports respond to the nominal weighted exchange rate, and depreciation of the RMB will increase its exports.[8] At the same time, an undervalued RMB also helps facilitate the inflow of FDI to China.

More profoundly, the RMB's exchange rate misalignment, while having a negative impact on domestic welfare, such as limiting China's consumption and hence living standards, also distorts international savings and investment flows and is central to any explanation of global imbalances (Makin 2009). Indeed, Beijing reinvested a majority (around 70%) of its foreign reserves back into the U.S. economy, which has helped reduce the yield on long-term U.S. Treasurys and similar assets below their equilibrium level, which is part of the explanation for Greenspan's (2005) conundrum concerning "the broadly unanticipated behavior of world bond markets." Ben Bernanke (2005) and others have referred to this phenomenon as a "global savings glut." The cheap credit that ensued from the flood of dollars held by sovereign investors, particularly China and Japan, is alleged to have formed a structural factor that helped fuel the U.S. subprime crisis (Ferguson 2008).

Nevertheless, before the outbreak of the subprime crisis and its subsequent pandemic into the GFC, major criticism of the RMB exchange rate revolved around the tightly managed yuan, which had created considerable friction with China's trading partners, who also argued that the more or less undervalued RMB awarded "unfair" competitive advantages for Chinese exporters. Serious international concerns about existing current account imbalances have been raised, most notably by Japan, the European Union, and particularly the United States. In the United States in particular, there has been a fierce political and policy debate on the issue on both sides of politics, between Capitol Hill and the White House, between "Dragon Slayers" and "Panda Huggers" among opinion leaders, and among a diverse range of industrial sectors and labor unions (Gifford 2010). This has spilled over into a wider public debate on how to deal with China as an emerging great power in the new century. Indeed, tensions have escalated into another nationwide mobilization on the China issue since 2001 when Washington was preoccupied with whether or not to grant China permanent normal trading relations status, which was essential in China's quest to enter the WTO, and which, in McGill's (2001) words, featured "empty but nevertheless noisy verbal fireworks." However, given record high (and still growing) trade deficits with China, Washington has made sure, through multilateral and bilateral engagements and facilitated by persistent pressure from Congress, that its signal to Beijing is unequivocally serious, clear, and (at times) credible, that Beijing has to revalue its currency and adopt a flexible exchange rate to avoid an all-out trade war with the United States, a vital export market for China.

A separate issue that is linked to RMB revaluation is the argument (particularly sanctioned by the IMF) for a discontinuation of the RMB-U.S. dollar peg with greater flexibility in the RMB exchange rate (IMF 2004). In fact, two-way traffic under a flexible RMB regime does not necessarily lead to appreciation. However, given China's persistent trade surplus, its rapid accumulation of foreign reserves, and international pressure for revaluation, the market saw the potential depegging as a synonym for appreciation, and politicians chose either of the phrases for their political convenience.

The Internal Dynamics

Like RMB exchange rate policymaking during the AFC, the international debate and political pressure on RMB revaluation has functioned as a direct pressure on Beijing to reform its foreign exchange regime. However, the decisions have to be made by the Chinese political leaders, who are also informed and thereby influenced by the push and pull of powerful economic ministries and domestic interests, according to their own preferences and agenda. In other words, and as usual, external pressures are strongly mediated by domestic institutions.

As discussed in Chapter 6, the change of leadership in 2003, from the Jiang-Zhu administration to the Hu-Wen administration, also led to a shift in emphasis from engaging the global economy to concerns over poverty and income inequality, embodied in regional and sectoral imbalances. Deng's strategy, followed by that of Jiang and Zhu, to develop export-oriented industries in the eastern coastal areas and to encourage entrepreneurship under the banner "to get rich is glorious," came with a cost. Development in agriculture and the inland western region has largely been stagnating compared with industry and the eastern coastal regions respectively. The increasing income gap has also rung the alarm. According to the World Bank (1997), China's Gini coefficient increased from 0.29 in the 1980s to 0.39 in the 1990s.[9] By 2009, according to some domestic estimates, the Gini coefficient rose to over 0.5 (Cong and Li 2010), becoming fertile ground for social instability. The central government, under Hu and Wen, has taken measures to reform the rural economy in a bid to raise the income of farmers, such as tax reductions, enhanced subsidies, and increased transfer payments. However, RMB revaluation would put considerable pressure on these efforts. Any appreciation will induce large imports of cheaper agricultural products from the rest of the world, lowering the price of agricultural products and therefore the income of Chinese farmers (Yi 2007).

Another grave concern of the Chinese leadership is unemployment. In Wen's policy proposal when he first became Chinese premier in 2003, how to solve unemployment was the first of "the three major economic problems." A revaluation of the RMB would have a seriously negative impact on export-oriented domestic enterprises, most of which are labor intensive, which would result in a rise in unemployment and again jeopardize social stability (Kaplan 2006).

Nevertheless, there are reasons for the new leadership to relax China's foreign exchange regime. First, as the limits of the otherwise successful export-oriented strategy emerge, the new administration has proposed a more balanced development model, which rests more on the promotion of domestic demand and consumption. Therefore, a pegged RMB, which served the previous development model well, may no longer be desirable for the new strategy. In fact, discontinuation of the dollar peg (and the associated revaluation) would encourage (or force) domestic industrial upgrading to acquire new competitive advantage. It would also help shift manufacturing capacity to the less developed inland areas as part of a cost reduction strategy and stimulate domestic consumption with the increased purchasing power of the domestic currency.

Macroeconomic stability, particularly inflation, has been another concern of the political leaders. Ronald McKinnon has been seen as an influential Western economist in China, and in a series of widely circulated essays (such as McKinnon and Schnabl 2004; McKinnon 2005a, 2005b) he warns that, although appreciation would make imports cheaper, demand in the tradable sector and inflow of foreign capital would also be reduced. The net effect, he argues, will be a domestic deflation and a near-zero interest rate trap, such as

Japan experienced from the late 1980s through the 1990s. However, the party leaders in Beijing are more comfortable dealing with deflation than with inflation. To them, the lessons from past experience are that deflation is somehow manageable, but, according to Chinese premier Wen Jiabao, inflation, in addition to corruption, has the capacity to topple the regime if not contained in a timely and effectively manner.[10] As we discuss later, China has already faced rising pressures of inflation under a pegged exchange rate regime; therefore it is in the interests of the Party for this reason at least to relax its currency regime.

Given these often contradictory preferences, the top leadership was hesitant to make a substantial move on this front. The international pressure did not help, either, since the leadership did not want to be seen to capitulate to foreign pressures on a critical policy issue such as the exchange rate, especially during the sensitive period immediately after the leadership transition. Indeed, given rising domestic sentiments of nationalism, largely sanctioned by the party-state, the top leaders have reiterated in public speeches that its main principle for its exchange rate policymaking is "independent initiative, controllability, and gradual progress" (Han 2005; Li 2010).

Institutional Dynamics

The major economic ministries that played an important role in China's foreign exchange rate policymaking during the AFC, namely the SDPC, MOFTEC, the MOF, and the PBC, have remained important players in this round of policy deliberations, albeit with divergent concerns and preferences.

The SDPC was restructured and reinvented as the National Development and Reform Commission (NDRC) in 2003 with greater responsibility and power in the bureaucracy in overseeing China's economic development. Apart from its traditional planning and policy research functions, one of the main functions of the NDRC in relation to exchange rate is to "control and monitor the total size of China's foreign debts . . . and maintain the balance of international payments" (NDRC 2006). The NDRC also has an Office of Policy Studies that aims to "organize studies on issues concerning economic and social development, reform and opening-up, and the international economy" (NDRC 2006). Therefore, the NDRC is able to stamp its influence on macroeconomic policymaking through its research into the social and political impacts of macroeconomic policy. As the leadership's policy priority shifted to addressing poverty and inequality, particularly rural poverty, the NDRC shared a similar concern in this regard, as any appreciation of the RMB was considered to disadvantage agriculture and farmers and to undo some of the efforts by the leadership for poverty reduction since 2004.

In recent years, the MOF's concern in relation to RMB revaluation has been its implication regarding the repayment of a considerable amount of money it has lent to local governments, which had reached US$17.4 billion by the middle of 2005 (Liew and Wu 2007, 205). The majority of the loans were used to settle the accounts of the customers of underperforming local financial institutions that the PBC had shut down. Given an already strained local budget (Yu 2005), RMB appreciation would lower prices and increase real interest rates, so that most of the poor counties would struggle to repay MOF loans since most of them rely on agriculture, which is affected negatively by a higher RMB.[11] At the same time, the MOF itself has overseen a series of budgetary deficits since 1996 with increasing commitments to support exports (during the AFC) and agriculture (since 2003). Therefore, it would prefer that these fiscal burdens be alleviated through exchange rate (devaluation) rather than through increased fiscal expenditures (Bowles and Wang 2008; Yang 2000). Alternatively, from the MOF's point of view, reducing or abolishing export rebates could reduce pressure on the state budget and pressure on RMB revaluation (without disadvantaging agriculture).[12] In regard to exchange rate flexibility, as a competitor with the PBC for policy influence, the MOF favors continuation of the RMB-U.S. dollar peg. A pegged regime potentially makes the MOF more influential vis-à-vis the PBC in determining macroeconomic policy since fiscal policy is more effective than monetary policy under a stable exchange rate in the presence of international capital mobility (Fleming 1962; Mundell 1963).

The Ministry of Commerce (MOFCOM) succeeded MOFTEC and merged with the former Ministry of Commerce into a megaministry mandated to oversee both domestic and foreign trade and investment. In terms of trade, the nontradable and import-competing sectors would favor a flexible exchange rate while the tradable and export sectors would favor a fixed rate. MOFCOM thus incorporates a much more diverse and more or less inherently contradictory set of interests in relation to the RMB exchange rate. Given the fact that the export sector remains a vital engine for the Chinese economy, MOFCOM has to support exports, and the RMB revaluation would have significant negative impact on exports and export enterprises. For Chinese exporters, a revaluation would increase their direct costs of goods sold, which would decrease their gross and operating margins if they were unable to pass the higher costs along into final prices. It was reported that if the RMB were to rise by 3–5% in 2005 against the U.S. dollar, the growth rate of China's exports might drop to 10% or below; a rise of 15% or more might cause export growth to go into decline.[13] It was not surprising that Bo Xilai, then minister of MOFCOM, stated that RMB appreciation could put many Chinese enterprises "in a difficult position" ("How Will RMB Exchange Rate Affect Trade?" 2006). Hence, MOFCOM was strongly against a large appreciation but could tolerate a gradual move to a more flexible exchange rate regime, which was believed to optimize China's import and export structure in the long term.

The Haunting Trilemma

So far in our discussion, all the major economic ministries except the PBC have been lukewarm at best, if not negative, on the issue of RMB depegging and revaluation. However, it has been the utmost concern of the PBC to liberalize the exchange rate regime primarily to gain greater monetary policy discretion. In this contest, the PBC was a critical player behind Beijing's move in 2005 to discontinue the RMB's dollar peg.

As discussed earlier, as an emerging market and increasingly open economy, China has been subject to the structural constraints posed by the policy trilemma, also known as the "impossible trinity." Two economists, Mundell (1963) and Fleming (1962), developed a model of international economics which posits that a country can achieve only two of the following three objectives at the same time: a fixed exchange rate, free capital movement, and an independent monetary policy. It thus implies that in an open economy (with limited capital control), a country that runs a pegged currency regime has no ability to set its nominal interest rate, and hence no independent monetary policy. In other words, the only way that the country could have both a fixed exchange rate and an independent monetary policy is if it can prevent arbitrage in the foreign exchange rate market from taking place and institutes capital controls on international transactions.

Capital controls prevent money from moving in and out of an economy easily, which can more or less insulate domestic monetary policy. To be sure, China's capital account is not open and cross-border capital is subject to a myriad of control measures. In the first reform era, China encouraged FDI (leading to current account convertibility in 1996) while other inflows and capital outflows were under heavy control (Lardy 1992b). Although in recent years China has sought to gradually liberalize controls on non-FDI capital flows, evidence suggests that the remaining capital account controls are indeed leaky and porous, given a diverse range of channels for foreign economic and financial exchanges as China steadily integrates with the global market (Glick and Hutchison 2008; Ma and McCaulty 2007). Most of the non-FDI capital inflows can be categorized as hot money that could potentially flow in and out of a country within a short time horizon.[14] According to Glick and Hutchison (2008), non-FDI inflows swung from an average of minus US$54 billion in 1998–2000 (outflows reflecting depreciation pressure on the RMB immediately after the AFC), to plus US$24 billion in 2001–4 (inflows due to lowered U.S. Fed interest rates, relatively stable Chinese interest rates, and RMB appreciation expectations) (see Figure 10.3). This turnaround of US$78 billion far exceeded the increase in the average current account surplus by US$18 billion over the same period. In addition, the development of the nondeliverable forward market of the RMB also facilitated the penetration of China's capital controls and international speculation on RMB appreciation (Fung et al. 2004; Huang and Sun 2007).

Therefore, given increasingly loosened capital control, the Chinese monetary authority has been left with a difficult choice between a fixed exchange

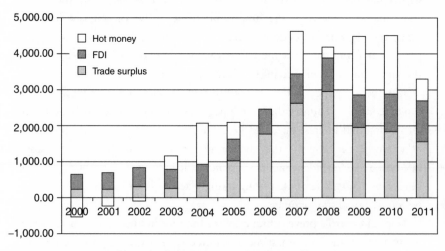

FIGURE 10.3. Hot money inflows, 2000–2011 (US$100 million).

Note: The figures for hot money are calculated in broad terms, that is, hot money = net increase of foreign reserve – trade surplus – FDI.

Source: National Bureau of Statistics of China, *China Statistical Yearbook,* various years.

rate and autonomy in interest rate setting, the latter being a central tool in fighting inflation. In fact, the ever-increasing supply of foreign exchange created a huge new dilemma for China's monetary authorities after the exchange rate unification in 1994. With the overriding policy target of a stable RMB exchange rate, which dictated that the RMB be virtually pegged to the U.S. dollar, the PBC's ability to control the money supply and hence to conduct domestic monetary policy has been circumscribed.

Since the PBC has had to buy all excess foreign exchange in the interbank market with RMB to stabilize the RMB's value, this is equivalent to the central bank issuing base money into the domestic economy. In making these purchases, the PBC typically credits the reserve accounts of commercial banks with an equivalent amount of RMB. Therefore, a substantial increase in the supply of foreign exchange translates into a corresponding increase in the domestic money supply. There has thus been a structural change in the PBC's monetary base since the 1994 unification. In 1990–93, the ratio of funds outstanding for foreign exchange (PBC's foreign exchange purchases in RMB, or *waihui zhankuan*) to the PBC's reserve money was less than 10% on average. However, this more than doubled to 25% in 1994 and increased further to around 44% between 1997 and 2002. In February 2005 it first jumped over 100% and has been hovering above that mark since then (see Figure 10.4). The significant increase in the foreign exchange component in the PBC's

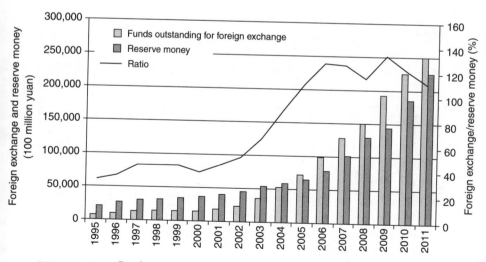

FIGURE 10.4. Funds outstanding for foreign exchange/reserve money, 1995–2011.
Source: PBC Annual Reports [Zhongguo renmin yinhang nianbao], various years.

monetary base suggests that the capacity of the PBC to control money supply, one of the key target variables, has been weakened if not paralyzed over the years, since this part of the reserve money represents the PBC's passive purchase of foreign exchange and therefore is largely beyond its control under the imperative of a fixed exchange rate.

An Unsustainable Sterilization

The massive buildup of money supply (in the form of M2) in the domestic market due to passive purchases of foreign exchange has thus caused serious inflationary pressures for the PBC (see Figure 10.5). To keep a lid on inflation, the PBC needs to subsequently remove liquidity from the banking system after its intervention in the foreign exchange market. This process is called "sterilization," with the aim being to equalize foreign and domestic asset transactions in opposite directions to nullify the impact of their foreign exchange operations on the domestic money supply (Y. Wu 2006). To be sure, some Asian central banks have routinely conducted such sterilization operations over the past two or three decades (Greenwood 2008), and the PBC has learned the relevant techniques from these experiences. However, the scale of the Chinese operations has been unprecedented. However, the hierarchical nature of the Chinese

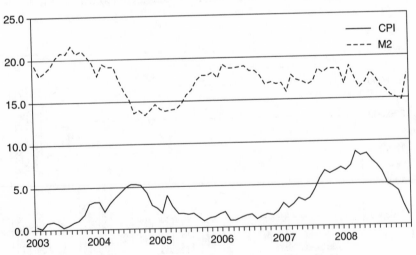

FIGURE 10.5. Money supply and CPI, 2003–8 (percentage growth rate on same period the previous year).

Source: PBC Research Bureau, *Almanac of China's Finance and Banking,* various years.

system and the economic transition awards the Bank more room for discretion in regard to the tools that it can utilize, in the form of an ad hoc combination of both administrative and indirect instruments in withdrawing liquidity from the market. This represents yet another case of the discretionary capacities of the PBC. For example, the shallow depth of the emerging bond market in the early 1990s used to hinder the PBC's open market operations. In the face of a flood of liquidity in the immediate aftermath of the 1994 unification, the PBC employed administrative means in a bid to offset inflationary impacts, such as recalling loans from the commercial banks as well as requiring the banks to increase their ad hoc deposits with the PBC.

In the new century, with the development of domestic financial markets and the increasing sophistication of the PBC's expertise, the Bank resorted to more market-oriented instruments to prevent a buildup of liquidity in the system while at the same time retaining the advantages of administrative leverage. Since 2002, the PBC has been mainly using two instruments in its sterilization interventions. One is to raise reserve requirements against deposits in commercial banks. A study by Yi Gang (2008), the then assistant governor of the PBC, suggests that from 2003 to 2007, by increasing the required reserve ratio fifteen times at a total of 8.5 percentage points, the PBC managed to mop up about 3.4 trillion RMB from the market.

The other means has been to issue RMB-denominated bills and bonds to the banks and other financial institutions. Given the relatively small scale of the treasury bond market in China in the early 2000s, the PBC decided to innovatively issue its own bonds, or PBC bills (yanghang piaoju), beginning in September 2002. These bills are auctioned to commercial banks at interest rates set by the PBC but can also be traded in the interbank market at market-determined rates (Y. Wu 2006). Facing a similar problem, the Indian central bank, the Reserve Bank of India, followed the PBC's innovation by issuing so-called Market Stabilization Scheme bonds in 2004 (Patnaik 2007). As of June 2011 the level of reserve requirements was 16.5% of bank deposits, while the value of the PBC bills had reached 10% of bank deposits. This means no less than 26.5% of Chinese commercial banks' deposits have been immobilized by the central bank.

The PBC's reliance on bank reserves and bond issuance in sterilization is clearly reflected in its balance sheet. Table 10.2 compares the Bank's position at the end of 2000 and 2011. First of all, the amount of foreign assets, most of which consist of the foreign exchange the Bank purchased from the foreign exchange market, has skyrocketed from 1.56 trillion yuan in 2000 to a whopping 23.79 trillion yuan. On the liability side, the outstanding PBC bills stood at 2.33 trillion yuan at the end of 2011, while bank reserves ballooned more than ten times during this period, from 1.6 trillion yuan to 16.88 trillion, as the Bank increased the requirement ratio over the years.

Since May 2006 the PBC has further refined the instrument by means of a "targeted issue" scheme in addition to selling through an auction. The targeted issue scheme forces specific targeted commercial banks to underwrite PBC bills at a yield lower than prevailing market rates (dingxiang zengfa, zhiding goumai).[15] The inclusion of the banks in the scheme (mainly the four dominant state banks) and the amount of the forced purchase has been at the discretion of the PBC.[16] This more flexible, sophisticated, but administrative approach is unlikely to be adopted in Western systems, but it nevertheless enabled the Bank to adjust overall liquidity management in the market as well as differential liquidity positions among the banks. By the end of 2011, outstanding PBC bills totaled 2.3 trillion RMB.

Although the massive scale of such sterilization could more or less delay inflation (or real exchange rate adjustment), it also comes with financial, economic, and structural costs. First, as interest-bearing bonds, the PBC bills incur financial costs for the central bank, especially under the sheer scale of the PBC's practice. Ljungwall et al. (2009) argue that up until 2008, the PBC was capable of carrying out effective monetary policy while keeping the exchange rate fixed at the same time, largely because of the relatively low cost of

Table 10.2.   PBC's balance sheet in 2000 and 2011 compared (RMB trillion)

Assets	2000	2011	Liabilities	2000	2011
Foreign assets	1.56	23.79	Currency issue	1.59	5.59
Claims on financial entities	2.22	2.09	Deposit reserves	1.60	16.88
Claims on government	0.16	1.54	Bond issue	0	2.33
Other assets	0	0.68	Other liabilities	0.75	3.30
Total assets	3.94	28.10	Total liabilities	3.94	28.10

Source: People's Bank of China. Figures for 2000 are from http://www.pbc.gov.cn/publish/html/2000-S2c.htm, those for 2011 are from http://www.pbc.gov.cn/publish/html/2011s04.htm.

Note: Deposit reserves in 2011 refers to the deposits of domestic financial institutions, but does not include deposits of financial corporations excluded from reserve money and the PBC's foreign liabilities (deposits of overseas financial institutions).

its sterilization operations, thanks to a high domestic savings rate under financial repression. According to their estimate, the PBC retained positive gains for every single year between 2000 and 2008 despite the explosive accumulation of foreign reserves during that period. Nevertheless, after a series of domestic interest rate hikes, the PBC's offset operations began to incur a net loss for the Bank. As of July 2011, for example, the PBC pays interest of 1.62% on required reserves. The yield on the one-year PBC bill is 3.5%. The equivalent U.S. Treasury bond—the instrument in which the bulk of the reserves are invested—is only 0.2% (Jones 2011). Even if the central bank had only soaked up three-fifths (insiders estimate four-fifths; see discussions below) of the base money created and used only reserve requirements, then that would still amount to an annual bill of 223 billion yuan (US$34.5 billion). The cost of using just the PBC bills comes in at 482 billion yuan (US$74.6 billion). These are against a payout of mere US$6.4 billion if it invested its entire stockpile in one-year U.S. Treasurys. And this is without taking into consideration the RMB's appreciation against the dollar (Jones 2011). Another perspective is the volume of interest the PBC has to pay. In the eight years between 2003 and 2011, the central bank paid nearly 1 trillion yuan in interest. As a result, more than half of the money raised by issuing PBC bills every year is used to pay the interest and principal due on maturing bills (Feng 2011). Although the PBC's net losses will eventually be written off by the state budget, such exposures could undermine its policy capacity.

The sterilization operations also distort interest rates and the asset portfolio of Chinese commercial banks. The PBC has to keep the interest rates of the bills at higher levels than their equilibrium levels to ensure clearance at auctions. At the same time, the banks are compelled (by higher reserve requirements) or induced (by purchase of PBC bills) to lend money back to the central bank, thus crowding out bank credits for their normal customers, firms and individuals. Most importantly, keeping an undervalued RMB tends to encourage the overexpansion of the export sector, contradictory to a wide consensus that China should develop a more consumption-based, domestically driven economy. In other words, sterilization could stabilize the Chinese economy for a while, but it is "no more than a temporary palliative, buying financial stability at the cost of real distortions" (Greenwood 2008, 216).

Certain studies argue that there is full monetary sterilization in China (see, e.g., Burdekin and Siklos 2008; Ouyang and Rajan 2005). However, despite the PBC's efforts, Ying Wu (2006) finds that sterilization in China falls short of being effective in neutralizing the expansionary impact of foreign exchange reserve accumulation. Based on the evidence of macroeconomic data and the empirical analysis of monetary aggregates, Wu suggests that sterilization applies effectively to only about two-fifths of the inflow of foreign exchange reserves. In an internal seminar at Peking University, Yi Gang, deputy governor of the PBC and head of SAFE, revealed that the PBC had released a gargantuan RMB20 trillion in exchange for its foreign reserve, which stands at US$3.18 trillion, by the end of 2010. The PBC has managed to sterilize about 80%, or RMB16 trillion of the total release through the PBC bills (Zhou 2011).

The New Regime

Beijing's announcement of the abolishment of the RMB's peg to the U.S. dollar as well as a one-off appreciation (albeit a modest 2.1%) caught many observers off guard, but for the political and policy insiders it marked a new era of foreign exchange management or, more generally, a new era of China's monetary and macroeconomic management. The road leading to the announcement was in fact marked by secret diplomacy, intensive internal and external bargaining, and adept maneuvers on the part of the PBC to push the reform.

International pressures for RMB revaluation, particularly those from the United States, had both propelled and hindered the process.[17] On one hand, domestic reformers, such as those in the PBC, utilized such external pressure to push for their reform agenda; on the other hand, as discussed above, these highly publicized criticisms limited the freedom of the Chinese leadership, who feared losing face in a potential nationalist reaction. Recognizing this, the Bush administration stepped up its quiet diplomatic talks at ministerial levels while the Congress had been increasingly wary of China's currency policy. U.S. Treasury Secretary John Snow conducted a series of shuttle visits to China starting in September 2003, meeting officials from the PBC, the MOF, and a range of political and business leaders in China. The messages conveyed back to Washington were mixed; Beijing was considering a reform, but would not proceed, or appear to proceed, on the timing and terms of "external forces."

By early 2005, the U.S. Congress lost its patience. On April 6, Congress lent support for a bipartisan amendment initiated by Sen. Charles Schumer, a New York Democrat, and Sen. Lindsey Graham, a South Carolina Republican, that would impose 27.5% tariff on all Chinese imports if Beijing didn't agree to revalue its currency. The overwhelming vote of support for the anti-China legislation surprised the Bush administration. On May 19, Mr. Snow appointed a special envoy to China on the currency issue, Olin Wethington, who made three unpublicized, weeklong trips to Beijing during the next seven weeks. The make-or-break message from Washington was made clear to the Chinese, who also made it clear that Beijing would not budge under foreign pressure. So on June 30, Fed Chairman Alan Greenspan and Secretary Snow went up to Capitol Hill for a highly staged closed-door session with senators Schumer and Graham. The senators announced after the meeting that they were delaying any vote on the amendment until after the August recess. Thus, with implicit cooperation by the White House and Congress, Beijing was able to make the final move on July 21, which was officially telegraphed to Washington hours before the rest of the world got the news from the Chinese media.

Apart from the high-politics diplomacy, the internal dynamics featuring a PBC-led campaign for reform were equally intensive and dramatic. The PBC, under the governorship of Zhou Xiaochuan (since December 2002) has played a key role behind Beijing's exchange rate reform. Zhou has been a staunch liberal economist and has worked in various key positions in China's financial sector, including head of SAFE (in charge of China's foreign exchange management under the PBC) between 1995 and 1998. Back in the 1990s, Zhou argued in a number of authored and coauthored books (Zhou et al. 1993; Zhou and Yang 1996; Zhou 1999b) that while the pegged regime was instrumental in promoting China's exports, it nonetheless has hampered the structural shift and sustainable development of the Chinese economy. As we have seen in Chapter 6, his expertise in monetary economics, coupled with his personal ties with successive leaders including Jiang, Zhu, and Wen, as well as his extensive connections with international central banking and finance, ensured that the PBC stands out in the policy circle. At the same time, the PBC's clash with the NDRC in the 2003–4 episode of monetary tightening led the latter to concede considerable authority to the PBC in Beijing's macroeconomic management (Chapter 9).

Another key figure from the PBC in China's foreign exchange rate policy-making is Yi Gang, who replaced Dai Genyou as director of the PBC's Monetary Policy Department in 2003 and was later promoted to assistant PBC governor in July 2004, and who was in charge of the substantial initiatives associated with the exchange rate reform. He was further promoted to vice governor of the PBC in December 2007 and to the head of SAFE in July 2009. A monetary economist with a PhD from the United States, Yi tends to take a liberal view on the exchange rate policy, which is reflected in his academic writings (Yi 2000, 2008; Yi and Tang 2001). In particular, Yi (2008, 189) argues, "A large economy like China cannot give up the independence of monetary policy. Therefore, China has to choose between a fixed exchange rate and the free flow of capital; in a sense, it has to choose between stability and efficiency. Over the long run, China is bound to have a free flow of capital and a floating exchange rate regime."

One of the major approaches of the PBC in persuading the leadership to relax the foreign exchange regime was to use the economic situation to argue for reform. The partial and incomplete sterilization and the inflow of foreign exchange and capital created inflationary pressure that the PBC has been struggling to reign in since 2003. In internal debate, the PBC pointed to the fact that its de facto exchange rate targeting regime could not be sustainable without leading to domestic inflation. The PBC managed to persuade top decision makers to increase interest rates in September 2004. However, this was not enough to contain the inflationary expansion. Driven by strong foreign capital inflow in anticipation of a possible RMB revaluation, the money supply measured as M2 grew by 14% from March 2004 to March 2005, which in turn had caused bank credits to expand by 11%. Although CPI was reduced to below 3% by early 2005 after peaking at 5.3% in July and August 2004, the PBC argued that irrational exuberance in the asset sector, if not contained properly and promptly, would cause inflation on a larger scale. The PBC has been attacking asset inflation bubbles since 2003 amid fierce resistance in the bureaucracy and the real estate sector (see Chapter 9). As property development is highly sensitive to bank loans in China, the flood of credit during this period triggered asset price inflation characterized by increases of nearly 10% the in residential property price index and 8% in the land rent price index, which created latent inflation risks (Y. Wu 2006). Therefore, the prospect of an emerging spiraling inflation provided the PBC an ideal context to argue for exchange rate reform and RMB revaluation in a bid to achieve greater monetary policy independence.

Various leads from our interviews suggest that a blueprint for reform was initiated in early 2003 after Zhou took over the PBC's governorship. Given the significance of exchange rate reform, the PBC took a very cautious approach and went to great lengths in making the necessary institutional and technical preparations. In the spring of 2003, the People's Bank stepped up its study of China's peg to the dollar and the implications of a potential shift to a new regime. It held staff seminars on exchange rate and macroeconomic management, and invited leading U.S. economists to Beijing to present their views. The central bank also sent officials to the Hong Kong Monetary Authority, the city's central bank, and the U.S. Federal Reserve for training. Between 2004 and 2005, the PBC was quietly stepping up its meetings with officials at the Monetary Authority of Singapore, the city-state's central bank, which is renowned for running a relatively successful managed float regime for decades and for the countercyclical nature of its exchange rate policy (Khor et al. 2007). Later, China's central bankers sent midlevel staff for extended visits to Singapore to learn how it managed its exchange rate regime.

With the help of Zhou's close colleague Guo Shuqing, then chief director of SAFE (administered by the PBC), a draft of the reform plan was finished in mid-2004.[18] It then took the PBC over a year to optimize the plan by adding emergency options, to coordinate, bargain, and reach consensus with other related institutions, and for the political leadership to give the green light and wait for an appropriate time. During this time, the PBC organized a series of conferences and symposiums. The most influential one was a joint conference on the issue of RMB by the PBC and the IMF at Dalian on May 26, 2004. The IMF had also been pushing Beijing for a transition to a basket-based regime. Almost all the senior officials from the PBC's management team in areas of monetary policy, exchange rate policy, and financial markets, as well as a number of internationally renowned experts and IMF officials, attended the meeting (Y. Li 2005). Zhou and his deputies listened to the arguments, both for and against a revaluation. For example, Stanford University's Ronald McKinnon and Columbia University's Nobel Prize-winner Robert Mundell saw no compelling case for depegging, while Harvard University's Jeffrey Frankel and Morris Goldstein of the Institute for International Economics in Washington supported reform, but warned that a crawling revaluation (appreciation in small incremental steps) could inflame speculation for more appreciation, which should be factored into the reform package. At the end of the conference, a senior Chinese central banker reportedly stood up and said China planned to follow Prof. Mundell's advice in the short term and Prof. Goldstein's advice in the long term, "only we're not going to tell you how long the short term will be" (Areddy et al. 2005).

At the same time, the PBC also endeavored to weather domestic debate. As the RMB became one of the central issues in macroeconomic management at that time, the related ministries all tried to swing the leadership and the public by issuing research reports through their think tanks. The PBC's moves on this front were the most notable, as it commissioned and published articles on the platforms (newspapers, magazines, and journals) under its sponsorship, such as *Jinrong shibao* (Financial News) and *Jinrong yanjiu* (Financial Research), as well as influential finance and economic magazines such as *Caijing*, featuring articles that conformed to the Bank's argument for revaluation. The PBC originally proposed a revaluation between 4.5% and 5%.[19] The leadership eventually played it safe in the face of fears about the implications for the country's exports and reduced the scale to 2.1% (Areddy et al. 2005).

As it turned out, the Chinese term of following Mundell's peg-as-usual advice was indeed "short." A little over a year later, on July 21, 2005, the PBC, after approval by the State Council, announced that the dollar peg regime would be replaced by a managed floating system with the RMB linked to a basket of currencies and permitted to fluctuate within a narrow band on a daily basis defined by the central bank.[20] At the same time, the RMB appreciated by 2.1% against the U.S. dollar. PBC Governor Zhou (2005) later revealed that the composition of its currency basket was dominated by the U.S. dollar, euro, Japanese yen, and South Korean won, with a smaller proportion made up of the British pound, Thai baht, Russian ruble, Australian dollar, Canadian dollar, and Singapore dollar. However, the weight of these currencies within the basket remained unspecified.

Every day, the PBC sets a new reference trading spot rate, the central parity rate, for the RMB exchange rate against the U.S. dollar. Before January 4, 2006, the central parity rate was announced by the PBC at the market close on each of the five days of the trading week and the announced rate was used for trading the following business day. On January 4, 2006, a more market-driven price mechanism was introduced to set the central parity rate. The PBC authorized the China Foreign Exchange Trading System to announce the central parity rate of the RMB early in the morning of each business day, which takes into account a number of market factors and conditions in the formation of the central parity rate (Pauwels and Liu 2011). Initially, the intraday fluctuation of the RMB exchange rate against the U.S. dollar was within a tightly controlled range of ±0.3%. The band was subsequently widened to ±0.5% on May 18, 2007.

Notwithstanding the associated appreciation, the 2005 exchange rate reform seems a small step in the liberalization of the foreign exchange rate. In fact it is a big step for China's macroeconomic management and a great achievement for the PBC, especially given the mounting political obstacles, especially concerns with revaluation-induced unemployment, and the various negative concerns by other economic ministries. The PBC managed to utilize international pressures as well as domestic inflationary pressures to initiate its own strategies and plans based on its institutional expertise, and to substantiate the strategies and plans into concrete, credible, and operationalized policy recommendations by coordinating among and bargaining with other economic ministries to establish a bureaucratic consensus. It has also weathered domestic policy debate and helped align this with its own preferences. Most importantly, it has swung support from the top leadership to approve its initiatives. In other words, the PBC was "pivotal" in forging a consensus for the landmark revaluation of the yuan in 2005 (Yao 2011). Zhou was subsequently dubbed "Mr. RMB" by the international media for his and the PBC's critical role in China's exchange rate debate.

The reform package, the purpose of which was "giving full play to the market's basic role in resources allocation," was inevitably a compromise, falling short of a radical overhaul of the pegged regime into a free-floating system ("PBOC on Reforming RMB" 2005). However, taking into account the hierarchical nature of the political regime and the political priority accorded to growth and employment, the 2005 reform represents an achievement by an increasingly authoritative and confident PBC, and a compromise regarding China's export-oriented development model.

Nevertheless, as the Chinese authorities had been warned, a revaluation of the RMB at a crawling pace against the U.S. dollar after 2005 only fueled international speculation on yet more RMB appreciation. This has been evidenced by a continuous surge of hot money into China, which can be generally calculated by the difference between the net inflow of foreign capital and China's current and capital accounts surpluses. As a result, after a relatively quiet period of low inflation in 2005 and 2006, headline inflation crept back above the 3% mark in March 2007 and peaked at 8.7% by February 2008. There was also a surge of asset prices during this period (see Chapter 9). The PBC painstakingly tightened monetary policy, raising interest rates nine times between 2004 and September 2008. In 2007 alone, the PBC raised interest rates six times. In addition, the Bank also resorted to raising required reserve ratios, with twenty-one such hikes, lifting the ratio from 7.5% to 17.5% during this period (see Figure 10.6). Despite these efforts aimed at withdrawing excess liquidity from the market through sterilization, the Bank struggled to put a lid on inflation, which was further strengthened by shocks in

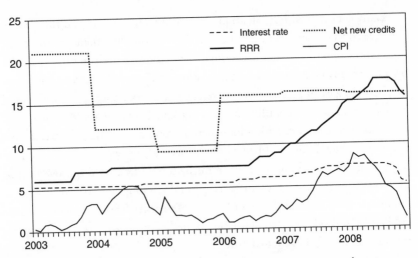

FIGURE 10.6. Monetary policy instruments and CPI (percentage growth rate on same period the previous year).

Note: Interest rate is based on the PBC's one-year benchmark lending rate.
Source: PBC Research Bureau, *Almanac of China's Finance and Banking,* various years.

food (such as pork) supply. Beijing's overconservative approach on RMB re-valuation has taken its toll in the PBC's monetary policy. The RMB in effect appreciated 20% against the U.S. dollar between July 2005 and July 2008 before the onslaught of the GFC.[21]

In the face of the GFC, however, the PBC has switched back to a de facto peg to the U.S. dollar since July 2008 to support a recovery in exports as part of Beijing's overall stimulation program. Nevertheless, as China's exports picked up speed and a balance of payments surplus reemerged in 2010, the PBC prepared for an early exit from a loose monetary policy and the dollar peg. Despite a vocal Ministry of Commerce that supported a "stable" RMB, Governor Zhou proclaimed in a high-profile press conference during the National People's Congress in March 2010 that the dollar peg was largely "an emergency anti-crisis policy" that "sooner or later will be withdrawn" (Dyer and Anderlini 2010). Meanwhile, Zhou's deputy, Hu Xiaolian, at the same time attempted to deconstruct the myth of the damaging impact of revaluation on China's foreign trade. In a rare high-profile media interview, Hu suggested that "between 2006 and 2008 [after the 2005 revaluation], China's exports increased by 23.4% annually, while imports increased by 19.7%, representing a golden age of foreign trade development. Looked at retrospectively, we can say that some have overestimated the negative impact of foreign exchange reform while underestimating the adaptive capacities of Chinese enterprises" (Ye et al. 2010).

As it turned out, after the State Council took severe measures to curb sky-rocketing housing prices in April 2010 (see Chapter 9), a gradually rising CPI compelled the Bank to resort to the exchange rate again to stem the formation of inflation expectations. On June 19, 2010, the PBC announced a switch back to its precrisis reference to a basket of currencies and to make the RMB more flexible, but ruled out a one-off appreciation like the 2005 reform. This "back-on-track" movement was interpreted as Beijing's bid to avoid international criticism of its exchange rate policy at an upcoming Group of 20 conference in Toronto, in which the RMB valuation was expected to be a major agenda item. It also represents the PBC's efforts to reign in emerging public infla-tion expectations given the record bank lending in 2009, and the interna-tional pressure facilitating the abandonment of the dollar peg in the after-math of the crisis. According to an estimate by Hongkong and Shanghai Banking Corporation, after the 2005 reform, the RMB rose in value by about 30% by the end of 2011 (see Figures 10.7 and 10.8). During this time, the PBC

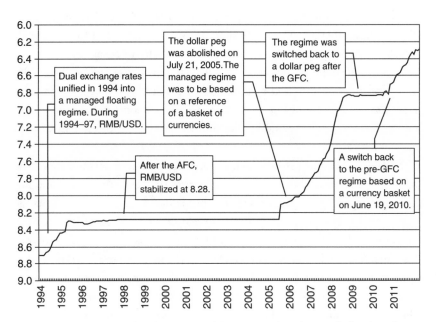

FIGURE 10.7. Nominal exchange rate of the RMB and evolution of China's exchange rate regime, 1994–2011 (RMB/US$).

Note: Nominal exchange rate is based on spot, monthly average figures.

Source: "Statistics" section on SAFE's Web site, http://www.safe.gov.cn; PBC (2008c).

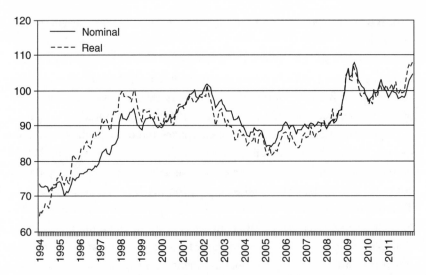

FIGURE 10.8. Nominal and real effective exchange rate of the RMB, 1994–2011.

Note: Monthly averages; 2010 = 100; broad indices; real effective exchange rate is based on CPI.
Source: BIS effective exchange rate indices (Broad Indices), Bank of International Settlement.

also beefed up its institutional capacity for dealing with exchange rate policies. In November 2009, it established the Monetary Policy Department II, which is in charge of exchange rate policy and the internationalization of the RMB. The department reports to Hu Xiaolian, vice governor of the PBC and the former head of SAFE (Li 2009a). The name of the department suggests the PBC's recognition of the intertwined relationship between monetary policy and exchange rate policy and the latter's importance in China's current context.

At the same time, Chinese central bankers have also taken note of the more or less successful experiences of countries such as Chile, Israel, and Poland that began with a pegged rate and then added flexibility to the exchange rate regime over time.[22] Some recent developments have also alleviated the pressure for RMB appreciation. In particular, China's balance of trade has been increasingly balanced. The share of trade surplus in the GDP peaked at 7.6% in 2007 but has since declined because of a slump in external demand, reaching 2% in 2011. China's current account surplus as a share of GDP has also declined from its peak of 10.1% in 2007 to a low of 2.8% in 2011 (Y. Li 2012). At the same time, China's terms of trade have also worsened in the postcrisis era. With a surge in import prices (given rising demand as a result of the stimulus program) and a stagnation of export prices, China's terms of trade dropped from 100 in June 2006 to 88.5 in December 2011 (Shen 2012). In addition, wages in China have also been on the rise, with local governments racing to boost minimum wages, "an annual ritual" in recent years. As a result, minimum wages rose nationwide by 22% on average over 2010 and 2011 (Tsui and Rabinovitch 2012).

Thus, the falling trade surplus, the deterioration of terms of trade, and rising labor costs have increased the RMB's real effective exchange rate, leading more observers, as well as policymakers, to conclude that the RMB's value is now approaching the equilibrium level. The PBC seized this opportunity to further increase the flexibility of the foreign exchange regime. On April 14, 2012, the PBC announced that the RMB's daily trading band against the U.S. dollar would be widened from the previous 0.5% to 1% above and below central parity, the daily reference exchange rate. For the IMF (2012), this is an "important step by the People's Bank of China to increase the flexibility of their currency. This underlines China's commitment to rebalance its economy toward domestic consumption and allow market forces to play a greater role in determining the level of exchange rates." Less than a week later, SAFE decreed on April 19, 2012, that it would end a six-year ban and allow small banks to hold overnight long positions in the RMB. This means these banks are now able to hold short positions in foreign currencies. By allowing even unsophisticated local institutions to assume greater currency risks, Chinese policymakers and the PBC are showing more confidence about the RMB's valuation. This is also likely part of a wider strategy of the internationalization of the RMB (Noble 2012). These developments also demonstrate the PBC's commitment to the reform of the exchange regime and the Bank's desire to establish credibility in the market, underlining the real meaning of a more flexible exchange regime, that depegging to the dollar does not necessarily mean appreciation in the short term.

A Three-Trillion-Dollar Question

Apart from exchange rate policy, another important mandate and authority of the PBC has been the management of China's foreign reserves. This was not a big issue in the 1980s and 1990s when China's foreign reserve holdings were relatively small. As discussed above, however, the pace of reserve accumulation greatly accelerated after the AFC, particularly after 2002.

There would be no foreign exchange reserves under a perfect, free-floating exchange rate regime. If a country ran the occasional current account surplus or deficit, it would quickly be neutralized by a stronger or weaker currency. In the not-so-perfect reality, countries tend to accumulate foreign reserves through imbalances in trade and investment. In this sense, China's ballooning foreign reserves in recent years represent an extreme case of state intervention to limit or contain currency appreciation. The conventional wisdom goes that the size of foreign reserves should be sufficient to cover three months of a nation's imports. However, many developing countries, especially the Asian countries that languished after the 1997 crisis, have renewed the motto "the more the better"—as a cushion of self-insurance to avert a currency crisis. But many see that China has gone too far. For instance, with almost US$2.4 trillion in Beijing's coffers by 2009, China owned more than a quarter of the world's total US$8.4 trillion in reserve assets, which is sufficient to cover thirty months of its imports (Lex 2010).

The argument that China should hold a large volume of foreign reserves prevailed in 2002 but lost ground as reserves have grown at an explosive 40% per year since then (Feng 2007b). While it has been the consensus within the policy circle that China now has a foreign reserve that is much more than it needs, disagreements exist about how to manage the huge holdings in an efficient manner. At the same time, analysts point to the opportunity costs associated with these enormous holdings. Notwithstanding the inflationary effect and growing international pressures, the reserves also incur huge financial costs to China. The surge in China's reserves occurred at a time when interest rates in major economies, including the United States, were at record lows. This means that the returns on China's reserves, 70% of which are dollar-denominated assets, are extremely low. However, the continuous influx of FDI into China means returns to foreign investment are apparently above the international average. Thus, the accumulation of extra reserves in the central bank effectively means China borrows at a much higher interest rate than the one at which it lends its reserves overseas.

The rapid surge of reserve holdings poses new challenges to the Chinese leadership and the reserve management team, who were preoccupied with the problems of a shortage of foreign exchange just a decade ago. Before 2007, China's foreign reserves were exclusively managed by SAFE. Although a subordinate of the PBC, SAFE is also directed by the State Council due to the traditional importance of foreign reserves to the government; therefore it is elevated above other agencies of the PBC in terms of dual leadership. In practice, however, SAFE conducts its major business under the administration of the PBC. Both the PBC and SAFE have been the major players in Beijing's reserve management, not only in everyday routine transactions and management but also in key policy decisions. As is discussed in Chapter 11, the foreign reserves under the PBC's control have been strategic and instrumental in awarding the central bank leadership in China's banking reform since 2003.

As China's foreign reserves reached a milestone of US$1 trillion in October 2006, Beijing began to seriously consider ways to increase the returns on its skyrocketing reserves. The MOF has long been vying for a way to secure some control over the foreign reserves. Despite its relatively declining (albeit still powerful) status, it managed to establish a sovereign wealth fund under its control, named China Investment Corporation (CIC), that has been in formal operation since September 2007. The key figure behind the launch of the CIC is Lou Jiwei, a former vice minister of the MOF. An official who has worked in the PBC, the Central Huijin Investment Company (Huijin hereafter), and CIC suggested that, despite the fact that the senior management of the CIC was drawn from a number of ministries, including SAFE (in a bid to placate the PBC), the MOF has the dominant influence over its major operations.[23]

The establishment of the CIC further extended institutional rivalry between the PBC and the MOF, which has intensified since 2003 when the PBC took over the control of two of the Big Four state-owned banks (the China Construction Bank and the BOC) from the MOF, with the MOF struggling to share the leadership of the third (the Industrial and Commercial Bank of China) with the PBC (see Chapter 11). Ideas about how to use foreign reserves were being floated as far back as 2003. Seeing it as its own turf, the PBC suppressed the idea of an alternative management fund, feeling that there was no need to gain a better return on their investment. The PBC resisted the MOF's push for dual management of foreign reserves, but as the foreign reserves jumped to over a trillion U.S. dollars in 2006, the PBC's position against a sovereign wealth fund was, not surprisingly, weakened. Eventually, the CIC was created under the control of the State Council, out of the bureaucratic reach of either ministry. However, it was staffed primarily with personnel tied to the MOF and the NDRC. The MOF also managed to merge the CIC with Huijin, an investment vehicle set up by the PBC during the recapitalization of the banks (see Chapter 11). The aim of the CIC is to diversify away from China's large holdings of low-yielding dollar-denominated fixed income securities. According to Lou, "the goals of the CIC will focus on overseas financial products to diversify investment and improve investment returns. . . . At the current stage, the company's investment will be focused on financial portfolios, trying to improve long-term investment returns while keeping risks in an acceptable range" ("Board Shows True Colours" 2007).

Since its inauguration, the CIC has been in the international limelight as the symbol of China's growing economic and political prowess. What is often neglected is the fact that the amount of funds that is under the CIC's management (US$200 billion) represents only a small fraction (less than 10%) of China's total reserve holdings, the majority of which is still under the control of the PBC and SAFE. If Huijin's funds of $140 billion are excluded, which are designated to recapitalize domestic financial institutions rather than overseas investment, the amount of funds that is at the CIC's disposal is only one-third of its original capital (US$67 billion) (McDonald 2007). The PBC also vetoed the MOF's proposal to directly transfer US$200 billion in foreign exchange reserves into the CIC's account as the latter's initial capital, forcing the MOF to issue RMB1.55 trillion yuan (US$208 billion) of special treasury bonds to buy the foreign reserves from the PBC in several phases.[24] The sale of the interest-bearing bonds as the CIC's capital thus placed a heavy financial burden on the CIC to repay the interest to the MOF. Moreover, before the formal launch of the CIC, the PBC made an investment on behalf of the CIC, buying a 0.46% stake in the BG Group, a British natural gas company, a move that is seen as a "power play" by the PBC (Amadan International 2007).

By forcing the sale of Treasury bonds to capitalize the CIC, the PBC made sure that the CIC is in a very difficult position. Given the average return of sovereign wealth funds of around 6% ("Beijing Tipped to Give" 2007),[25] the demand from the top leadership for higher returns forced the CIC into risky investments. In fact, the initial investment by the CIC in the initial public offering of the Blackstone Group, a private equity and investment company, yielded a loss of 40%. CIC's failure in the Blackstone investment attracted nationwide criticism of the CIC and of Lou personally (Amadan International 2007). Given the interest costs to its capital and the appreciation of the RMB, the CIC must have a return of 10–13% to break even. But according to a senior CIC management official, with assets totaling US$410 billion at the end of 2010, the average annualized return on capital between 2008 and 2010 had been a mere 6.3% (Feng 2011). This helps strengthen the central bank's argument that SAFE was the more experienced institution in investment management.

As the CIC's original funds were fully allocated by July 2011, it has been arguing for arrangements for its recapitalization to be formalized. It has called for an automatic mechanism that links its capital to a proportion of Beijing's ever-increasing reserves, but, given its dismal performance, the argument for automatic recapitalization has lost momentum. Instead, the CIC was allocated US$30 billion at the end of 2011 on an ad hoc basis, short of the US$200 billion the CIC had been seeking (Wei 2012). What is notable from this round of capital injection is this that time the funds were directly transferred from SAFE's account, not through the MOF purchasing the reserves by issuing bonds. While this will reduce the CIC's finance costs, it also implies that SAFE may have become a stakeholder in the CIC, an institutional victory for the PBC that implies more influence over the fund.

With the CIC drawing worldwide attention, the PBC and SAFE have been quietly strengthening their capacity in reserve management in a bid to outclass the CIC. In this regard, Hu Xiaolian played an important role. Hu is a veteran of Beijing's foreign exchange management, working in almost all the key departments of SAFE (including the director of the core Reserve Management Department) for twenty years until she was appointed chief administrator of SAFE in April 2005. In one of her few public speeches, Hu stressed that SAFE will explore "more efficient means to use its reserve assets, will further optimize the currency and asset structure of the foreign reserves, and continue to expand its investment channels" ("Waihui guanli gaoshou Hu Xiaolian" 2006).

Given the CIC's mandate to invest in overseas financial equities, SAFE was expected to maintain its conservative strategy in investing the bulk of the foreign reserves. However, largely in a bid to demonstrate its competency and prestige, SAFE initiated a series of attempts at more aggressive investments. For example, in late 2007, it was reported that a SAFE subsidiary in Hong Kong built stakes in three of the biggest banks in Australia (John 2008). While these stakes are minor (less than 1% in each bank), it was a significant event, since up until November 2007, SAFE had never bought into any foreign equities or currencies. In 2008, SAFE allocated $2.5 billion in a US$17 billion fund managed by TPG for private equity investments, around $2 billion in shares of British Petroleum and around $2.5 billion in shares in France's Total ("SAFE, Not CIC," 2008). In reality, as many of these equity purchases are likely below the ownership thresholds requiring disclosure, and given the PBC and SAFE's penchant for secrecy, SAFE has likely been far more active in overseas equity purchases than is known. These expanded equity investments by SAFE were consistent with a report by an influential domestic magazine, *Caijing*, that the State Council had authorized SAFE in April 2008 to invest 5% of China's foreign exchange reserves in non-fixed-income investments (Yu 2008). As of the end of April 2008, 5% of China's foreign exchange reserves would form a potential equity investment pool of US$87.8 billion, which would be larger than the US$67 billion that is at the CIC's disposal. It appears that during this round of institutional turf wars, the MOF and CIC initially gained an upper hand, but the PBC and SAFE have generated more dynamic momentum as China's chief foreign reserve manager.

Although Beijing expanded its equity investment through SAFE and the CIC, China's foreign reserves face a long-term trend of capital loss given the highly likely depreciation of the U.S. dollar due to spiraling deficits in the United States. For instance, it is calculated that since China unpegged its currency from the U.S. dollar in July 2005, the country's foreign reserves have suffered a loss of 157 billion yuan (Yu 2008). Beijing's concern was so grave that Premier Wen aired his concerns publicly. In a press conference during the National People's Congress in March 2009, Wen told international reporters "We have lent a huge amount of money to the U.S., so of course we are concerned about the safety of our assets. Frankly speaking, I do have some worries." Wen called on the United States to "maintain its credibility, honor its commitments and guarantee the security of Chinese assets" (Batson and Browne 2009). In a highly coordinated fashion, Zhou Xiaochuan (2009), as governor of the PBC, published an essay on the PBC's Web site later that month. Reflecting China's dilemma of having to park the majority of its foreign reserves in a currency that faces long-term depreciation, Zhou called for an internationally endorsed shift away from the U.S. dollar as the world's reserve currency "as soon as possible" and urged the IMF to expand the use of its Special Drawing Rights and move toward a "super-sovereign reserve currency." Zhou's article attracted immense coverage by the world media and stirred a round of intense debate on the infrastructural framework of the global financial and economic system, particularly in the context of the GFC and an expansionary U.S. monetary policy. The article may reflect Zhou's interests, but more likely it was a proclamation of the Chinese leadership's views and concerns about the structural imbalances in the global economy. If so, the fact that Zhou was chosen to represent Beijing's voice is an indication of the PBC's key institutional authority in China's exchange rate policy and reserve management, as well as Zhou's personal reputation in the international financial community as perceived by the leadership.

The PBC and the Internationalization of the RMB

An eye-catching development in the international monetary scene in recent years, particularly since 2010, has been the blistering growth in the use of the RMB outside China, especially among its neighboring countries. This is represented by a rapid increase in RMB deposits in Hong Kong, as well as the emergence and diversification of domestic and offshore RMB-denominated bond markets, and a series of bilateral currency swap agreements (Ren 2011). Again, the PBC and SAFE have been the major driver behind the trend, with PBC governor Zhou convincing the leadership to make the RMB an international currency in 2009.

Apart from Beijing's apparent strategic ambition to increase its clout in global finance, the recent acceleration of RMB internationalization is more the result of the PBC's concern over potential losses in China's foreign assets, the desire to avoid exchange rate risk, and a unilateral action reflecting frustration over global structural problems and regional inactivity. First of all, the acute U.S. dollar shortage effect on trade experienced in the aftermath of the GFC, and a long-term prospect of a weak dollar on the back of record-breaking fiscal deficits in the United States, have triggered a need for diversification of its trade settlement and reserve currency from China. The domestic consensus that emerged was that the dollar's global reserve status is irreplaceable, at least in the short to medium term, largely because there has been no credible alternative to the dollar (especially given the ongoing fragility of the euro). Therefore, China's strategy has been "growing out of the dollar," that is, promoting a diversification of international currencies (including the RMB) without challenging the established position of the U.S. dollar.

In the meantime, China has been engaging in regional financial cooperation, which is based on the Chiang Mai Initiative. Although China has achieved some tangible results together with its East Asian neighbors, progress has been largely limited and slow. Therefore, compared with the creation of a regional financial architecture and reforms to the international financial system, internationalization of the RMB seems to be achievable, giving some scope for China to act positively rather than passively on global and regional issues. In other words, RMB internationalization seems to be a partial strategy aimed at trying to safeguard China's financial interests as well as its stability.

According to Kenen (2009), an international currency is one that is used and held beyond the borders of the issuing country for transactions with both that country's residents and between nonresidents. An international currency has to be capable of playing the roles of a store of value, a medium of exchange, and a unit of account for both residents and nonresidents. More specifically, it can be used for private purposes as a substitute currency, for invoicing and denominating investments, and for trade and financial transactions. It can also be used for public purposes as official reserves, a vehicle currency for foreign exchange intervention, and an anchor currency for pegging (Chinn and Frankel 2005).

One of the major developments in the RMB's internationalization has been its increasing use as a trade settlement currency. In April 2009, China's State Council approved a pilot scheme by SAFE, promoting cross-border trade settlement in RMB in Shanghai, four other cities in Guangdong Province, and Hong Kong. In June 2010, the scheme was expanded to cover twenty of the thirty-one mainland Chinese provinces and to companies located in and outside Hong Kong. As a result, the amount of trade settled in the Chinese currency has surged, with more than 800 billion yuan (US$125 billion) of such transactions passing through Hong Kong in the first half of 2011.

At the same time, the PBC allowed an expansion of the scope of RMB business in Hong Kong in July 2010 in a bid to facilitate the latter to become a major offshore RMB center. Corporations were allowed to open and use RMB accounts for any purpose, no longer just for trade settlement. Moreover, RMB deliverable spot and forwards started trading and banks were allowed to introduce RMB-linked products. This significantly expanded the RMB's functional domains, which led to a corresponding surge of RMB deposits in Hong Kong, reaching almost 600 billion yuan by the end of 2011 (see Figure 10.9). As a result, the RMB has accumulated rapidly in the banking system, crowding out Hong Kong dollars and U.S. dollars, the traditional source of bank funding. As of July 2011, RMB deposits made up 9.5% of the total US$947 billion of deposits in Hong Kong, up from less than 2% just a year ago. There are signs that Beijing is preparing for an expansion of the offshore market. Six months after opening the RMB to trading in Hong Kong, China launched RMB trading in the United States in January 2011 (albeit on a limited scale) (Wei 2011).

The rapidly expanding pool of offshore RMB holdings set the stage for the development of an offshore bond market, primarily in Hong Kong. An RMB-denominated bond market has emerged in Hong Kong since 2007, called "dim sum" bonds, as the issuance of such bonds is still a tiny fraction of the total bond issuance.[26] The first such bond was issued in July 2007 by the China Development Bank. The list of authorized issuers was further expanded in 2010 by the authorities to most domestic and foreign companies under light-touch regulation. Despite the economic downturn, at least fifty companies, including McDonald's, Caterpillar, and the UK-based retailer Tesco, sold RMB bonds in Hong Kong worth the equivalent of US$8.8 billion by September 2011 (see Table 10.3). In April 2011, HSBC helped arrange the first initial public offering outside mainland China to be denominated in RMB (Ren 2011).

Apart from dim sum bonds for offshore markets, another pillar of the PBC's international strategy is to promote an onshore bond market for foreign institutions, the so-called panda bonds. Compared with advanced countries, China's domestic bond market, especially the corporate bond sector, is relatively shallow. Panda bond issuance thus helps to widen the bond market,

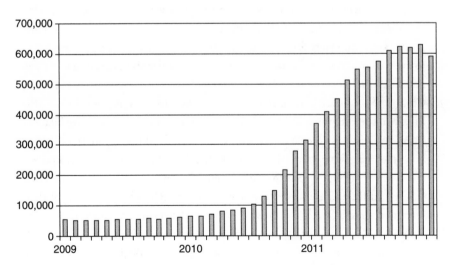

FIGURE 10.9. RMB deposits in Hong Kong, 2009–11 (RMB million).
Source: Monthly Statistical Bulletin, Hong Kong Monetary Authority.

Table 10.3.   Landmark RMB bond issues in Hong Kong

Time	Bond	Issuer
July 2007	First RMB bond	China Development Bank
September 2009	First RMB government bond	Ministry of Finance
July 2010	First RMB corporate bond	Hopewell Highway
September 2010	First RMB corporate bond by a foreign entity	McDonald's
December 2010	First speculative-grade RMB corporate bond	Galaxy
October 2011	First RMB Islamic (Sukuk) bond	Khazanah Nasional Berhad*

Source: Ren (2011) and KNB (2011).
*Khazanah Nasional Berhad is Malaysia's sovereign wealth fund.

to enrich the financing structure, and to enhance opportunities for investing in RMB-denominated bonds. The PBC and SAFE have been relaxing the rules regarding the proceeds of bond issuance. Since September 2010, international institutions, upon SAFE's approval, can opt to remit overseas proceeds from panda bond sales in foreign currencies. This policy change is another step in the experiment on liberalizing the capital account and internationalizing the use of the RMB.

Another notable development in this regard is a series of bilateral currency swap agreements (BSAs) the PBC has arranged with its counterparts in other economies. These swaps, allowing the economies to offer RMB trade financing to local importers for Chinese exports, were first seen as policy measures to alleviate the trade contraction effect of U.S. dollar shortages in a crisis scenario. A number of such BSAs were signed with member countries under the Chiang Mai Initiative framework after the AFC. In the wake of the GFC, the PBC has been stepping up the scheme since December 2008, signing bilateral BSAs with seventeen economies with a combined value of more than 1.5 trillion yuan (see Table 10.4). More profoundly, the RMB is emerging as a potential reserve currency (Smith 2012). Central banks of Malaysia, Thailand, Chile, and Iceland are reported to have acquired RMB bonds as part of their foreign reserves. South Korea was also considering such a move in January 2012. On March 12, 2012, Japan announced its plan to purchase US$10.3 billion equivalent of China's treasury bonds pending Beijing's approval (Hu 2012). China and Japan started direct trading of their currencies in both markets on June 1, 2012 (Lu 2012). The direct trading between the currencies of

Table 10.4. Bilateral currency swap agreements with the PBC

Date	Counter party	Size of swap lines	Maturity (year)	Renewable
Dec. 12, 2008	Bank of Korea	RMB180bn/KRW38tn	3	Yes
Jan. 20, 2009	Hong Kong Monetary Authority	RMB200bn/HKD227bn	3	Yes
Feb. 8, 2009	Bank Negara Malaysia	RMB80bn/MYR40bn	3	Yes
March 11, 2009	National Bank of the Republic of Belarus	RMB20bn/BYR8,000bn	3	Yes
March 23, 2009	Bank Indonesia	RMB100bn/IDR175tn	3	Yes
April 2, 2009	Central Bank of Argentina	RMB70bn/ARS38bn	3	Yes
June 9, 2010	Central Bank of Iceland	RMB3.5bn	3	Yes
July 23, 2010	Monetary Authority of Singapore	RMB150bn/SGD30bn	3	Yes
April 18, 2011	New Zealand Reserve Bank	RMB25bn	3	Yes
April 19, 2011	Central Bank of Uzbekistan	RMB700m	3	Yes
May 6, 2011	Central Bank of Mongolia	RMB5bn	3	Yes
June 13, 2011	National Bank of Kazakhstan	RMB7bn	3	Yes
June 23, 2011	Central Bank of the Russian Federation	Not publicly specified	N/A	N/A
Jan. 17, 2012	Central Bank of the United Arab Emirates	RMB35bn	3	Yes
Feb. 8, 2012	Bank Negara Malaysia	RMB180bn	3	Yes
Feb. 21, 2012	Central Bank of the Republic of Turkey	RMB10bn	3	Yes
March 20, 2012	Bank of Mongolia	RMB10bn	3	Yes
March 22, 2012	Reserve Bank of Australia	RMB200bn	3	Yes
June 26, 2012	National Bank of Ukraine	RMB15bn	3	Yes

Source: Author-collected data.

the second and third largest economies in the world, without using the U.S. dollar as an intermediate currency, is likely to further foster bilateral trade and raise the RMB's international profile.

Nevertheless, the rapid development in the internationalization of the RMB will ultimately face fundamental hurdles, namely capital controls that hamper cross-border flow of the currency and a lack of full convertibility of the RMB that limits the ready availability of the currency. The PBC's key role in Beijing's RMB campaign in recent years led to speculation about the real motivations on the part of the PBC and Zhou. For example, Zhou was seen by one analyst as having

> conned the leadership into approving it, . . . us[ing] the language of economic nationalism to push an agenda that ultimately would loosen state control of the economy by making the yuan . . . more dependent on market forces than government orders. Call it a Trojan horse strategy. Make the policy arguments so attractive that decision makers will approve the ideas without realizing the implications—like the Trojans accepting that beautiful horse from the Greeks without realizing what was inside. (Davis 2011b)

Although the internationalization of a currency is not tantamount to capital account liberalization and full convertibility of the domestic currency, the latter issues are, to a very significant degree, indeed prerequisites for internationalization. In addition, a full liberalization of capital controls and the foreign exchange regime is also in the PBC's interests as this will free up the Bank's hands regarding monetary policy. Although conspiracy theories and speculation were brushed off during our interviews with PBC officials, there was a consensus that the issues of capital account liberalization and a currency float have to be addressed down the road; that the central bank should seize the "historical opportunity" to internationalize the RMB amid a dented dollar and a damaged euro.[27]

In fact, since early 2012, the PBC has strongly hinted that it is ready to accelerate the pace of exchange rate reform. On February 23, 2012, a position paper was published by a PBC research team led by Sheng Songcheng, chief of the PBC's Statistics and Analysis Department (Sheng 2012b). The essay argues that China has entered "a period of strategic opportunity for capital account liberalization, and that RMB could be freely convertible in ten years." In the subsequent debate in which some called for a more gradual liberalization, a second essay from the PBC was published on April 17, further arguing that the time for a "speedy adjustment" had arrived in the face of Western weakness, and that capital account liberalization should be accelerated alongside exchange rate reform and interest rate reform, which would eventually entail the market setting the interest rates of the banks (Sheng 2012a). According to these essays, the PBC's position is that there should be no fixed, step-by-step procedure for the reforms. Rather, they can be achieved through coordination and cooperation, and in a way that provides mutual support among the reform areas, a timely reminder of Zhou's long-term integrated approach to financial reform in China. The PBC's initiative and future policy developments on this front will no doubt have profound implications for the prospects of China's economy and the world market.

Conclusion

The unification of a dual-track exchange rate regime in 1994 marked one of the major events that have shaped China's macroeconomic management. It established a linkage between the exchange rate and China's domestic monetary policy, largely because the central bank needed to intervene in the foreign exchange market, which has had a direct impact on the domestic money supply. It was also in the 1990s that the PBC began to enjoy growing authority in the exchange rate policy process, leading to its pivotal role in the partial liberalization of the fixed regime in 2005 and again in Beijing's recommitment of a flexible RMB exchange rate in 2010, as well as in China's reserve management and the RMB's internationalization strategy.

In terms of exchange rate policy, strong external pressures, particularly from the United States, have been mediated by domestic institutions, such as the PBC. It is also worth noting that the PBC's discretion in this case, especially the Bank's conscious strategy of utilizing both administrative and more market-oriented instruments to sterilize its market interventions, is a typical pragmatic case of "central banking, Chinese style." But we should also keep in mind that these operations, although awarding the PBC more room to neutralize the money supply, could not fully contain the inflationary impact of its purchases of U.S. dollars on such a gigantic scale. Therefore, the Bank cannot fundamentally defy the standard policy trilemma, despite the presence of a wider than normal array of policy instruments, some of which are no doubt seen as a luxury by many Western central bankers.

Although it has so far fallen short of a free-floating regime, the PBC has sought to reform and relax its foreign exchange rate regime, to realign RMB valuations more to market forces, and to promote the international use of the

RMB. The long-term trend of currency liberalization partly reflects the growing weight of the PBC in China's monetary policy and macroeconomic management. On the other hand, exchange rate liberalization has also facilitated the rise of the PBC as more market-oriented elements become increasingly involved in the exchange rate regime. The significance of this event cannot be underestimated. In the long run, full convertibility of the RMB is to be expected, and the PBC is likely to gain more independence for its monetary policy, which in turn should boost its profile and authority within the party-state.

11

The PBC and Financial Reforms
in China since 2003

The large state-owned banks (SOBs) in China have emerged as among the largest but perhaps the most challenged banks in the world. Banking reform has become a key aspect of wider financial reforms in China and an essential component of the PBC's quest to build a more market-oriented monetary and financial system. The 1995 Central Bank Law assigned the formal task to the PBC of ensuring overall stability in the financial system, which had been constantly jeopardized by a problematic banking sector plagued with mounting bad loans. Government intervention and irregular practices have also significantly distorted the banking sector and the PBC's monetary policy transmission mechanisms. In a wide range of countries, notional central bank responsibility for overall financial stability has been a noticeably vague commitment. However, we argue in this chapter that, as the PBC increasingly gained authority in the financial arena, it spearheaded a series of reforms of the Chinese financial system, particularly in the banking sector, in a bid to increase the effectiveness of its monetary policy and to establish a sustainable foundation for China's long-term financial and economic stability.

The PBC's leading role in the financial reforms, especially since 2003, again reflects a broader transition of authority in financial governance from the old planning regime to a new, more market-oriented framework underpinned by central bank activism. Beijing's largely failed attempt to bail out the state banks in 1998, centered on arm's-length fiscal injections by the Ministry of Finance (MOF), largely discredited the conventional wisdom of older practices and institutions and paved the way for a new approach espoused by the PBC in 2003. Apart from the institutional competition between the MOF and the PBC, the PBC's reformist role since 2003 illustrates the sources of the central bank's empowerment in a transition context. In particular, the PBC used innovative ideas and managed to convince the party leaders to tap China's burgeoning foreign reserves, under the PBC's control, to recapitalize the banks, thus seizing reform leadership from the MOF. Externally, China's commitment to financial opening, partly dictated by its accession to the World Trade Organization (WTO), provided an anticipated shock to Chinese financial institutions, especially increased competition with global players. Key reformist agents, especially in the PBC, used this to boost commitment within the party leadership to support structural reforms of the financial and banking system.

The story of China's financial reforms from the perspective of the evolving authority and status of its central bank should also inform the ongoing debate on the state and future of the financial system and its implications for the overall Chinese economy, particularly regarding ongoing worries about the stability of the banking sector. Walter and Howie (2011, 32) see the Chinese banking system as a fragile financial behemoth, where the party-state "treats its banks as basic utilities that provide unlimited capital to the cherished state-owned enterprises." They further argue that the so-called reforms of the banking sector have been nothing more than an "accounting legerdemain," manipulating the books in order to hide nonperforming loans (NPLs) rather than addressing them, thereby delaying the day of reckoning. This view is more or less echoed in Shih's (2005, 2008) works on the politics of Chinese finance, which suggest that key party leaders, such as Premier Zhu Rongji, have intentionally postponed serious banking reforms, despite the Asian financial crisis providing a good opportunity for bank restructuring.

While these arguments are partly questioned in the following sections, some general points can be made in relation to our case regarding PBC-led financial reforms. First, banking and financial reforms, in any national setting, are inevitably a political process, often subject to intensive and extensive bargaining among the stakeholders. As we show, banking reforms in China have thus far been limited, with a number of significant issues left unaddressed, particularly the state's control over the banks that are weighed down with NPLs. However, these deficiencies do not necessarily warrant a denial of the progress that has been made thus far, especially since 2003. In fact, if the overall reform trajectory is taken into account, the banking system has been substantially transformed, albeit gradually, from part of the state bureaucracy to one that increasingly embraces ownership diversification, modern modes of corporate governance and risk management, and growing scrutiny by the international market. This general trend reflects wider dynamics of positive institutional change within the state that will help redefine its contours within the market in the future.

In addition, the accounts above tend to oversimplify the drivers and therefore the momentum of the reforms, sometimes leading to contradictory arguments. For Walter and Howie (2011), the series of alleged accounting maneuvers and the establishment of an array of modern financial markets are largely seen as a conspiracy by the party-state to erect a market-friendly image designed to lure domestic and international investors to fund the state bank's bad loans. On the other hand, however, they claim that the financial reforms under Zhu Rongji were "remarkable," "comprehensive, transformational, and pursued consistently" (Walter and Howie 2011, 21). For his part, Shih (2008) seeks to unpack the party-state, but stops at attributing the reform dynamics exclusively to elite-centered factional politics. However, as we argue here, institutional actors, such as the PBC, helped drive the reform momentum. In this case, the formal and informal relationships and exchanges between the PBC and the party leadership, and between the PBC and other powerful bureaucratic institutions, as well as the leadership transition, have all shaped the path of institutional change in the financial sector. As we show, a largely liberal-dominated PBC has injected market elements into the redesign of the banking system. Although the core issue of insulating the banks from political intervention has not been unaddressed, the PBC's strategy of shareholding reforms and public listing of the banks nevertheless has planted the seeds for further reforms.

In this chapter, we first examine Beijing's past experience in establishing and reforming its banking system in the reform era. Despite rapid progress in erecting a rudimentary banking system from scratch in the early days, we argue that no major breakthrough was made in the 1980s and the first half of the 1990s to address politically difficult issues in the banking sector, which led to the accumulation of gigantic levels of NPLs in the bank system. Subsequently, the massive recapitalization program in the aftermath of the Asian financial crisis was more of a short-term rescue than a long-term solution, as problems of moral hazard via profligate bailouts brought the banking sector to the verge of collapse. We then concentrate on the efforts of the PBC, under the governorship of Zhou Xiaochuan and the legacy of Zhu Rongji, to lead a restructuring of China's financial system, including the banking and securities sectors since 2003. We also discuss the Bank's efforts to foster the development of a corporate bond market and to painstakingly upgrade China's payment and settlement system, a vital and essential infrastructure for the financial and economic system.

The Ailing Banking Sector

Given the fact that more than 70% of savings and credits are handled by the major banks, the banking system has arguably been the most critical part of the financial system and the overall Chinese economy. Yet a significant discrepancy in the Chinese economy in the reform era has been a pattern of generally robust economic growth on the back of a more or less dysfunctional banking system. The banks, mostly owned by the state, have been plagued and haunted by mounting bad loans, persistent political intervention, intimate ties with state enterprises, poor corporate governance and regulation, a lack of knowledgeable and experienced personnel, and rampant corruption and fraud (Allen et al. 2008; Chen and Shi 2004; Girardin 1997; Pei 1998). Structural reforms, badly needed to rejuvenate the banking sector, remained a remote priority of the leadership in the 1980s and 1990s. Even when Beijing got more serious about the banking sector in the aftermath of the Asian financial crisis, deep-seated reforms were still lacking.

Banking Reforms in the 1980s

The key to understanding the lagging nature of banking restructuring again lies in the political strategy of reform. To ensure that the cause of wider economic reforms was not derailed by entrenched conservatives, the reformist leadership had to forge a pro-reform bandwagon (Shirk 1993). One of the main consequences was that reforms were carried out in a gradual and sequential manner, in which crucial sectoral reforms were conducted in order of their political viability. Because of the critical significance of financial resources as a component of political capital in China, the financial system was always a highly politicized and contested arena in domestic politics (Liew

2004; Shih 2008). The political sensitivity surrounding the financial system meant that banking reform was strategically delayed and postponed, if not avoided, compared with rural and industrial reforms that had topped the leadership's agenda in the 1980s and 1990s respectively. As a result, the banking sector shouldered and accumulated the systemic costs of reforms in other sectors and thus increasingly became the Achilles' heel of the overall economy, the weakest link in an otherwise rapid growth model.

Developments in the financial sector in the 1980s focused mainly on institution building, featuring the establishment of a banking system and its early diversification. As discussed in Chapter 7, by 1984, the monobank system of the planning era had been transformed into a two-tiered system in which the PBC became an exclusive central bank, while its commercial banking function was taken over by four newly established or reestablished specialized SOBs, the Agricultural Bank of China (ABC), the Bank of China (BOC), the People's Construction Bank (later renamed the China Construction Bank, CCB), and the Industrial and Commercial Bank of China (ICBC). The four SOBs have since dominated China's banking and financial system and are collectively called the Big Four. Despite their dominance, there was also a level of diversity in the financial sector, such as the emergence of small regional banks, limited access to the domestic market by foreign banks, and the emergence of nonbank financial institutions, such as urban and rural credit cooperatives, insurance companies, trust and investment companies, leasing firms, and so on. In terms of ownership, apart from the SOBs, early experiments were also made to set up joint stock banks (Pei 1998, 322).

Despite Beijing's early efforts to build a more forward-looking financial system as a part of its economic liberalization reforms, the financial intermediaries fell well short of operating on market-based principles. This was mainly due to the fact that the majority of the financial system was owned by the state and therefore was subject to political intervention and command. Under pressures from central and local governments, the SOBs performed fiscal functions of providing directed credit and subsidized capital to state-owned enterprises (SOEs) and to projects of political priority. This tied the bank's balance sheets to the fate of the state sector. In addition, competition among financial institutions was very limited, especially within the Big Four, since their businesses were arbitrarily divided along industrial sectors, thus largely operating in exclusive territories.[1] At the same time, the institutionally weak PBC was inexperienced and incapable of regulating the emerging financial market as its traditional means of credit control, the Credit Plan, was increasingly circumvented and exploited by the Big Four, and particularly by the nonbank financial institutions (Pei 1998; Tam 1986).[2]

Banking Reforms, 1990–97

The PBC's weak supervision over a largely distorted market was one of the major factors in the economic chaos in 1992–93, represented by gigantic flows of banking funds channeled into speculative real estate ventures, the newly opened stock market, and the prevalence of an active black interbank market, built upon rapid monetary expansion and high inflation (Girardin 1997). This prompted the authorities to adopt a broad reform initiative for the financial sector, spearheaded by Zhu Rongji, then vice premier and governor of the PBC, which was approved by the Party in November 1993 and formally cemented in the Central Bank Law and the Commercial Bank Law in 1995. These laws included measures to strengthen the PBC's autonomy and regulatory capacity over the financial institutions and markets (Chapter 7).

As for banking, three specialized policy banks were established in 1994 to assume the role of financing investment projects of national priority.[3] This move was a major step in offloading the heavy burden of policy lending and bad assets from the large SOBs, whose policy loans accounted for one-third of their outstanding loan portfolios. The aim was to turn the latter into more commercially oriented banks (Balfour and Roberts 2004). To achieve this, authority within the Big Four was centralized within their head offices, which were made responsible for their own liquidity management and credit control. There had also been attempts to force the banks to adopt international standards of financial accounting and operational practices (Li 1996; Okazaki 2011; Qian 1996). Another dimension was to further diversify the financial institutions and to increase competition. This was demonstrated by the establishment of the first private bank in China, the Min Sheng Banking Corporation, in 1995. There were also moves to increase access by foreign banks and experimentation to allow them to conduct local currency business (albeit under territorial restrictions) beginning in 1997. There was also a consolidation of urban credit cooperatives into urban cooperative banks (Guo 2002).

This round of reform had mixed results. While bank supervision was boosted with new management guidelines, market entry barriers were still high and the Big Four remained the dominant players in the market. Although the large SOBs no longer issued policy loans, outstanding loans remained on their balance sheets. Moreover, the policy banks suffered a number of problems, including poor capitalization, lack of institutional capacity in the localities, and a lack of autonomy from other powerful government departments (Boyreau-Debray and Wei 2005).

The Black Hole in the Banking Sector

Crucially, the banking reforms did not address the most important cause of the financial weakness of the Chinese banking system, the huge portfolio of bad loans owed by the SOEs to the banks. As state revenues dwindled rapidly after the decentralization process in the 1980s, the central government could no longer provide new equity for its SOEs, which forced it to transfer the responsibility of financing the SOEs to the banking system. The banks were effectively treated "as another treasury" (Pei 1998, 332), channeling 80% of their credit to the SOEs in the mid-1990s (Blanchard 1997, 17). To be sure, SOEs and SOBs share one thing in common in the Chinese context: they are both legacies of the socialist system that suffer from soft budget constraints, by which an organization expects that financial difficulties will lead to a bailout rather than liquidation or closure (Kornai 1986). Repaying bank loans was thus not considered essential by the SOEs since the borrowers believed these loans were fiscal funds, while the SOBs did not care much about recovering the loans from the SOEs since they believed the loan losses would ultimately be written off by the government one way or another. As a result, the deeply indebted SOEs led to the accumulation of NPLs in the banking sector.

To make things worse, in 1996, for the first time, overall losses exceeded profits by the SOEs, which in turn saw a further deterioration in the bank's balance sheets. Strictly speaking, the Big Four were technically insolvent by 1993–94. In 1994, they had total capital of 240.5 billion yuan, while their NPLs were estimated by the PBC to be over 530 billion yuan, more than double their total capital. By 1996, the entire banking sector faced technical bankruptcy. The share of NPLs rose to 25% of total outstanding bank loans. The combined amount of bank capital and loan loss reserves totaled 307 billion yuan, compared with the 330 billion yuan in overdue and unrecoverable loans (Pei 1998, 336). Another estimate by an expert from the Central Party School painted an even more pessimistic picture, with the NPL ratio reaching 25–50% of all loans outstanding in 1995, or between 21% and 43% of GDP at the time (Shih 2004, 931). Although the figures were alarming, the issue was only recognized as one among many of the problems confronting the regime, and was certainly not at the top of the elite agenda.

Banking Reforms, 1997–2002

China largely escaped the worst of the Asian financial crisis in 1997 thanks to its limited financial opening, yet the financial disaster that had unfolded in China's neighbors one after another served as a wake-up call for the top policymakers in Beijing to get serious about the health of the banking sector. A flood of reports from within the government subsequently tied a potential looming crisis to China's NPL problem.

The solution that was eventually given the green light, however, turned out to be a short-sighted recapitalization program rather than long-term structural reform. The central government injected 270 billion yuan (US$32.6 billion) into the Big Four banks by issuing the same amount of special treasury bonds by the MOF, increasing the capital adequacy ratio of the banks to the Basel requirement of 8% (up from 3.5%) at the end of 1997.

However, this only recovered a tiny fraction of the estimated 3.3 trillion yuan in NPLs. After Zhu Rongji became premier, the State Council decided to split the bulk of the existing NPLs into asset management companies (AMCs). This was an early reflection of somewhat similar current efforts to remove toxic assets from Western banks amid the post-2007 global financial crisis (GFC). Four AMCs—Xinda, Changcheng, Huarong and Dongfang—were established in 1998 and took over NPLs from the CCB, the ABC, the ICBC, and the BOC respectively. The general approach was that the four AMCs issued 1.4 trillion yuan in financial bonds to the Big Four and used the funds to purchase 1.4 trillion in NPLs from the same banks at face value. The AMCs each had a charter of ten years and were supposed to recover as many of the NPLs as possible through debt-to-equity swaps, bankruptcy, and debt restructuring. The remaining NPLs not recovered at the end of the ten-year period were supposed to be written off by the MOF (Shih 2004). The 1.4 trillion bill was broken down into three parts, 40 billion yuan in initial capital for the four AMCs (each with 10 billion yuan) from the MOF, 570 billion yuan for refinancing from the PBC, and 820 billion yuan in bonds purchased by the Big Four at fixed interest rates underwritten by the MOF. Together with 270 billion in special treasury bonds, Beijing footed a total bill of 1.71 trillion yuan for the entire package during 1998–99. To put the figure in perspective, the bailout accounted for a staggering 25% of total state revenue in the fifty years since the PRC was founded in 1949 (Ye 2009).

The plan seems to have appealed to everyone in the game. The SOBs replaced 1.4 trillion of NPLs with the same amount of sound assets made up of MOF-backed and interest-bearing bonds. But the plan failed to address the core issue. Instead of a fiscal injection of capital that could have wiped out the NPLs in one clean stroke, this set of complicated capital maneuvers between institutional accounts did not remove the NPLs from the bank's balance sheets, but simply hid them within the AMC bonds that the banks held (Walter and Howie 2011). The AMCs "bought" the NPLs at their face value, but their recovery rate has been dismal at best, averaging 20% by 2011 (CBRC 2012). This means the MOF will ultimately have to foot the bill. The time bomb thus embedded in the plan appears to contradict Zhu's vision and ambition of restructuring the banking sector, which led Shih (2005) to argue that even seemingly staunch reformers such as Zhu were subject to short-term political calculations for financial reforms, leaving the hot potato to his successors. However, given the dire political environment, Zhu was disinclined to set off yet another political landmine with a bold overhaul of the banking system. In charge of China's financial affairs for years, Zhu was well aware of the problems, but the imperative of political survival saw bank restructuring strategically postponed (see Chapter 5).

During this period, the PBC became a formal member of the Bank of International Settlements in 1996. This provided the PBC with more opportunities to discuss issues in relation to bank supervision. Within this context, the PBC committed to full compliance with the Core Principles for Effective Banking Supervision under the Basel Capital Accord, which is the international standard for capital adequacy ratios for globally operating commercial banks (Okazaki 2011). This encouraged the PBC to improve banking regulation. Regarding the issue of bank recapitalization, the PBC had grave concerns over possible moral hazards induced by the one-way injection of capital into the SOBs without complementary reforms of the banks, but was not in a position to provide a politically better alternative for Zhu.[4] At the time the Bank was more concerned with strengthening overall financial stability. Since a majority of the costs were borne by the MOF, the PBC did not oppose the package. The PBC's worries were confirmed soon after, however. As one PBC official recalled, "The government reiterated its warnings to the banks that this round of capital injection was 'the last dinner.' Not clear about Beijing's

Table 11.1.   NPL ratio and capital adequacy ratio of the Big Four in 2002 (%)

	ICBC	ABC	BOC	CCB
NPL	25.41	36.63	23.37	15.17
Capital adequacy ratio	5.54	N/A	8.15	6.91

Source: Adapted from Okazaki (2011).

strategic intentions, the SOBs did not disclose their NPLs in full at the beginning. The banks eventually realized that this [the recapitalization] was actually a free lunch—therefore the deeply concealed figure [of NPLs] subsequently popped up to the surface."[5]

Apart from the existing pile of bad loans, the banks were also pushed by political pressures for more relaxed credits to state enterprises and the real estate sector in a bid to boost aggregate demand in the wake of an export slump in the post-Asian crisis period. According to Dai Xianglong, then PBC governor, this round of capital injection had reduced the bank's combined NPLs from 35% of the total loan portfolio at the end of 1999 to 25% by the end of 2000. However, according to Lardy (2001), the RMB 2 trillion in NPLs on the SOBs' balance sheets could be as high as RMB 5 trillion by international accounting standards, which amounted to a whopping 40–75% of GDP in 2000. Moreover, the NPLs piled up again to an average of 17.8% of total portfolio by 2002 according to H. Wang (2004) of the China Banking Regulatory Commission (CBRC), while the average capital adequacy ratio of the Big Four fell to 4.61% at the end of 2002 (see Table 11.1), well below the 8% requirement of the Basel Accord (Ye 2009). Liu Mingkang (2004), chairman of the CBRC, later admitted that the government had been focused on reducing the financial difficulties of banks rather than on addressing inherent structural problems in the 1998 program, and that it had become clear that the banks' financial distress had been more deeply rooted than had been previously realized.

PBC-Led Financial Reform, 2003–5: A New Approach

China's banking reform experienced renewed momentum after China acceded to the WTO in December 2001, by any standards a significant structural shift in the transition process. To speed up its accession negotiations, Beijing made a number of concessions from its previously held position, including financial opening (Feng 2006c). One major commitment was that Beijing would allow foreign banks full access to the Chinese market by December 2006, a five-year phase-in period after the WTO membership. Therefore, Beijing had to prepare the moribund banking sector for the looming showdown with global financial giants. As the clock was ticking on this brief window of opportunity for substantial institutional change, a consensus was finally reached within the political elite to undertake radical reforms of the banks. Political will had to be substantiated into strategies and actions, which set the scene for the increasingly authoritative and ambitious PBC. Wider structural and political shifts were thus setting the stage for significant institutional change at the PBC. Hand in hand with its growing prominence in the monetary arena was the Bank's critical role in this round of banking and wider financial reforms under the governorship of Zhou Xiaochuan. This included the shareholding reforms of the major state banks, defusing risks in the domestic stock market by restructuring the stock brokerages, and embarking on integrated operations on financial intermediaries.

Any structural reform package, however, first needed to deal with the "historical burdens" of the banking sector, namely, the existing stocks of NPLs that had piled up over the previous three decades. However, options available to Beijing in terms of the source of recapitalization were indeed limited. The earlier approach of a state bailout had already overstretched the fiscal resources of the central government. Alternatively, inviting in domestic private capital was financially viable, given China's high savings ratio and the rapid development of the private sector in the 1990s. Nevertheless, liberalizing domestic private investment in the financial sector could be politically risky for the Communist Party since this meant that the regime could lose control of key financial resources. Thus, foreign investment in a supervised partnership with domestic institutions was instead put on the table.

The more important issue, however, was how to prevent the creation of new NPLs and make the banks operate on sounder commercial principles. In other words, the key issue that emerged was about disciplining the banks. Beijing's previous strategy of blind capital injection and reliance on industry self-discipline and party supervision (through the Central Financial Work Committee) had turned out to be a major failure. Back in the 1990s, current PBC leaders, such as Zhou Xiaochuan (Wu and Zhou 1999; Zhou 1999a) and Wu Xiaoling (1992) (PBC vice governor, 2000–7) had explored various options for realigning the SOBs' incentives in a market economy. Based on their theoretical understanding and past experience, Zhou formed the view that, given the institutional settings in China's political and financial sector, structural reforms would not be driven by corporate insiders. The way out, argued Zhou, was to subject the banking industry to more effective market and shareholder discipline and international scrutiny.

Under this principle, there was a step beyond the earlier fiscal solutions centered on the MOF and a shift toward more structural reforms advocated by the PBC. In this manner the PBC designed and carried out a new road map for banking reform. The first step was to replenish the bank's capital to internationally accepted levels and turn it into shareholding enterprises. After cleaning their balance sheets, the banks would then engage in attracting foreign financial institutions (foreign strategic investors, FSIs) for equity investment so that the domestic banks could gain management expertise and market confidence. The next step was to list the banks in an overseas stock market. Walter and Howie (2011) argue that the state bailout in 1998 and the program since 2003 can be seen as one unified reform round, which was dismissed by the Bank officials we interviewed.[6] We instead see them as two distinctive phases of banking restructuring. Indeed, it was the disastrous aftermath of the 1998 program that paved the way for a more market-oriented reform attempt in 2003.

The PBC's reform strategy has thus far been implemented in an encouraging way. The Big Four have all been subjected to the PBC's therapy. Their balance sheets had a clean start after massive capital injection. At the same time, the government also conducted a second round of NPL disposal in which more than RMB 1.2 trillion NPLs were transferred to the AMCs. Compared with the AMCs receiving the NPLs at their face value in the 1998 program, this time the disposal mechanisms were more market oriented to the extent that auction systems were introduced and the direct relationship between the state banks and AMCs was largely severed (Okazaki 2011). Except the ABC, the banks further managed to persuade a number of internationally renowned financial institutions to come on board as FSIs, and have successfully launched their initial public offerings (IPOs) in Hong Kong or Shanghai. This pattern of equity reforms with foreign participation is not confined to the major state banks, but has spread to other banks as well. By October 2005, nineteen foreign institutions invested in sixteen Chinese banks with a total capital of over US$16.5 billion, or a substantial 15% of China's total banking portfolio (Shen 2006) (see Tables 11.2 and 11.3).

Table 11.2. Reform arrangements of the five largest SOBs since 2003

Bank	Capital injection Institution	Amount (RMB billion)	Date	Disposal of NPLs (RMB billion)	Foreign strategic investment Investment (RMB billion)	Initial share in capital (%)	Initial public offerings Location	Date	Amount (RMB billion)
ABC	Huijin[a]	130.0	Nov. 2008	815.6[c]			Hong Kong	July 2010	12.2 (HKD)
							Shanghai	July 2010	68.5
ICBC	Huijin[b]	124.0	April 2005	705.0[d]	30.5	10	Hong Kong	Oct. 2006	126.6
BOC	Huijin	186.4	Dec. 2003	308.1	43.0	17	Hong Kong	June 2006	90.0
							Shanghai	July 2006	20.0
CCB	Huijin	186.2	Dec. 2003	185.8	32.8	14.2	Hong Kong	Oct. 2005	74.6
BOCOM	MOF	5.0	June 2004	53.0	14.5	19.9	Hong Kong	June 2005	18.0
	Huijin	3.0	June 2004				Shanghai	May 2007	25.2
	Social Security Fund	10.0	June 2004						
Totals		644.6		2,067.5	120.8				601.0

Source: Okazaki (2011) and *Almanac of China's Finance and Banking 2011.* Beijing: Zhongguo jinrong chubanshe.

a. The MOF keeps its original invested capital of RMB 124.0 billion.
b. The MOF keeps its original invested capital of RMB 130.0 billion.
c. This amount of NPLs was transferred to a comanaged account between the MOF and Huijin, with MOF giving receivables to the Bank. The receivables are expected to be offset in fifteen years against a refund of income tax, the Bank's future dividends to the MOF, and/or the MOF selling part of its equity in the Bank.
d. The Bank transferred the NPLs, worth 246 billion yuan, to Huarong Asset Management Company in June 2005 at book value. Huarong then set up a comanaged account with the MOF, with the latter giving receivables to the Bank. The receivables were to be offset against the Bank's future profits and dividends to the MOF.

Table 11.3. Foreign investment in Chinese banks since 2002

Chinese bank	FSI	Nationality	Date of agreement	Deal size (US$ million)	Share in capital (%)
Guangdong Development Bank	Citigroup	USA	Nov. 2006	723	20.0
United Rural Cooperative Banks of Hangzhou	Rabobank Group	Netherlands	July 2006	20	10.0
	IFC	International	July 2006	10	5.0
ICBC	Goldman Sachs/Amex/Allianz	USA/Germany	Jan. 2006	3,780	10.0
Ningbo City Commercial Bank	OCBC Bank	Singapore	Jan. 2006	71	12.2
Tianjin City Commercial Bank	ANZ Group	Australia	Dec. 2005	120	19.9
Huaxia Bank	Deutsche Bank	Germany	Oct. 2005	325	14.0
	Pangaea Capital Management	Singapore	Oct. 2005	125	6.9
	Standard Chartered Bank	UK	Sept. 2005	123	19.9
Bohai Bank	Royal Bank of Scotland/Merrill Lynch/Li Ka Shing Foundation	UK/USA/ Hong Kong	Aug. 2005	3,048	10.0
BOC	Temasek	Singapore	Sept. 2005	1,524	5.0
	UBS	Switzerland	Sept. 2005	500	1.6
	Asian Development Bank	International	Oct. 2005	75	0.2
	Mitsubishi UFJ	Japan	June 2006	180	0.2
Nanchong City Commercial Bank	German Investment and Development Bank	Germany	July 2005	5	13.3

Bank	Strategic investor	Country	Date	Amount	%
CCB	Bank of America	USA	June 2005	2,500	9.1
	Temasek	Singapore	July 2005	1,466	5.1
Hangzhou City Commercial Bank	Commonwealth Bank of Australia	Australia	April 2005	76	19.9
Bank of Beijing	ING Group	Netherlands	March 2005	215	19.9
	IFC	International	March 2005	50	5.0
Jinan City Commercial Bank	Commonwealth Bank of Australia	Australia	Nov. 2004	17	11.0
BOCOM	HSBC	UK	Aug. 2004	1,747	19.9
Shenzhen Development Bank	New Bridge Capital	USA	June 2004	149	17.9
	GE Finance	USA	Oct. 2005	100	7.0
Industrial Bank	Hang Seng Bank	Hong Kong	Dec. 2003	208	16.0
	GIC	Singapore	Dec. 2003	50	5.0
	IFC	International	Dec. 2003	70	4.0
Shanghai Pudong Development Bank	Citigroup	USA	Sept. 2003	72	4.6
Mingsheng Bank	International Finance Corp.	International	May 2003	24	1.2
	Temasek	Singapore	Nov. 2004	106	4.6
Xi'an City Commercial Bank	Bank of Nova Scotia	Canada	Sept. 2002	7	5.0
	IFC	International	Sept. 2002	20	12.5
Everbright Bank	IFC	International	June 2002	19	4.9
Nanjing City Commercial Bank	IFC	International	Nov. 2001	27	5.0
	BNP Paribas	France	Jan. 2006	87	19.2

Source: Okazaki (2011), Ma (2006), and author-collected data.

Behind the Scenes

The 2003 reform campaign was conducted under the general oversight of the new premier, Wen Jiabao, and Vice Premier Huang Ju, but the actual steward-ship went to the PBC and Zhou Xiaochuan, who took over the governorship of the PBC in December 2002. This is a major sign of the rising clout of the PBC. Emphasizing the PBC's rising institutional resources, a PBC official summa-rized the reason for the PBC's leadership role succinctly: "We have the man-date, we have the idea, and we have the funds."[7] Although the authority for banking regulation had been split off from the PBC to the newly established prudential regulator, the CBRC, the PBC managed to regain its superiority over the subsidiary regulators and became a metaregulator in the financial sys-tem, responsible for overall financial stability (see Chapter 7). For the central bank, reforming the SOBs was not only a long-term goal to build a more market-oriented and sophisticated financial infrastructure in China, but also an imminent challenge given the "short notice" of Beijing's WTO commit-ment, which the PBC took as an urgent renewed mandate for radical therapy for the banks. In addition, the PBC was now equipped with both expertise and experience to devise a reform strategy that was both politically viable and that seemed technically sound.

Given a resurgence of NPLs after the 1998 bailout and international atten-tion on the solvency of Chinese banks, the idea of a second-round capitaliza-tion was floated after 2000. However, there was a lack of viable plans on the table and the agenda stalled over the following two years. The MOF lacked both the financial capacity and incentive to be once again entangled with the risky business of banking recapitalization and reform.[8] The PBC also easily defeated proposals for a second fiscal injection. As a PBC official stated, "Re-capitalization using fiscal capital had been totally discredited [since 1998]. Look what happened last time. Everyone in our circle knew that such a pro-posal stood no chance of passing in the People's Congress this time."[9] Cru-cially, however, this time the central bank had access to a critical institutional resource: the capital to deliver its strategy. The PBC "innovatively" proposed to tap into China's foreign reserves, which it administered, to recapitalize the banks.[10] As with other Asian countries, China had started to build a large amount of foreign reserves after the 1997 crisis "for the rainy days" and also to better shield itself from international pressures. This was made possible by rapidly growing surpluses from its national current and capital accounts fueled by WTO accession. China's foreign reserves reached US$403.25 billion at the end of 2003, triple the 1997 figure of US$139.89 billion. The reserves had been growing at a phenomenal pace of around US$200 billion a year since 2003 (Feng 2007b). Therefore, the PBC argued convincingly that it was well placed to use part of the excess reserves to recapitalize the SOBs without damaging fiscal health. Moreover, this allocation of capital from a PBC-managed fund did not need approval by the People's Congress. This move thus saved time and a potentially sensitive debate in the legislature, another case of PBC agents carving out a degree of discretion within their institutional context. The State Council's eventual approval of this plan effectively awarded the PBC institutional leadership in the reform campaign. Institutionally, the roles of the PBC and the MOF have been "reversed" this time; the latter has been sidelined in this round of reform (Walter and Howie 2011).

To be sure, institutionally speaking, banking reform since 2003 has been led by the ad hoc State Council Leading Group on Shareholding Reforms of State Banks, which was chaired by Vice Premier Huang Ju, who was in charge of the nation's financial affairs. But in effect the Group was directed by Zhou, who had trust and support from Huang (Davis 2011a). In addition, the secretariat office of the Group also operated within the Financial Stability Bureau (FSB) of the PBC.[11] In the Chinese bureaucratic setting, this means that in practice, the PBC was the central coordinating body on this issue and therefore the PBC was the leading and most influential institution in this arena. As Naughton (2004b, 5) observed, "Zhou is the technocrat with lead authority in this area. The fact that the program went ahead in December 2003 demonstrates that Wen Jiabao has accepted Zhou Xiaochuan's overall blueprint for financial reforms and has assembled a workable political consensus around the proposals."

Huijin: A Special Policy Vehicle

Crucially, the PBC's ambitious reforms of the state banks and the wider financial restructuring were carried out by the establishment of the PBC-sponsored Central Huijin Investment Company (also named SAFE Investment Company; Huijin hereafter) in December 2003. Through Huijin, the PBC injected US$45 billion from its foreign reserves into the CCB and the BOC in January 2004. In addition, the Bank of Communications, China's fifth largest bank, received US$365 million from Huijin in June 2005 (Feng 2006b). After a series of capital injections and restructuring, Huijin became the predominant sole shareholder of China's banking system (see Table 11.4).

Huijin is thus a special policy vehicle, effectively a proxy of the PBC. The institutional design and daily operation of the company is under the instruction of the FSB of the PBC. Although the personnel are from various ministries, the executives and the backbone staff came from the PBC and the State Administration of Foreign Exchange, which manages China's foreign reserves, which is also subordinate to the PBC. Moreover, Huijin's then general manager, Xie Ping, a liberal reformer, is a former chief of the Research Bureau and director of the FSB of the PBC and the right-hand man of Zhou Xiaochuan.[12]

The shareholding reform and Huijin's predominance in the share structure of the banks enabled the PBC to take control of financial risks in the banking

Table 11.4.   Huijin's investment in China's financial institutions

Date	Financial institutions invested	Amount of initial investment	Stakes (%, at the end of 2011)
December 2003	BOC	US$22.5 billion	67.6[a]
December 2003	CCB	US$20 billion	57.13[a]
December 2003	Jianyin Investment	US$2.5 billion	100[a]
June 2004	BOCOM	RMB 3 billion	0[b]
April 2005	ICBC	US$15 billion	35.43[a]
June 2005	Galaxy Securities	RMB 10 billion	N/A
July 2005	Export-Import Bank of China	US$5 billion	N/A
August 2005	Shenyin Wanguo Securities	RMB 2.5 billion	37.2[a]
August 2005	Guotai Jun'an Securities	RMB 1 billion	21.3
August 2005	Galaxy Holdings	RMB 5.5 billion	78.57[a]
January 2007	China Reinsurance Corporation	US$4 billion	85.5[a]
December 2007	Everbright Bank	RMB 20 billion	48.37[a]
December 2007	China Development Bank	US$20 billion	48.7
November 2008	ABC	RMB 130 billion (US$19 billion)	40.12[a]
November 2009	New China Life Insurance	RMB 4 billion	31.23[a]

Source: PBC and CBRC.

a. Huijin was the controlling shareholder.

b. Huijin transferred its equities in the BOCOM (6.12%) to the MOF in March 2008.

sector and to dictate the desired pattern of reform. Like SOEs, SOBs suffered from the problem of "virtual" state ownership, meaning that a number of government bureaucracies shared authority over the administration and management of the banks, which effectively meant the banks were accountable to no one. Being the controlling shareholder of the banks, Huijin became a "visible hand" in promoting banking reform, mandated to take proactive measures to ensure the safety of the state's capital injection and to obtain a reasonable return on investment. As a state investment company, Huijin's injections are not fiscal allocations but capital investment; therefore a return is expected.

Both the PBC and the Huijin officials stress that the bank's public listing is not an end, but a means to address their chronic problems of poor credit analysis and risk management, rampant insider control, and, most importantly, poor corporate governance. Wang Jianxi, vice chairman of Huijin, made said, "We are their [the banks'] shareholders and they need to report to us. One of our important tasks is to help them restructure" (Shi 2005). First, the PBC and Huijin, being the majority shareholder, regained the authority from the Communist Party's Central Organization Department to appoint desirable senior management of the Big Four, thus considerably weakening political intervention in the financial sector. For instance, Guo Shuqing, chairman of Huijin, was sent to chair the board of the CCB when the then board chairman, Zhang Enzhao, was allegedly involved in financial mishandlings. The size of CCB's board of directors was drastically cut from sixty to fifteen, making it more efficient in overseeing management and operations. Huijin introduced independent directorship to the boards of the CCB and the BOC, assigning four directors to the former and six to the latter ("With Xie Ping's Steering" 2004). The directors assigned by Huijin are no longer government officials but employees of Huijin, who are awarded with higher personal income and more flexible incentives to look after state investment in the banks. Foreign expertise was also invited onto the board, with Bank of America's head of corporate planning and strategy taking up a directorship on the board of the CCB ("With Xie Ping's Steering" 2004).

At the same time, supervisory boards were taking shape in the CCB and BOC to ensure better compliance with the principles of international best practice in the financial sphere. In terms of income and promotion, banking personnel were increasingly linked to their performance rather than their years of service. Xie Ping declared, "the board must provide me with written reports on the performances of all the senior managers and board directors, and I will decide how much they will get paid" (Shi 2005).

Other notable progress has been the establishment of high-level committees charged with prudential risk management on a commercial basis, thus consolidating the authority of loan approvals to the committee. The long-term problem of overstaffing has also been a target of internal restructuring. In 2004, one-third of the CCB's branches were scrapped and the number of its employees was reduced by nearly a quarter (Thomas and Li 2006).

Huijin and the PBC also played a critical role in attracting external interest in Chinese banks. The fact that the series of banking reforms was underwritten by the Chinese central bank, an institution that increasingly has substantial credibility and professionalism in the emerging market economy and one dominated by liberal reformers, has appealed to hesitant international investors and lessened suspicion and doubt about Beijing's latest banking revamp. Huijin is also directly involved in the negotiations with foreign institutions for strategic shareholding before the bank's IPOs (T. Li 2005).

The PBC's targets were not limited to the state banks, however, but extended to the existing shareholding commercial banks and policy banks (see Table 11.4). Indeed, the reform plans for the individual policy banks were initially designed by the research bureau of the PBC under the personal supervision of Zhou Xiaochuan (W. Li 2006). The reform agenda also spread to China's emerging stock market.

Restructuring the Stock Market

The Chinese stock market, since its inauguration in 1990, mainly served the government's political imperative to finance the deeply troubled SOEs through public investment (Tan 2004). The state's domination of the market, characteristic of the country's economic transition, resulted in an extremely distorted and corrupt market (Bell and Feng 2009; Green 2004). One obvious manifestation of this was the coexistence of China's high rates of annual GDP growth juxtaposed with a persistent bearish stock market. Public listing did not "rejuvenate" the enterprises as hoped, but instead fostered low-efficiency and highly corrupt institutional arrangements (Bell and Feng 2009).

For the PBC, which is mandated to oversee China's financial stability, these problems in the stock market held the potential to trigger a financial crisis. After years of market downturn and excessive speculation, more than 90% of the 25 million domestic investors faced absolute losses, and more than half of the brokerages were effectively bankrupt (Bell and Feng 2009, 128). More alarmingly, the huge amount of bad loans in the banks that resulted from shaky investments could extend the risks in the stock market to the entire financial system, given the dominance of state banks in the system.

As the market was on the verge of a collapse, the leadership in Beijing finally implemented the long-awaited institutional reform of the capital market in 2005, addressing the fundamental problem of state ownership by allowing the full floatation of state shares in the market (Bell and Feng 2009). In the meantime, the PBC initiated the restructuring of the financial intermediaries in the market. Again, Huijin acted as the chessman of the PBC, with its approach to banking reform essentially copied to revitalize the stock market. The PBC's strategy has been to recapitalize and take control of large national brokerages through Huijin and the medium-sized regional brokerages through the Construction Investment Co., also owned by Huijin. In 2005, Huijin finalized its recapitalization of Galaxy Securities, Southern Securities, Shenyin Wanguo Securities, and Guotai Jun'an Securities. By the end of 2005, the State Council approved thirteen brokerages to receive US$37.5 billion of capital injections from Huijin. It is estimated that the overall recapitalization could double that amount, reaching US$75 billion (Liu 2006).

Similar to the banking reforms, the bailout by Huijin is the first step, to be followed by internal reforms. Huijin's majority control of the securities companies enabled the PBC to regain some supervisory authority from the China Securities Regulatory Commission (CSRC). The CSRC suffered the contradictory roles of maintaining stability in the stock market as a regulator while at the same time being charged with propelling market prices for SOE listings. This left ample room for corruption and speculation by the brokerages under such regulation. With the PBC partly taking control of the securities companies, exerting stricter scrutiny in relation to financial stability and pushing for internal reforms, the risks are expected to be contained and lessened. Moreover, the PBC also set up a protection fund for ordinary stock investors to compensate their losses due to mishandling by securities firms. "The purpose of this," commented Wu Xiaoling, then vice governor of the PBC, "is not simply to save the brokerages, but to establish sound market rules and to establish market confidence. . . . What the market lacks is confidence, not capital" (Shi 2005).

To Zhou, who was chairman of the CSRC before taking the governorship of the central bank, restructuring the stock market was also essential for the inevitable market opening in the future. Once again the structural dynamics of the transition were having an impact on institutional change. In Zhou's words, "now that the globalization challenge is looming, China's stock market must learn to adapt to and utilize this trend. Some say we should open in a slower pace or control the rhythm [of opening]. This might be the case, but it would also elicit other risks" (Feng and Cai 2005). To Zhou, the implicit risks were rudimentary regulation and the fragile financial intermediaries in the market pitched against fully fledged foreign rivals, a situation that needed to be dealt with proactively rather than reactively. In late 2002 the CSRC approved the participation of foreign capital in China's RMB-denominated A share market, albeit on a limited scale, under the scheme of Qualified Foreign Institutional Investors. However, the PBC has been the major driver behind this initiative.[13] Its introduction is significant to the Chinese market in that it brings fresh liquidity, plus greater market confidence and financial expertise that have been largely absent among domestic investors. More importantly, domestic companies will also need to improve their transparency and corporate governance given the much tighter scrutiny of international investors and institutions.

Other PBC Endeavors

Apart from banking and stock market restructuring, the PBC has also been working on several other fronts in terms of reforming the financial system. These include its efforts to foster corporate financing by breathing new life into China's corporate bond markets and to establish an advanced payment and settlement system.

In terms of corporate financing, the PBC set up a short-term commercial paper (bond) market in 2005 to break the direct-financing logjam. Issuing bonds with a term of up to one year, the market was popular with the large number of companies unable to navigate the lengthy and difficult approval process for longer-term bonds, which was managed by the NDRC (later adding the CSRC for listed companies) and which was mostly limited to large SOEs and state infrastructure projects.

Since the early 1990s, the PBC has also been endeavoring to upgrade China's financial infrastructure, particularly the old, mostly manual-based payment and settlement system inherited from the planning era.[14] The payment system is the bloodline of any country's financial infrastructure, and maintaining the operation of the system usually becomes the direct or indirect responsibility of a central bank, such as the PBC. A sound payment system provides low-cost, fast, and efficient clearing services, which ensures the smooth flow of financial markets and facilitates the implementation of monetary policies. Any problem in the system can pose a systemic risk to the entire financial system. Compared with its Western counterparts, the Chinese central bank faced an especially daunting task to transform the fragmented and rudimentary payment system of the planned economy into one that is efficient and robust for an emerging market economy.

China's payment system has evolved in three phases: the manual processing system in the 1980s, the Electronic Interbank System (EIS) between 1991 and 2005, and the more recently deployed China National Advanced Payment System (Feng 2006a). The payment and settlement system in the planning era worked mostly as an accounting and book-entry system, mainly to provide financial records of the economic activities under central planning. Facing the explosive demand for fast and reliable clearance in the financial sector, the PBC has been continuously upgrading the national payment system. Under a direct push by the then PBC vice governor, Chen Yuan, an electronic system (EIS) was established in 1991, which greatly improved the speed and accuracy of the system, sparking enormous interest among the PBC leadership and the wider financial sector with a consensus that computer-based processing networks bring not only efficiency but also rationalization of operational procedures. Furthermore, the PBC's experience of designing, building, and maintaining the electronic network laid the foundation for a more advanced system.

Financial liberalization in China further deepened as the economic transition to greater market orientation accelerated in the early 1990s. The existing payment system could not meet the seemingly insatiable demands of further market development. Back in 1991 when the EIS had just started its full operation, the PBC began preliminary planning for a new payment and settlement infrastructure for the near future. A Payment System Decision-Making Committee was set up by the PBC to oversee the design and construction of the system, with a vice governor of the PBC taking over the committee chairmanship (Feng 2006a). The PBC managed to extract external support from the international community, including funding support from the World Bank and the Asian Development Bank and advice from an international advisory committee composed of experts from central banks of the United States, Japan, Britain, Germany, and Switzerland. Running since 2005, the China National Advanced Payment System became the artery of financial flows and the nucleus for financial modernization in China. With the application of cutting-edge technologies, the system "position[s] China amongst the best of breeds in the payments system world" (Keppler 2005). Using fiber-optic networks to link PBC branches and banking outlets throughout China, the new system permits both large and small sums to be handled and cleared electronically and enables such transactions to be done both quickly and accurately. At the same time, from the 1990s, the PBC has also nurtured an interbank bank card information exchange system on its own initiative. These efforts at building a more capable and reliable financial infrastructure have paid off as they further enhanced the PBC's institutional capacity to govern the financial system, implementing its monetary policy, and improving the effectiveness of monetary policy.

2005: The Death of Financial Reform in China?

In *Red Capitalism*, Walter and Howie (2011, 19–21) argue that the year 2005 marked a turning point for comprehensive financial reform under the leadership of Zhu Rongji and Zhou Xiaochuan, mostly due to the fact that Zhou's key ally at the top, Jiang Zemin, eventually stepped down from his supreme position, as did his key supporter in the State Council, Vice Premier Huang Ju, who had been in charge of financial affairs but who became terminally ill during that year.

Certain empirical evidence seems to support this argument, particularly a subsequent rebalancing of power within the bureaucracy against the PBC's "radicalism." The above discussion of the PBC-led financial reforms since 2003 suggests that the increasingly authoritative central bank began to flex its muscle not just in the traditional monetary policy arena, but also by aggressively extending its reach to other sectors, which inevitably challenged and encroached on the jurisdictions of other institutional players. For example, the PBC's often unilateral actions through window guidance annoyed the banking regulator, the CBRC; Huijin's dominance of some of the major securities companies alerted the CSRC; the PBC's initiative on the corporate bond market was at loggerheads with the NDRC and the CSRC; and, most serious was the MOF's concern over the PBC's wresting of the Big Four from its control.

The fact that the PBC has been more or less on the defensive on the financial reform front since 2005 is best reflected in its turf war against the MOF. The MOF used to be considered the owner of the banking system, including the Big Four, under a vague corporate law. In particular, the MOF's Finance Department was directly in charge of the operation of the banks, albeit often with lax supervision. However, as the CCB and BOC were recapitalized by Huijin under the PBC, the MOF found itself instantly deprived of its privilege over the banks. Since the two banks were allowed to allocate all of their initial capital (the existing net equity held by the MOF) to a special fund to write off the bad loans, the MOF's equity in these banks was effectively wiped out, and therefore it lost its control of the banks to Huijin.

A fierce debate in China as the two SOBs were publicly listed on the stock exchanges helped the MOF to regain part of its lost territory. Skeptics of the reform saw potential strategic damage to China's future development by foreign participation, pointing to the allegedly limited transfer of banking expertise to domestic banks, marginalization of domestic investors, the prospect of eventual foreign control of China's financial system, on top of a cheap share price for FSIs in what some saw as a "garage sale" ("You zhuanjia dui guoyou" 2005; Naughton 2006b). The criticisms of the reform were largely framed within a wider debate between liberals, nationalists, and New Leftists on the orientation of economic policy. This, combined with the opposition from the MOF and other institutions that had been reluctantly under the shadow of the PBC, created pressure on the Bank and particularly on the newly installed Hu-Wen regime, which felt pressured to restore a power balance to placate the major bureaucratic players.

Subsequently, the MOF managed to retain its half equity in the ICBC with a US$15 billion investment equal to that by Huijin in April 2005. By doing so, the existing bad loans worth 240 billion yuan were to be gradually written off from the Bank's income tax, equity returns, and potential sales of the ICBC shares by the MOF (Liu 2005). This model of equally split ownership, between the MOF and Huijin, was copied to the recapitalization of the last of the Big Four, the ABC, in November 2008, as Huijin injected 190 billion U.S.-dollar-equivalent yuan into the Bank. Further, in September 2007, the MOF managed to convince the State Council to establish a sovereign wealth fund, the China Investment Corporation (CIC), under its control, and to merge Huijin into the CIC. In Chapter 10 we discussed the battle over reserve management between the PBC and the State Administration of Foreign Exchange on one side and the MOF and the CIC on the other. However, losing Huijin to the CIC meant the PBC lost a key vehicle in its financial restructuring plan.

Despite the setbacks for the PBC during this period, we argue that 2005 did not mark the death of financial reform in China; rather, it initiated a new phase of reform, one in which the PBC remains a major player but deliberates through a more inclusive, consensus-seeking process, compared with its previous unilateralism. Importantly, the PBC and Zhou still also find support from the top leadership. The new Hu-Wen administration maintains a generally reformist line, despite a professed change in priority toward more social and equitable development (Chapter 6). Moreover, Premier Wen Jiabao, who is in charge of overall economic and financial affairs, has been a veteran reformer and a major supporter of Zhou and the PBC. Zhou's reappointment as the PBC governor in 2008 reflected confidence and trust by the top leadership. At the same time, a number of important PBC-initiated reforms after 2005, such as banking and exchange rate reforms, would not have proceeded without support from the leadership. The inclusiveness of the new policy process also improves coordination and reduces conflict during policy implementation.

More importantly, the trajectory of financial policies after 2005 followed the track of Zhu's legacy and Zhou's rationale. For instance, in the banking sector, despite the MOF acquiring Huijin from the PBC, it could not provide a credible alternative to the PBC's approach, which had proved successful in the CCB's and the BOC's IPOs. Therefore, the restructuring of the remaining ICBC and the ABC also followed the PBC's model. In particular, the ICBC was listed in Hong Kong and Shanghai in October 2006, raising US$19.1 billion. The ABC eventually went public in July 2010. Listed on the exchanges in both Shanghai and Hong Kong, the Bank raised a total capital of US$22.1 billion (with both overallotment options exercised), smashing the ICBC's record of the world's largest IPO in history (Tudor 2010).

At the same time, the PBC under Zhou has also been active in shaping the path of reform on a number of fronts. In the case of the ABC's public listing, which was widely regarded as the most difficult challenge for the government because of its high NPL ratio and historical debt burdens, Zhou managed to have Xiang Junbo, vice governor of the PBC since 2004, appointed as the president of the ABC in 2007. He has been instrumental in the Bank's reform and IPO.

Another example of PBC activism after 2005 is the development in the bond market. Despite the Bank's initial reform of the sector in 2005, the overall bond market remained tiny and tangled up in red tape under fragmented regulation. Frustrated by the deadlock and insisting on the benefits of a direct finance market, Zhou Xiaochuan and the PBC took matters into its own hands. In an archetypical example of discretionary institutional behavior, the central bank extended the term of bills from one year to five years in April 2008, which effectively created a new, medium-term corporate bond market "at the stroke of a pen" (Wheatley 2008). More importantly, the bonds are issued under a market-oriented process through a dealer's association overseen by the PBC, and also came with much less onerous issuance requirements than traditional types of bonds. As a result, such bond issuance surged from $25 billion in 2008 to $101 billion in 2009, taking up almost half of the total bond issuance in 2009 (Cookson 2010). Again, this is a case of the PBC muscling in on the territory of the powerful NDRC and sectoral regulators, and utilizing and extending its existing authority in an underlegalized arena. Beyond this, other examples of assertiveness include the PBC's major role in pushing for a switch back to a more market-oriented exchange rate regime in 2010, in an ambitious campaign to lift the RMB's international profile (see Chapter 10), and in its "active coordination" with the CSRC to introduce an international board to China's stock market in 2011 (Li 2011). In addition, the PBC's argument for structural reforms, such as capital account liberalization and interest rate marketization, have been gaining traction in 2012 (see Chapters 9 and 10, also Su 2012; Feng 2012).

Assessing the Banking Reforms

The PBC's approach to banking and financial reform represents a dramatic departure from the traditional state socialist model espoused by the MOF. It is an *ex ante*, proactive strategy to tackle institutional deficiencies of the financial system, rather than the *ex post facto*, passive reaction to bank insolvency. It centers on the idea of market discipline, upgrading expertise and institutional innovation, rather than the traditional approach of lax supervision and fiscal bailouts offered by the old regime. In other words, it seeks to establish sound and sustainable financial intermediation in the emerging market. In describing the PBC's strategy, one of its officials used a Chinese saying, "It's more desirable to teach someone to fish than to offer someone a fish."[15]

The PBC-led bank restructuring represents a systemic effort to tackle difficult challenges in the financial sector. Despite PBC's loss of control of Huijin to the MOF, the reform campaign has been relatively successful in terms of the PBC's initial objectives. The PBC's recapitalization of the banks and the subsequent IPOs helped reduce their NPLs to internationally acceptable standards ("You zhuanjia dui guoyou" 2005). According to the CBRC (2012), the average NPL ratio of Chinese banking institutions stood at 1.77% by the end of 2011, well within the current Basel standards.

To some observers, Chinese banks have been transformed into "the world's most valuable and profitable lenders in terms of market capitalization and abso- lute profits" (Anderlini 2010a). The *Banker's Top 1000 World Banks 2011* ranking listed 101 Chinese banks, including three of the top ten in terms of capital strength (ICBC, CCB, and BOA, measured by Tier 1 capital), the top two larg- est banks by market capitalization (ICBC and CCB), four of the top ten in profits (the Big Four), and fifteen of the top twenty-five movers (see Table 11.5).

In terms of asset structure, Chinese banks are also better positioned than most of their Western counterparts, as they were not drawn into the "toxic" mortgage-backed securitization markets. The banks also appear to have a large stock of profits, at least in the short term. Chinese banks now account for the largest slice of global banking profits. Their profits soared by 95% be- tween 2008 and 2010, accounting for 21% of total global banking profits in 2010 ("Chinese Banks Dominate" 2011).

Nevertheless, in the longer term, this round of banking reform is likely to yield mixed results. First, according to Bergera and colleagues (2009), foreign investment will likely improve the efficiency of Chinese banks. Foreign invest- ment appears to have substantial presence in the domestic banking sector, taking over 15% of total equity, and according to Y. Yang (2009), there has been extensive cooperation between Chinese banks and the FSIs (see Table 11.6). Yet given the current restriction on foreign equity in individual banks, the FSIs have had more or less limited presence in the boards and therefore influence. The PBC's intention of introducing international banking expertise was further hampered by the GFC, as some of the major cash-strapped inves- tors withdrew from their Chinese investments.

Despite the seemingly dazzling figures of Chinese banks in world rank- ings, serious observers would take a rather more sober view of their books. Although major banks in China appear to possess a better asset structure than many of their beleaguered Western counterparts, this may be primarily due to the relative closure of China's domestic financial system to the wider trend of financial globalization, and to the relative underdevelopment of domestic financial intermediation, such as derivatives and securitization. As a CBRC official commented during the global financial meltdown, "we did

Table 11.5. World ranking of Chinese banks, 2011

World rank	Bank	Tier 1 capital (US$ million)	Pretax profits (US$ million)	ROA (%)	CAR (%)	NPL (%)
1	Bank of America	163,626	−1,323	−0.06	7.22	3.27
2	JP Morgan Chase	142,450	24,859	1.17	6.73	6.42
3	HSBC Holdings	133,179	19,037	0.78	5.43	2.36
4	Citigroup	126,193	12,273	0.64	6.59	4.76
5	Mitsubishi UFJ	119,732	9,125	0.37	4.83	1.68
6	Industrial and Commercial Bank of China	113,393	32,528	1.6	5.58	1.08
7	Wells Fargo	109,353	18,700	1.49	8.69	6.96
8	China Construction Bank	95,834	26,448	1.62	5.87	1.14
9	Bank of China	94,579	21,463	1.36	5.99	1.10
10	Royal Bank of Scotland	94,091	−1,471	−0.06	4.14	5.31
14	Agricultural Bank of China	79,285	18,230	1.17	5.08	2.03

Source: "Top 1000 World Banks" (2011).
Notes: ROA, return on assets; CAR, capital assets ratio; NPL, nonperforming loans. End of 2010 figures.

Table 11.6.   Business cooperation between Chinese banks and FSIs

Chinese bank	FSI	Area of business cooperation
CCB	Bank of America	Corporate governance, risk management, IT and accounting management, human resources, retail banking, and liquidity management
BOC	Royal Bank of Scotland	Credit cards, financial management, corporate business, and personal insurance
	UBS	Investment banking
	Asian Development Bank	Internal administration, anti–money laundering
ICBC	Goldman Sachs	Investment banking, corporate governance
	Allianz	Insurance, capital management
	American Express	Credit cards

Source: Adapted from Yang Y. (2009).

not drown not because we were good at swimming but because we were far from the water" (Li 2009b).

In fact, China did at one point have a toe in the water. Take securitization, for example, a process that involves packaging the anticipated cash flows of instruments such as loans or receivables into asset-backed securities, which are then sold to investors. It is one of the ways in which assets can be hedged in a derivative market. China launched a pilot program on asset securitiza-tion in 2005, but the experiment was put on hold in 2008 in the wake of the GFC when the technique became a byword for problems in the West ("China Revives Credit" 2012). But this did not stop the banks from venturing further into this area. Previous reforms aimed at improving disclosure have had the opposite effect, which saw the banks seek to avoid formal capital adequacy ratios and circumvent credit quotas through informal securitization, moving credit to the off–balance sheet activities, particularly in wealth management products. According to a Fitch estimate, about RMB 2.3 trillion in securi-tized loans was sitting in off–balance sheet accounts in Chinese banks by the first half of 2010 (Cotterill 2010). The growing popularity of this activity in recent years, particularly since 2009, could result in a pervasive understate-ment of credit growth and credit exposure, all under the radar of banking regulators. According to the IMF (2011), informal securitization could aug-ment a potential shock and undermine monetary policy effectiveness.

Considering this, the PBC tried to broaden financing categories under its watch, from traditional bank credits to "society-wide financing," involving a range of emerging financing channels including securitization (see Chapter 8). The CBRC also responded by temporarily stopping all informal securitization deals between trust companies and banks. It also asked the banks to bring all off–balance sheet assets that underlay wealth management assets back on their books by the end of 2011 and to set up loss provisions as well as capital against potential losses.[16] In May 2012, after a four-year hiatus, the PBC and CBRC felt comfortable enough to revive the securitization program with a trivial quota of 50 billion yuan, compared with the country's 61 trillion yuan worth of loans (Zheng 2012). Therefore, the reaction by the Chinese financial authorities to the GFC has not seen a halt on reforms, but a cautious and progressive attitude, "a never-ending dance between regulation and allowing much-needed financial innovation."[17] According to Li Daokui, a former member of the PBC's Monetary Policy Committee, "Asset securitization is the road one must follow to achieve modern finance. The key is how to regulate it in a proper manner" (Wang 2012).

Although buoyant about the bank's volume of profits, Zhang Jianhua (2009) of the PBC admitted that profitability remains the weakest link in the bank's performance, which largely rests on interest rate spreads, rather than the diversity and quality of their services. According to the CBRC (2012), total profits of the Chinese banks almost tripled between 2007 and 2011, but their average return on asset ratio (showing how profitable a bank's assets are in generating revenue) and average return on equity ratio (measuring a bank's efficiency at generating profit) had increased by only 0.4% and 3.7% respectively during the same period. This indicates very low profitability on the part of the banks, largely due to their rudimentary business model. Indeed, despite the institutional reforms initiated by the PBC, the banks continue to run on a mostly similar business model of relying on a generous interest rate spread set by the central bank. In a bid to provide a lifeline, the PBC (including Zhou Xiaochuan) believes this is necessary to spur the bank's "maturity" (Shen 2010). As a result, the growth in profitability was mainly attributed to the increase in the size of interest-bearing credit assets, with the bank's net interest income accounting for 66.2% of the total income in 2011 (CBRC 2012).

However, this model, dubbed "eating capital" *(chi ziben)* in China, essentially encourages banks to lend as much as they can until their balance sheets are eroded, forcing them to return to the capital markets for funds in order to meet regulatory requirements. In fact, the banks have quickly "eaten up" their newly raised capital in the post-GFC lending extravaganza to finance the massive government stimulation program, so much so that they have extended hands to market investors again for refinancing after their IPOs. In 2011 alone, fourteen of the sixteen listed banks announced their refinancing programs totaling almost 520 billion yuan ("2011nian shangshi yinhang rongzi" 2011). According to the CBRC, the recently installed international banking regulatory standard, Basel III, will have a "further impact on capital replenishment on China's banking sector" and shareholders' fear of dilution (Ma 2010). This situation has been made even more difficult by the MOF's insistence that the banks pay high levels of dividends. Between 2009 and 2011, the big four commercial banks have raised 622 billion yuan in new capital through bonds and share offerings while paying out 402 billion yuan in dividends (Borst 2011).

More importantly, the PBC-led reform has yet to address the fundamental issue of government intervention in commercial banking as the state remains the largest shareholder of the listed banks. A major setback happened when Huijin was merged into the MOF-controlled CIC, which means the MOF resumed its status as the state supervisor of the banks and therefore its old practices of lax discipline and accountability (Walter and Howie 2011). This was apparently behind the bank's lending spree in 2009, with record lending of 9.6 trillion yuan, under the party-state's pressure to finance its gigantic stimulus package (Chapter 9). Indeed, ICBC admitted in its shareholder circular in 2009 that the Bank was "conscientiously implementing the State's macro economy policy" (Smith 2010).

In addition, the ties between the banks and local governments remain intimate. Such ties saw a large part of the recent credit boom go to finance platforms that are controlled by and serve for local government. According to the National Audit Office, local government debt stood at 10.7 trillion yuan by the end of 2010 (about a quarter of China's GDP), of which 79% was financed by bank credit (Huang 2012). According to a self-assessment by the banks, a minimum of 20% of these debts were unlikely to be repaid (Anderlini 2010a). About 35% of the loans to local governments will be due over the next three years after 2012, but many of them went to infrastructure investments that have not yet started to generate revenues, raising the risk of defaults (Rabinovitch 2012). Facing a pending peak in maturity, Beijing ordered a rollover of local debt of almost 500 billion yuan in 2011, near 18% of the total repayable for the year (Zhong 2012).

In this sense, the latest round of recapitalization by the PBC and the bank's public listing has perhaps only temporarily reduced their NPL ratios to an acceptable level, which, according to the CBRC, stood at 0.9% by November 2011 (Wu and Min 2012). The banks' extremely high exposure to local governments' largesse and real estate projects (see Chapter 9) have given rise to concerns of a potential new wave of NPLs in the medium term. If a further fall of housing prices and a rise of local government defaults are factored in, the NPL ratio could rise by about 5.4 trillion yuan, to 13.4% of total loans (Anderlini 2010c). An investigation by Fitch Ratings (2010) on the irregular practice of "informal securitization" of the Chinese banks, or the repackaging of bank loans into investment products, led to more pessimistic views by the agency with the conclusion that "future asset quality deterioration is a near-certainty—the question is only when, to what degree, and whether it will lead to a crisis."

A more comprehensive assessment of China's financial system stability by the IMF in 2011 was more upbeat. Based on stress tests of the largest seventeen commercial banks jointly conducted with the Chinese authorities, the findings indicate that most of the banks appear to be "resilient" to isolated shocks, including a sharp deterioration in asset quality, a correction in the real estate markets, shifts in the yield curve, and changes in the exchange rate. However, "if several of these risks were to occur at the same time, the banking system could be severely impacted" (IMF 2011, 7).

The early achievement of the banking reforms and the remaining worrying signs of a systemic failure in the banking sector remind us that there is no silver bullet for the myriad chronic problems. Addressing these issues will be an ongoing business for the Chinese authorities, especially as the banks remain state owned and therefore state controlled, eventually backed by "the perpetual put option" (Walter and Howie 2011, 68–73), or the readiness of the state to bail out distressed banks. Despite the various setbacks and deficiencies, the PBC's efforts nevertheless represent a serious first step of a long march to establish more efficient and effective financial intermediation in China. Nevertheless, more bold and radical reforms are needed to build sustainable business models for Chinese banks and to help them toward more commercially oriented lending.

The mixed results of the PBC-led financial reforms also reflect the fragility of market reforms in a transition context, in which progress is often subject to drawn-out battles on two fronts. In ideational terms, as discussed earlier, liberal reformers have to defend their rationale against a surging wave of economic nationalists. More importantly, the fate of the reforms, such as that of the recent round of bank restructuring, hangs on the competition between divergent agendas within the state, between the old planning, administrative allocation agenda and practice, and the new liberal agenda that tries to forge ahead with market reforms and commercial banking practices. The administrative agenda is still apparent, representing a relatively easier, more direct, and more "familiar" solution for the party-state when quick results are imperative, and it often appears more effective than a market approach in China's institutional setting. However, as the costs associated with this short-term strategy emerge, the reformers may be able to gather momentum for further reforms. This largely prescribes the dynamics of institutional change in reform China, which are often embodied in the form of one step forward, two steps back, or two steps forward, one step back. Indeed, gradualism is not just a politically convenient strategy, but also often a result of the conflicts and compromises within the party and bureaucratic elite.

Conclusion

Banking reform in China is a microcosm of the larger, heated struggle to redefine the distribution of authority and the future of China's economic and political institutions. While earlier reforms such as the 1998 recapitalization program was a mostly failed attempt by a politically hesitant leadership and the old planning apparatus, the recent round of reforms initiated in 2003 benefited from the development of new, market-oriented institutions, especially the PBC, that have been taking shape with growing authority and credibility, aided by the pressures of external integration.

Hence, despite substantial inertia and resistance, the key role of the PBC in building a modern financial infrastructure is significant. Through Huijin, the Chinese central bank drew on 10% of the foreign reserves and controlled more than half of the state's financial assets, which enabled substantial financial reforms following the PBC's own liberal agenda. The reforms, which aimed at weakening the central state's dominance in the (distorted) market and transforming the domestic financial intermediaries into more market-oriented commercial institutions, have helped reassure international investors regarding China's banking reforms. However, there are problems with this model, especially continued state intervention in the banking sector under the control of a more conservative MOF, and the bailout of securities companies that are owned by central and local governments, which could generate moral hazard. Overall, however, the PBC's efforts have thus far laid a more solid foundation for China's financial stability and development in a post-WTO era. Further substantial reforms are, however, required.

12

Conclusion

During an interview, a PBC official gave a vivid analogy of the politics of reform amidst transition, and the complex institutional challenges it entails: "China is very much like a giant leaking ship. We cannot stop and repair the ship, otherwise it is bound to sink. We have to mend it while it sails until reaching the shore. In other words, we have to reform amidst development, and to develop amidst reform. There is no other alternative."[1] The rise of the People's Bank and the modernization of China's monetary policy that we have examined in the book, illustrates the many complexities, dilemmas, and achievements of an adaptive Leninist party-state in dealing with the gigantic project of systemic transition. We have argued that the process of establishing a more market-oriented central banking system and monetary policy framework is deeply embedded in Beijing's quest for a managed transition featuring drawn-out tensions between planning and market institutions.

Most Chinese political and intellectual elites view the big bang transition approach in Russia and its former satellites as having failed—akin to demolishing the ship and trying to build a new one at sea. The Chinese trajectory has instead featured a more or less "managed" transition, entailing the gradual transformation of the economic system, allowing a market-oriented framework slowly but steadily to grow out of the plan. This dualism in China's transition has put heavy demands on the state to establish a sound institutional infrastructure for the emerging market economy, while at the same time attempting to sustain a political consensus around reform while avoiding political instability.

As we have seen, the first reform era of the 1980s was dominated by the heritage of the planning apparatus, ambivalent ideological lines, and a constant political battle between reformers and conservatives, all of which had a constraining impact on the newly established central banking system. The PBC largely operated on the sidelines of macroeconomic policymaking and institutionally in the shadow of the SPC and the MOF. A general shift of the PBC's operational context in the 1990s marked a second reform era, which featured an elite aversion to inflationary risks due to episodes of traumatic price volatilities in the late 1980s and early 1990s, and a stronger political and ideational consensus in favor of market-oriented reform and external integration. These shifts empowered reformers within the party leadership as well as within the PBC, which in turn accelerated the reform process as the market drive deepened and complementary institutions were established. This propelled further institutional changes on the part of the PBC, as it developed critical institutional and policy capacities that saw it evolve into a policy heavyweight in Beijing's macroeconomic management circle. The rise of the central bank reflects the changing power structure in economic and financial policymaking within the Chinese state, as demonstrated by key policy clashes between the PBC and traditional power holders such as the National Development and Reform Commission and the Ministry of Finance.

Most centrally, however, the rise of the PBC reflects the growth of strong mutual dependencies between the PBC and the leadership of the Communist Party, which has helped underpin the growing authority of the PBC within the steep hierarchy of the party-state. By building its institutional capacity, particularly its expertise in modern central banking and monetary policy, by establishing a credible policy record, and by fostering informal though powerful ties with key figures in the top party leadership, the PBC has won increased authority by becoming an indispensable ally for the political leadership in macroeconomic management as well as in providing political support. These political and institutional dynamics of mutual dependency, set within facilitative change contexts, have been the key to explaining the puzzle of the rise of the PBC's authority. Hence through our historical and institutional lens, we have deconstructed the myth of the PBC as a puppet agency, which is widely and readily taken for granted even by some experienced China watchers. At the same time we have rejected the notion of a high level of central bank independence in China, as some studies suggest. In reality, as we have argued, the party leaders have increasingly recognized the PBC's monetary expertise and authority, especially since the 1990s. In the hierarchical Chinese context, this is a significant outcome.

The leaders of the PBC were also able to exploit informal relations and opportunities to exercise considerable discretion in the making and implementation of monetary policy. Beijing's lingering reliance on administrative means in governing an emerging market awarded the PBC extra channels and tools that are not typically available to Western central banks. This can be illustrated by the PBC's battle against asset price inflation during 2003–4 to circumvent the approval of the State Council, the Bank's innovative sterilization programs amid the pressure for RMB revaluation, the PBC's seizure of banking reform leadership by utilizing China's foreign reserves that are under its control, and the PBC's almost single-handed efforts to revive China's corporate bond markets, all of which represent adept efforts by the PBC to navigate, exploit, and maneuver in the discretionary space created by legal and wider institutional arrangements. These efforts in turn boosted the PBC's credibility in the market and ultimately its authority within the party-state.

The interplay between contextual impacts and agent assertiveness has also been witnessed in the evolution of China's monetary policy. The dual-track economy that persisted during the first reform era saw economic administration engaged in cautious and often limited experiments in economic management featuring indirect policy tools, while monetary policy still mostly took the form of direct financial planning. As market reforms accelerated in the 1990s, however, these initial efforts were expanded into more ambitious and systematic strategies, partly reflecting the PBC's rising authority. For example, the abolition of the Credit Plan in 1998 was monumental in that it formally marked the end of financial planning as the PBC began to embrace a new more market-oriented monetary policy framework centering on aggregate controls and a mixture of direct and indirect policy tools.

We have thus shown how an increasingly assertive and authoritative central bank has served as a vital building block in the transformation from a command-oriented administrative state in China to a more market-oriented "regulatory state," at least in the arena of monetary and financial policy. Here our argument largely counters those that are skeptical about Chinese institutional reform. For example, Feng (2010) points to the challenges of policy coordination across a fragmented bureaucracy, while Dyer (2010a) questions the competency of China's large bureaucracy and form of state capitalism that is alleged to have "a much less impressive record at producing the innovation that Chinese leaders believe is crucial to the long-term future of the economy." It may also be true, as Pearson (2005) argues, that the emergence of a professionalized "regulatory state" in China is being stymied by the centralizing hand of the party-state. Pearson's account, however, does not fully square with the case of the PBC, which has experienced a very substantial increase in professionalism and authority. Our argument also raises questions about accounts such as Pei's (2006), who argues that China's gradualist strategy for economic reform under a "developmental autocracy" lacks the dynamics and incentives for further and more fundamental reforms to sustain economic growth and instead has resulted in a predatory state, a grabbing hand that adversely interferes in the economic sphere with rampant and widespread corruption. True, corruption is a major problem in China, but our account of the rise of a more professionalized central bank is more aligned with arguments from scholars such as Yang (2004), who argues that the Chinese state has undergone positive and incremental transformations to help better govern an emerging market economy. One problem with an exclusive focus on institutional dysfunction or on the economic and social costs associated with corruption is that it overlooks widespread pressures on the leadership, not least from market opening and the economic transition, to continue to reform the state and build new, more effective institutions. The rise of the PBC is evidence of the latter. Nevertheless, the polarized debate on China's institutional trajectory will no doubt continue. Sectoral and institutional differences and variations, as this case suggests, are worth greater examination, suggesting the need for detailed case-by-case assessments across different institutional arenas to arrive at a more comprehensive picture of China's state capacity than we have at present.

Our depiction of the Chinese central bank gaining authority within an authoritarian regime poses a puzzle that we have attempted to explain, but this also suggests broader comparative analysis, especially regarding central bank independence (CBI). Here, for obvious reasons, we have not focused CBI in the China context but on a more nuanced analysis of rising central bank authority (CBA). As we have argued, many comparative studies of CBI are overgeneralized and oversimplified, often using formal proxy measures in quantitative analysis that are simply too crude to assess the texture of key historical developments, in China or elsewhere. Instead we have examined real institutional life, deeply embedded in domestic historical contexts and political and bureaucratic power plays. Notwithstanding the formal, nonindependent status of the PBC, we have argued that rising CBA in China has marked a significant change in Chinese monetary institutions and policy. We have traced the domestic institutional roots of this change in China's case and argued that the unique institutional capacities and expertise of the PBC have been a major factor underpinning its rising authority and helping it forge wider alliances. We suspect this kind of institutionally based CBA story regarding rising authority, both in its formal and informal dimensions, has been a widespread one amongst many central banks.

Beyond such embedded institutional analysis, we have also emphasized domestic causation and heavily mediated policy diffusion from overseas. The standard external drivers of rising central bank authority that are typically depicted in the literature have not been at work in China's case, especially the structural forces from financial markets and the requirement for external signaling of creditworthiness. Nor has the cognitive spread of CBI as an idea if not ideology expressed through a transnational epistemology community of central bankers been influential in China. Indeed, the impact of such international diffusion mechanisms has been quite limited. This is partly because, as we have argued, China is not dependent on external credit, but is instead a major international supplier of credit. Nor has China simply mimicked others or sought to achieve normative recognition or approval by jumping on the CBI international bandwagon. Indeed, this pressure or mechanism, widely discussed in the international policy diffusion literature (see, e.g., Dobbin et al. 2005; Sharman 2008) has been noticeably absent in China. The same applies with respect to China's limited and largely self-directed agenda on exchange rate liberalization. On the other hand, the main area where international influences have been apparent is the influence of Western economic ideas on Chinese policymakers, as manifested, for example, in the search for more market-oriented policy instruments or the input of Western agencies such as the IMF in helping to train local monetary officials. Yet we have also argued that the need to heavily tailor and adapt imported economic nostrums and Western doctrines of best practice to suit local conditions has been crucial in Chinese monetary policy reform and institution building. The rise of the

PBC and the reshaping of Chinese monetary policy have not primarily been an externally driven, policy convergence process. Based on past lessons and experiences, central bankers and other key economic policymakers came to the view that China needs to find its own way, at its own pace, to deal with the extra and in many ways unique difficulties and complexities entailed in the transition process.

The influence of such adapted or "indigenous" policy solutions has also been apparent in other transition cases. A good example is the Reserve Bank of India (RBI). As with the original PBC, the RBI, at its establishment in 1951, was mandated to support the state's developmental projects through deficit monetization and directed credits under economic planning (albeit less rigidly than that in China) (Reddy 2001). Like China, the transition from a planned economy to an increasingly marketized economy in the 1990s saw the RBI confront new inflationary pressures. The RBI experimented briefly in 1985–86 and 1997–98 with a "flexible monetary targeting approach," with M3 growth as a nominal anchor, reserve money as the operating target, and bank reserves as the operating instrument (Mohan 2005). The monetary policy framework was further changed to a multiple indicator approach in which a host of macroeconomic variables were monitored (Jadhav 2003). As with the PBC, the monetary authorities in India thus had to work with both quantitative and qualitative (price-based) instruments in order to harness monetary conditions to achieve desired macroeconomic objectives. This pragmatic, mixed-bag approach may be a wider comparative lesson from transition cases. For example, echoing similar dilemmas in China, the former RBI governor, Jalan, summarized the Bank's position:

> There is growing consensus now—in theory as well as in practice—that the central bank should have instrumental independence, and concentrate on a single target of inflation control with the use of a single instrument. The position, no doubt, is theoretically sound, but as I look at the history of economic thought and changing fashions in economic policy making, I must confess to a sense of discomfort on whether the current dominant view on "one target, one instrument" will survive the test of time. . . . In developing countries this whole question of trade-offs—particularly at the margin— and during periods of external or domestic uncertainties, becomes even more relevant because of a large non-monetized and agricultural economy. It seems to me that a certain amount of target flexibility and balancing of conflicting objectives are unavoidable. (quoted in Jadhav 2003, 46)

Likewise, China's monetary policy has had to accommodate a range of priorities, particularly a fine short-term balance between growth and price stability, and utilize to its full advantage a combination of direct and indirect policy instruments. It has also needed to situate monetary reforms within a wider pattern of institutional reforms, especially in relation to banking reform, financial market development, and the exchange rate system. For example, the exchange rate system is likely to be further liberalized, but this will need to be in step with wider major reforms in the banking and financial sector and a gradual shift to a more domestically driven development model.

A similar focus on the importance of domestic drivers of central bank reform can be found in Russia. Reflecting international pressures, Johnson (2006a, 96) argues that CBI was introduced in the early 1990s (Hinton-Braaten 1994; Hochreiter and Riesinger 1995) "without much discussion," in a process that mimicked the practices of Western counterparts and the impact of "a transnational policy network" or "epistemological community." Elsewhere, however, Johnson (1997, 2003) has explained the rise of CBI in Russia as also a result of domestic politics, indeed, "extreme politics" in the immediate aftermath of the fall of communism. By installing CBI, the then president, Boris Yeltsin, sought to achieve a dual goal: to ensure monetary stability in the face of economic turmoil after the collapse of the Soviet Union, and to gain an important ally in his bitter battle for supremacy against the parliament. Johnson's approach here, instead of just being framed as part of a wider generalized international CBI trend under the banner of market pressures or institutional diffusion or mimicry, arguably provides a more nuanced account of domestic institutional and political dynamics.

This domestic orientation has infused much of the extant explanatory literature dealing with the politics of China's economic opening and reform. Although scholars of China's opening, such as Howell (1993), Lardy (1992b), Pearson (2001), and others, have paid attention to external pressures, it is still largely the case, as Zweig (2002, 14) argues, that China scholars have tended to focus on elite or domestic political explanations and have tended to "downplay external factors." After an extensive review of the literature, Moore (2002, 35) agrees: "If there is a single dominant theme within this literature . . . it is that domestic politics have been the primary source of policy changes in China's reform and opening." He goes on to argue that such a bias may be inappropriate because "the structuring impact of the international political economy has been seriously underestimated in the literature on post-Mao China" (43). We have concurred with this view in a study of China's attempts to develop indigenous high technology in the wireless sector, a case where international (especially U.S.) pressures subverted China's attempts in the early 2000s to develop domestic wireless standards (Bell and Feng 2007).

On the other hand, domestic political actors ultimately remain the ones that actually make policy decisions. A large literature also argues that the effects of external pressure will be mediated by domestic institutional arrangements (e.g., Keohane and Milner 1996; Weiss 2003). As Gourevitch (1978, 900) argues, "The international system is underdetermining. . . . The environment may exert strong pulls, but short of actual occupation, some leeway in response to that environment remains. The explanation of choice among the possibilities therefore requires some examination of domestic politics." In the case at hand, we have emphasized domestic drivers of change, but it is clear that the relative weight of external and domestic pressures for change will vary across different sectors and cases. We need a clearer understanding of how and under what conditions domestic and external pressures might shape domestic policy choices.

Our domestic institutional and political focus is reflected in our account of the rise of the PBC and our focus on the development of strong mutual dependencies between the party leadership and the PBC. This endogenous process of institutional change in China suggests that with the right nexus of institutional capacity and political reciprocity, an authoritative and more market-oriented central banking system is achievable within a Leninist system. This process also highlights the importance of building institutional capacity and wider reciprocity in forging strong institutional supports and foundations, something not as apparent in many central banks in eastern Europe (Johnson 2006b).

In explaining the rise of the PBC as a major institutional change within the Chinese state, we have traced a set of mutually shaping interactions between key agents within the PBC and a wider set of shaping contexts that have constrained and empowered the PBC. The contexts have included exogenous crises, changing political and power configurations (especially within the party-state), changes in public policy, and evolving ideational as well as structural contexts, especially the economic transition. The interaction between key agents and such contexts has been central, we argue, in shaping change at the PBC. Our explanatory approach is thus critical of sticky versions of historical institutionalism (HI), which explain substantial patterns of change largely through exogenous shocks. To help explain this case of large scale, occasionally punctuated, but mostly incremental change, we opted instead for a more agency-centered version of HI featuring a more active notion of agency than that found in sticky versions of HI. We see agents as active players with varying and contingent degrees of discretion, operating in environments that are not only constraining but also potentially empowering. We have also modeled agents as operating in multiple institutional and wider contexts that constantly evolve and potentially open up new opportunities for agents. Certain external contexts are important, especially the changing power structure within the party-state, as well as China's transition economy. Changes in these wider contexts helped empower agents and facilitate change within the PBC. The degree of empowerment and flexibility we traced also questions rigid theoretical notions of "path dependency." We instead suggested it is more useful to focus on specific mechanisms such as institutional legacies or increasing returns to explain how agents deal with "path contingency." As Schneiberg (2007, 50) argues, "It is hard to explain fundamental change and the rise of new paths using arguments about path dependency and the constraining power of context." Our approach is more open-ended and historically contingent. Our empirical account of China's dynamically evolving monetary institutions covers over three decades of historical change. The sheer scale and dynamism of the changes in question sit oddly with the determinacy often implied by accounts of postcommunist transitions that emphasize a pattern of constraining path dependency born of the legacies of communist central planning. The Chinese story is more complex and dynamic than this. Over time, systems of institutional change can unwind earlier patterns of constraint and shift to new institutional accretions on a new contingent path.

According to a study by the Standard Chartered Bank in early 2012, the total assets of the PBC have ballooned 119% since 2006 to a whopping 28 trillion yuan (US$4.5 trillion) by the end of 2011, making it the world's biggest central bank in terms of total assets, ahead of the European Central Bank (US$3.5 trillion) and the U.S. Federal Reserve (US$3 trillion). The PBC, instead of the traditional central bank lenders such as the European Central Bank or the Federal Reserve, is now the major supplier of global liquidity. According to the report, the PBC has become the world's number 1 in terms of both the stock of M2 money (85.2 trillion yuan, or US$13.7 trillion) and newly added M2 money. In 2011 alone, China's M2 supply accounted for 52% of the world's total. This led the Standard Chartered Bank to call Zhou Xiaochuan, governor of the PBC, "the world's central banker" (Mackenzie 2012; "PBOC Tops Central Banks" 2012).

For Chinese central bankers, however, being crowned the "global boss" in this way was rather awkward, with the official newspaper, the *People's Daily* ("Global Boss" 2012), calling it "false flattery." Indeed, the spate of seemingly flattering figures have only highlighted the economic pain behind the huge assets of the Chinese central bank, 80% of which was in the form of foreign exchange assets at the end of 2011. Under the imperative of a "managed" exchange rate regime, the PBC has had to resort to an inflation of its balance sheet, by purchasing excess dollars in the market, to absorb the inflation of China's external surpluses (Chapter 10). More importantly, this also highlights the distortion and compromises imposed on domestic monetary policy as well as overall economic management in China. All this reflects the fact that monetary policy has operated in a highly politicized policy arena dominated by the party elite and contending bureaucracies that have in various ways prioritized the short-term pursuit of low inflation and economic growth. This has seen the PBC embroiled in the crossfire among often conflicting objectives, amid both internal and external pressures.

Within this difficult context, the PBC's achievements have so far been impressive. After all, it has only been a little more than three decades since China began to dismantle the monobank system and build a modern central bank. Compared with its Western counterparts whose institutions and policy frameworks are often relatively well developed and fine tuned, the PBC is a novice player at best in terms of its relatively brief history. Over the years, the PBC has been inundated with a variety of challenges, many of which have not been encountered by overseas central banks. So far policy outcomes have been mixed. The PBC has been largely successful since the 1990s in controlling consumer price index inflation. Progress has also been made with institutional reforms. Steps have been taken to liberalize China's interest rate regime, but major reforms on this front have remained limited since 2000. The exchange rate regime is marked by more flexibility, but there is still a long way to go toward a full float of the RMB. The major banks also have been restructured into shareholding enterprises and listed in stock markets, but state intervention remains the major problem in hampering their commercial operations.

Moreover, the PBC's rising authority does not lead one to expect substantial moves toward an autonomous or fully independent central bank, similar to many Western counterparts. As we have seen, the institutional authority and policy capacity of the PBC have been enhanced by its mutual relationship with the party leadership. Yet the leadership is unlikely to relinquish ultimate authority over monetary and financial affairs given their central position in the leadership's economic strategy. Also, the informal dimensions of the PBC's authority have been built on personal ties and contingent allegiances. In the long run, therefore, apart from continuously building up its institutional capacity, a more authoritative PBC will need to rest on the further reform of China's economic and financial policymaking framework. The fact that the central bank is now firmly located in the power center of China's macroeconomic management suggests at least a degree of forward-looking change within the party-state as it faces the challenges of economic liberalization and external integration.

We have also argued in this book that the PBC's growing authority has partly hinged on its relatively successful monetary policy track record. But this also poses challenges, largely because the PBC's track record is potentially vulnerable in the face of some future significant policy error or miscalculation on the part of the Bank. The rise of the PBC is thus very much a contingent work in progress. The future of Chinese central banking largely rests on how the PBC will face up to the complex challenges in the years ahead, many of which have no easy fix. These challenges require not only understanding of modern money and the economy but also a consciousness of and a readiness to adapt them to China's unique process of market transition. They also require politically difficult decisions.

Looking ahead, a major challenge for the PBC will be to increase its monetary policy autonomy by minimizing or severing the link between its foreign exchange purchase and base money expansion. The PBC's intervention in the foreign exchange rate market has been directly responsible for the rapid expansion of broad-based money, which is, in the words of Li Daokui (2012), a former member of the PBC's monetary policy committee, a "perennial destabilizing force for the entire economy." China has had a similar experience with the West in its quest for an appropriate anchor for monetary policy. According to Frankel (2012), the Western fashion was money supply targeting in the early 1980s, which was derived from the prevailing monetarist doctrine, but this approach succumbed rather quickly to violent money demand shocks. The next anchor of choice was exchange rate targeting, as various countries increasingly adopted "stricter" fixed exchange rate regimes (Petursson 2000). Subsequently, in the face of the liberalization of international financial transactions and the huge increase in their volume, particularly in the wake of the currency crises of the 1990s when pegged exchange rates came under fatal speculative attack in many of these countries, exchange rate targeting was replaced by a new monetary policy anchor with wider acceptance, namely, interest rate targeting.

In China's case, the PBC adopted the intermediate regime of money supply targeting in the mid-1990s, which evolved into de facto exchange rate targeting in the early 2000s when the PBC was preoccupied with defending first a fixed exchange rate and then a crawling peg to the dollar. Although China is in a strong position to fend off any speculative attack on the RMB given its vast pool of reserves, exchange rate as the PBC's policy anchor increasingly appears unsustainable due to the huge costs associated with its sterilization programs. More importantly, it severely limits the room and effectiveness of the PBC's anti-inflation mandate. On the other hand, as we have argued, the Chinese economy has increasingly become more inflation prone. Constraints on the PBC's core business of monetary policy will over time damage its credibility and therefore its authority in the party-state and wider government, as well as in the market. Therefore, the stakes are high for the PBC to further liberalize the exchange rate regime and make it more market oriented. Fierce resistance will be encountered from the tradable sector and its bureaucratic and party elite representatives, but the reform will be pivotal for the strategic transition from an export-led economy to one that is driven by domestic consumption. In the longer term, both the political and monetary authorities will need to make a choice between effective inflation control and a stable exchange rate. A welcome sign for the PBC emerged in early 2012, with the RMB's real exchange rate approaching its equilibrium, given a reduction in China's trade surplus and capital outflow due to a slump in external demand and risk aversion by international capital in the wake of widespread sovereign debt crises. This could pose an opportunity for the PBC to push and convince the leadership on structural reforms, such as capital account liberalization, more flexibility in the exchange rate system, and the RMB's eventual full float, which would help free the hands of the PBC in its monetary policy deliberations.

Fueling short-term inflation concerns, another challenge has been the rapid increase in labor costs in China since the beginning of 2010, amid credible signs of labor shortage (5–8 million for the coastal regions annually), emerging cases of collective bargaining (despite a lack of independent unions), and increasingly tense industrial relations. After all, a repressed labor market in the last two decades has helped the PBC contain inflation. This time around, more organized and higher-waged labor will become an increasing structural force to be reckoned with in terms of its direct impact on inflation. A study has found that every 10% increase of labor costs will result in a 3% rise in manufacturing costs, and eventually a 1.5% increase in consumer price index ("Gongzi shangzhang" 2008). The recent wage increases are not a one-off phenomenon. An annual increase of 20–30% in the low-end labor market is expected by some economists in the three to four years after 2010 (Y. Chen 2010). Neither are they local. In 2011, for example, twenty-four of the thirty-one provinces in China had raised their minimum wage levels by an average of 22% ("24 ge shengfen" 2011). This led the French bank Natixis to forecast that labor costs in China would match those of the United States within four years, catching up with eurozone countries in five years and with Japan in seven ("China Labour Costs" 2012).

The nationwide wage rise has led to an increase in the real exchange rate and will be instrumental in China's long-term transition to a consumption-based economy. It may trigger not an immediate exodus of foreign investment (Holmes 2011) but more likely a relocation of manufacturing to the inland regions where wage levels are still relatively low, as well as a gradual upgrade to the higher value-added segments of the supply chain. In the short term, however, this poses upward pressure on production costs in China and will reduce the (already thin) margins of Chinese exporters. The wage increases also have mixed consequences for macroeconomic and monetary management. In the short term, the wage increases are less likely to translate into significant price increases, largely due to a consistent increase of labor productivity in China (averaging more than 9% a year since 2005) (Batson and Shirouzu 2010). Nevertheless, in the mid to long term, the PBC and more broadly the Chinese authorities will have to deal with and factor in this new variable in their strategies of price stabilization.

The abolition of financial repression and the marketization of interest rates will also be a fundamental challenge for the PBC. Financial repression, which is centered on limiting capital outflow and regulating deposit and lending rates, has enabled the government to transfer cheap financial resources from the household sector to the state sector. This has been a crucial foundation of

China's investment-driven and export-oriented growth model (Zhang 2011). According to Zhang (2012), such a system also formed a cost-sharing mechanism in which the household sector also bore some of the sterilization costs of the PBC through negative real deposit rates. Nevertheless, this form of systemic exploitation is no longer sustainable. On the one hand, as Beijing's priority switches gradually to more socially equitable development and to a more consumption-based economy, traditionally high household savings levels will fall. On the other hand, however, the increasingly porous capital controls and growing access to international financial markets will gradually break the monopoly of the banks over domestic savings. Therefore, interest rate liberalization will become an imperative, rather than a policy trend. However, in the short to medium term, a liberalized rate regime will put pressure on the banks, which have been enjoying easy profitability from relatively high interest rate spreads, as well as on China's local governments, many of which have been highly leveraged and therefore will face higher finance and repayment costs.

We have argued that the rise of the PBC has reflected important informal relationships between its leaders and key political figures within the party leadership. The fear of inflation among the party leaders, which has been proved to be destabilizing to the regime, forms the incentive for the authoritarian regime to delegate greater monetary authority to a professional body to help rein in inflation. So far, the political regime has defied a number of doomsday predictions of a sinking ship and has managed to keep the leaking ship afloat with significant institutional changes. But ultimately, the political deficiencies of authoritarian rule may have to be addressed to further secure the institutional achievements of the reforms. As part of this broader process, the extent and pace of institutionalization of the central bank's authority, and ultimately perhaps its institutional independence, hinge on further economic liberalization, but perhaps also more importantly on political democratization.

Notes

1. Introduction

1. "China's Commercial Banks Need Freer Interest Rates, Banking Tsar," *Asia-Pulse News,* March 22, 2005.

2. Zhou Xiaochuan, "Reform the International Monetary System," People's Bank of China, March 23, 2009, http://www.pbc.gov.cn/publish/english/956/2009/20091229104425550619706/20091229104425550619706_.html.

3. See, for example, political magazines such as *Cheng Ming* and *Trend Magazine.*

3. The People's Bank in the Shadow of the Plan, 1978–92

1. The bargaining and deal making became a major drain on the state's fiscal resources. By the end of this reform era, budget revenues as a percentage of GDP had declined from around 35% to just over 10% of GDP.

2. Although Deng and Chen were closely allied at the beginning of the reform period, the differences of the two lines began to emerge in the early 1980s when Deng rejected Chen's approach to urban reform. Deng's line was to emphasize a higher rate of growth, bolder experimentation, allowing nonsocialist economic forms to grow, rapid and full integration into the world economy, and extensive marketization of the economy. In contrast, Chen's more conservative policy orientation was to work

within the basic framework of the planned economy, maintain the leading position of the state-owned enterprises, and emphasize concerns of dependence on the outside world. The conflict between the two groups has shaped the dynamics of domestic reform (see Dittmer 1992; Teiwes 1995).

3. For a discussion of the evolution of the official terms for the aim of the reform, see J. Xu (2008).

4. Harding (1986) sees the post-Mao polity as a "consultative authoritarianism," while Barnett (1986) suggests that China's evolution under Deng has moved "from totalitarianism toward liberalized authoritarianism."

5. For state-society interactions in China, see Falkenheim (1987), Goldman (1994), Perry and Selden (2000), and T. Shi (1997).

6. A fine collection of essays on elite politics in the reform era is Unger (2002), which collects a series of articles solicited and published by *China Journal* in 1995 and 2001.

7. The number of PSC members is not stipulated in the CCP's charter and has varied over the years, particularly in the post-Mao era. For example, there were seven PSC members during the party's fourteenth and fifteenth congresses, and the PSC expanded its membership to nine during the sixteenth and seventeenth party congresses, but reduced it again to seven during the eighteenth congress.

8. Author's interview with a former staff member from the CCP's Central Committee (interviewee number 21), July 27, 2006, Beijing.

9. For example, as of April 2012, the CLGFEA is headed by Premier Wen Jiabao and his deputy, Vice Premier Li Keqiang. The Group's members include Hui Liangyu, vice premier in charge of agriculture; Zhang Dejiang, vice premier in charge of industries; Wang Qishan, vice premier in charge of finance and commerce; Ma Kai, secretary-general of the State Council; Zhang Ping, director of the NDRC; Xie Xuren, the finance minister; Zhou Xiaochuan, governor of the PBC; Li Rongrong, head of the state-owned Assets Supervision and Administration Commission; Shang Fulin, head of the CBRC; Wu Dingfu, head of the CIRC; and Zhu Zhixin, vice director of the NDRC.

10. See the CLGFEA's official Web site, http://www.114zf.com/chinese/party/finan cial_and_economic_leading_group_of_the_cpc_central_committee.

11. As of the end of 2011, there are five bureaus within the CLGFEA in charge of fiscal affairs, economics and finance, macroeconomic management, comprehensive business, and secretarial support.

12. Author's interview with a former staff member from the CCP's Central Committee (interviewee number 21), July 27, 2006, Beijing.

13. The latest evidence of the NDRC's shrinking influence can been seen in its loss of the authority to approve corporate bond issuance to the China Securities Regulatory Commission, and part of its authority in formulating industrial policies to the newly amalgamated Ministry of Industry and Information in 2008.

14. The Big Four state banks are the Industrial and Commercial Bank of China, the Agricultural Bank of China, the Bank of China, and the China Construction Bank.

15. For a detailed discussion of the soviet economic system in general, see Nove (1986). The theoretical foundation of the study was laid out by Grossman (1963).

16. For a detailed discussion of the role of the SPC in China's economic management, see Wang and Fewsmith (1995).

17. The Gosbank was separated from the Ministry of Finance in 1954.

18. The approval appeared in the State Council's decree, "Several Decisions on Reorganizing and Strengthening Banking Works" released in November 1977 (China Economic Research Group 1999).

19. Author's interview with a PBC official (interviewee number 25), July 17, 2009, Beijing.

20. Ibid.

21. State Council (1983). Despite being an announcement of the executive arm of the Chinese government, the State Council, rather than the legislature, the National People's Congress, the 1983 Decree is a legal document given the fact that government documents also enjoy legal status and that the government has often been more active in legislation than the National People's Congress.

22. These variables include the targeted rate of economic and investment growth, expected price levels, and the variation of the circulation velocity of money. The circulation velocity of money is the rate at which money in circulation is used for purchasing goods and services, usually measured as a ratio of GNP to a country's total money supply. In theory, it should be factored into the Credit Plan. However, since its variations were hard to calculate in an annually based planning period, it was largely neglected in the actual planning process. Author's interview with a PBC official (interviewee number 28), July 25, 2006, Beijing.

23. Ibid.

4. Monetary Policy in the Shadow of the Plan, 1978–92

1. Author's interview with a PBC official (interviewee number 14), October 12, 2010, Beijing.

2. Between 1980 and 1988, for example, the number of industrial goods under central mandatory planning was reduced from 120 to 60, and the number of the capital goods allocated by the central government was reduced from 256 to 27 (see Jin 1994, 24).

3. Also, author's interview of a veteran PBC official (interviewee number 19), July 26, 2006, Beijing.

4. Ibid.

5. The transmission mechanism of monetary policy is the process that describes how changes in monetary policy affect other parts of the economy. A good illustration

of the main transmission channels of monetary policy decisions can be found at the Web site of the European Central Bank at http://www.ecb.europa.eu/mopo/intro /transmission/html/index.en.html.

6. Broad money here includes cash in circulation, household savings deposits, and demand and time deposits of enterprises.

5. The Second Reform Era: A New Context for the PBC

1. "Decisions of the CCP Central Committee on Issues Concerning the Establishment of a Socialist Market Economic Structure," China.com.cn, November 14, 1993, http://www.china.com.cn/chinese/archive/131747.htm.

2. Author's interview with a PBC official (interviewee number 28), July 25, 2006, Beijing.

3. Author's interview with a PBC official (interviewee number 4), October 9, 2010, Beijing.

4. Author's interview with a former PBC official (interviewee number 7), October 10, 2010, Beijing.

5. Ibid.

6. Author's interview with a PBC official (interviewee number 11), October 12, 2010, Beijing.

7. Author's interview with a PBC official (interviewee number 4), October 9, 2010, Beijing.

8. Author's interview with a PBC official (interviewee number 14), October 12, 2010, Beijing.

9. Author's interview with a PBC official (interviewee number 4), October 9, 2010, Beijing.

10. Author's interview with a PBC official (interviewee number 2), August 3, 2006, Beijing.

6. The Growth of Mutual Dependency between the PBC and the Party Leadership

1. Core members of the fourth generation, such as Hu Jintao and Wen Jiabao, managed to graduate from college before the beginning of the Cultural Revolution, while the key figures of the coming generation, such as Xi Jinping and Li Keqiang, were sent to the countryside after high school.

2. Author's interview with an NDRC official (interviewee number 30), April 9, 2012, Beijing.

3. Author's interview with a PBC official (interviewee number 28), July 25, 2006, Beijing.

4. 'History," http://www.pbcsf.tsinghua.edu.cn/publish/pbcsfen/7367/index .html.

5. Author's interview with a PBC official (interviewee number 28), July 25, 2006, Beijing.

6. For public access to these statistics and reports, go to http://www.pbc.gov.cn/publish/zhengwugongkai/1047/index.html.

7. Based on comments from one of the anonymous reviewers of the manuscript.

8. Author's interview with a PBC official (interviewee number 14), October 12, 2010, Beijing. Zhongnanhai is the compound in Beijing hosting the headquarters of the Communist Party and the government, hence synonymous with the leadership and government administration in China.

9. For a comprehensive biography of Zhu in the 1980s and 1990s, see Brahm (2002).

10. Author's interview with a PBC official (interviewee number 17), October 14, 2011, Beijing.

11. Ibid.

12. Ibid. For an example of the PBC's harsh financial discipline, see "A Circular of the General Office of the State Council in Forwarding the Statement of the PBC on the Punishment of Financial Institutions Violating the Three Regulations," May 12, 2006, http://www.gzzb.gov.cn/zc/Print.asp?ArticleID=3495. Gazette of Guizhou People's Government, http://www.gzzb.gov.cn.

13. Author's interview with a PBC official (interviewee number 17), October 14, 2011, Beijing.

7. Formal Institutional Change and the Rise of the PBC in the Second Reform Era, 1992–2011

1. The nine regional branches are located in Shanghai, Tianjin, Nanjing, Shenyang, Guangzhou, Jinan, Wuhan, Xi'an, and Chengdu. After the reform, the central bank's organizational structure included the head office (in Beijing), nine regional branches, two business administration offices (Beijing and Chongqing), 333 city-level central subbranches, and 1,660 county-level subbranches. See Tao (2003).

2. For example, Wu Xiaoling, the first governor of the Shanghai branch, which covers Shanghai, Zhejiang, and Fujian, was transferred from PBC's head office in Beijing. Tan Jingshun, governor of the Shenyang branch, was transferred from his governorship of the Gansu provincial branch. "Da dongzuo: Yanghang kuasheng she fenhang" [A big move, the central bank set up cross-provincial branches], China Economic Analysis Group, March 2, 1999, http://www.js.cei.gov.cn/zhjj/text/analysis/BBL/BBL30401.txt.

3. "Speech of Governor Zhou Xiaochuan at the Inauguration Ceremony of the People's Bank of China Shanghai Head Office," People's Bank of China, http://www.pbc.gov.cn/publish/english/956/1943/19432/19432_.html.

4. There had been a number of bankruptcies in the banking industry in the wake of the Asian financial crisis, most notably the collapse of the Guangdong International Trust Investment Corporation, which triggered a standoff between the central government and the international lending community.

5. Author's interview with a PBC official (interviewee number 14), October 12, 2010, Beijing.

6. For an empirical discussion of the variety of supervisory models, see Arnone and Gambini (2007).

7. Author's interview with a PBC official (interviewee number 14), October 12, 2010, Beijing.

8. For example, the number of staff in charge of financial regulation in a provincial-level central branch is set at twenty-five, compared to 400 who deal with monetary policy issues. See "Yinjianhui dansheng ji" (2006).

9. One PBC official involved in the process of establishing the CBRC admitted that the PBC had submitted several options for institutional structures of banking regulation, all of which centered on the PBC's monopoly. These options were eventually vetoed by the State Council. Author's interview with a PBC official (interviewee number 25), July 17, 2009, Beijing.

10. Ibid.

8. In Search of a New Monetary Policy Framework

1. The three policy banks are the China Development Bank, the Export-Import Bank of China, and the Agricultural Development Bank of China. According to Mehran (1996, 14), policy lending can be defined as that part of bank lending that is "made at the request of (or strongly encouraged by) the government to promote its economic, industrial, and sectoral policies and to assure funding for priority activities."

2. Author's interview with a PBC official (interviewee number 28), July 25, 2006, Beijing.

3. Author's interview with a PBC official (interviewee number 6), August 5, 2006, Beijing. This view is shared by other interviewees (numbers 2, 5, 11, 18, and 22).

4. Author's interview with a PBC official (interviewee number 19), July 26, 2006, Beijing.

5. Author's interview with a PBC official (interviewee number 4), October 9, 2010, Beijing.

6. Monetary base is the central bank's monetary liabilities, equal to bank reserves plus currency in circulation.

7. In China's categorization, M0 refers to cash in circulation, M1 (narrow money) refers to M0 plus demand deposits by enterprises, and M2 (broad money) refers to M1 plus time deposits by enterprises and savings deposits of household.

8. According to Krugman 2009, moral hazard refers to "any situation in which one person makes the decision about how much risk to take, while someone else bears the cost if things go badly."

9. Author's interview with a PBC official (interviewee number 23), July 20, 2009, Beijing.

10. Author's interview with a PBC official (interviewee number 14), October 12, 2010, Beijing.

11. Author's interview with a PBC official (interviewee number 28), July 25, 2006, Beijing.

12. Author's interview with a PBC official (interviewee number 19), July 26, 2006, Beijing.

13. Ibid.

14. CHIBOR is an acronym for China Interbank Offer Rate, which is based on actual traded rates on interbank deals, with the seven-day rate for bond maturity as the benchmark. In terms of market sensitivity, the Shanghai Interbank Offer Rate, launched in January 2007, is seen as a more accurate benchmark for the interbank market since it is based on quoted rates rather than on actual traded rates. "Reference Rates," AsianBondsOnline, http://asianbondsonline.adb.org/china/structure/buying _selling/description.php.

9. Monetary Policy in the Second Reform Era, 1992–2011

1. Author's interview with a veteran PBC official (interviewee number 19), July 26, 2006, Beijing.

2. Ibid.

3. Author's interview with an MOF official (interviewee number 9), September 27, 2005; interview with a PBC official (interviewee number 17), October 14, 2011; and an academic from the Central Party School (interviewee number 16), October 11, 2011. See also Liew (2003).

4. "Quanguo fangdichan ye zongshu" [The domestic real estate sector], Central People's Government of the People's Republic of China, http://www.gov.cn/test /2005-06/30/content_11329.htm.

5. PBC, "The PBC Circular on Further Strengthening the Management of Real Estate Credit," China.com, http://www.china.com.cn/chinese/PI-c/348886.htm.

6. Author's interview with a veteran PBC official (interviewee number 19), July 26, 2006, Beijing.

7. Ibid.

8. Author's interview with an NDRC official (interviewee number 30), April 9, 2012, Beijing.

9. The rollback is embodied in policy statement titled "The State Council's Circular on Promoting a Sustainable and Healthy Development of the Real Estate Sector"

(commonly referred to as Document No. 18), Central People's Government of the People's Republic of China, http://www.gov.cn/zwgk/2005-08/13/content_22259.htm.

10. Author's interview with a veteran PBC official (interviewee number 19), July 26, 2006, Beijing.

11. Author's interview with a PBC official (interviewee number 22), October 12, 2011, Beijing.

12. Author's interview with an NDRC official (interviewee number 24), April 10, 2012, Beijing.

13. Data retrieved from end-of-year data at National Bureau of Statistics of China, http://www.stats.gov.cn/tjsj/.

14. Key tax reforms in 1994 were aimed at rebalancing the fiscal decentralization of the 1980s and early 1990s. Subsequently, the central government was able to get a larger share of the tax revenue, but local governments were left with similar liabilities as before the reform. The result was that local government had to rely on extrabudgetary income (such as increased fees) to sustain local development. After 2000, sales of local land became the most vital channel for local governments to raise funds.

15. "Highlights—China Premier Wen Jiabao's Comments at NPC Press Conference," Reuters, March 14, 2012.

16. Gray income here refers to legal income people do not disclose and illegal income, such as bribes, unreasonable monopolistic revenues of some resource-based and monopoly industries, and corruption of some government officials, which is not included in the levy of personal income tax.

17. "China's Urban Population Exceeds Countryside for First Time," Bloomberg News, January 17, 2012.

18. Author's interview of a CBRC official (interviewee number 1), April 9, 2012, Beijing.

19. According to Frankel (2012), a Harvard professor and former member of President Clinton's Council of Economic Advisers, "Perhaps the biggest setback hit in September 2008, when it became clear that central banks that had been relying on IT [inflation targeting] had not paid enough attention to asset-price bubbles. . . . The lack of response to asset bubbles was probably IT's biggest failing."

20. Author's interview with a PBC official (interviewee number 18), October 12, 2011.

21. For a detailed discussion of the contents of Beijing's anticrisis stimulation package, see Naughton (2009).

22. "Further Reform the RMB Exchange Rate Regime and Enhance the RMB Exchange Rate Flexibility," People's Bank of China, June 19, 2010, http://www.pbc.gov.cn:8080/publish/english/955/2010/20100622144059351137121/20100622144059351137121_.html.

10. The PBC and China's Foreign Exchange Rate Policy

1. Author's interview with an MOF official (interviewee number 9), September 27, 2005, Beijing.

2. Author's interview with a PBC official (interviewee number 28), July 25, 2006, Beijing.

3. Author's interview with a PBC official (interviewee number 17), October 14, 2011, Beijing. Beidaihe Conference is held at a scenic resort in Hebei Province near Beijing, a frequent site of official meetings of the CCP, where senior party and government officials gather in the summer to discuss important issues.

4. Ibid.

5. Ibid.

6. Author's interview with an MOF official (interviewee number 10), April 10, 2012, Beijing.

7. For a good review of these studies, see Dunaway and Li (2002).

8. According to the study, devaluation of the RMB against the U.S. dollar by 1% will increase exports by 0.3%, but devaluation of the RMB by 1% against a basket of currencies of China's main trading partners will increase exports by between 2.7% and 2.9%.

9. The Gini coefficient (also known as Gini index or Gini ratio) is a measure of the inequality of income distribution, a value of 0 expressing total equality and a value of 1 maximal inequality.

10. "Inflation, Corruption Could Hurt China: Wen," *The Age*, October 4, 2010.

11. According to N. Yu (2005), loans owed by poor counties to the MOF have exceeded 100% of county revenue in many cases, driving these counties into deficit.

12. Chinese governments at different administrative levels provide direct and indirect financial support to promote exports. Export rebates are found to have a significant influence on exports, with 1% absolute increase in the export rebate rate producing about a 5% increase in exports. Rebates actually paid out are not the same as announced rebate rates, since rebates are often issued as IOUs to manipulate fiscal expenditures, which are paid only when there is an urgent need to increase exports (see Bowles and Wang 2008).

13. "RMB Appreciation Would Affect Exports," *China News*, May 11, 2005.

14. This includes net securities, other capital inflows, and errors and omissions.

15. For instance, on June 14, the PBC made a targeted issue of one-year maturity bills worth 100 billion yuan at a yield of 2.1138%, 0.4% lower than the prevailing market rate (see Patnaik 2007).

16. Ibid. For example, of the PBC bills issued, 42 billion yuan were forced on China Construction Bank, 30 billion yuan on the Agricultural Bank of China, 12 billion yuan on the Industrial and Commercial Bank of China, 10 billion yuan on the Bank of Communications, and the remaining 6 billion yuan on others.

17. The discussion of diplomacy behind China's 2005 reform, unless otherwise specified, is based on a *Wall Street Journal* account by Areddy et al. (2005).

18. Author's interviews with PBC officials (interviewee number 3, October 14, 2010; interviewee number 7, October 10, 2010; interviewee number 17, October 11, 2011), Beijing.

19. Author's interview with a PBC official (interviewee number 17), October 11, 2011, Beijing.

20. The actual mechanism, by April 2008, was that the PBC would set a reference rate before the start of each day's trading on the China Foreign Exchange Trade System in Shanghai, and then would allow the dollar-yuan exchange rate to rise or fall within a band of 0.5% in the session.

21. Calculated from data at State Administration of Foreign Exchange, http://www.safe.gov.cn.

22. Author's interview with a PBC official (interviewee number 14), October 12, 2010, Beijing.

23. Author's interview with a former PBC and CIC official (interviewee number 2), August 3, 2006, Beijing.

24. Author's interview with a PBC official (interviewee number 25), July 17, 2009, Beijing.

25. Of the 10–13% figure, 4.5% is used to pay for the interest bonds, the yuan appreciates 5% against the dollar, and the operating cost of such an organization is around 2–3%.

26. For example, as of October 2010, only US$1.46 billion of dim sum bonds had been issued for the year, amounting to about 1% of US$145 billion of yuan-denominated debt issued in mainland China.

27. Author's interviews with PBC officials (interviewee number 18, October 12, 2011; number 17, October 14, 2011), Beijing.

11. The PBC and Financial Reforms in China since 2003

1. For example, the ICBC was in charge of urban deposit and lending; the ABC was in charge of rural finance; the BOC was in charge of all foreign-related transactions; and the CCB provided loans to major state infrastructural projects.

2. The uneasy relationship between the PBC and the nonbank financial institutions, particularly the trust and investment companies, resulted in several rounds of crackdowns in the 1980s and early 1990s (see Pei 1998, 329–30).

3. The three policy banks are the China Development Bank, the Agricultural Development Bank of China, and the Export-Import Bank of China.

4. Author's interview with a PBC official (interviewee number 19), July 26, 2006, Beijing.

5. Ibid.

6. Author's interviews with PBC officials (interviewee number 22, October 12, 2011; number 17, October 14, 2011), Beijing.

7. Author's interview with a PBC official (interviewee number 25), July 17, 2009, Beijing.

8. Author's interview with a PBC official (interviewee number 14), October 12, 2010, Beijing.

9. Author's interview with a PBC official (interviewee number 25), July 17, 2009, Beijing.

10. Ibid.

11. Ibid.

12. Ibid.

13. Author's interview with a PBC official (interviewee number 14), October 12, 2010, Beijing.

14. The following discussion on the PBC and China's payment and settlement system is based on Feng (2006c).

15. Author's interview with a PBC official (interviewee number 19), July 26, 2006, Beijing.

16. "Shall We Dance?," *China Economic Review,* October 1, 2010.

17. Ibid. See also Tong (2009).

12. Conclusion

1. Author's interview with a PBC official (interviewee number 5), September 21, 2005, Beijing.

References

Adler, Emanuel. 1992. "The Emergence of Cooperation: National Epistemic Communities and the International Evolution of the Idea of Nuclear Arms Control." *International Organization* 46(1): 101–45.

Aizenman, Joshua, and Glick Reuven. 2008. "Pegged Exchange Rate Regimes, a Trap?" *Journal of Money, Credit and Banking* 40(4): 817–35.

Allen, Franklin, Jun Qian, and Meijun Qian. 2008. "China's Financial System: Past, Present and Future," in Loren Brandt and Thomas Rawski, eds., *China's Great Transformation*, 506–69. Cambridge: Cambridge University Press.

Alloway, Tracy. 2011. "China's New, Wider Financing Measure." FTAlphaville, http://ftalphaville.ft.com/blog/2011/04/15/547231/China's-new-wider-financing-data/.

Amable, Bruno. 2000. "Institutional Complementarity and Diversity of Social Systems of Innovation and Production." *Review of International Political Economy* 7(4): 645–87.

Amadan International. 2007. *The Creation of the China Investment Corporation.* Washington, DC: Amadan International.

Anderlini, Jamil. 2010a. "China Banks Resigned to Defaults." *Financial Times,* July 28.

———. 2010b. "China Inflation Rises as Growth Slows." *Financial Times,* October 21.

———. 2010c. "Uniform Results Highlight Risks Building Up for China's Lenders." *Financial Times*, August 30.

Archer, Margaret. 1995. *Realist Social Theory: The Morphogenetic Approach*. Cambridge: Cambridge University Press.

———. 1996. *Culture and Agency: The Place of Culture in Social Theory*. Cambridge: Cambridge University Press.

———. 2000. "For Structure: Its Reality, Properties and Powers: A Reply to Antony King." *Sociological Review* 48: 464–72.

———. 2003. *Structure, Agency and the Internal Conversation*. Cambridge: Cambridge University Press.

Areddy, James T. et al. 2005. "Behind Yuan Move, Open Debate and Closed Doors." *Wall Street Journal*, July 25.

Arnone, M., and A. Gambini. 2007. "Financial Supervisors Architecture and Banking Supervision," in D. Masciandaro and M. Quintyn, eds., *Designing Institutions for Financial Stability: Independence, Accountability and Governance*. Cheltenham, UK: Edward Elgar.

Arnone, Marco et al. 2009. "Central Bank Autonomy: Lessons from Global Trends." *IMF Staff Papers* 56: 263–96.

Arthur, W. Brian. 1989. "Competing Technologies, Increasing Returns, and Lock-In by Historical Events." *Economic Journal* 99: 116–31.

Aslund, Anders. 1994. "Lessons in the First Four Years of Systemic Change in Eastern Europe." *Journal of Comparative Economics* 19: 22–38.

Bach, David, Abraham L. Newman, and Steven Weber. 2006. "The International Implications of China's Fledgling Regulatory State: From Product Maker to Rule Maker." *New Political Economy* 11(4): 499–518.

Back, Aaron, and Victoria Ruan. 2010. "People's Bank of China Survey Stokes Fears for Real Estate Bubble." *The Australian*, September 20.

Balfour, Frederik, and Dexter Roberts. 2004. "The Leak in China's Banking System." *Business Week* 3908: 67.

Banaian, King, Leroy Laney, and Thomas D. Willett. 1986. "Central Bank Independence: An International Comparison," in E. Toma and M. Toma, eds., *Central Bankers, Bureaucratic Incentives, and Monetary Policy*, 199–219. Boston: Academic.

Barnathan, Joyce. 1994. "China: Is Prosperity Creating a Freer Society?" *Business Week*, June 6, 94–99.

Barnett, A. Doak. 1981. *China's Economy in Global Perspective*. Washington, DC: Brookings.

———. 1986. "Ten Years after Mao." *Foreign Affairs* 65: 37–65.

Batson, Andrew, and Andrew Browne. 2009. "Wen Voices Concern over China's U.S. Treasurys." *Wall Street Journal*, March 13.

Batson, Andrew, and Norihiko Shirouzu. 2010. "Power to the People: Strikes in China Signal Shift Towards Domestic Consumption." *The Australian*, June 10, 23.

Beckert, Jens. 1999. "Agency, Entrepreneurs, and Institutional Change: The Role of Strategic Choice and Institutionalized Practices in Organizations." *Organization Studies* 20(5): 777–99.

"Beijing Tipped to Give $3USb Mandate to Buyout Fund." 2007. *Hong Kong Standard Newspapers,* May 19.

Bell, Stephen. 2004. *Australia's Money Mandarins: The Reserve Bank and the Politics of Money.* Cambridge: Cambridge University Press.

———. 2011. "Do We Really Need a New Constructivist Institutionalism to Explain Institutional Change? Defending an Agent-Centred Historical Institutionalism." *British Journal of Political Science* 41: 883–906.

Bell, Stephen, and Hui Feng. 2007. "Made in China: IT Infrastructure Policy and the Politics of Trade Opening in Post-WTO China." *Review of International Political Economy* 14(1): 49–76.

———. 2009. "Reforming China's Stock Market: Institutional Change Chinese Style." *Political Studies* 57(1): 117–40.

———. 2010. "The Selective State and the Domestic Mediation of International Policy Diffusion: Evidence from Chinese Monetary Policy and Central Banking." Unpublished manuscript.

Bergera, Allen N., Iftekhar Hasan, and Mingming Zhou. 2009. "Bank Ownership and Efficiency in China: What Will Happen in the World's Largest Nation?" *Journal of Banking and Finance* 33(1): 113–30.

Bernanke, Ben. 2005. "The Global Saving Glut and the U.S. Current Account Deficit." Federal Reserve Board, http://www.federalreserve.gov/boarddocs/speeches/2005/200503102/.

Beyer, Jurgen, and Jan Wielgohs. 2001. "On the Limits of Path Dependency Approaches for Explaining Postsocialist Institution Building: In Critical Response to David Stark." *East European Politics and Societies* 15(2): 356–88.

Blanchard, Raymond. 1997. "The Heart of Economic Reform." *China Business Review,* January–February.

Blyth, Mark. 1997. "'Any More Bright Ideas?' The Ideational Turn of Comparative Political Economy." *Comparative Politics* 29(2): 229–50.

———. 2002. *Great Transformations: Economic Ideas and Institutional Change in the Twentieth Century.* Cambridge: Cambridge University Press.

"Board Shows True Colours of National's New Sovereign Fund." 2007. *South China Morning Post,* October 6.

Bofinger, Peter. 2001. *Monetary Policy: Goals, Institutions, Strategies, and Instruments.* Oxford: Oxford University Press.

Borio, C. 2006. "Monetary and Prudential Policies at the Crossroads: New Challenges in the New Century." BIS Working Paper No. 216.

Borst, Nicolas. 2011. "Huijin's Purchase of Chinese Bank Shares." *China Economic Watch,* Peterson Institute of International Economics.

Bowles, Paul, Osvaldo Croci, and Brian MacLean. 2000. "Creating the Institutions of the Global Economy? Central Bank Independence in Japan and Italy," in Stephen McBride and John Wiseman, eds., *Globalization and Its Discontents*, 55–68. London: Macmillan.

Bowles, Paul, and Baotai Wang. 2008. "The Rocky Road Ahead: China, the US and the Future of the Dollar." *Review of International Political Economy* 15(3): 335–53.

Bowles, Paul, and Gordon White. 1993. *The Political Economy of China's Financial Reforms: Finance in Late Development.* Boulder, CO: Westview.

———. 1994. "Central Bank Independence: A Political Economy Approach." *Journal of Development Studies* 31(2): 235–65.

Boyreau-Debray, Genevieve, and Shang-Jin Wei. 2005. "Pitfalls of a State-Dominated Financial System: The Case of China." NBER Working Paper No. W11214.

Brada, J., and A. Kutan. 2002. "The End of Moderate Inflation in Three Transition Economies?" William Davidson Institute Working Papers Series Number 433. Ann Arbor: William Davidson Institute at the University of Michigan.

Brada, Josef C. 1993. "The Transformation from Communism to Capitalism: How Far? How Fast?" *Post Soviet Affairs* 2(9): 87–110.

Brahm, Lawrence J. 2002. *Zhu Rongji and The Transformation of Modern China.* New York: Wiley Eastern.

Brandt, Loren, and Xiaodong Zhu. 2000. "Redistribution in a Decentralized Economy: Growth and Inflation in China under Reform." *Journal of Political Economy* 108(2): 422–39.

Breslin, Shaun. 1996. "China: Developmental State or Dysfunctional Development?" *Third World Quarterly* 17(4): 689–706.

———. 2003. "Paradigm Shifts and Time-Lags? The Politics of Financial Reform in the People's Republic of China." *Asian Business and Management* 2(1): 143–66.

———. 2005. "Power and Production: Rethinking China's Global Economic Role." *Review of International Studies* 31(4): 735–53.

Brodsgaard, Kjeld Erik, and Zheng Yongnian. 2006. *The Chinese Communist Party in Reform.* London: Routledge.

Brzezinski, Z. K. 1960. *The Soviet Bloc: Unity and Conflict.* Cambridge, MA: Harvard University Press.

Bucknall, Kevin B. 1989. *China and the Open Door Policy.* Sydney: Allen and Unwin.

Burdekin, R. C. K., and P. L. Siklos. 2008. "What Has Driven Chinese Monetary Policy: Some Lessons and an Overview." *Journal of International Money and Finance* 27(5): 847–59.

Burns, John P. 1993. "China's Administrative Reforms for a Market Economy." *Public Administration and Development* 13(4): 345–60.

———. 1999. "The People's Republic of China at 50: National Political Reform." *China Quarterly* 159: 580–94.

Campbell, John. 1997. "Mechanisms of Evolutionary Change in Economic Governance: Interaction, Interpretation and Bricolage," in L. Magnusson and J. Ottoson, eds., *Evolutionary Economics and Path Dependence*. London: Edward Elgar.

———. 2002. "Ideas, Politics, and Public Policy." *Annual Review of Sociology* 28: 21–38.

———. 2004. *Institutional Change and Globalization*. Princeton, NJ: Princeton University Press.

CBRC. 2012. *2011 Annual Report*. Beijing: China Banking Regulatory Commission.

Chai, J. 1997. *China: Transition to a Market Economy*. New York: Clarendon.

Chan, Che-Po, and Gavin Drewry. 2001. "The 1998 State Council Organisational Streamlining: Personnel Reduction and Change of Government Function." *Journal of Contemporary China* 10(29): 553–72.

Chen, Bin. 2010. "Ruhe yingdui tongzhang zhuanjia guandian buyi" [Experts diverge on inflation-busting measures]. *Shanghai zhengquan bao*, May 5.

Chen, Jianxun, and Huici Shi. 2004. *Banking and Insurance in the New China: Competition and the Challenge of Accession to the WTO*. Cheltenham, UK: Edward Elgar.

Chen, Xiao, and Qiu Lian. 2011. "Wenzhou minjian jiedai weiji diaocha" [Investigation of the private lending crisis in Wenzhou]. *Lifeweek*, November 11.

Chen, Yong. 2010. "Zhang gongzi: shi fu shi huo?" [Wage rise: fortunate or unfortunate?]. *Jingji guanchabao*, September 7.

Cheng, Yong. 2005. "Zhou Xiaochuan: guoyou yinhang gaige bu cunzai jianmai" [Zhou Xiaochuan: reforming state-owned banks no cheap sale]. *Shanghai Zhengquan bao*, November 30.

China Economic Research Group. 1999. "Da dongzuo, yanghang kuasheng she fenhang" [A big move, the PBC establishes cross-provincial branches]. Jiangsu Economic Information Network, http://webcache.googleusercontent.com /search?q=cache:mVo9uoKgoU4J:www.js.cei.gov.cn/zhjj/text/analysis/BBL/BBL 30401.TXT+%E5%A4%A7%E5%8A%A8%E4%BD%9C+%E5%A4%AE%E8%A1 %8C%E8%B7%A8%E7%9C%81%E8%AE%BE%E5%88%86%E8%A1%8C&cd=1 &hl=en&ct=clnk&gl=au.

"China Labour Costs like U.S. 'Within Years.'" 2012. *The Australian*, August 2.

"China Revives Credit Asset-Backed Securitization." 2012. MarketWatch, http:// www.marketwatch.com/story/china-revives-credit-asset-backed-securitization -2012-06-03-224853843.

"Chinese Banks Dominate the Bankers Top 1000 Ranking." 2011. *Financial Times*, July 1.

Chinn, Menzie, and Jeffrey Frankel. 2005. "Will the Euro Eventually Surpass the Dollar as Leading International Reserve Currency?" Paper presented at the NBER conference, G7 Current Account Imbalances: Sustainability and Adjustment. Cambridge, MA: National Bureau of Economic Research.

Chovanec, Patrick. 2009. "China's Real Estate Riddle." *Far Eastern Economic Review* (June): 23–27.

———. 2012. "China Real Estate Unravels." Patrick An American Perspective from China, October 10, http://chovanec.wordpress.com/2012/05/16/china-real-estate -unravels/.

Clark, William R. 1998. "Agents and Structures: Two Views of Preferences, Two Views of Institutions." *International Studies Quarterly* 42: 245–70.

Cong, Yaping, and Changjiu Li. 2010. "Zhongguo Gini xishu shi yi chao 0.5, caifu liangji fenhua" [China's Gini coefficient has increased to over 1.5, reflecting income polarizations]. *Jingji cankao bao,* May 21.

Cookson, Robert. 2010. "China: Regulators' Turf War Helps Market Take Root." *Financial Times,* March 10.

Cookson, Robert, and Peter Garnham. 2010. "Beijing's Closer Look at the Renminbi." *Financial Times,* October 25.

Cortell, Andrew P., and Susan Peterson. 1999. "Altered States: Explaining Domestic Institutional Change." *British Journal of Political Science* 29(1): 177–203.

Cotterill, Joseph. 2010. "Fitch Goes Aaaagh on Chinese Securitisation." *Financial Times,* July 14.

Coudert, Virginie, and Cecile Couharde. 2005. "Real Equilibrium Exchange Rate in China." *CEPII Working Paper* No. 2005–01. Centre d'Études Prospectives et d'Informations Internationales.

Courtis, N. 2006. *How Countries Supervise Their Banks, Insurers and Securities Markets.* London: Central Banking.

Cover, James Peery. 1992. "Asymmetric Effects of Positive and Negative Money Supply Shock." *Quarterly Journal of Economics* (November): 1261–82.

Crawford, Beverly, and Arend Lijphart, eds. 1997. *Liberalization and Leninist Legacies: Comparative Perspectives on Democratic Transitions.* Berkeley: University of California Press.

Crouch, Colin. 2005. *Capitalist Diversity and Change.* Oxford: Oxford University Press.

———. 2007. "How to Do Post-determinist Institutional Analysis." *Socio-Economic Review* 5: 527–67.

Crouch, Colin, and M. Keune. 2005. "Changing Dominant Practice: Making Use of Institutional Diversity in Hungary and the United Kingdom," in W. Streeck and K. Thelen, eds., *Beyond Continuity: Institutional Change in Advanced Political Economies,* 83–102. Oxford: Oxford University Press.

Dai, Meixing. 2006. "Inflation-Targeting under a Managed Exchange Rate: The Case of the Chinese Central Bank." *Journal of Chinese Economic and Business Studies* 4(3): 199–219.

Dai, Xianglong, ed. 1998. *Zhongguo renmin yinhang 50 nian: zhongyang yinhang zhidu de fazhan licheng 1948–1998* [Fifty years of the People's Bank of China:

The evolution of a central banking system 1948–1998]. Beijing: Zhongguo jinrong chubanshe.

———. 2002a. "Zai Zhongguo Yinhang 'Jingji Quanqiuhua yu Yinhang ye de Weilai' guoji jinrong gaoceng yantaohui shang de yanjiang." *Zhongguo zhengquan bao,* March 20.

———. 2002b. "Zhongguo jinrongye zai gaige zhong fazhan" [The development of the Chinese financial industry with reform]. http://ru.china-embassy.org/chn /xwdt/t73693.htm.

David, Paul A. 1985. "Clio and the Economics of QWERTY." *American Economic Review* 75: 322–27.

Davies, Howard, and David Green. 2010. *Banking on the Future: The Fall and Rise of Central Banking.* Princeton, NJ: Princeton University Press.

Davis, Bob. 2011a. "Political Overlords Shackle China's Monetary Mandarins." *Wall Street Journal,* April 15.

———. 2011b. "Were China's Leaders Conned?" *Wall Street Journal,* June 1.

Dittmer, Lowell. 1992. "Patterns of Leadership in Reform China," in Arthur L. Rosenbaum, ed., *State and Society in China: The Consequences of Reform.* Boulder, CO: Westview.

———. 1995. "Chinese Informal Politics." *China Journal* 34(July): 1–34.

Dittmer, Lowell, and Yu-shan Wu. 1995. "The Modernization of Factionalism in Chinese Politics." *World Politics* 47(July): 467–94.

Dobbin, F., B. Simmons, and G. Garret. 2005. "The Global Diffusion of Public Policies: Social Construction, Coercion, Competition or Learning?" *Annual Review of Sociology* 33:449–72.

Donnithorne, Audrey. 1967. *The Chinese Economic System.* New York: Praeger.

Drezner, Daniel W. 2001. "Globalisation and Policy Convergence." *International Studies Review* 3: 53–78.

Du, Liang. 2003. "Renshi huobi zhengce, jiedu yanghang fangdai tiezheng" [The PBC's stringent policy toward property development loans]. *Zhongguo qiyejia* [The Chinese Entrepreneurs] 7: 5–7.

Dunaway, Steven, and Xiangming Li. 2002. "Estimating China's equilibrium real exchange rate." IMF Working Paper No. 202.

Dyer, Geoff. 2010a. "China's Market-Leninism Has Yet to Face Biggest Test." *Financial Times,* September 16.

———. 2010b. "Land Loans Threaten to Dig Big Hole for China." *Financial Times,* March 29.

Dyer, Geoff, and Jamil Anderlini. 2010. "Beijing Remains Divided over Currency Peg." *Financial Times,* March 8.

Economist Intelligence Unit. 2003. "China Finance: Credit and Credibility." *EIU ViewsWire,* July 14.

———. 2011. "Building Rome in a Day: The Sustainability of China's Housing Boom." EIU's Access China Service. http://www.excellentfuture.ca/sites/default/files/Building%20Rome%20in%20a%20Day_0.pdf.

Edwards, Sebastian, and Eduardo Levy Yeyati. 2005. "Flexible Exchange Rates as Shock Absorbers." *European Economic Review* 49(8): 2079–105.

Eichengreen, Barry. 1999. "Kicking the Habit: Moving from Pegged Rates to Greater Exchange Rate Flexibility." *Economic Journal* (March): C1–C14.

Elster, Jon, Claus Offe, and Ulrich K. Preuss. 1998. *Institutional Design in Post-Communist Societies: Rebuilding the Ship at Sea.* Cambridge: Cambridge University Press.

Epstein, G. 1992. "Political Economy and Comparative Central Banking." *Review of Radical Political Economics* 24(1): 1–30.

Ericson, Richard E. 1991. "The Classical Soviet-Type Economy: Nature of the System and Implications for Reform." *Journal of Economic Perspectives* 5(4): 11–27.

Falkenheim, Victor, ed. 1987. *Citizens and Groups in Contemporary China.* Ann Arbor: University of Michigan Center for Chinese Politics.

Feng, Hui. 2006a. "The Emergence of a Modern Payment Infrastructure in China." *Settlement, Payment, E-money and E-trading Development* 1(2): 17–21.

———. 2006b. "How the People's Bank Is Shaping China's Financial Sector." *Central Banking* 17(1): 35–41.

———. 2006c. *The Politics of China's Accession into the World Trade Organisation: The Dragon Goes Global.* London: Routledge.

———. 2007a. "Broken China: Fixing a Fragile Regulatory Framework." *Financial Regulator* 12(2): 43–48.

———. 2007b. "China's New Reserve Strategy." *Central Banking* 17(3): 29–36.

———. 2009. "Beijing's Precarious Balancing Act." *Central Banking* 20(2): 39–43.

———. 2010. "Are We There Yet? The Regulatory State, Metagovernance and China's Post-WTO Financial Regulation." Unpublished manuscript.

———. 2011. "The Three Trillion Dollar Question." *Central Banking* 21(4): 26–30.

———. 2012. "The Beginning of the End?" *Central Banking* 23(1): 43–47.

Feng, Ju, and Zhanbo Cai. 2005. "Zhou Xiaochuan qiangdiao ziben shichang kaifang manle ye you fengxian" [Zhou Xiaochuan stresses risks associated with a slow opening of capital market]. *Meiri jingji xinwen,* October 19.

Ferguson, Niall. 2008. *The Ascent of Money: A Financial History of the World.* New York: Penguin.

Fewsmith, Joseph. 1994. *Dilemmas of Reform in China: Political Conflict and Economic Debate.* Armonk, NY: M. E. Sharpe.

———. 1996. "Institutions, Informal Politics, and Political Transition in China." *Asian Survey* 36(3): 230–46.

———. 1998. "Jiang Zemin Takes Command." *Current History* (September): 250–56.

————. 1999. "China and the WTO: The Politics behind the Agreement." *NBR Analysis* 10(5): 23–39.

————. 2001. *Elite Politics in Contemporary China.* Armonk, NY: M. E. Sharpe.

Fitch Ratings. 2010. "Chinese Banks: Informal Securitisation Increasingly Distorting Credit Data." *China Special Report,* July 14.

————. 2011. "Chinese Banks: Growth of Leverage Still Outpacing GDP Growth." *China Special Report,* July 14.

Fleming, J. 1962. "Domestic Financial Policies under Fixed and under Floating Exchange Rates." *IMF Staff Papers* 9: 369–79.

Fligstein, Neil. 2001. "Social Skill and the Theory of Fields." *Sociological Theory* 19: 105–25.

Forder, J. 1998. "The Case for an Independent Central Bank: A Reassessment of Evidence and Sources." *European Journal of Political Economy* 14: 53–71.

Frankel, Jeffrey. 1999. "No Single Currency Regime Is Right for All Countries or at All Times." NBER Working Paper No. 7388. Washington, DC: National Bureau of Economic Research.

————. 2004. "On the Renminbi: The Choice between Adjustment under a Fixed Exchange Rate and Adjustment under a Flexible Rate." NBER Working Paper No. 11274. Washington, DC: National Bureau of Economic Research.

————. 2012. "The Death of Inflation Targeting." Project Syndicate, May 16, http://www.project-syndicate.org/commentary/the-death-of-inflation-targeting.

Friedrich, C. J., and Z. K. Brzezinski. 1956. *Totalitarian Dictatorship and Autocracy.* Cambridge, MA: Harvard University Press.

Fung, Hung-Gay, Wai K. Leung, and Jiang Zhu. 2004. "Nondeliverable Forward Market for Chinese RMB: A First Look." *China Economic Review* 15(3): 348–52.

Gao, Xin, and Pin He. 1993. *Zhu Rongji zhuan: cong fandang youpai dao Deng Xiaoping jichengren* [A biography of Zhu Rongji: from anti-party Rightist to one of Deng Xiaoping's successors]. Taipei: Xin xinwen wenhua.

Garud, Raghu, and Peter Karnoe, eds. 2001. *Path Dependence and Creation.* Mahwah, NJ: Lawrence Erlbaum.

Garvy, George. 1977. *Money, Financial Flows, and Credit in the Soviet Union.* Cambridge: Ballinger.

Geiger, Michael. 2008. "Instruments of Monetary Policy in China and Their Effectiveness: 1994–2006." Discussion Papers No. 187. New York: United Nations Conference on Trade and Development.

Gifford, Rob. 2010. "Panda-Huggers and Dragon-Slayers: How to View Modern China Today." *Social Education* 74(1): 9–11.

Gilley, Bruce, and David Murphy. 2001. "Why China Needs a Real Central Bank." *Far Eastern Economic Review* 164(20): 48–52.

Girardin, Eric. 1997. *Banking Sector Reform and Credit Control in China.* Paris: OECD Development Centre.

Glick, Reuven, and Michael Hutchison. 2008. "Navigating the Trilemma: Capital Flows and Monetary Policy in China." Working Paper Series 08-32. San Francisco: Federal Reserve Bank of San Francisco.

"Global Boss False Flattery for PBOC." 2012. *People's Daily*, May 2.

Goldman, Merle. 1994. *Sowing the Seeds of Democracy in China: Political Reform in the Deng Xiaoping Era*. Cambridge, MA: Harvard University Press.

Goldstein, M. 2004a. "Adjusting China's Exchange Rate Policies." Paper presented at the International Monetary Funds Seminar on China's Foreign Exchange Rate System, Dalian, China, May 26–27.

———. 2004b. "Adjusting China's Exchange Rate Policies." IIE Working Paper WP04-1. Washington, DC: Institute for International Economics.

Gomulka, Stanislaw, Yong-Chool Ha, and Cae-One Kim, eds. 1989. *Economic Reforms in the Socialist World*. Armonk, NY: M. E. Sharpe.

"Gongzi shangzhang hui yakua Zhongguo zhezuo 'shijie gongchang' ma" [Will rising wage level bear down China "the world factory"]. *Shanghai zhengquan bao*, April 21.

Goodman, John. 1991. "The Politics of Central Bank Independence." *Comparative Politics* 23(3): 329–49.

Gourevitch, Peter. 1978. "The Second Image Reversed: The International Sources of Domestic Politics." *International Organization* 32(4): 881–911.

Green, Stephen. 2004. *The Development of China's Stock Market, 1984–2002: Equity Politics and Market Institutions*. London: RoutledgeCurzon.

Greenspan, Alan. 2005. *Federal Reserve Board's Semiannual Monetary Policy Report to the Congress* Before the Committee on Banking, Housing, and Urban Affairs, U.S. Senate, February 16, http://www.federalreserve.gov/boarddocs/hh/2005 /february/testimony.htm.

———. 2007. *The Age of Turbulence*. New York: Penguin.

Greenwood, John. 2008. "Costs and Implications of PBC Sterilization." *Cato Journal* 28(2): 205–17.

Gries, Peter Hays. 2001. "Tears of Rage: Chinese Nationalist Reactions to the Belgrade Embassy Bombing." *China Journal* 46: 25–43.

Grossman, Gregory. 1963. "Notes for a Theory of the Command Economy." *Soviet Studies* 15(2): 101–23.

Guo, Yong. 2002. *Banking Reforms and Monetary Policy in the People's Republic of China: Is the Chinese Central Banking System Ready for Joining the WTO?* Basingstoke, UK: Palgrave Macmillan.

Haas, Peter M. 1992. "Introduction: Epistemic Communities and International Policy Coordination." *International Organization* 46(1): 1–35.

Hall, Peter. 1989. *The Political Power of Economic Ideas*. Princeton: Princeton University Press.

Halper, Stefan. 2010. *The Beijing Consensus: How China's Authoritarian Model Will Dominate the Twenty-First Century*. Philadelphia: Basic Books.

Halpern, Nina. 1992. "Information Flows and Policy Coordination in the Chinese Bureaucracy," in Kenneth Lieberthal and David M. Lampton, eds., *Bureaucracy, Politics, and Decision Making in Post-Mao China*. Berkeley: University of California Press.

Hamrin, Carol Lee. 1992. "The Party Leadership System," in Kenneth Lieberthal and David Lampton, eds., *Bureaucracy, Politics, and Decision Making in Post-Mao China*. Berkeley: University of California Press.

Hamrin, Carol Lee, and Suisheng Zhao. 1995. "Introduction: Core Issues in Understanding the Decision Process," in Carol Lee Hamrin and Suisheng Zhao, eds., *Decision-Making in Deng's China: Perspectives from Insiders*. Armonk, NY: M. E. Sharpe.

Han, Yonghong. 2005. "Wen Jiabao: renminbi huilu gaige buneng jiyuqiucheng" [Wen Jiabo: RMB exchange rate reform not to be handled in hastened steps]. *Lianhe Zaobao,* May 29.

Hannan, Kate. 1998. *Industrial Change in China*. London: Routledge.

Harding, Harry. 1986. "Political Development in Post-Mao China," in A. Doak Barnett and Ralph N. Clough, eds., *Modernizing China: Post-Mao Reform and Development*, 13–39. Boulder, CO: Westview.

Harty, S. 2005. "Theorising Institutional Change," in A. Lacours, ed., *New Institutionalism: Theory and Analysis*. Toronto: Toronto University Press.

Hay, Colin. 2002. *Political Analysis*. Basingstoke, UK: Palgrave.

———. 2006. "Globalisation and Public Policy," in M. Rein, M. Moran, and R. E. Goodin, eds. *Oxford Handbook of Public Policy*. Oxford: Oxford University Press.

———. 2007. "Constructivist Institutionalism," in R. Rhodes, S. Binder, and B. Rockman, eds., *The Oxford Handbook of Political Institutions*. Oxford: Oxford University Press.

Hay, Colin, and Ben Rosamond. 2002. "Globalization, European integration and the Discursive Construction of Economic Imperatives." *Journal of European Public Policy* 9(2): 147–67.

Hay, Colin, and Daniel Wincott. 1998. "Structure, Agency and Historical Institutionalism." *Political Studies* 46(5): 951–57.

He, Guoqian. 1998. "Zhongguo jingji shichanghua jincheng zhong de huobi zhengce gaige" [China's monetary policy reform in the process of economic liberalization]. PhD diss., Peking University.

He, Y. 1998. *Zhongguo baipishu* [China's White Paper]. Beijing: Gaige chubanshe.

Heilmann, Sebastian. 2005. "Regulatory Innovation by Leninist Means: Communist Party Supervision in China's Financial Industry." *China Quarterly* 18: 1–21.

Hinton-Braaten, K. 1994. "Central Banking in Economies in Transition," in Thomas D. Willett et al., eds., *Establishing Monetary Stability in Emerging Market Economies*. Boulder, CO: Westview.

Hochreiter, E., and S. Riesinger. 1995. "Central Banking in Central and Eastern Europe: Selected Institutional Issues." *ECU Journal* 32: 17–22.

Holz, Carsten. 1992. *The Role of Central Banking in China's Economic Reforms.* Ithaca, NY: Cornell University, East Asia Program.

Homles, Frank. 2011. "With Rising Wages, Will China Remain a Manufacturing Hub?" marketoracle.co.uk, http://www.marketoracle.co.uk/Article31808.html.

Horsman, Mathew, and Andres Marshall. 1994. *After the Nation States.* London: HarperCollins.

Howell, Jude. 1993. *China Opens Its Doors: The Politics of Economic Transition.* Boulder, CO: Lynne Rienner.

"How Will RMB Exchange Rate Affect Trade?" 2006. *People's Daily*, June 2.

Hu, Angang. 1999. "Kuaru xinshiji de zuida tiaozhan: woguo jinru gaoshiye jieduan" [The biggest challenge in the new century: China enters a period of high unemployment]. *Zhongguo renkou kexue* 6: 11–14.

Hu, Angang, and Shaoguang Wang. 1994. *A Report on State Capacity in China.* Hong Kong: Oxford University Press.

Hu, Xiaobo. 2000. "The State, Enterprises, and Society in Post-Deng China." *Asian Survey* 40(4): 641.

Hu, Xiaolian. 2010. "A Managed Floating Exchange Rate Regime Is an Established Policy." Bank of International Settlement, http://www.bis.org/review/r100721d.pdf.

Hu, Yifan. 2012. "Chiyou renminbi: geguo yanghang xin qushi" [Holding RMB: new trend among the central banks]. *Wall Street Journal* online Chinese edition, April 16.

Huang, Guabo. 1994. "Problems of Monetary Control in China: Targets, Behavior and Mechanism," in Qimiao Fan and Peter Nolan, eds., *China's Economic Reforms: The Costs and Benefits of Incrementalism.* New York: St. Martin's.

Huang, Qianwei. 2012. "Difang rongzi pingtai huo da guimo zhanqi" [Local platform finance may face a massive rollover]. *Nanfang ribao*, February 15.

Huang, Xuejun, and Wenjing Sun. 2007. "Opening Up of the NDF Market under Foreign Exchange Liberalization: Experience from Emerging Markets." *Studies of International Finance* 3: 12–15.

Huang, Yasheng. 1996. *Inflation and Investment Controls in China: The Political Economy of Central-Local Relations during the Reform Era.* Cambridge: Cambridge University Press.

———. 2002. "Managing Chinese Bureaucrats: An Institutional Economics Perspective." *Political Studies* 50(1): 61–79.

———. 2008. *Capitalism with Chinese Characteristics: Entrepreneurship and the State.* Cambridge: Cambridge University Press.

Huber, John D., and Charles R. Shipan. 2002. *Deliberate Discretion? The Institutional Foundations of Bureaucratic Authority.* Cambridge: Cambridge University Press.

"Huigai huo kending Zhou Xiaochuan liuren yanghang hangzhang" [Zhou to remain as the PBC governor for positive reviews of the exchange rate reform]. 2008. *Takunpao*, February 27.

Hung, Ho-fung. 2008. "The Rise of China and the Global Overaccumulation Crisis." *Review of International Political Economy* 15: 149–79.

Huo, Kan, and Hairong Yu. 2010. "Interest Rate Hike May Be Fire, or Just Flash." Caixin Online,http://english.caing.com/2010-10-28/100193168_1.html.

Huo, Kan et al. 2009. "Keen Eyes Fixed on China's Monetary Policy." *Caijing*, July 29.

Ikenberry, G. John. 1988. "Conclusion: An Institutional Approach to American Foreign Economic Policy." *International Organization* 42(1): 219–43.

Ikeya, M. 2002. "China-Unique Strengths and Weaknesses of Monetary Policy: Diehard Socialism behind Window Guidance." R&I Asian Focus. January 22. Rating and Investment Information Inc.

IMF. 2004. "People's Republic of China: 2004 Article IV Consultation." IMF Country Report 04/351.

———. 2011. *People's Republic of China: Financial System Stability Assessment.* IMF Country Report No. 11/321.

———. 2012. "Statement by IMF Managing Director Christine Lagarde on the People's Bank of China Exchange Rate Action." International Monetary Fund, Press Release No. 12/133.

Jadhav, Narendra. 2003. "Central Bank Strategies, Credibility and Independence: Global Evolution and Indian Experience." Dr. Narendra Jadhav, http://www.drnarendrajadhav.info/drnjadhav_web_files/Published%20papers/Final%20Paper%20on%20Central%20Banking%20Strategies1.pdf.

Jessop, Bob. 1996. "Interpretive Sociology and the Dialectic of Agency and Structure." *Theory, Culture and Society* 13: 119–28.

Ji, Zhibin. 2011. "Zhongyang yinhang nenggou yindao jinrong shichang yuqi ma: jiyu 2006–2010 nian shuju de fenxi" [Can central bank communications guide financial market expectations? An analysis based on the 2006–2010 data]. China International Finance Conference 2011.

Jiang, P. 1999. *The RMB Convertibility and Capital Controls.* Shanghai: Fudan University Press.

Jin, Leroy. 1994. *Monetary Policy and the Design of Financial Institutions in China: 1978–1990.* New York: St. Martin's.

Jing, X. 2001. *Development of International Finance and China's Financial Reforms.* Beijing: China Finance Press.

"Jinrong jianguan daibian" [Financial regulation set to change]. 2005. *Jingji Magazine*, December 30.

John, Danny. 2008. "China Buys Australian Bank Stakes." *Sydney Morning Herald*, Business Day, http://www.smh.com.au/business/china-buys-australian-bank-stakes-20080104-1k8w.html.

Johnson, Juliet. 1997. *Path-Dependent Independence: The Central Bank of Russia in the 1990s.* Political Science Series. Vienna: Institute for Advanced Studies.

———. 2002. "Financial Globalization and National Sovereignty: Neoliberal Transformations in Post-Communist Central Banks." Paper presented at the annual meeting of the American Political Science Association, Boston, Massachusetts.

———. 2003. " 'Past' Dependence or Path Contingency? Institutional Design in Postcommunist Financial Systems," in Grzegorz Ekiert and Stephen Hanson, eds., *Capitalism and Democracy in Central and Eastern Europe: Assessing the Legacy of Communist Rule,* 289–316. Cambridge: Cambridge University Press.

———. 2006a. "Postcommunist Central Banks: A Democratic Deficit?" *Journal of Democracy* 17(1): 90–103.

———. 2006b. "Two-Track Diffusion and Central Bank Embeddedness: The Politics of Euro Adoption in Hungary and the Czech Republic." *Review of International Political Economy* 13(3): 361–86.

Johnston, M. Francis, and Huimin Li. 2002. "Estimating China's Urban Unemployment Rate: Background, Mechanics, and an Alternative." *Journal of Contemporary China* 11(31): 189–207.

Jones, Claire. 2011. "The Costs to the PBoC of China's Reserves." *Financial Times* blog, July 11, http://blogs.ft.com/money-supply/2011/07/18/the-costs-to-the-pboc -of-china%E2%80%99s-reserves/?Authorised=false#axzz1UWvs9SQ.

Jordan, Jerry L., and John B. Carlson. 2000. "Money, Monetary Policy, and Central Banking." *Journal of Financial Services Research* 18(2–3): 241–53.

Jowitt, Kenneth. 1992. *New World Disorder: The Leninist Extinction.* Berkeley: University of California Press.

Kaplan, Stephen B. 2006. "The Political Obstacles to Greater Exchange Rate Flexibility in China." *World Development* 34(7): 1182–200.

Karras, Georgios. 1996. "Are the Output Effects of Monetary Policy Asymmetric? Evidence from a Sample of European Countries." *Oxford Bulletin of Economics and Statistics* 58(2): 267–78.

Katznelson, Ira. 2003. "Periodization and Preferences: Reflections on Purposive Action in Comparative Historical Social Science," in J. Mahoney and D. Rueschemeyer, eds., *Comparative Historical Analysis in the Social Sciences.* New York: Cambridge University Press.

Kay, Adrian. 2005. "A Critique of the Use of Path Dependency in Policy Studies." *Public Administration* 83(3): 553–71.

Kenen, P. 2009. "Currency Internationalisation: An Overview." Paper presented at the conference, "Currency Internationalisation: Lessons from the Global Financial Crisis and Prospects for the Future in Asia and the Pacific," Seoul, Korea.

Keohane, Robert O., and Helen V. Milner, eds. 1996. *Internationalisation and Domestic Politics.* Cambridge: Cambridge University Press.

Keppler, Robert. 2005. "Developing a Modern Payments System: Ambitious Vision Becomes a Reality." *Access Finance* 5(June): 11–13.

Khor, Hoe Ee. 1991. "China—Macroeconomic Cycles in the 1980s." IMF Working Paper 91/85. Washington, DC: International Monetary Fund.

Khor, Hoe Ee et al. 2007. "Managed Float Exchange Rate System: The Singaporean Experience." *Singapore Economic Review* 52(1): 7–25.

KNB. 2011. "Khazanah Issues Inaugural Offshore RMB Denominated Sukuk of RMB500 Million (Equivalent to RM246 Million)." Media statement, Khazanah Nasional, October 13, http://www.khazanah.com.my/docs/KNB_Sukuk_131011 .pdf.

Koelble, Thomas A. 1995. "The New Institutionalism in Political Science and Sociology." *Comparative Politics* 27(2): 231–43.

Koreh, M., and M. Shalev. 2009. "Dialectics of Institutional Change: Transformation of Social Insurance Financing in Israel." *Socio-Economic Review* 7: 553–84.

Kornai, Janos. 1980. *The Economics of Shortage.* Amsterdam: North-Holland.

———. 1982. *Growth Shortage and Efficiency: A Macrodynamic Model of the Socialist Economy.* Oxford: Blackwell.

———. 1986. "The Soft Budget Constraint." *Kyklos* 39(1): 3–30.

Krasner, Stephen D. 1984. "Approaches to the State: Alternative Conceptions and Historical Dynamics." *Comparative Politics* 16: 223–46.

Krugman, Paul. 2009. *The Return of Depression Economics and the Crisis of 2008.* New York: W. W. Norton & Company Limited.

———. 2011. "Will China Break?" *New York Times,* December 18.

Lam, Willy. 1999. *The Era of Jiang Zemin.* Singapore: Prentice Hall.

Lampton, David. 1987a. "Chinese Politics: The Bargaining Treadmill." *Issues and Studies,* 23(3), 11–41.

———, ed. 1987b. *Policy Implementation in Post-Mao China.* Berkeley: University of California Press.

Lampton, David, and Kenneth Lieberthal, eds. 1992. *Bureaucracy, Politics, and Decision Making in Post-Mao China.* Berkeley: University of California Press.

Lan, Xinzhen. 2010. "Taming the Real Estate Market." *Beijing Review,* April 30.

Lardy, Nicholas. 1992a. "Chinese Foreign Trade." *China Quarterly* 131: 691–720.

———. 1992b. *Foreign Trade and Economic Reform in China, 1978–1990.* Cambridge: Cambridge University Press.

———. 2001. "China's Worsening Debts." *Financial Times,* June 22.

———. 2005. "Exchange Rate and Monetary Policy In China." *Cato Journal* 25(1): 41–47.

Lau, Ka Man, and Si-ming Li. 2004. "Commercial Housing Affordability in Beijing, 1992–2001." Paper presented at the conference, "Housing and Social Development: Emerging Theoretical Issues in Asia-Pacific," Hong Kong.

Lau, Lawrence J., Yingyi Qian, and Gerard Roland. 2000. "Reform without Losers: An Interpretation of China's Dual-Track Approach to Transition." *Journal of Political Economy* 108(1): 120–43.

Laurenceson, James. 2012. "Busting the Myth of China's Property Bubble." The Conversation, April 4, http://theconversation.edu.au/busting-the-myth-of -chinas-property-bubble-5961.

Laurenceson, James, and Danielle Rodgers. 2010. "China's Macroeconomic Volatility—How Important Is the Business Cycle?" *China Economic Review* 21(2): 324–33.

Lavlan, M. Yves, ed. 1973. *Banking, Money and Credit in Eastern Europe.* Brussels: North Atlantic Treaty Organization.

Lee, Hong Yung. 1991. *From Revolutionary Cadres to Party Technocrats in Socialist China.* Berkeley: University of California Press.

Lee, Martin Lishexian. 2002. "Chinese Central Bank, Prudential Regulation and Political Reform." *Australian Business Law Review* 30(1): 32–44.

Lenin, Vladimir. [1918] 1964. *Collected Works,* vol. 26. Moscow: Progress Publishers.

Levi-Faur, David. 2005. "The Global Diffusion of Regulatory Capitalism." *Annals of the American Academy of Political and Social Science* 598(1): 12–32.

Lex. 2010. "To Reserve and Protect." FTChinese, July 26, http://www.ftchinese. com/story/001033751/en.

Li, Cheng. 2001. *China's Leaders: The New Generation.* Lanham, MD: Rowman and Littlefield.

Li, Daokui. 2012. "My Lessons from Life as a Chinese Central Banker." *Financial Times,* May 10.

Li, Kui Wai. 1996. *Some Thoughts on China's 1995 Bank Reform.* Hong Kong: Department of Economics and Finance, City University of Hong Kong.

Li, Qianchuan. 2011. "Yanghang zhuoli tuijin guojiban" [The central bank seeks to promote an international board]. *Jingji guancha bao,* November 2.

Li, Tao. 2005. "Yingai yuannian jinzhi diaocha" [First year of banking reform, a prudential investigation]. *Chanquan shichang* [Ownership Market] 1(1): 6–8.

———. 2009a. "Yanghang queding chengli huobi zhengce er si" [The PBC is set to establish Monetary Policy Department II]. *Caijing,* October 10.

———. 2009b. "Yinjianhui fahua: yinhangye hai budao ziman de shihou" [CBRC: No time for complacency yet for the banks]. *21 shiji jingji baodao,* November 11.

Li, Weiling. 2006. "Sanjia zhengcexing yinhang gaige jinnian qidong Zhou Xiaochuan qinzi zhihui" [Reform of the three policy banks to be launched this year under personal leadership of Zhou Xiaochuan]. *Guoji jinrong bao,* February 27.

Li, Xiaobi. 2010. "Hu Jintao: renminbi huilu gaige bu qufu yu waibu yali" [Hu Jintao: RMB reform will not succumb to external pressures]. *China Daily,* April 13.

Li, Yang. 2005. "Huilu gaige bixu gaodu guanzhu huobi cuopei fengxian" [Foreign exchange reform must pay great attention to the risk of currency mismatch]. *Jingji cankao bao,* October 24.

Li, Yuqian. 2012. "Yuan Move Linked to More Reforms." Caixin Online, http:// english.caixin.com/2012-04-16/100380441.html.

Lieberman, R. C. 2002. "Ideas, Institutions, and Political Order: Explaining Institutional Change." *American Political Science Review* 96: 697–712.

Lieberthal, Kenneth, and Michel Oksenberg. 1988. *Policy Making in China: Leaders, Structures, and Processes.* Princeton, NJ: Princeton University Press.

Liew, Leong. 1995. "Gradualism in China's Economic Reform and the Role of the Strong Central State." *Journal of Economic Issues* 29(3): 883–95.

———. 2003. "The Role of China's Bureaucracy in Its No-Devaluation Policy during the Asian Financial Crisis." *Japanese Journal of Political Science* 4(1): 61–76.

———. 2004. "Policy Elites in the Political Economy of China's Exchange Rate Policymaking." *Journal of Contemporary China* 13(38): 21–51.

———. 2005. "China's Engagement with Neo-liberalism: Path Dependency, Geography and Party Self-Reinvention." *Journal of Development Studies* 41(2): 331–52.

Liew, Leong, and Harry X. Wu. 2007. *The Making of China's Exchange Rate Policy: From Plan to WTO Entry.* Cheltenham: Edward Elgar.

Lin, Guijun. 1997. *Study of the RMB Exchange Rate.* Beijing: University of International Business and Economics Press.

Lin, Guijun, and Ronald M. Schramm. 2003. "China's Foreign Exchange Policies since 1979: A Review of Developments and an Assessment." *China Economic Review* 14(3): 246–80.

Liu, Feng. 2007. Woguo gongkai shichang yewu caozuo gongju de xuanze jiqi youhua" [The selection and optimisation of operational instruments for open market operations in China]. *Jinrong jingji* [Finance and Economy] 18: 146–47.

Liu, Jinquan, and Zhiqiang Liu. 2002. "Zhongguo huobi zhengce fei zhongxing" [China's monetary policy is not neutral]. *Jilin Daxue Xuebao* 4: 20–22.

Liu, Liang. 2006. "Huijin: jinrong hangmu chuhai" [Huijin: the financial aircraft carrier sets sail]. *Zhongguo jingji shibao,* June 8.

Liu, Mingkang. 2004. "The State-Owned Banks in China: Reform, Corporate Governance and Prospects." Speech at the Beijng International Financial Forum, Beijing, CBRC.

Liu, Xiaojun, and Xiaofeng Chen. 2008. "Woguo gongkai shichang yewu de fazhan yu wanshan" [The development of China's open market operations]. *Fazhan yanjiu* [Development Research] 5: 32–33.

Liu, Xiaowu. 2005. "Gonghang zhuzi fangan pilu Caizhengbu Yanghang ge chi 50% guquan" [ICBCs recapitalisation plan revealed, MOF and the PBC both holding 50% equity]. *Zhongguo jingying bao,* April 25.

Ljungwall, Christer, Xiong Yi, and Yutong Zou. 2009. "Central Bank Financial Strength and the Cost of Sterilization in China." CERC Working Paper 8, May.

Lohmann, Susanne. 1994. *Federalism and Central Bank Autonomy: The Politics of German Monetary Policy, 1957–1992.* Los Angeles: Department of Political Science, UCLA.

Long, Weiying, ed. 1997. *Zhongguo waihui shichang nianjian* [Almanac of China's foreign exchange market]. Beijing: Zhongguo jinrong chubanshe.

"The Looming Revolution." 2004. *The Economist*, November 13, 77–79.

Lowndes, V. 2010. "The Institutionalist Approach," in D. Marsh and G. Stoker, eds., *Theory and Methods in Political Science*. London: Palgrave.

Lu, Hui. 2012. "China Starts Direct Currency Trading with Japan," *Xinhua*, June 4.

Lü, Xiaobo. 2000. "Booty Socialism, Bureau-preneurs, and the State in Transition: Organizational Corruption in China." *Comparative Politics* 32(3): 273–94.

Ma, G., and Robert McCaulty. 2007. "Do China's Capital Controls Still Bind? Implications for Monetary Autonomy and Capital Liberalisation." BIS Working Paper No. 233.

Ma, Guonan. 2006. "Sharing China's Bank Restructuring Bill." *China and World Economy* 14(3): 19–37.

Ma, Yuan. 2010. "Banking Regulator Denies Higher CAR Requirement." Caixin Online, http://english.caing.com/2010-09-17/100182125.html.

MacFarquhar, Roderick. 1981. *Origins of the Cultural Revolution*, vol. 1. Cambridge, MA: Oelgeschlager, Gunn, and Hain.

Mackenzie, Kate. 2012. "That's Governor Zhou to You." *Financial Times*, April 17.

Mah, Fenghwa. 1971. *The Foreign Trade of Mainland China*. Chicago: Aldine Atherton.

Mahadeva, L., and G. Sterne. 2000. *Monetary Policy Frameworks in a Global Context*. London: Routledge.

Mahoney, James. 2000. "Path Dependence in Historical Sociology." *Theory and Society* 29: 507–48.

Mahoney, James, and Kathleen Thelen. 2010. "A Theory of Gradual Institutional Change," in James Mahoney and Kathleen Thelen, eds., *Explaining Institutional Change: Ambiguity, Agency and Power*. Cambridge: Cambridge University Press.

Makin, Anthony J. 2009. "Is China's Exchange Rate Policy a Trade Protection?" *Business Economics* 44: 80–86.

Malpezzi, Stephen, and Stephen Mayo. 1997. "Housing and Urban Development Indicators: A Good Idea Whose Time Has Returned." *Real Estate Economics* 25(1): 1–12.

Maman, Daniel, and Zeev Rosenhek. 2007. "The Politics of Institutional Reform: The Declaration of Independence of the Israeli Central Bank." *Review of the International Political Economy* 14(2): 251–75.

Manion, Melanie. 1993. *Retirement of Revolutionaries in China*. Princeton, NJ: Princeton University Press.

Marcussen, Martin. 2005. "Central Banks on the Move." *European Journal of Public Policy* 12: 903–23.

Maxfield, Sylvia. 1997. *Gatekeepers of Growth: The International Political Economy of Central Banking in Developing Countries*. Princeton, NJ: Princeton University Press.

McAnulla, Stuart. 2006. "Challenging the New Interpretivist Approach: Towards a Critical Realist Alternative." *British Politics* 1(1): 113–38.

McCubbins, Mathew, and Thomas Schwartz. 1984. "Congressional Oversight Overlooked: Police Patrols vs. Fire Alarms." *American Journal of Political Science* 28(1): 165–79.

McDonald, Joe. 2007. "China's $200 US Billion Fund to Invest Two-Thirds at Home; Foreign Plans Less Ambitious." Associated Press, November 8, http://www.investorvillage.com/smbd.asp?mb=4368&mn=940&pt=msg&mid=3410415.

McGill, Doug. 2001. "The PNTR Debate Is Pointless." In These Times, http://www.inthesetimes.com/article/1646/the_pntr_debate_is_pointless/.

McKinnon, Ronald. 1993. *The Order of Economic Liberalization: Financial Control in the Transition to a Market Economy.* Baltimore, MD: Johns Hopkins University Press.

———. 2005a. "China's New Exchange Rate Policy: Will China Follow Japan into a Liquidity Trap?" Stanford Institute for Economic Policy Research, http://siepr.stanford.edu/publicationsprofile/257.

———. 2005b. "Exchange Rate or Wage Changes in International Adjustment? Japan and China versus the United States." Economics Department Working Paper, http://www.stanford.edu/~mckinnon/papers/swp05007.pdf.

McKinnon, Ronald, and Gunther Schnabl. 2004. "The East Asian Dollar Standard, Fear of Floating, and Original Sin." *Review of Development Economics* 8: 331–60.

McNamara, K. R. 2002. "Rational Fictions: Central Bank Independence and the Social Logic of Delegation." *West European Politics* 25(1): 47–76.

Mehran, Hassanali. 1996. *Monetary and Exchange System Reforms in China: An Experiment in Gradualism.* Washington, DC: International Monetary Fund.

Miao, Yan, and Dandan Li. 2008. "Yanghang qiantou, jinrong xietiao jianguan yi buji lianxi huiyi chuchang" [The PBC taking the leading role, financial regulation takes the form of inter-ministerial joint meeting]. *Shanghai zhengquan bao,* August 15.

Miller, Alice. 2005. "Hu's in Charge?" *China Leadership Monitor,* No. 16.

Miyashita, Tadao. 1966. *The Currency and Financial System of Mainland China,* trans. J. R. McEwan. Tokyo: Institute of Asian Economic Affairs.

Mohan, R. 2005. "Globalisation, Financial Markets and the Operation of Monetary Policy in India." *BIS Papers* 23: 161–70.

Montinola, Gabriella, Yingyi Qian, and Barry R. Weingast. 1996. "Federalism, Chinese Style: The Political Basis for Economic Success." *World Politics* 48(1): 50–81.

Moore, Thomas G. 2002. *China in the World Market: Chinese Industry and International Sources of Reform in the Post-Mao Era.* Cambridge: Cambridge University Press.

Moran, Michael. 2002. "Understanding the Regulatory State." *British Journal of Political Science* 32: 391–413.

Mundell, Robert. 1963. "Capital Mobility and Stabilisation Policy under Fixed and Flexible Exchange Rates." *Canadian Journal of Economics and Political Science* 29(4): 475–85.

Murphy, David. 2003. "Bank on Zhou." *Far Eastern Economic Review* 166(1): 30.

Nathan, Andrew J. 1973. "A Factionalism Model for CCP Politics." *China Quarterly* 53: 34–66.

National Bureau of Statistics of China. *China Statistical Yearbook.* Beijing: China Statistics Press. Published annually.

Naughton, Barry. 1987. "The Decline of Central Control over Investment in Post-Mao China," in David M. Lampton, ed., *Policy Implementation in Post-Mao China,* 51–79. Berkeley: University of California Press.

———. 1991. "Why Has Economic Reform Led to Inflation?" *American Economic Review* 81(2): 207–11.

———. 1992. "Hierarchy and the Bargaining Economy: Government and Enterprise in the Reform Process," in Kenneth Lieberthal and David M. Lampton, eds., *Bureaucracy, Politics, and Decision Making in Post-Mao China.* Berkeley: University of California Press.

———. 1995. *Growing Out of the Plan: Chinese Economic Reform, 1978–1993.* New York: Cambridge University Press.

———. 2002. "Zhurongji: The Twilight of a Brilliant Career." *China Leadership Monitor,* 1(Winter).

———. 2004a. "An Economic Bubble? Chinese Policy Adapts to Rapidly Changing Conditions." *China Leadership Monitor* 9(Winter).

———. 2004b. "Financial Reconstruction: Methodical Policymaking Moves into the Spotlight." *China Leadership Monitor* 10(Spring).

———. 2004c. "Hunkering Down: The Wen Jiabao Administration and Macroeconomic Recontrol." *China Leadership Monitor* 11.

———. 2005. "The New Common Economic Program: China's Eleventh Five Year Plan and What It Means." *China Leadership Monitor* 16.

———. 2006a. "Another Cycle of Macroeconomic Crackdown." *China Leadership Monitor,* 19(Fall).

———. 2006b. "Waves of Criticism: Debates over Bank Sales to Foreigners and Neo-liberal Economic Policy." *China Leadership Monitor* 17(Winter).

———. 2008a. "The Inflation Battle: Juggling Three Swords." *China Leadership Monitor* 25.

———. 2008b. "A Political Economy of China's Economic Transition," in Loren Brant and Thomas Rawski, eds., *China's Great Economic Transformation,* 91–135. Cambridge: Cambridge University Press.

———. 2009. "Understanding the Chinese Stimulus Package." *China Leadership Monitor*, 28, http://www.hoover.org/publications/china-leadership-monitor /article/5588.

NDRC. 2006. "Main Functions of the NDRC." National Development and Reform Commission, http://en.ndrc.gov.cn/mfndrc/default.htm.

Ning, Lu. 2001. "The Central Leadership, Supraministry Coordinating Bodies, State Council Ministries, and Party Departments," in David M. Lampton, ed., *The Making of Chinese Foreign and Security Policy in the Era of Reform, 1978– 2000*. Stanford, CA: Stanford University Press.

Noble, Josh. 2012. "China's Banks Can Now Short the Dollar." *Financial Times*, April 19.

North, Douglas. 1990. *Institutions, Institutional Change and Economic Performance*. Cambridge: Cambridge University Press.

Nove, Alec. 1986. *The Soviet Economic System*. London: George Allen and Unwin.

Nuti, D. M. 1986. "Hidden and Repressed Inflation in Soviet-Type Economies: Definitions, Measurements and Stabilisation." *Contributions to Political Economy* 5: 37–82.

Obstfeld, M., J. C. Shambaugh, and A. M. Taylor. 2005. "The Trilemma in History: Tradeoffs among Exchange Rates, Monetary Policies, and Capital Mobility." *Review of Economics and Statistics* 3: 423–38.

O'Donnell, Guillermo A. 1979. *Modernization and Bureaucratic-Authoritarianism: Studies in South American Politics*. Berkeley: Institute of International Studies, University of California.

Ohmae, Kenichi. 1990. *The Borderless World: Power and Strategy in the Interlinked Economy*. London: Harper Collins.

———. 1995. *The End of the Nation State: The Rise of Regional Economies*. London: HarperCollins.

Oi, Jean C. 1999. *Rural China Takes Off: Institutional Foundations of Economic Reform*. Berkeley: University of California Press.

Okazaki, Kumiko. 2011. "Banking System Reform in China: The Challenges of Moving Toward a Market-Oriented Economy." RAND Corporation Occasional Paper Series.

Oksenberg, Michael. 1982. "China's Economic Bureaucracy." *China Business Review* (May–June).

Olsen, J. P. 2009. "Change and Continuity: An Institutional Approach to Institutions and Democratic Government." *European Political Science Review* 1: 3–32.

Orlik, Tom. 2011. "Why Pork Prices Are Such a Big Deal in China." *Wall Street Journal*, July 11.

Orren, Karen, and Stephen Skowronek. 1994. "Beyond the Iconography of Order: Notes for a 'New Institutionalism': Approaches and Interpretations," in Larry

Dodd and Calvin Jillson, eds., *The Dynamics of American Politics.* Boulder, CO: Westview.

Ou, Jiawa. 1995. "Policy Choices of the Central Bank," in On Kit Tam, ed., *Financial Reform in China.* London: Routledge.

Ouyang, Alice Y., and Ramkishen S. Rajan. 2005. "Monetary Sterilisation in China since the 1990s: How Much and How Effective." Discussion Paper No. 0507, University of Adelaide.

Patnaik, Ila. 2007. "Comparing Monetary Policies." *Financial Express,* August 23, http://openlib.org/home/ila/MEDIA/2007/fe_comparing.html.

Pattis, Michael. 2008. "Chinese Inflation: It's Money Not Pork." *Far Eastern Economic Review*, April.

Paulson, Henry. 2009. "Wang Qishan." *Time,* April 30.

Pauwels, Laurent, and Ligang Liu. 2011. "Do External Political Pressures Affect the Renminbi Exchange Rate?" OME Working Paper Series. Sydney: Business School, University of Sydney.

PBC. 2001a. *China Monetary Policy Report, Quarter One 2001.* Beijing: People's Bank of China.

———. 2001b. *China Monetary Policy Report, Quarter Two 2001.* Beijing: People's Bank of China.

———. 2003a. *China Monetary Policy Report, Quarter Four 2002.* Beijing: People's Bank of China.

———. 2003b. *China Monetary Policy Report, Quarter Two 2003.* Beijing: People's Bank of China.

———. 2003c. *Monthly Statistical Report.* Beijing: People's Bank of China.

———. 2003d. "Zhongguo Renmin Yinhang yuanyu jinyibu jiaqiang fangdichan xindai yewu guanli de tongzhi" [The PBC Circular on Further Strengthening the Management of Real Estate Credit]. China.com, http://www.china.com.cn /chinese/PI-c/348886.htm.

———. 2004. *China Monetary Policy Report, Quarter Two 2004.* Beijing: People's Bank of China.

———. 2005. "Deputy Governor Xiang Junbo Answers Questions Regarding the PBC Shanghai Head Office." People's Bank of China, http://www.pbc.gov.cn /publish/english/956/1943/19437/19437_.html.

———. 2006. *China Monetary Policy Report Quarter Four 2006.* Beijing: People's Bank of China.

———. 2007. *China Monetary Policy Report, Quarter Two 2007.* Beijing: People's Bank of China.

———. 2008a. *China Financial Stability Report, 2007.* Beijing: People's Bank of China.

———. 2008b. *China Monetary Policy Report, Quarter Two 2008.* Beijing: People's Bank of China.

———. 2008c. "China: The Evolution of Foreign Exchange Controls and the Consequences of Capital Flows." BIS Papers. Beijing: People's Bank of China.

———. 2008d. "2003 nian yilai Zhongguo renmin yinhang gongzuo zhuyao qingkuang" [The operation of the PBC since 2003]. People's Bank of China, http://www.pbc.gov.cn/publish/redianzhuanti/1101/2009/20090707093339951477 957/20090707093339951477957_.html

———. 2009a. *China Monetary Policy Report, Quarter Three 2009.* Beijing: People's Bank of China.

———. 2009b. *China Monetary Policy Report, Quarter Four 2009.* Beijing: People's Bank of China.

———. 2010. "Financial Statistics." People's Bank of China, January, www.pbc.gov.cn.

———. 2011. *China Monetary Policy Report, Quarter One, 2011.* Beijing: People's Bank of China.

PBC Research Bureau. *Almanac of China's Finance and Banking.* Beijing: Almanac of China's Finance and Banking Press. Published annually.

"PBOC on Reforming RMB Exchange Rate Regime." 2005. *People's Daily*, August 6.

"PBOC Tops Central Banks in Total Assets." 2012. *China Daily*, April 23.

Pearson, Margaret M. 2001. "The Case of China's Accession to GATT/WTO," in David M. Lampton, ed., *The Making of Chinese Foreign and Security Policy in the Era of Reform, 1978–2000.* Stanford, CA: Stanford University Press.

———. 2005. "The Business of Governing Business in China: Institutions and Norms of the Emerging Regulatory State." *World Politics* 57(2): 296–322.

Peebles, Gavin. 1991. *Money in the People's Republic of China: A Comparative Perspective.* Sydney: Allen and Unwin.

Pei, Minxin. 1998. "The Political Economy of Banking Reforms in China, 1993–1997." *Journal of Contemporary China* 7(18): 321–50.

———. 2006. *China's Trapped Transition: The Limits of Developmental Autocracy.* Cambridge, MA: Harvard University Press.

Perry, Elizabeth J., and Mark Selden, eds. 2000. *Chinese Society: Change, Conflict, and Resistance.* New York: Routledge.

Peters, B. Guy. 2005. *Institutional Theory in Political Science: The New Institutionalism.* London: Continuum.

Peters, B. Guy, Jon Pierrea, and Desmond S. King. 2005. "The Politics of Path Dependency: Political Conflict in Historical Institutionalism." *Journal of Politics* 67: 1275–300.

Petursson, Thorarinn G. 2000. "Exchange Rate or Inflation Targeting in Monetary Policy?" *Monetary Bulletin* 1: 36–45.

Pierson, Paul. 2000a. "Increasing Returns, Path Dependence, and the Study of Politics." *American Political Science Review* 94(2): 251–67.

———. 2000b. "The Limits of Design: Explaining Institutional Origins and Change." *Governance* 13: 474–99.

Polillo, Simone, and Mauro F. Guillen. 2005. "Globalization Pressures and the State: The Worldwide Spread of Central Bank Independence." *American Journal of Sociology* 110(6): 1764–802.

Politi, James. 2010. "House to Hit Back on Renminbi." *Financial Times,* September 30.

Pontussen, Jonas. 1995. "From Comparative Public Policy to Political Economy: Putting Institutions in Their Place and Taking Interests Seriously." *Comparative Political Studies* 28: 117–47.

Portes, R. 1981. "Central Planning and Monetarism: Fellow Travellers?" NBER Working Paper No. 782. Cambridge, MA: National Bureau of Economic Research.

Posen, Adam. 1993. "Why Central Bank Independence Does Not Cause Low Inflation: There Is No Institutional Fix for Politics," in R. O'Brien, ed., *Finance and the International Economy.* Oxford: Oxford University Press.

Pye, Lucian W. 1968. *The Spirit of Chinese Politics.* Cambridge, MA: MIT Press.

Qian, Andrew Xuefeng. 1996. "Transforming China's Traditional Banking Systems under the New National Banking Laws." *Georgia Journal of International and Comparative Law* 25: 479–95.

Raadshelders, J. C. N. 1998. "Evolution, Institutional Analysis and Path Dependency." *International Review of Administrative Sciences* 64: 565–82.

Rabinovitch, Simon. 2012. "China Details Local Debt Rollover Plan." *Financial Times,* March 20.

Ramo, Joshua Cooper. 2004. *The Beijing Consensus.* London: Foreign Policy Centre.

Ramseyer, Mark J., and Frances McCall Rosenbluth. 1993. *Japan's Political Marketplace.* Cambridge, MA: Harvard University Press.

Reddy, Y. V. 2001. "Autonomy of the Central Bank: Changing Contours in India." Speech at the Indian Institute of Management at Indore, October 3.

Ren, Daniel. 2012. "China's Central Bank Governor, Zhou Xiaochuan, Led Financial Reform." *South China Morning Post,* September 14.

Ren, Kangyu. 2011. "Tracking China's Currency." *Central Banking* 22(2): 56–63.

Riskin, Carl. 1991. *China's Political Economy: The Quest for Development since 1949.* New York: Oxford University Press.

Roach, Stephen S. 2011. "Myths Debunked: Why China Will Have a Soft Landing." Economy Watch, http://www.economywatch.com/economy-business-and -finance-news/myths-debunked-why-china-will-have-a-soft-landing-stephen-s -roach.05-10.html?page=full.

———. 2012. "Beijing Teaches a Masterclass in Macro Policy Strategy." *Financial Times,* March 9.

Roche, Cullen. 2010. "An Interview with a Chinese Real Estate Insider." Pragmatic Capitalism, http://pragcap.com/an-interview-with-a-chinese-real-estate-insider.

Rogoff, K. 2008. "What If China Sputters?" *Financial Times,* February 4.

Roland, Gérard. 2002. "The Political Economy of Transition." *Journal of Economic Perspectives* 16(1): 29–50.

Rolnick, Art. 2003. "Interview with Ping Xie." Federal Reserve Bank of Minneapolis, http://minneapolisfed.org/publications_papers/pub_display.cfm?id=3339.

Rosen, Stanley, and Joseph Fewsmith. 2001. "The Domestic Context of Chinese Foreign Policy: Does Public Opinion Matter?" in David M. Lampton, ed., *The Making of Chinese Foreign and Security Policy.* Stanford, CA: Stanford University Press.

Saez, Lawrence. 2003. *Banking Reform in India and China.* London: Palgrave Macmillan.

"SAFE, Not CIC, Makes a Strategic Move on France's Total." 2008. China Stakes, April 8, http://www.chinastakes.com/2008/4/safe-not-cic-makes-a-strategic -move-on-frances-total.html.

Saich, Tony. 2000. "Negotiating the State: The Development of Social Organizations in China." *China Quarterly* 161: 124–41.

———. 2001. *Governance and Politics of China.* New York: Palgrave Macmillan.

Schapiro, Leonard. 1972. *Totalitarianism.* New York: Praeger.

Scharpf, Fritz. 1997. *Games Real Actors Play: Actor-Centered Institutionalism in Policy Research: Theoretical Lenses on Public Policy.* Boulder, CO: Westview.

Schmidt, Vivien A. 2006. "Institutionalism," in Colin Hay, Michael Lister, and David Marsh, eds., *The State: Theories and Issues,* 121–46. London: Palgrave.

———. 2008. "Discursive Institutionalism: The Explanatory Power of Ideas and Discourse." *Annual Review of Political Science* 11: 303–26.

Schneiberg, Marc. 2007. "What's on the Path? Path Dependence, Organizational Diversity and the Problem of Institutional Change in the US Economy, 1900–1950." *Socio-Economic Review* 5(1): 47–80.

Schwartz, H. 2005. "Down the Wrong Path: Path Dependence, Increasing Returns and Historical Institutionalism." Unpublished manuscript.

Shambaugh, David. 2008. *China's Communist Party: Atrophy and Adaptation.* Washington, DC: Woodrow Wilson Center Press.

———. 2009. *China's Communist Party: Atrophy and Adaptation.* Berkeley: University of California Press.

Sharman, J. C. 2008. "Power and Discourse in Policy Diffusion: Anti-Money Laundering in Developing States." *International Studies Quarterly* 52: 635–56.

Shaw, Edward S. 1973. *Financial Deepening in Economic Development.* New York: Oxford University Press.

Shen, Jianguang. 2012. "Quanqiu zai pingheng yu renminbi huilu" [Global rebalance and the RMB exchange rate]. *Financial Times Chinese edition,* May 8.

Shen, Jianli. 2010. "Zhou Xiaochuan: yinhang nengli xiufu reng xu licha jili" [Zhou Xiaochuan: restoration of banking capacities needs rate spreads as incentives]. *21 Shiji jingji baodao,* September 10.

Shen, Linying. 2006. "2005 nian yinhangye gaige datisu, cong fenye jingying dao hunye jingying" [Banking reform speeds up in 2005, from separate operations to mixed operations]. *Zhengquan ribao* [Securities Daily], December 31.

Sheng, Songcheng. 2011. "Shehui rongzi zongliang de neihan ji shijian yiyi" [The content of society-wide financing and its practical implications]. People's Bank of China, http://www.pbc.gov.cn/publish/diaochatongjisi/866/2011 /20110217180043605992604/20110217180043605992604_.html.

———. 2012a. "Woguo jiakuai ziben zhanghu kaifang tiaojian jiben chengshu" [Conditions almost ready to speed up our country's capital account liberalization]. *Zhongguo zhengquan bao,* February 23.

———. 2012b. "Xietiao tuijin lilu huilu gaige he ziben zhanghu kaifang" [Coordinating the promotion of interest rate and exchange rate reforms and capital account liberalization]. *Zhongguo zhengquan bao,* April 17.

Shi, Chaoge. 2005. "Zhou Xiaochuan chonggou Zhongguo jinrong bantu, zhengjiu quanshang shuxie ziben shichang" [Zhou Xiaochuan reframes China's financial landscape, bailing out stock brokerages and infusing the capital market]. *Shanghai zhengquan bao,* November 5.

Shi, Tianjian. 1997. *Political Participation in Beijing.* Cambridge, MA: Harvard University Press.

Shih, Victor. 2004. "Dealing with Non-performing Loans: Political Constraints and Financial Policies in China." *China Quarterly* 180: 922–44.

———. 2005. "Elite Decision-Making in China's Financial Sector: A Quasi-Market Analysis." Presentation at the Centre d'Etudes Prospectives et d'Informations Internationales (CEPII) Conference, Paris, France, September 19.

———. 2007. "Partial Reform Equilibrium, Chinese Style: Political Incentives and Reform Stagnation in Chinese Financial Policies." *Comparative Political Studies* 40(10): 1238–62.

———. 2008. *Factions and Finance in China: Elite Conflict and Inflation.* New York: Cambridge University Press.

Shirk, Susan. 1992. "The Chinese Political System and the Political Strategy of Economic Reform," in Kenneth Lieberthal and David M. Lampton, eds., *Bureaucracy, Politics, and Decision Making in Post-Mao China,* 59–91. Berkeley: University of California Press.

———. 1993. *The Political Logic of Economic Reform in China.* Berkeley: University of California Press.

———. 1994. *How China Opened Its Door: The Political Success of the PRC's Foreign Trade and Investment Reforms.* Washington, DC: Brookings Institution.

———. 1996. "Internationalization and China's Economic Reforms," in Robert O. Keohane and Helen V. Milner, eds., *Internationalization and Domestic Politics,* 186–206. Cambridge: Cambridge University Press.

Si, Tingting. 2009. "Healthy Economy in August Points to a Sustained Recovery." *China Daily,* September 12.

Siklos, Pierre L. 2002. *The Changing Face of Central Banking: Evolutionary Trends since World War II.* Cambridge: Cambridge University Press.

Smith, David. 2010. "China's Changing Bank Balance." *Wall Street Journal,* June 25.

Smith, Gary. 2012. "Renminbi to Shake up Reserves Management Status Quo." *Central Banking* 22(4): 61–66.

Song, Hefeng. 2004. "Jihua jingji xia shangpin shichang lingyu yizhixing tonghuo pengzhang duliang" [Measuring repressed inflation in the commodity market in the planned economy]. *Lilun yuekan* 9: 93–95.

State Council. 1983. *Decision of the State Council Concerning the People's Bank of China Exclusively Performing Central Bank Functions.* China.com, September 17, http,//www.china.com.cn/law/flfg/txt/2006-08/08/content_7060345.htm.

———. 1986. *Provisional Regulations on Banking Administration.* Beijing: State Council.

———. 1996. *Zhonghua Renmin Gongheguo waihui guanli tiaoli* [Regulations on the Foreign Exchange System of the People's Republic of China]. http://www.geocities.jp/ps_dictionary/c/waihui.htm

———. 2008. *Zhongguo renmin yinhang zhuyao zhize, neishe jigou he renyuan bianzhi guiding* [Provisions of the PBC's major responsibilities, internal institutions and personnel scale]. Central People's Government of the People's Republic of China, http://www.gov.cn/gzdt/2008-08/14/content_1072077.htm.

Steinfield, Edward S. 2004. "Market Visions: The Interplay of Ideas and Institutions in Chinese Financial Restructuring." *Political Studies* 52: 643–63.

Steinmo, Sven. 1993. *Taxation and Democracy.* New Haven, CT: Yale University Press.

Streeck, Wolfgang, and Kathleen Thelen, eds. 2005. *Beyond Continuity: Institutional Change in Advanced Political Economies.* Oxford: Oxford University Press.

Su, Manli. 2012. "Zhou Xiaochuan: lilu shichanghua gaige daikuan xianxing" [Zhou Xiaochuan: interest rate marketization should give priority to lending rates]. *Xin jing bao,* April 24.

Sullivan, Arthur, and Steven M. Sheffrin. 2003. *Economics: Principles in Action.* Upper Saddle River, NJ: Pearson Prentice Hall.

Sun, Tianqi. 2008. "Zhongguo jinrong gaige: gaige kaifang 30 nian de licheng yu fazhan qushi" [China's financial reform: the 30-year experiences of reform and opening up and its future prospects]. China Securities Journal, http://www.cs.com.cn/xwzx/01/d37/03/200807/t20080715_1527253.htm.

Tam, On-Kit. 1986. "Reform of China's Banking System." *World Economy* 9(4): 427–40.

Tan, Qingshan. 2004. "State, Institution Building, and Emerging Stock Markets in China." *Communist and Post-Communist Studies* 37: 373–94.

Tang, Wei. 2008. "2008 nian huobi zhengce zao zhiyi, Zhou Xiaochuan yali da toufa bian bai" [Zhou Xiaochuan's hair turns white as monetary policy in 2008 questioned]. *Zhongguo zhengquan bao,* December 29.

Tang, Wencheng. 2000. "An Inside Story of Zhongnanhai's Handling of China's Admission to the WTO." *Mirror Monthly,* January.

Tang, Yuankai. 2003. "Central Bank to Focus on Policy." *Beijing Review* 46(17): 32.

Tao, Shigui. 2003. "Yanghang daqu fenhang de qu yu liu" [The future of the central bank's regional branches]. *Vanke Weekly,* http://www.vankeweekly.com/asp/bbs2 /showAnnounce.asp?id=649980.

Taylor, Matthew M. 2009. "Institutional Development through Policy-Making: A Case Study of the Brazilian Central Bank." *World Politics* 61(3): 487–515.

Teiwes, Frederick C. 1979. *Politics and Purges in China: Rectification and the Decline of Party Norms, 1950–1965.* White Plains, NY: M. E. Sharpe.

———. 1995. "The Paradoxical Post-Mao Transition: From Obeying the Leader to Normal Politics." *China Journal* 34: 55–94.

Thelen, Kathleen. 1999. "Historical Institutionalism in Comparative Politics." *Annual Review of Political Science* 2: 369–404.

———. 2000. "Timing and Temporality in the Analysis of Institutional Evolution and Change." *Studies in American Political Development* 14: 101–8.

———. 2003. "How Institutions Evolve: Insights from Comparative Historical Analysis," in James Mahoney and Dietrich Rueschemeyer, eds., *Comparative Historical Analysis in the Social Sciences.* Cambridge: Cambridge University Press.

———. 2004. *How Institutions Evolve: The Political Economy of Skills in Germany, Britain, the United States and Japan.* Cambridge: Cambridge University Press.

Thelen, Kathleen, and Sven Steinmo. 1992. "Historical Institutionalism in Comparative Politics," in K. Thelen, F. Longstreth, and S. Steinmo, eds., *Structuring Politics: Historical Institutionalism in Comparative Analysis.* New York: Cambridge University Press.

Thomas, Stephen, and Chen Li. 2006. "Banking on Reform." *China Business Review,* May–June.

"Three Chinese Banks Rank High in Global Profit List." 2009. *International Business Times,* http://www.ibtimes.com/articles/20090624/three-chinese-banks -rank-high-global-profit-list.htm.

Tong, Fei. 2009. "Fansi jinrong weiji Yinjianhui jingshi yinhang sanda tiaozhan" [Revisiting the GFC, the CBRC warns of three challenges for banks]. *21 shiji jingji baodao,* June 3.

"Top 1000 World Banks." 2011. *The Banker,* July.

Tsai, Kellee S. 2006. "Adaptive Informal Institutions and Endogenous Institutional Change in China." *World Politics* 59: 116–41.

Tsebelis, George. 2002. *Veto Players: How Political Institutions Work.* Princeton, NJ: Princeton University Press.

Tseng, W. et al. 1994. "Economic Reform in China: A New Phase." IMF Working Paper No. 114. Washington, DC: International Monetary Fund.

Tsou, Tang. 1986. *The Cultural Revolution and Post-Mao Reforms: A Historical Perspective.* Chicago: University of Chicago Press.

———. 1995. "Chinese Politics at the Top: Factionalism or Informal Politics? Balance-of-Power or a Game to Win All?" *China Journal* 34: 95–156.

Tsui, Enid, and Simon Rabinovitch. 2012. "China Pushes Minimum Wage Rises." *Financial Times,* January 4.

Tudor, Alison. 2010. "Agricultural Bank of China IPO raises $US19.21bn." *Wall Street Journal,* July 7.

"24 ge shengfen nian nei tiaozheng zuidi gongzi biaozhun pingjun zengfu 22%" [24 provinces adjusting their minimun wage level by an average 22%]. 2011. *Xinhua,* December 30.

"2011nian shangshi yinyang rongzi paihang Jianshe yinhang 800 yi yuan ju shou" [CCB tops refinancing chart in 2011 with 80 billion yuan]. 2011. *Xinhua,* July 22.

UNCTAD. 2007. "UNCTAD Investment Brief No. 2." Investment Issues Analysis Branch, UN Conference on Trade and Development.

Unger, Jonathan, ed. 2002. *The Nature of Chinese Politics.* Armonk, NY: M. E. Sharpe.

"Waihui guanli gaoshou Hu Xiaolian caopan: zhangguang 8000 yi waihui chubei" [Hu Xiaolian the master in operation: overseeing $800 billion foreign reserves]." 2006. *Shichang Bao,* March 31.

Walter, Carl E., and Fraser J. T. Howie. 2011. *Red Capitalism: The Fragile Financial Foundation of China's Extraordinary Rise.* Singapore: Wiley.

Wang, Huaqing. 2004. "Shangye yinhang fengxian kongzhi he yewu fazhan" [Risk control and business development of commercial banks]. China Banking Regulatory Commission staff report.

Wang, Jianjun. 2004. "Jinrong tiaokong zaoyu tizhi xianjing er 'guo re'" [Financial regulation trapped in existing institutions leading to overheating]. *Liaowang,* July 12.

Wang, Linxin, and Joseph Fewsmith. 1995. "Bulwark of the Planned Economy: The Structure and Role of the State Planning Commission," in Carol Lee Hamrin and Suisheng Zhao, eds., *Decision Making in Deng's China: Perspectives from Insiders.* Armonk, NY: M. E. Sharpe.

Wang, Tao. 2004. "Exchange Rate Dynamics," in Eswar Prasad, ed., *China's Growth and Integration into the World Economy: Prospects and Challenges.* Washington, DC: International Monetary Fund.

Wang, Xiaolu. 2010. "Huise shouru yu guomin shouru fenpei." *Bijiao* 48: 21–27.

Wang, Xiaotian. 2012. "Trial of Asset Securitization." *China Daily,* March 19.

Wang, Yong. 2000. "China's Domestic WTO Debate." *China Business Review* 27(1): 54–62.

———. 2001. "China's Stakes in WTO Accession: The Internal Decision-Making Process," in Heike Holbig and R. Ash, eds., *China's Accession to the World Trade Organization: National and International Perspectives.* London: RoutledgeCurzon.

Ward, Benjamin. 1980. "The Chinese Approach to Economic Development," in R. Dernberger, ed., *China's Development Experience in Comparative Perspective.* Cambridge, MA: Harvard University Press.

Weber, Max. 1976. "Essay on Bureaucracy," in Frances E. Rourke, ed., *Bureaucratic Power in National Politics.* Boston: Little, Brown.

Wedeman, Andrew. 2012. *Double Paradox: Rapid Growth and Rising Corruption in China.* Ithaca, NY: Cornell University Press.

Wei, Lingling. 2011. "New Move to Make Yuan a Global Currency." *Wall Street Journal,* January 12.

———. 2012. "Q&A with CIC's Wang Jianxi." *Wall Street Journal,* March 6.

Weiss, Linda, ed. 2003. *States in the Global Economy: Bringing Domestic Institutions Back In.* Cambridge: Cambridge University Press.

———. 2005. "The State-Augmenting Effects of Globalisation." *New Political Economy* 10(3): 345–53.

Wessel, David. 2009. *In the Fed We Trust: Ben Bernanke's War on the Great Panic.* New York: Crown Business.

Weyland, Kurt. 2005. "Theories of Policy Diffusion Lessons from Latin American Pension Reform." *World Politics* 57(2): 262–95.

———. 2008. "Toward a New Theory of Institutional Change." *World Politics* 60(2): 281–314.

Wheatley, Alan. 2008. "Turf Wars Hobble China's Financial Markets." Reuters, http://www.reuters.com/article/idUSPEK33204820080428.

White, Gordon, Jude Howell, and Xiaoyuan Shang. 1996. *In Search of Civil Society: Market Reform and Social Change in Contemporary China.* Oxford: Clarendon.

Wilenski, P. 1986. *Public Power and Public Administration.* Sydney: Hale and Iremonger.

"With Xie Ping's Steering, the Central Huijin Company Turns Out to Be Solid." 2004. *Jingji guancha bao,* September 27.

World Bank. 1997. *China 2020.* Washington, DC: World Bank.

———. 2009. *China Quarterly Update, November 2009.* Washington, DC: World Bank.

Wrong, Dennis H. 1961. "The Oversocialized Conception of Man in Modern Sociology." *American Sociological Review* 26: 183–93.

WTO. 2010. "Trade Policy Review: China." World Trade Organization, http://www.wto.org/english/tratop_e/tpr_e/tp330_crc_e.htm.

Wu, Fulong, ed. 2006. *Globalization and the Chinese City.* London: Routledge.

Wu, Hong, and Ran Min. 2010. "Cai Esheng: 0.9% de buliang daikuan lu shi zhenshi shuju" [Cai Esheng: An NPL rate of 0.9% is a true figure]. Caixin, November 17.

Wu, Jinglian, and Xiaochuan Zhou. 1999. *Gongsi zhili jiegou, zhaiwu chongzu he puochan chengxu: chongwen 1994 nian Jinglun huiyi* [Corporate governance, debt

restructure and bankruptcy procedures: revisiting the 1994 Jinglun Conference].
Beijing: Zhongyang bianyi chubanshe.

Wu, N., and Q. Chen. 1989. *Study of the RMB Exchange Rate Policies*. Beijing:
China Finance Press.

Wu, X. et al. 2001. *Zhongguo waihui guanli* [China foreign exchange management].
Beijing: China Finance Press.

Wu, Xiaoling. 1992. *Zhongguo de jinrong shenhua yu jinrong gaige* [Financial
deepening and reform in China]. Tianjin: Tianjin People's Publisher.

———. 2007. "Lijie Yanghang" [Understanding the central bank]. http://old.ccer
.edu.cn/cn/ReadNews.asp?NewsID=9053.

Wu, Yan. 2004. "Sida jiedian kan tiaokong" [Macroeconomic managment in four
cases]. *Huadong xinwen* [Eastern China News], May 26, 1.

Wu, Ying. 2006. "The RMB Exchange Rate and Monetary Sterilisation in China."
China: An International Journal 4(1): 32–59.

Xia, Bin, and Qiang Liao. 2001. "Huobi gongyingliang yi buyi zuowei dangqian
woguo de huobi zhengce zhongjie mubiao." *Jingji yanjiu* 8: 33–43.

Xia, Ying. 2003. "Yanghang shuangchong juese bichi chongtu Yinjianhui 'taidong'"
[Central bank's dual role conflicts with each other, CBRC on the horizon].
Nanfang zhoumo, January 17, 6.

Xie, Andy. 2010. "Chinese Real-Estate Bust Is Morphing into a Slow Leak."
Bloomberg Opinion, http://www.bloomberg.com/news/2010-09-26/chinese
-property-bust-is-morphing-into-a-slow-leak-commentary-by-andy-xie.html.

Xie, Ping. 1995. "Zhongguo zhangyang yinhang de dulixing" [The independence
of the Chinese central bank]. *Shanghai zhengquan bao* [Shanghai Securities
Daily], April 5.

———. 2000. "Xin shiji Zhongguo huobi zhengce de tiaozhan" [Monetary policy
challenges in the new century]. *Jinrong yanjiu,* 1: 1–10.

———. 2004. "Zhongguo huobi zhengce fenxi 1998–2002." *Jinrong Yanjiu* 8: 11–15.

Xie, Ping, and Qiao Yu. 1999. "Money Aggregates Management: Problems and
Prospects in China's Economic Transition." *Contemporary Economic Policy* 17(1):
22–26.

Xie, Ping, and Xiaopu Zhang. 2002. "Huobi zhengce yu huilu zhengce de sanci
chongtu: 1994–2000 Zhongguo de shizheng fenxi" [Tensions between monetary
policy and exchange rate policy: an empirical analysis of China's case between
1994 and 2000]. *Guoji jingji pinglun* 3: 30–36.

Xu, Jingan. 2008. "Wo suo qinli de gaige juece guocheng" [The reform decision-
making that I have experienced]. Xu Jing'an the Blog, http://blog.sina.com.cn/s
/blog_4aaf6ed301000b9q.html.

Xu, Shenglan. 2009. "An Affordable Home for Every Family, Chongqing Official
Promises." *Huangqiu shibao* [Global Times], September 8.

Xu, Yixian. 1996. "Qiantan xingzheng jiguan gongwen chuli zhong de huiqian gongzuo" [A brief discussion of collective signatures in administrative documentation]. *Hebei zheng bao* 3: 21–23.

Yan, Jiaqi. 1995. "The Nature of Chinese Authoritarianism," in Carol Lee Hamrin and Suisheng Zhao, eds., *Decision Making in Deng's China: Perspectives from Insiders,* 3–14. Armonk, NY: M. E. Sharpe.

Yang, Dali. 2004. *Remaking the Chinese Leviathan: Market Transition and the Politics of Governance in China.* Stanford, CA: Stanford University Press.

Yang, Fan. 1993. "Renminbi huilu zoushi yanjiu" [Research on trends in the RMB exchange rate]. *Zhongguo wujia* 3: 20–21.

———. 2000. *Renminbi huilu yanjiu: jianlun guoji jinrong weiji yu Zhongguo shewai jingji* [On the RMB exchange rate: international financial crisis and China's external economy]. Beijing: Shoudu jingji maoyi daxue chubanshe.

Yang, Hongxu, Yan Su, and Liu Liu. 2012. *2011 nian tiaokong xiaoguo chuxian, fangjia shouru bi lianxu dier nian huiluo* [Effects of macro control emerge in 2011 with price-to-come ratio dropping for a second consecutive year]. Beijing: E-house China R&D Institute.

Yang, Peixin. 1984. "Banking," in Guangyuan Yu, ed., *China's Socialist Modernization,* 405–36. Beijing: Foreign Language Press.

Yang, Taixing. 2009. "Channeng guosheng hangye Q2 da 22 ge" [Overcapacity industries reaching 22 in Q2]. *Gongshang shibao,* October 21.

Yang, Yi. 2009. "Guanyu Zhongguo nongye yinhang yinjin zhanlue touzizhe wenti de sikao" [Some thoughts on the issue of strategic investors for the ABC]. *Shidai jinrong* 386: 29–31.

"Yanghang meizhou zengjia yici piaoju baxing" [The central bank increases its bill issuance once a week]. 2004. *Jinrong shibao,* August 4.

Yao, Kevin. 2011. "China Central Bank Strives for More Policy Influence." Reuters, March 24.

Ye, Hewen. 2002. "Bu bianzhi yu bu shengzhi: renminbi wunian zhilu" [Non-devaluation and non-appreciation: RMB in five years]. *Jingji guancha bao,* September 8.

Ye, Tan. 2008. "Zhou Xiaochuan: Mr RMB with Half Mission Accomplished." *Juece tansuo* 11: 71–75.

———. 2009. *Na shenma zhengjiu Zhongguo jingji* [How to salvage the Chinese economy]. Beijing: CITIC Press.

Ye, Weiqiang, Shuo Wang, and Kan Huo. 2010. "Gouxiang Renminbi" [Contemplating RMB]. *Xinshiji Weekly* 411: 20.

Yi, Gang. 2000. "Selection of Exchange Rate System." *Jinrong Yanjiu* [Journal of Financial Research] 9: 46–52.

———. 2008. "Renminbi Exchange Rates and Relevant Institutional Factors." *Cato Journal* 28(2): 187–96.

Yi, Gang, and X. Tang. 2001. "Theoretical Foundations of 'Corner Solution Assumption' of the Exchange Rate System." *Financial Research* 8: 5–17.

Yi, Jingtao. 2007. "China's Exchange Rate Policymaking in the Hu-Wen Era." Briefing Series. Nottingham, UK: China Policy Institute, University of Nottingham.

"Yinjianhui: dangqian Zhongguo yinhangye fazhan mianlin sanda tiaozhan" [CBRC: Chinese banks facing three major challenges]. 2010. *Caijing,* September 16.

"Yinjianhui dansheng ji" [The leadup to the establisment of the CBRC]. 2006. *China Business News,* April 29.

"You zhuanjia dui guoyou yinhang xiyin waizi moshi biaoshi danyou" [Experts' concern over foreign participation in state-owned banks]. 2005. *Zhongguo zhengquan bao,* September 23.

Yu, Liang. 2008. "Yanghang piaoju de faxing chengben ji ke chixu xing yanjiu" [The issuance costs of central bank bills and their sustainability]. *Inner Mongolia Banking Research* 10: 3–6.

Yu, Ning. 2005. "Central Bank Loans 'Free-for-All.'" *Caijing,* July 27.

———. 2008. "Foreign Reserves Seek Higher Investment Returns." *Caijing,* April 28.

Yu, Ning, and Tao Li. 2008. "Yanghang gongbu sanding fangan" [The PBC publishes the internal review]. *Caijing,* August 14.

Yu, Qiao. 1997. "Economic Fluctuation, Macro Control and Monetary Policy in the Transitional Chinese Economy." *Journal of Comparative Economics* 25: 180–95.

Yu, Yongding. 2000. "China's Deflation during the Asian Financial Crisis, and Reform of the International Financial System." *ASEAN Economic Bulletin,* August.

Zarathustra, W. 2011. "China: The Forgotten Real Estate Bubble of the 1990s." *Business Insider,* March 23.

Zeng, Xiaopeng. 2003. "Yanghang chushou yizhi fangdichan" [The central bank set to put brakes on the real estate sector]. *Zhongguo zhengquan bao,* June 28.

Zhang, Jianhua. 2009. "Guoyou shangye yinhang yingli nengli zuicha" [Zhang Jianhua: state-owned banks fare last in profitability]. Ifeng.com, http://finance.ifeng.com/topic/money/qqzkfh4/bank/zzyh/20090704/888019.shtml.

Zhang, Lei. 2009. "Huobi zhengce gongju dui huobi zhengce xiaoguo de yingxiang." *Jingjishi* 3: 201–2.

Zhang, Ming. 2011. "The transition of China's development model," in Wilhelm Hofmeister, ed., *G20 Perceptions and Perspectives for Global Governance.* Singapore: Konard Adeuauer Stiftung.

———. 2012. "Chinese Stylized Sterilization: The Cost-Sharing Mechanism and Financial Repression." *China and World Economy* 20(2): 41–58.

Zhang, Ran. 2009. "Monetary Policy Should Be Fast and Heavy-Handed." *China Daily,* March 6.

Zhang, Tianlei. 1999. "90 niandai jingji gongzuo dui dangxia de jiaoxun" [The lessons from the economic work in the 1990s for the current situation]. *Beijing Daily,* December 11.

Zhang, Xiaohui. 2009. "Guanyu huobi zhengce yu zichan jiage" [On monetary policy and asset price]. *Caijing,* July 20.

Zhao, Hongmei. 2010. "Zhongguo yanghang Huobi zhengce yao jieshou guo neiwai jianyan RMB guojihua mianlian xin tiaozhan-fu hangzhang" [The PBC monetary policy to be tested at home and abroad; the internationalisation of the RMB facing new challenges—vice governor]. Reuters, http://cn.reuters.com /article/currenciesNews/idCNnCN11761952010070?pageNumber=2&virtual BrandChannel=0.

Zhao, Suisheng. 1995. "The Structure of Authority and Decision-Making: A Theoretical Framework," in Carol Lee Hamrin and Suisheng Zhao, eds., *Decision-Making in Deng's China: Perspectives from Insiders,* 233–45. Armonk, NY: M. E. Sharpe.

Zhao, Ziyang. 1987. "On the Separation of Party and Government." Speech to the Preparatory Meetings for the Seventh Plenary Session of the Twelfth Central Committee, Beijing, October.

Zheng, Joan. 1995. "Battling China's Inflation." *Far Eastern Economic Review,* March 30, 34.

Zheng, Shiping. 1997. *Party vs. State in Post-1949 China: The Institutional Dilemma.* Cambridge: Cambridge University Press.

Zheng, Zhi. 2012. "500yi dangao lai le, xindai zichan zhengquanhua zhengshi chongqi." *21 Century Business Herald,* June 2.

Zhong, Hua. 2012. "Qunian yingchang difang zhai zhong jin 5,000 yi yuan huo zhanqi" [Rollover of almost 500 billion yuan worth of repayable local government debt last year]. *Wall Street Journal Chinese edition,* March 22.

Zhou, Mubing. 1993. *Xifang huobi zhengce lilun yu Zhongguo huobi zhengce shijian* [Western theories on monetary policy and the Chinese experience]. Beijing: Zhongguo jinrong chubanshe.

Zhou, Qiren. 2011. "Huobi tiaokong de Zhongguo tese" [Monetary management, Chinese characteristics]. Caijing.com, http://blog.caijing.com.cn/expert_article -151195-18420.shtml.

Zhou, Xiaochuan. 1999a. *Chongjian yu zaisheng: huajie yinhang buliang zichan de guoji jingyan* [Restructuring and rejuvenating: international experiences of reducing nonperforming loans]. Beijing: Zhongguo jinrong chubanshe.

———. 1999b. *Zhuangui qijian de jingji fenxi yu jingji zhengce* [Economic analysis and policy in the era of transition]. Beijing: Zhongguo jingji chubanshe.

———. 2005. "Speech at the Inaugural Ceremony of the PBC's Second Head Office in Shanghai." ChinaNews, http://www.chinanews.com.cn/news/2005 /2005-08-10/26/610367.shtml.

———. 2006. "Zhongguo huobi zhengce de tedian he tiaozhan" [The characteristics and challenges of China's monetary policy]. *Caijing* 175(26)December 25.

———. 2009. "Reform the International Monetary System." Bank of International Settlements, http://www.bis.org/review/r090402c.pdf.

Zhou, Xiaochuan, and Zhigang Yang. 1996. *Maixiang kaifangxing jingji de siwei zhuanbian* [A change of mentality in the face of an open economy]. Shanghai: Shanghai yuandong chubanshe.

Zhou, Xiaochuan et al. 1993. *Renminbi zou xiang ke duihuan* [RMB's Road to Convertibility]. Beijing: Jingji guanli chubanshe.

"Zhou Xiaochuan huo jiang liren weilai tian bianshu [Zhou Xiaochuan may leave the pbc adding uncertainty for the future]." 2007. *Wall Street Journal* Chinese Online, http://www.peacehall.com/news/gb/china/2007/10/200710120214.shtml.

Zhou, Xin, and Kirby Chien. 2009. "China Banks NPL Ratio Falls to 1.66 Pct End-Sept, Updated 29 October)." Reuters, http://uk.reuters.com/article/idUK PEK14296620091029.

Zweig, David. 2001. "China's Stalled 'Fifth Wave.'" *Asian Survey* 41(2): 231.

———. 2002. *Internationalizing China: Domestic Interests and Global Linkages.* Ithaca, NY: Cornell University Press.

Acknowledgments

China's economic transition to a more market-oriented economy since 1978 has entailed profound institutional changes to the structure of the state, including the governance of the financial system. By putting the institutional evolution of the Chinese central bank, the People's Bank of China (PBC), under the microscope, this study seeks to inform ongoing debates on the dynamics and nature of institutional change in general and the empirical developments in China in particular.

This book builds upon the work of a wide range of scholars of Chinese politics and political economy, and on our own theoretical and comparative works over the years. It also benefits from the firsthand interview materials and from the contribution by a range of officials, within the PBC and beyond, who graciously offered their time and views on the rise of the People's Bank of China. Between 2005 and 2012, we made six field trips to China and conducted intensive interviews, mostly with officials from the PBC as well as other related ministries. The materials from these interviews have formed a key facet of this book. Given the political and diplomatic sensitiveness of monetary and particularly exchange rate policy at the time of our interviews, most of the interviewees requested anonymity, which we have honored. Many of the officials were willing to help in the hope that their contribution to this project could facilitate better understanding in the outside world of the various ideas, debate, dilemmas, and challenges the Chinese authorities have had to face in the fast-changing environment of China's economic transition. We hope that this book can live up to such expectations and take a step forward in this direction. We are also greatly indebted to those who have helped us arrange and coordinate our interviews.

Over the years we have benefited from discussions with many scholars and friends whose contributions to this volume are important but cannot be singled out. In particular, however, our thanks go to Leong Liew, James Laurenceson, and Andrew Hindmoor, who have taken the time to read earlier drafts of the manuscript. Their critical reading and constructive suggestions are most appreciated. Two anonymous readers of an early version of the manuscript also added valuable perspectives and comments that have been incorporated into the book. Any remaining errors in the book, however, are our own.

We would also like to thank Michael Aronson of Harvard University Press, who has put tremendous efforts into reviewing the manuscript, arranging the reviews, and securing the project. Thanks also to Andrew Schuller, who helped with our negotiations with the Press.

We should also acknowledge the Australian Research Council for funding the bulk of the research on this project over the years. As usual, the School of Political Science and International Studies at the University of Queensland has provided an ideal base for our research activities.

Special acknowledgment must be made to our families, especially to Jo, Hillary, Qian, and Ellie, for their love, care, and tolerance over the years of research and writing.

Index

The letter *f* following a page number denotes a figure and the letter *t* denotes a table.